CLASSICS IN THEORY

General Editors
BROOKE A. HOLMES   MIRIAM LEONARD   TIM WHITMARSH

Emanuela Bianchi is Associate Professor of Comparative Literature at New York University.

Sara Brill is Professor of Philosophy at Fairfield University.

Brooke Holmes is Robert F. Goheen Professor in the Humanities and Professor of Classics at Princeton University.

Praise for *Antiquities beyond Humanism*

'To be sure, the book is of significant interest to those who study subjects in continental philosophy like psychoanalysis, feminist theory, queer theory, and object-oriented ontology. But this excellent volume also should be read by those with broader interest in antiquity, as it demonstrates ways in which the ancient texts continue to be of the greatest value to promising new movements in contemporary thinking.'

Colin C. Smith, *Bryn Mawr Classical Review*

'The book is recommended reading for anyone interested in contemporary continental philosophy and the ancient world. It includes thought-provoking and surprising [...] openings for approaching antiquity from posthuman perspectives. The collection succeeds in showing that ancient texts are blooming with non-human life.'

Pieta Päällysaho, *Arctos: Acta Philologica Fennica*

CLASSICS IN THEORY

Classics in Theory explores the new directions for classical scholarship opened up by critical theory. Inherently interdisciplinary, the series creates a forum for the exchange of ideas between classics, anthropology, modern literature, philosophy, psychoanalysis, politics, and other related fields. Invigorating and agenda-setting volumes analyse the cross-fertilizations between theory and classical scholarship and set out a vision for future work on the productive intersections between the ancient world and contemporary thought.

Antiquities beyond Humanism

Edited by
Emanuela Bianchi
Sara Brill
Brooke Holmes

UNIVERSITY PRESS

Great Clarendon Street, Oxford, OX2 6DP,
United Kingdom

Oxford University Press is a department of the University of Oxford.
It furthers the University's objective of excellence in research, scholarship,
and education by publishing worldwide. Oxford is a registered trade mark of
Oxford University Press in the UK and in certain other countries

© The editors and Oxford University Press 2019

The moral rights of the authors have been asserted

First published 2019
First published in paperback 2021

All rights reserved. No part of this publication may be reproduced, stored in
a retrieval system, or transmitted, in any form or by any means, without the
prior permission in writing of Oxford University Press, or as expressly permitted
by law, by licence or under terms agreed with the appropriate reprographics
rights organization. Enquiries concerning reproduction outside the scope of the
above should be sent to the Rights Department, Oxford University Press, at the
address above

You must not circulate this work in any other form
and you must impose this same condition on any acquirer

Published in the United States of America by Oxford University Press
198 Madison Avenue, New York, NY 10016, United States of America

British Library Cataloguing in Publication Data
Data available

Library of Congress Cataloging in Publication Data
Data available

ISBN 978–0–19–880567–0 (Hbk.)
ISBN 978–0–19–284583–2 (Pbk.)

Links to third party websites are provided by Oxford in good faith and
for information only. Oxford disclaims any responsibility for the materials
contained in any third party website referenced in this work.

ACKNOWLEDGMENTS

Antiquities beyond Humanism began life as a conference, "Posthuman Antiquities," that the three of us organized at New York University on November 14–15, 2014. We would like to thank the original participants in that conference. We have had the great fortune to work with extraordinary scholars on this project, and we thank all of them for their incisive thinking, patience, and grace as this project made its way from idea to conference to publication. We are also indebted to the original sponsors for the conference without whom this project would not have been possible: the Department of Comparative Literature at NYU, the NYU Center for Ancient Studies, the Gallatin Fund for Classics and the Contemporary World, the Office of the Dean of the College of Arts and Science at Fairfield University, Global Research Initiatives of the Office of the Provost at NYU, Postclassicisms (supported by a Global Collaborative Networks Fund grant at Princeton University), the Department of Classics at Princeton, the NYU College of Arts and Science, the NYU Office of the Dean of the Faculty of Arts and Science, the NYU Humanities Initiative, the NYU Office of the Dean for Humanities, the Center for the Study of Gender and Sexuality at NYU, the NYU Department of Philosophy, the NYU Department of Classics, the NYU Department of Media, Culture, and Communication, the NYU Department of English, and the A. S. Onassis Program in Hellenic Studies at NYU. For tireless organizational assistance with the conference, we thank NYU Comparative Literature's then Administrative Director, Kit Frick, our assistant Elizabeth Benninger, Agata Tumilowicz for help on the day, videographer Tiffany Salone, and Anastassia Kostrioukova for her wonderful conference poster and program design. We thank the three anonymous readers who made invaluable comments on the manuscript. Deep gratitude is also due to Tim Whitmarsh, who as the one member of the Classics in Theory editorial team with distance on the project saw it through the vetting and editorial process with care and professionalism, and to Georgina Leighton and Charlotte Loveridge at OUP, and Lydia Shinoj at SPi, who have smoothed the path to publication with panache. The editorial assistantship of Erik Fredericksen and Malina Buturovic has been a true sine qua non, as has Timothy Beck's copyediting and Cashman Kerr Prince's indexing—we thank them all. We are truly grateful to Allyson Vieira for the stunning cover image. Finally, we would like to thank our partners, families, and friends for their support during the many stages of this project—you know who you are.

CONTENTS

LIST OF CONTRIBUTORS ix

1 Introduction 1
Emanuela Bianchi, Sara Brill, and Brooke Holmes

PART 1 POSTHUMAN ANTIQUITIES?

2 The human reconceived: back to Socrates with Arendt 31
Adriana Cavarero

3 Hearing voices: the sounds in Socrates' head 47
Ramona Naddaff

4 Song and dance man: Plato and the limits of the human 63
Michael Naas

5 Precarious life: tragedy and the posthuman 77
Miriam Leonard

PART 2 ALTERNATE ZOOLOGIES

6 Aristotle's meta-zoology: shared life and human animality in the *Politics* 97
Sara Brill

7 Sounds of subjectivity or resonances of something other 123
Kristin Sampson

8 Shared life as chorality in Schiller, Hölderlin, and Hellenistic poetry 141
Mark Payne

9 Apples and poplars, nuts and bulls: the poetic biosphere of Ovid's *Metamorphoses* 159
Giulia Sissa

PART 3 ANTHRO-EXCENTRIC

10 Hyperobjects, OOO, and the eruptive classics—field notes of an accidental tourist 189
James I. Porter

11 Nature trouble: ancient *physis* and queer performativity   211
    Emanuela Bianchi

12 On Stoic sympathy: cosmobiology and the life of nature   239
    Brooke Holmes

13 Immanent maternal: figures of time in Aristotle, Bergson,
    and Irigaray   271
    Rebecca Hill

14 In light of *eros*   287
    Claudia Baracchi

INDEX   305

LIST OF CONTRIBUTORS

Claudia Baracchi is Associate Professor of Moral Philosophy at the University of Milano-Bicocca, Italy.

Emanuela Bianchi is Associate Professor of Comparative Literature with affiliations in Classics and Gender and Sexuality Studies at New York University, USA.

Sara Brill is Professor of Philosophy at Fairfield University, USA.

Adriana Cavarero is Professor of Political Philosophy at the University of Verona, Italy.

Rebecca Hill is Senior Lecturer in the School of Media and Communication at RMIT University, Australia.

Brooke Holmes is Robert F. Goheen Professor in the Humanities and Professor of Classics at Princeton University, USA.

Miriam Leonard is Professor of Greek Literature and its Reception at University College London, UK.

Michael Naas is Professor of Philosophy at DePaul University, USA.

Ramona Naddaff is Associate Professor of Rhetoric at the University of California, Berkeley, USA.

Mark Payne is Professor of Classics and the College at the University of Chicago, USA.

James I. Porter is Irving G. Stone Professor in Literature and Professor of Rhetoric and Classics at the University of California, Berkeley, USA.

Kristin Sampson is Associate Professor of Philosophy at the University of Bergen, Norway.

Giulia Sissa is Professor of Political Science and Classics at the University of California, Los Angeles, USA.

Introduction

*Emanuela Bianchi, Sara Brill,
and Brooke Holmes*

In the third book of his *Histories*, Herodotus tells the story of the death of the Persian king Cambyses. Startled by a dream revealing a coup at home, he leaps on his horse with the intent to march on the capital and is immediately wounded by his own sword, whose sheath has fallen off in the commotion (3.64). The wound, Herodotus reports, occurs at exactly the site where Cambyses had himself struck the sacred bull Apis in Egypt, and as was the case with Apis, it proves fatal to Cambyses. The story is cited centuries later by the travel writer Pausanius as a particularly vivid and apparently famous example of inanimate objects "of their own accord inflicting righteous retribution on humans" (1.28.11). These impersonal agents of justice could also be perpetrators of injustice, as Pausanius recognizes, with the result that any assessment of the place of the human in the ancient Greco-Roman world must accommodate itself to the fact that the category of legal subject—if by this we mean any entity that may be brought to trial—included not only human beings but also dogs and oxen, statues and axes, javelins, stones, and wooden beams. Ensnared in webs of pollution and expiation but also of blame, the legal status of these non-human animals and "lifeless things" reminds us that the concepts of agency and subjectivity are capacious in the ancient Mediterranean, with deep consequences for the concepts of animacy, materiality, embodiment, personhood, and responsibility.

The entanglement of human and non-human within social, ethical, legal, and political spaces stands as an invitation to reflect more broadly on the place of the human within the larger category of *zōē*, the kind of life that for the Greeks encompassed animals, plants, the cosmos, and the divine in addition to the human. The ax that remembers the injustice of its use to slay Agamemnon, the river that rises up in anger against Achilles, or the stone that Ajax comes to resemble—all defy any modern reduction to "mute" materiality.[1] These objects instead insist upon their contribution to a sphere of action, efficacy, and justice that

---

[1] Sophocles, *Electra* 484–6 (the ax); Homer, *Iliad* 21.233–71 (river); Schol. D. *Il.* 6.5 (wall of stone, see also Purves (2015)).

may be seen at work in *kosmos*, *physis*, and *theos* alike, one that far exceeds the realm of the human.

It is in this sphere of life that ancient Greek thinking about the cosmological character of justice, so striking in the earliest extant philosophical fragment from Anaximander,[2] comes together with conceptions of the dynamic and at times intentional capacities of objects and elements and the exuberant, distributed powers of self-renewal present in even the most basic living things, exemplified by Theophrastus' observation that a plant has "the power of growth in all its parts, inasmuch as it has life in all its parts" (*Enquiry into Plants* 1.1.4). We can see here glimmers of a history of thinking which undercuts and challenges the somatophobia that is all too frequently taken to be isomorphic with "ancient Greek thought," traces of an alternate lineage that includes variegated, rhizomatic strands whose intersections and divergences run rough-shod over contemporary distinctions between zoological, ethical, juridical, and political theorizing. Throughout much of ancient Greek and Roman thinking, the concepts of *bios*, *ēthos*, and *polis* are so deeply intertwined as to render terms like "bioethics" and "biopolitics" nearly redundant. Ancient Greek and Roman literary, medical, and philosophical texts are resplendent with sites at which materiality, embodiment, and the boundaries between living and non-living, human and animal, divine and beastly, erupt into a field of questioning, deliberation, care, and experimentation.

It is therefore not surprising that ancient philosophy has been especially formative for the field of biopolitics, preeminently through Michel Foucault's last two volumes on the *History of Sexuality* and his now published lectures at the Collège de France and through Giorgio Agamben's oft-cited appropriation of an ostensibly Aristotelian division between *bios* and *zōē*.[3] Yet the very power and authority of these foundational works has made classical antiquity more of a trope, a site of philological gesture and received wisdom, than a dynamic and productive conceptual resource for the various forms of posthumanism and new materialism that have flourished in the past decade in a wide range of disciplines. Moreover, the force of the post- in the concept of posthumanism, akin to the geological rupture that attends the newly christened Anthropocene, has encouraged the sense of a decisive epochal break with the past.

---

[2] "Whence things have their origin, there they must also pass away according to necessity; for they must pay penalty and be judged for their injustice, according to the ordinance of time" (DK12 B1).

[3] Brill's contribution to this volume challenges the Aristotelian lineage of Agamben's construction of *zōē* and *bios*.

Countering this unflagging modernist infatuation with the new, *Antiquities beyond Humanism* maps out the ground for a richer and more sustained encounter with Greco-Roman antiquity, excavating an ante-humanism that nonetheless does not seek any kind of return to a pre-humanist arcadia. The volume arises from a commitment to actively engage this ancient philosophical tradition as a powerful field through which to tackle some of the most urgent questions addressed by the new materialisms and forms of post- and non-humanism. The papers gathered here take up ancient Greek philosophical and literary texts as at once live with possibilities for the present and uncannily distant. Collectively, they approach antiquity as neither origin nor telos but as asynchronous or untimely in Nietzsche's sense. By bringing together a range of international scholars actively working at the intersections of ancient philosophy, literature, continental philosophy, feminist theory, and political theory, we aim to open up new vectors for thinking beyond the human that are responsive to the contemporary world while also proposing a complex set of relationships within the *longue durée* of the intellectual traditions shaped by the profound strangeness and unsettling familiarity of the Greco-Roman world. In this way, the volume resists and displaces the seductions of presentism, scientism, and technological determinism that often limit the horizons of new materialist thinking.

Nonetheless, like the new and still emerging fields of posthumanism, biopolitics, chaos theory, complexity theory, quantum theory, neovitalism, new materialism, cyborg studies, affect studies, object-oriented ontologies, sound studies, ecocriticism, and animal and plant studies, classical thinking displaces and complicates the modern notion of subjectivity and finds movement and life inherently at work in both organic and inorganic phenomena. While the very notion of Renaissance humanism was founded on a return to the centrality of the human in cultural and political life conceived as a classical ideal, ancient texts reveal themselves as teeming with competing narratives. Greek philosophy begins, after all, with those whom Aristotle calls the *physikoi*, who turn to explanations of the cosmos grounded in observations of the natural world. And while the ethical tradition in Greek philosophy centrally addresses the question of what kind of life human beings should live, this question was inextricably linked to investigations of plant life and animal life and, indeed, even stone life; the *technai* (political, medical, rhetorical, ethical) that are fundamental to human life; and the ontological status of living being as such (including questions about the motion and animacy of non-living things). From this perspective, antiquity gives rise not only to a humanist tradition but also to lines of thought that are better understood as non-humanist.

The life of the body and non-human life in Greco-Roman antiquity have of course been the subject of much important classical scholarship over the last fifty years. Such work has predominantly focused, however, on the negative valuation of these concepts in Greek philosophy, functioning as the (typically feminized) foil to the life of divine reason and proper human flourishing. These inquiries into ancient philosophical formations continue to be fundamental in exposing the subtle and often unconscious ways in which the body is still pathologized and caught up in unproductive binaries in contemporary thought, and they warn against easy or reactive returns to humanist ideals in the wake of post-structuralism and posthumanism. But there is also work to be done tracing out other strains of ancient thought that take up a more nuanced relationship to animals, plants, and embodied life. We need to better understand how inquiries into vulnerability and care are also opportunities to think about contingency, mindfulness, ephemerality, value, and affinity in ways that resist polarization and instead dynamically knot and unfold around different problems. The non-human is not simply the negated Other of the human in Greek thought—either as its binary opposite or as the familiar structuralist poles of god and animal—but a plural, unpredictable, and richly articulated field that intertwines with attempts to think the human from Homer into late antiquity and beyond. In staging an encounter with "the Greeks" along these lines, *Antiquities beyond Humanism* contributes, too, to the theorization and enactment of the very history of philosophy and ideas. Rather than retelling narratives of origin, return, legacy, and linear temporality, the essays gathered in this volume trust in the creative potential of classical antiquity under contemporary conditions while refusing its conventional role as grounding ideal or inaugural nightmare.

1.1. **Humanism, the human, and classical antiquity**

What does it mean to be human? The question is never posed in a vacuum. For centuries of European intellectual history, the coordinates of an inquiry into the human were dominated by various strains of humanism, that is, scholarly-pedagogical movements to make man—and man was uncontroversially equivalent to the human—the privileged object of study and contemplation as a means to ethical self-formation. The human in humanism is not a biological-evolutionary category to be uncovered through positivist investigation (if it ever is). Rather, within traditional forms of humanism it is an ideal category, exemplified unevenly and requiring careful cultivation. We are not born human but at least some of us can become genuinely, *essentially*, human.

In the search for perfect specimens, humanism has historically zeroed in on the ancient Greeks and Romans. Renaissance humanism is founded on an investment in the ancients, especially the Latin authors, as exemplars of a grace and nobility that can be acquired in the present through detailed study of their extant texts, and the humanist revolution in education of the fifteenth and sixteenth centuries takes it as an "article of faith" that its foundations must lie in the Greco-Roman classics.[4] It is to the Greeks as singular representatives of "true humanness," defined above all by physical beauty, nobility of spirit, and freedom, that the eighteenth- and nineteenth-century German neo-humanists—Winckelmann, Wolf, Schiller, Humboldt—turn in seeking a model on which to found spiritual renewal at the level of both the individual and the collective (and the Greeks are again at the center of Werner Jaeger's "Third Humanism" in Weimar Germany).[5] When in "What is a Classic?" (1944), T. S. Eliot reaches for the paragon of "a classic," which he defines as a work whose genius should be recognized by all human beings, he turns to Latin and Greek and, more specifically, to Virgil's *Aeneid*. In contemporary American universities, even if the humanities can hardly be said to be synonymous with a classical education, their self-definition continues to owe much, albeit controversially, to the study of Greco-Roman antiquity. As long as the idioms of humanism persist, the Greeks (and to a lesser degree, the Romans) never seem to be far away. To take just one example: when the political theorist Bonnie Honig undertakes a critique of what she calls "mortalist humanism," a humanism that she argues is founded not on ideals of beauty and freedom but on a shared capacity for suffering, she is both targeting readings of *Antigone* and developing a position through her own pioneering reading of the play: Sophocles is still the site for a debate about humanism.[6] In short, the "ancients" have been and continue to be integral to how the human has been defined in a wide range of philosophical, political, aesthetic, literary, and historical traditions that have contributed to the self-definition of modern Europe and "the West."

What this means is that any inquiry into the boundaries of the human in ancient Greek and Roman texts intervenes in a long and consequential history. This history is also one of exclusionary and coercive norms that have licensed enormous physical, symbolic, and epistemic violence. The

---

[4] "Article of faith": Grafton and Jardine (1986) xiv.
[5] See Marchand (2003) 3–35 on German neo-humanism, 302–40 on the Third Humanism of Jaeger, and 21 on Wolf's belief that the Greeks alone represent "true humanness."
[6] Honig (2013).

humanist project, especially over the past few centuries, has systematically argued for the superiority of the ancient Greeks at the expense of other peoples (among them the Egyptians, Persians, Phoenicians, Indians, and Jews, as well as the Greeks in the modern period, seen as unworthy of their illustrious past). In so doing, it has laid the groundwork—and at times supplied the justification—for modern European and American racial formations as well as modern forms of imperialism, colonialism, and slavery.[7] The misogyny of ancient authors and their refusals to grant women full humanity have licensed the oppression and abuse of women among modern adherents of classical humanism, and the persistent gendering of agency, autarchy, and freedom in Greek and Roman authors have often, for their readers, naturalized associations between femininity and powerlessness, with deep consequences for the self-determination not only of women but also of other groups demeaned by feminization: "barbarians," slaves, and "sexual deviants."[8] These legacies make it clear that if we are to look to antiquity at all, it should be an antiquity beyond humanism as it has been historically defined.

But we could hardly suggest that what makes this volume distinctive is that it heeds for the first time the call for an antiquity beyond the humanist vision. Notwithstanding tensions within that vision from its earliest articulations, the decentering of "classical" antiquity and challenges to its ideal bodies and subjects have been ongoing projects for at least over a century, from the rise of comparative anthropology at the end of the nineteenth century and Nietzsche's invention of Dionysus, to investments in the prehistoric and the pre-classical in modernist art, to the antihumanism of postwar European philosophy. In classical scholarship, E. R. Dodds's mid-century classic, *The Greeks and the Irrational* (1951), and the anthropological turn in the group of postwar French scholars of antiquity associated with the Centre Louis Gernet—Jean-Pierre Vernant,

---

[7] Work on the Eurocentrism and racism of classical humanism has been shaped for the past thirty years by Martin Bernal's trilogy *Black Athena*, and especially the first two volumes (Bernal (1987) and (1991)) and the controversy attending their publication; McCoskey (2012) 167–99 provides a useful overview of the debates. The papers in Orrells, Bhambra, and Roynon (2011) bear witness to the ways in which reception studies and studies in black classicism have shifted the terms of the *Black Athena* debate and opened up more sophisticated, difficult, and far-reaching conversations about race and classical antiquity. See also Rankine (2006), esp. 30–3, on the pernicious ways in which the racial logic of the old humanism can resurface in reception studies through the framing of the study of classical antiquity as humanizing, civilizing, or universalizing.

[8] For the problem of sexual difference at the heart of Western metaphysics and issuing from ancient Greece, see especially Irigaray (1985), Cixous (1986), Lloyd (1984), Tuana (1993), Cavarero (1995), Holmes (2012), and Bianchi (2014) as well as the collections of Tuana (1994) and Freeland (1998), especially the contributions of duBois (1994), Saxonhouse (1994).

Pierre Vidal-Naquet, Nicole Loraux, Marcel Detienne—remain landmarks within a field of work marked by a commitment to the otherness of the ancients (and especially "the Greeks") and a non-idealizing vision of the past. If anything, antiquity beyond humanism in its historically dominant forms has been the norm rather than the exception over the past half a century (which is not to say that these humanist traditions don't survive in all kinds of ways into the present, not least when the value of engaging classical antiquity is being contested and the discipline is fielding challenges to its place in the university). The papers in this volume emerge from this rich landscape as much as they engage new theoretical work around and beyond the category of the human in twenty-first-century scholarship. It is therefore worth charting very briefly the background to this volume within classical studies.

The idea of the human in Renaissance humanism and German philhellenism had been premised on an essence in human nature or an ideal quality of humaneness in the Roman or Greek embodiment of man. By contrast, the powerful influence of structuralism on Vernant and other postwar French classicists, as well as on some of their most important interlocutors in the US and the UK, provided an impetus to think the ancient human in relational terms. According to this line of thought, the human lies between the gods and the animal world, defined through the negotiation of taxonomic boundaries rather than through a given essence. Vidal-Naquet's reading of the *Odyssey*, for example, charts the "fantasy world" of the wanderings in Books 9–12 as "a world that is not the world of men, a world which is by turns superhuman and subhuman." The story of the epic, he goes on, "is in one sense the story of Odysseus's return to normality, of his deliberate acceptance of the human condition."[9] The human condition crystallizes through a study in what a human is not (e.g. immortal, omniscient, monstrous, cannibalistic, etc.).

The human, then, can be reread in antiquity as a relational term. Accordingly, its meaning shifts in response to changing ideas of the divine and the animal. Vernant was as deeply interested in the fifth century BCE as a privileged site for the emergence of Greek ideas about the human as previous scholars of the "Greek miracle." But what occupied him was not the fleeting triumph of the classical spirit between archaism and decadence. Rather, he focused on how a nascent legal culture in Athens and the flourishing of Attic tragedy came to redraw the boundaries between the gods and humans by situating human agency in new vocabularies of blame and responsibility, as well as the ways in

---

[9] Vidal-Naquet (1986) 19.

which the rise of the democratic *polis* redefined man against the animal in terms of the idealized image of the autarchic male citizen and his participation in the political community.[10] The gods and the animal remain determining coordinates within the definition of the human. But the human they help produce starts to acquire new qualities. It also arguably acquires sharper lines, as the very categories of "the human" (*ho anthrōpos*) and "human nature" (*hē anthrōpinē physis*) become increasingly determinate, especially in the new genres of prose writing (rhetorical, historiographical, medical, cosmological, prescriptive and so on), which inform, too, the representation of the human body in sculpture. Still, even with the advent of the Protagorean creed, "man is the measure of all things," it is undeniable that the human continues to be measured against the superhuman and the subhuman, whether that means telling stories of early human life that focus on the divergence of anthropology and zoology (in the Hippocratic text *On Ancient Medicine*, for example, or the myth of Protagoras in Plato's eponymous dialogue), creating a *scala naturae* (in Aristotle, for example, or the Stoics), or charting a vision of how a human being might become godlike through philosophical inquiry (e.g. Plato's *Phaedo*, or Aristotle's *Nicomachean Ethics*).

The human can be situated in relationship to the divine and the bestial but it can also be read as a fundamentally gendered category, synonymous with "man" not because of a shared invocation of the universal but because of the implicit assumption that human must mean male. The work of Vernant was not insensitive to the category of gender, but in the 1970s and 1980s, structuralist anthropology met feminism more deliberately in the work of French and American classicists such as Marilyn Arthur Katz, Ann Bergren, Page duBois, Nancy Felson, Helene Foley, Nicole Loraux, Nancy Rabinowitz, Giulia Sissa, and Froma Zeitlin, which exposed the female as a critical foil within the definition of the human in antiquity, now read more explicitly as *man*. The flourishing of feminist readings within a gendered anthropology helped lead to an explosion of interest in the coming decades in the strategies by which Greek and Roman authors defined the category of the human, especially within the "sciences of man," against its many others: not only women but also non-Greek "barbarians," slaves, non-elites, and "sexual deviants," all categories that contaminate one another (purported barbarians and pathic homosexuals are often feminized, women are defined as unfree and requiring male control).

---

[10] See especially the essays in Vernant and Vidal-Naquet (1988).

As the universal category of man became increasingly fissured by difference, critical methodological questions also began to arise about the integrity of categories of identity within the category of the human across time. The privileging of historical difference and the refusal of universalism had been guiding commitments of the Centre Louis Gernet, but the growth of cultural studies and the New Historicism in the 1980s encouraged an even greater fidelity to the specificities of the historical record. The rise of gender studies destabilized the category of "woman" in antiquity, as in other domains, while at the same time fueling the development of sexuality studies and queer theory. Greece and Rome became frontlines in Foucault-inspired debates about the trans-historical validity of "sex" and the changing role played by sexuality in the definition of human norms in different cultures (often in accordance with claims about human nature), as well as in the self-definition of historical actors.[11] Much of the debate turned on just how radically different the classical past was and the ethical stakes of acknowledging the persistence of pernicious ideas and categories from classical antiquity into the present. Debates over ancient racial formations have negotiated these questions as well. In recent years, scholars have acknowledged the groundbreaking work of Frank Snowden Jr. in demonstrating the apparently negligible role played by skin color in our ancient Greek and Roman sources, both textual and material, while at the same time dissecting the logic of ancient racial formations, different from the present but nevertheless persistent and still operative within the functioning of the categories of human and subhuman today.[12]

Instead of simply accepting the free Greek adult male as the natural synonym of the human and a target of mimesis in the present, then,

---

[11] The status of the category of "pathic homosexual"—that is, *kinaidos/cinaedus*—has been highly contested in the history of sexuality. For some of the key positions in the debate, see Winkler (1989) esp. 45–6 and Halperin (2002) 35 (arguing for the largely fictional status of the *kinaidos/cinaedus*) and, for arguments that see more continuity between ancient and contemporary queer identities and subcultures, Richlin (1993) and Taylor (1997). For further discussion of the "sexuality wars," see Holmes (2012). The very stakes of what it means to seek sameness or difference in the history of sexuality have been vigorously debated in medieval, Renaissance, and early modern studies over the past decade—see e.g. the essays and introduction in Fradenburg and Freccero (1996), Goldberg and Menon (2005) and Traub (2013)—but these conversations, while responding in key ways to the arguments of Halperin (1990) and (2002) and advancing the theoretical conversation significantly—have had a relatively negligible effect on work in ancient Greco-Roman sexuality. Matzner (2016) has started to open up the conversation.
[12] See Snowden (1970) and (1983); Dee (2003–4) defamiliarizes "white" as a self-descriptor of ancient Greeks and Romans. On proto-racism in antiquity, see Isaac (2004). McCoskey (2012) provides a useful overview of the turn towards "ethnicity" and argues for the importance of keeping race as a central term in work on Greco-Roman antiquity.

scholars of antiquity have in recent decades relentlessly and painstakingly interrogated the exclusions constituting the human in ancient texts, exposing the category as ever more vulnerable to the encroachment of the ostensibly subhuman. They have aimed to make more far-reaching claims about the exclusionary logic of the construction of the human in Greek thought or Greek culture as a whole, at times working with the resources of psychoanalysis and anthropology. There has been pushback in some quarters against the broad sweep of some of this work and what is seen as the tendency, in some early structuralist work in particular, to draw freely from a corpus of heterogeneous material from distinctive cultures within a period of time spanning over a thousand years. Yet even working at the granular level of the case study or the individual text, it is difficult to miss the persistent definition of norms, which in antiquity are ethical rather than statistical, in terms of gender, race, class, social status, sexuality, and species. We can no longer *not* notice the ways in which being human in the majority of our ancient texts is restricted to a small group of people who have to overcome the parts of themselves that pull towards the subhuman and the non-human in order to *become* human and *stay* human, thanks to a robust tradition of work on an antiquity beyond humanism. The essays in this volume are at once deeply indebted to this tradition, participate within it, and hope to contribute to its continued flourishing.

Yet for all that women, slaves, or barbarians are read as failing to achieve full humanity by many ancient authors, they remain in an important way within the category of the human. They may be "mutilated" specimens, as in Aristotle's infamous definition of the female, but they are still specimens. These kinds of differences have emerged as decisive for the posthuman or non-human turn within the broader theoretical humanities and social sciences, which has focused attention on a space beyond the human qua species and interrogated how changes in technology, global economy, and ecological conditions have transformed or will soon transform the very definition of the human as a species.

The essays gathered in this volume resist the idea that such changing conditions sever our present and future selves from millennia of reflection on what it means to be human, and those in the first Part, in particular, interrogate directly the relevance of posthumanism to our engagement with ancient texts. At the same time, they share with the broader theoretical humanities a focus on zones of the non-human constituted more by an understanding of the human qua species than by an understanding of the human qua ideal state, zones that can be glossed as the animal, the vegetal, the cosmic, the material, or the daemonic. Of course, it can be difficult to parse the difference between these two versions of the human. The human in antiquity is never a value-neutral category, though this is not to say that the human always comes out ahead of the animal: in 1935, Lovejoy and Boas compiled a whole dossier of texts supporting what they call "animalitarianism," exemplified most spectacularly by Plutarch's *Gryllus*, where the men turned into swine by Circe resist a return to human form by extolling the virtues of animal life and insisting on the superiority of animals to humans.[13] Nevertheless, the space "beyond humanism" that these essays traverse expands to encompass things and bodies and beings that are classed not so much as ostensibly *failed* humans but as not human at all.

In this respect, these essays re-engage questions that have been central to the structuralist project: the relations among the human and the animal, the divine and daemonic realms.[14] At the same time, the work gathered here shares a desire to avoid the strict polarities that have at times become straitjackets within structuralist analyses, even when those analyses have insisted on a poetics of ambiguity.[15] They share an interest in taking up the animal world, the cosmos, and the daemonic as categories that function not just to delineate the human but which are also mapped as spaces demanding exploration on their own terms, as much as possible. They take seriously the relationships between the human and the non-human worlds together with forms of non-human sociality in ancient texts that share features with distinctively human modes of sociality (e.g. political, choral, affective) but cannot be reduced to their purely human manifestation. They expand beyond the animal and the divine to encompass, too, material objects, plants, and the cosmos as a whole. And much as an important strain of work in non-human studies more generally has dealt with the ways in which the human self—and usually the human body—is imagined to incorporate the non-human (the germ cell, e.g., or the microflora of the biome), a number of the chapters here interrogate and reflect on how facets of the human can become portals to the non-human (the voice, for example, or the experience of desire).

None of this is to say that a body of work on animals in antiquity, or plants, or humans in relation to the larger cosmos does not exist. But the majority of such work has been done primarily in subfields in ancient philosophy and science that often remain isolated from broader

---

[13] Lovejoy and Boas (1935) 389–420.
[14] This is not a surprise, given that some important work in non-human studies, especially in anthropology, is avowedly neo-structuralist, perhaps most notably that of Philippe Descola: see Descola (2013a) and (2013b).
[15] See, for example, the critique of Wohl (2005) 137–8 of the analysis of sexual difference in Charles Segal's structuralist-inspired reading of the *Bacchae*.

interdisciplinary theoretical conversations. It is true that there is a rich tradition within Classics of attending to the many ways human selves are permeable to non-human forces. Indeed, important work has recognized how the forces that course through the warrior lusting for battle or the lover flooded with desire or the person ingesting a meal are not exclusively human at all but rather conduits of energy that also pass through rivers and trees and clouds, creating bonds between bodies that are subject to increasingly complex examination in ancient cosmological, biological, and medical writings.[16] But contemporary theoretical preoccupations with the limits of the human—and with what lies beyond those limits—warrant a rethinking of the implications of these ancient ways of imagining force, emotion, and desire as points of connectivity between human and non-human.

The point is not, however, that an agenda set by contemporary theory needs to be now simply applied to ancient material. As we have stressed, the papers here are deeply committed to the idea that ancient texts actively contribute to contemporary discussions and harbor an untimely potential to disrupt and extend them. Indeed, the particular constellation of concerns captured by the "non-human turn" invites us to read ancient texts from new angles as we seek to imagine anew in the present. Some of this work is beginning to get underway. While classical archaeology has for some time now been reconceptualizing objects as agents within human and non-human networks of power, more attention is being paid these days to the semiotic and agential power of objects within ancient texts.[17] Recent work on animals in antiquity has probed the ways in which ancient authors sympathetically imagine animal life, the ways in which narratives of metamorphosis disclose forms of otherness irreducible to binary taxonomy, and the contributions that ancient philosophy might make to contemporary debates about interspecies ethics.[18] The ferment of activity within the environmental humanities and ecocriticism is starting to be channeled into readings of Greco-Roman texts, as are the resources of environmental history.[19] The ways in which nature and organisms are imagined through the thinking of machines, a deep vein of work in contemporary non- and posthuman studies, have been traced in recent

---

[16] See Onians (1951); Padel (1992); Clarke (1999).

[17] See e.g. Purves (2015); Mueller (2016); and the essays in Greenstine and Johnson (2017) ; Telò and Mueller (2018); and Chesi and Spiegel (Forthcoming).

[18] See e.g. Payne (2010) and (2016); Bell and Naas (2015); Hutchins (2016). On ancient philosophy and interspecies ethics, Sorabji (1993) remains relevant.

[19] See the recent edited collection Schliephake (2016). On environmental history, Harper (2016).

work with due attention to the specific nature of *technē* and mechanism in ancient writers.[20]

So while rethinking the human within the framework of a rigorously materialist cosmos has a long history, the project is now being undertaken from a range of new perspectives in the theoretical humanities and continental philosophy. The essays gathered here engage deeply with this work, sometimes sympathetically and sometimes critically but always as active participants in contemporary conversations. By publishing these essays together, we hope to encourage further work in these areas in many different communities working on material from Greco-Roman antiquity.

1.2. Posthumanism, the non-human, and contemporary theory

Antiquities beyond Humanism thus also joins a fast-moving stream of critical-theoretical work that, since the early 1990s, has shifted attention to objects, affects, bodies, matter and materialisms, living and non-living animacies, and the networks and ecologies that connect them, across disciplines as wide-ranging as philosophy, feminist theory, queer theory, cultural studies and the social sciences more generally, science studies, and political theory. While a comprehensive mapping of these movements and their many-tentacled and burgeoning strands is beyond the scope of this introduction, the question of what our untimely, anachronistic engagement with antiquity contributes to this field is worth tarrying with. Of the various starting points one might choose for this "turn," especially in the Anglo-American context, one might usefully point to Elizabeth Grosz's 1994 text, *Volatile Bodies*. Here, Grosz lays out an alternative to thinking about the corporeal that rescues it from the "profound somatophobia" of the Western tradition. She traces this somatophobia from Plato and the Judaeo-Christian tradition to the present, finding its zenith in Cartesian dualism. Most twentieth-century feminist theory, with its understandable emphasis on gender rather than sex, that is, in its focus on human practices, culture, language, and history in the project of diagnosing and seeking to remediate misogyny and sexism, unthinkingly repeats this devaluation of the body. Grosz responds to this complicity of feminism and somatophobia by reactivating an alternate non-Cartesian ontological tradition, monist rather than

---

[20] See e.g. Berryman (2009); Roby (2013).

dualist, committed to the immanence of bodies, earthliness, affectivity, and materiality, and found in thinkers such as Nietzsche, Bergson, Foucault, Simondon, and, above all, Deleuze. Spinoza has been a key predecessor here but in her most recent work on "the incorporeal," Grosz follows Deleuze in going back to ancient philosophy, and the Stoics in particular (from whom she borrows "the incorporeal"), thereby responding, too, to the ancient and, more specifically, Stoic roots of Spinozist philosophy.[21]

Now Grosz also thoroughly embraces an inclusion of human practices in forming, shaping, inscribing, indeed in materializing bodies, so to call her position one that is committed primarily to the posthuman or non-human would be patently false. And yet, as the title *Volatile Bodies* suggests, she also affords bodies and materiality their own motility and a capacity for effective action. This concern for the ways that bodies, matter, and things move and exist independently of the human capacity to explicitly know them became the focus of much of the thinking that followed in the first decades of the twenty-first century, in the various incarnations of what have come to be called new materialisms, speculative realisms, affect theories, and object-oriented ontologies. Along with feminist philosophers such as Moira Gatens, Rosi Braidotti, and Donna Haraway, and other contemporaneous thinkers such as Manuel DeLanda, Brian Massumi, and Pheng Cheah, Grosz was thus a pivotal figure in reopening a philosophical genealogy that had been left relatively fallow during the era of twentieth-century "high theory" and that, especially in the face of accelerating environmental crisis, opened inevitably on to questions of the posthuman and the non-human. This is not to say that materiality, the body, the non-human, the affective, or the objectal were not also key thematic concerns within the dominant strands of twentieth-century theorizing. Psychoanalysis, Marxism, structuralism, phenomenology, the Foucaultian understanding of power, theories of performativity, and deconstruction have after all attended assiduously to these phenomena, evidenced for example par excellence by Derrida's extended engagement with the question of the animal in his later work.[22] Nonetheless, it would be hard to argue that a seismic shift has not taken place, one conditioned at once by the rise of neo-liberal global capitalism, climate change and accelerating environmental destruction, new understandings of colonial and decolonial historical dynamics, and new configurations of gender, among which *Antiquities beyond Humanism* is inalienably situated.

---

[21] See Grosz (2017) and Deleuze (1990). For Deleuze and the Stoics, see Bénatouïl (2003); Sellars (2007); Johnson (2017); and Holmes in this volume.

[22] See, in particular, Derrida (2008).

One hallmark of this turn in the intellectual sphere, then, has been to draw on an alternate genealogy of modern philosophy that sidesteps the aporias of Cartesianism by taking Spinoza's *Ethics* as a foundational text, a text which proposes, in Deleuze's interpretation, "a *common plane of immanence* on which all bodies, all minds, and all individuals are situated."[23] This sense of immanence, in which nothing stands apart from the world that might function as a transcendent foundational principle of it or for it, gives on to a scene where all things are in continual becoming, expression, proliferation, diffusion, interconnection, and—to use Karen Barad's word—intra-action.[24] The hierarchical binaries so central to structuralist and poststructuralist thinking—here we might include not just mind and body, but reason and passion, intellect and sensation, outside and inside, depth and surface, reality and appearance, presence and absence, lack and satisfaction, among many others—dissolve in a field of plenitude that rigorously flattens such hierarchies. Moreover, things are no longer specified according to static form but are understood as emergent and processual, and boundaries are understood as connective tissue as much as barriers that separate. Many of these binaries are central to modern philosophical paradigms, but some of them, such as form and matter, are established in ancient Greek thought, perhaps sometimes in different form (*psychē*, often translated as soul but deriving from breath, certainly over time becomes opposable in antiquity to *sōma* or body), and continue to hold sway throughout the dominant Western tradition.

In a signal intervention, Deleuze and Guattari begin their 1972 opus *Anti-Oedipus* by designating bodies, organs, and individuals as *machines*, the famous desiring machines that engage in desiring-production— desiring machines plugging into organ machines: "The breast is a machine that produces milk, and the mouth a machine coupled to it."[25] In one short sentence Deleuze and Guattari dispense not just with Oedipus and his primal transgression, but also with Hecuba's organic maternal connection with Hector and with Orestes' matricide, indeed with all Greek foundational scenes and the logics of sacrifice they both produce and support. They also annul the distinctiveness of Pandora, for if the first woman is a deadly artifact, the infant is no less a machine, and both have been thrown free of any death-drive into a profusion of machinic liveliness. Not only is sexual difference, strictly speaking, hereby rendered irrelevant but perhaps the most profound and enduring of ancient distinctions, that between *technē* and *physis*—art or craft, and

---

[23] Deleuze (1988) 122.   [24] Barad (2007) 33 and *passim*.
[25] Deleuze and Guattari (1983) 1.

nature—is also destroyed insofar as the figure of the machine comes to encompass both.

Echoes resonating back to antiquity, at least to Plato, may also be found in Deleuze's interest in what he calls Spinoza's expressionism, insofar as the distinction between the One and the Many still may be seen to be in operation in the distinction between the unified substance that Spinoza famously designates, almost in passing, as "god, or nature," and the infinite attributes and modes which it expresses. The problem of the One and the Many is of course a central issue for Plato, notably in the *Parmenides*, in which the question of their relation remains steadfastly unresolved. Plotinus turns the problem of participation of the Many in the One on its head: instead of asking how it is possible for the Many to participate in the One, he proposes that the One is a source from which the Many emanates through an overflow that is essentially a giving, a donation, a divine unity which necessarily exceeds and overflows itself as emanation and expression. Joshua Ramey, in *The Hermetic Deleuze*, carefully traces these precursors to Deleuze's thought throughout a long tradition, from Plotinus through Porphyry, Iamblichus, and John Scotus Eriugena, all the way to figures like Nicolas of Cusa and Giordano Bruno. Ramey contends that these later Christian thinkers could be understood to have instituted a subversive "plane of immanence" within theology itself.[26]

In this way, then, an immanentist strand could be said to stretch or echo all the way back to Greek antiquity, finding its richest metaphor in and as the *rhizome*, which is—in addition to being one of the most persistent motifs of Deleuze and Guattari—the central term in Empedocles' natural philosophy. *Rhizōmata pantōn*, the "roots of all things," normally (mis)translated as "elements," encompass for Empedocles fire, air, earth, and water, and their divine counterparts: "bright Zeus, life-giving Hera, and Aidoneus, and Nestis who moistens the springs of men with her tears" (DK31 B6). Divine and material at once, but indeterminately so, since there has been controversy since antiquity over how the four ancient elements should be correlated with each deity, as well as some mystery as to the identity of "Nestis"—a *hapax legomenon* in the tradition, often glossed conveniently as a Sicilian water goddess— these four elemental beings are bound by the vegetal figure of the rhizome. Rhizomatic vegetality, that of the tuber as well the multi-stranded hyphae of mycological and fungal networks, eschews the logic of the unified and vertical radicle or root. Embedded in earth and *in*

---

[26] Ramey (2012) 37; a careful and detailed account of this genealogy ensues, 37–47.

extremis indistinguishable from it (drinking up water, spreading in all directions like fire, opening up possibilities like air), at once material and divine, the rhizome cannot properly figure either Greek origin or Greek miracle in any traditional sense. It also dissolves the compositional and partitional logic of the element as building block, as part that makes up a whole, and thereby separates itself from any possible atomism. Instead, like *Antiquities beyond Humanism*, it multiplies origins, rendering them unstable and only partially knowable, partially revealed and yet always partially concealed.

This evocation of Empedocles also returns us to the arguably non-humanist strands of early nineteenth-century German romanticism and *Naturphilosophie*, and in particular to Hölderlin's several iterations of his play *The Death of Empedocles*, in which the philosopher's own self-immolation in the magma of Mount Etna represents the culmination of the merging of the human with nature, a kind of natural apotheosis.[27] And yet the insistent organicism of romanticism poses dangers too. The fantasy of an unbroken connection between Germany and Greece is rendered perhaps all too material and literal in the watery flow of "Der Ister," Hölderlin's hymn to the Danube which rises in the mountains of the Black Forest and spills out into the Black Sea, a natural link between these two great nations powering an ultimately genocidal national imaginary. Nietzsche's later call to "remain faithful to the earth" will explicitly eschew such organicism along with any philological aspiration to Indo-European or Aryan unity, even as he harks back to the glory of the Greeks' tragic age.[28] Instead, he seeks the tragic intensifications of life in the midst of embracing the facticity of death, prior to the turn toward what he calls, with famous disparagement, the "Greek cheerfulness" characteristic of both Socrates and Euripides.[29] One task, then, to which this volume hopes to contribute is a decoupling of such classicizing organicism, or approach to "the natural," from any possible nationalism, any possible localism, any project that may seek to delimit the West from and contrast it with its Eastern or African or Semitic others. It thus aims to deterritorialize the Greco-Roman tradition, thereby setting in motion, anti-imperialistically, varied and uneven lines of flight. At times it also re-engages that tradition, as Cavarero does with her Arendtian Socrates, and deploys it in an explicitly critical, anti-totalitarian, politically resistive mode.

While many of the chapters in *Antiquities beyond Humanism* do not address these lines of thinking explicitly (Mark Payne's essay evokes the

---

[27] Hölderlin (2008).   [28] Nietzsche (1954) 125.
[29] Nietzsche (1967) 97 and *passim*.

German Romantics, but in a quite different register, that of the multiplicity of chorality), they are nonetheless situated, as we are, in a philosophical milieu that has emerged, along Spinozist lines, as a countertradition to that of Cartesian dualism and the reign of the philosophy of the human subject inaugurated therein. Rather than directly countering this dominant architecture of modernity with a suppressed philosophical alternative, *Antiquities beyond Humanism* seeks a renewed encounter with the strangeness of the Greek texts and the Greek world that is at once indelibly marked by modernity and capable of disrupting its terms. The essays here address anew the voices and echoes that populate these texts and worlds, attending to the dynamic multiplicity of its dramas, its goddesses, gods, heroes, women, objects, affects, animals, plants, cosmos, and the lives of its mortals and their political forms, drawing out unexpected resonances and connections. We are situated within such beings' entanglements with nature, with fate, with necessity, within a landscape vastly distant in space and time, barely knowable and yet all too familiar, thinking with those who, like us and yet not like us, grapple with philosophical problems of mortality, immortality, body, soul, matter, life, morality, war, kinship, desire, love, space and time, origin, and what it might mean to live well together in the city and in the cosmos. *Antiquities beyond Humanism* renews these questions in thoroughly surprising ways, radically different from and yet uncannily familiar to those found in the hegemonic systems and discourses of modernity.

1.3. Antiquities beyond humanism

At turns critical and speculative, the chapters in this volume mark both sites of rupture in what is often represented as a seamless celebration of the human and the opening of new vistas unremarked in the majority of scholarship. In gathering them together, we have no ambition to comprehensive coverage but aim rather for provocations to thought. The current organization reflects one way in which its chapters overlap, but there are others, and our hope is that this structure will invite the reader to draw connections as she sees fit. For instance, a concern with vocality and meaning, with the uneasy coupling of speech and reason in ancient Greek *logos*, animates several of these chapters. More than one author observe a startling divergence between anthropocentrism and humanism in certain aspects of ancient thought. Several chapters gesture towards a radical ecological dimension of ancient thought that demands further attention and exploration.

Part 1 stages a lively exchange about the merits and limits of the volume's theoretical enterprise and contains a set of challenges that illuminate the stakes of bringing this collection of questions to classical antiquity. Adriana Cavarero throws into question the figure of the posthuman itself through a reading of Arendt. "The Human Reconceived: Back to Socrates with Arendt" locates the production of the posthuman in a very particular time and place. In the wake of the deliberate and orchestrated attempt to strip humanity of its constitutive plurality and produce in its stead an anonymous mass, the posthuman emerges not as a means of critiquing anthropocentrism but as a "material outcome of totalitarianism." For Arendt, the figure of Socrates serves as a focal point, a figure whose fearless public scrutiny of his time and place recommends him as an antidote to the Platonic disavowal of plurality and thus as a model of resistance to the processes of dehumanization that produces the posthuman. For Cavarero, Arendt's Socrates is a potent reminder of the political work of thinking with and against the posthuman.

In the exemplary character of Socrates, Ramona Naddaff, too, finds rich theoretical fodder, and in "Hearing Voices: The Sounds in Socrates' Head" she investigates the most vivid and controversial sign of this exemplarity, Socrates' daemonic voice. Drawing upon Roland Barthes's taxonomy of listening, Naddaff calls attention to the peculiar form of responsiveness that Socrates exercises and its effect on his character, emphasizing the simultaneously diremptive and constitutive operation of Socratic listening. For Naddaff, Socrates' response to this voice transforms him onto something other than human and presents the figure of the philosopher as an anticipation of the posthuman.

Michael Naas queries the antiquity of the posthuman from another direction and in a more critical vein, calling attention to the depth of anthropocentrism in ancient thought by focusing upon the unusual construction of the difference between human and animal in Plato's *Laws*: only humans, claims Plato's Athenian Stranger, can sing and dance. In "Song and Dance Man: Plato and the Limits of the Human" he takes this claim as a measure of Plato's commitment to the primacy of the human and finds in it a springboard for investigating other moments in Plato's dialogues where this prioritization comes to the fore: an emblem of what must be wrestled with in attempting to find resources for thinking the posthuman in ancient thought.

On the opposite end of this line of inquiry, Miriam Leonard illuminates the anti-humanist character of one of the figures most frequently presented as a champion of the human: Sophocles. Working within a psychoanalytic framework, she sees in Sophoclean tragedy a traumatizing decentering of the human via the wound that tragedy inflicts to human self-love. Leonard shows how this wound is reopened in Freud's location of the life and death instincts across a broad spectrum of organisms, making the human no more or less bound to them than, for instance, the germ cell. But further, by denying a necessary division between human and animal and insisting instead that one hold oneself open to the non-human, positioning its protagonists, "on a spectrum of sub and super-human possibilities" (16), tragedy moves beyond those strains of contemporary posthuman thought that are mired in a needless dichotomy.

Several of the chapters in Part 1 call for a nuanced study of the various moments in ancient thought in which animality itself is present to inquiry via the vivid intersection of human and non-human animal life. The chapters in Part 2 respond to this call by charting a certain fluidity and permeability between categories of living beings and natural forces. They offer glimpses of an account of life, a zoology, strikingly different from both Linnaean taxonomy and Heideggerian phenomenology, with its insistence on the ontological distinction between human and animal. These alternate zoologies invite a rethinking of the divisions that shape the human experience of social and political life and of the images by means of which we venture to understand the cosmos.

In Part 1, Leonard's work on Sophocles invited a critical reappraisal of those thinkers most associated with privileging the human, a reappraisal based on careful attention to moments in antiquity in which the interpenetration of human and non-human animal worlds comes to the fore. Sara Brill opens Part 2 by turning to the relationship between zoology and politics in Aristotle's thought. "Aristotle's Meta-Zoology: Shared Life and Human Animality in the *Politics*" argues that the particular political forms of human intimacy that arise from the possession of language and the capacity for choice—intimacies collectively understood as arising from the sharing of life—can only be fully understood when measured on a zoological scale. Here, they emerge not as categorically distinct from forms of shared animal life, but rather as an intensification of them. Political community, in turn, emerges from Aristotle's *Politics* as the properly human habitat (*topos*) by merit of its foundation in the shared perception of advantage and disadvantage. The tenuousness of this shared perception creates an instability that requires a very particular form of ecological thought, one that must attend to all that is shared between human and non-human animals.

Kristin Sampson turns to Homeric epic to consider what the voice might mean in the absence of a Platonic emphasis on the autonomy of the speaking subject, that is, on speaking in one's own voice. In "Sounds of Subjectivity or Resonances of Something Other" she investigates how the voice might possibly sound "if the body and the soul are not established as entities that can function as a ground for an autonomous identity" (124). In the fluidity of Homeric *phōnē*, Sampson finds a conception of voice tied neither to the actions of a subject, nor even to what we would normally call a living entity at all. In the bellows of the wave, the roar of fire, and the howling of the wind we confront a voice that signifies without a subject, or, as Sampson puts it, we encounter corporeality without body and a living world "breathing and full of voice" (131).

In broaching the fluid boundaries between humans, non-human animals, and natural forces, Sampson identifies a permeability that Mark Payne also finds in the polyvocal character of the Hellenistic poets' approach to nature, echoed too in the nineteenth-century sentimental poetry of Schiller and Hölderlin. In "Shared Life as Chorality in Schiller, Hölderlin, and Hellenistic Poetry," Payne excavates a very particular sensibility—the human feeling of its own organicity, of itself as a subject of life—by means of which it moves beyond merely human sociality to a shared life with all living beings. This sensibility takes the form of participating in a chorus, of being immersed in a plurality of voices, breaths, and rhythms; it is the recovery of this chorality that sentimental poetry takes as its aim. We can thus read in Hölderlin's Calauria or Wordsworth's River Derwent an ecological poetics that attempts to revive and pay homage to a sense of the shared organicity from which self-formation arises.

It is to yet another fluidity that Giulia Sissa directs our attention: the perpetual flux of Pythagoras' great speech in Ovid's *Metamorphoses*, a speech she reads as illuminating the eccentricity of the poetic metaphysics at work in the poem. For Ovid, the change that forms and permeates the cosmos follows a certain logic and operates as a very particular kind of becoming, one that produces stabilities that endure for a time and then flow away. Out of this form of becoming emerges not only a taxonomy of animals and plants but also an ethics of eating. Or, as Sissa puts it, Ovid's *Metamorphoses* "respects a vegetarian *contrainte*, which is logical, structural, and literary" (162). To be sure, this is an ethics born not out of respect for non-human life but out of the fear of anthropophagy, and in this the poem remains an anthropocentric text. But, as Sissa demonstrates, its metamorphic fluidity undermines any sense of human exceptionalism and thus presents us with the paradoxical formation of an anthropocentrism that is also posthuman.

Sissa's paradox invites consideration of forces in antiquity that operate entirely beyond the human sphere. The chapters collected in Part 3 look to the resources in ancient thought for thinking the materiality of natural forces and their often gendered scenes of emergence and interaction in a manner that is firmly anthro-excentric.

James I. Porter finds in a collection of ancient texts evidence of an array of materialisms that resonate with object-oriented ontology, speculative realism, and the objects that provide a primary provocation for these schools of thought. In "Hyperobjects, OOO, and the Eruptive Classics—Field Notes of an Accidental Tourist," he investigates these resonances along three trajectories: views of nature in which we encounter some conception of a hyperobject; a collection of materialist and sensualist perspectives on nature in which matter is conceived as operating independently of a human phenomenology; and object-oriented philosophies of nature that treat human phenomena as one object among others. Porter's wide-ranging study is double-faced. It illuminates the existence of object-oriented tendencies in the ancient Greek and Roman worlds, but it also indicates the greater ease with which those philosophies meld the ethical with the material and the natural. And it is in its latent ethical significance that Porter views the primary value of contemporary object-oriented thought. Without the risk and danger of conceiving of the contingency and ungrounded character of the human world, we miss not only the fullest possibilities of ethical life, and some clarity regarding its stakes, but also the very means by which we might measure the full catastrophic scale of climate change.

As Porter makes clear, the conceptions of matter at work in these texts are inextricable from a conception of nature, and it is to a few of the most ancient figurations of *physis* that Emanuela Bianchi directs our attention, finding in Presocratic thought an account of nature whose performative dimension holds profound significance for both phenomenological studies of nature and for the treatment of nature in feminist and queer theory. In "Nature Trouble: Ancient *Physis* and Queer Performativity" Bianchi interrogates the common impulse for a final unveiling of truth that drives the search for origin in classical antiquity and the search for an underlying reality in contemporary physics. Drawing on Butler's notion of gender performativity as well as a phenomenological approach to the natural world that brings to bear the thinking of John Sallis, Alphonso Lingis, and Luce Irigaray upon its readings of early Greek texts, Bianchi develops a phenomenological account of nature as itself thoroughly performative, a theater of display, unpredictable effect, and response that may never succumb to full epistemic illumination. In so doing, she at once radicalizes the Heideggerian account of ancient *physis*, while mounting an intervention into what she sees as the reductionism and scientism of contemporary theorists of the posthuman such as Karen Barad.

While Porter and Bianchi highlight the material and dramaturgical impulses in ancient Greek thinking about nature, Brooke Holmes approaches the complex tensions within what she calls "capital-N" Nature—Nature as a totality, rather than an individual nature, as in Aristotle—through the Stoic concept of sympathy (*sympatheia*). In "On Stoic Sympathy: Cosmobiology and the Life of Nature," Holmes shows how the Stoics contribute to the conceptualization of a web of interconnected natures in antiquity by making sympathy visible as a feature of the world. Asking why sympathy mattered so much to the Stoics, she demonstrates its role in reconciling parts and wholes and establishing the unity of unified bodies, including the unity of the cosmos, before working through the tensions within sympathy as a mark of organic life and, especially, as a sign of the cosmic organism. By taking cosmobiology to an extreme, the Stoics have to deal with how to affirm the integrity of individual natures within a cosmos organized not only by a nature but by Nature as a determined life, to which each part must be subordinated. Revisiting Deleuze's reading of the Stoics in the *Logic of Sense*, she argues that sympathy must be seen as the surface effect par excellence in the Stoic cosmos, naming the paradoxical reality of god's becoming.

Rebecca Hill shifts attention away from the space of the cosmos to the concept of time, arguing in "Immanent Maternal: Figures of Time in Aristotle, Bergson and Irigaray" that in Aristotle's account of time we find an unexpected precursor to the account of time as difference in the work of Luce Irigaray and Henri Bergson. As with Naas's reading of Plato, Hill attends to Aristotle's illumination of a metaphysics that frames what is supposed to be beyond the human within human terms, in this case the hierarchically sexed terms that color so much of Aristotle's ethical and political thought. And, like other authors in the volume, she sees the merit of such a reading as working in two directions, telling us something significant about ancient thought but also illuminating important aspects of contemporary theory. That is, Hill's account of time in Aristotle recommends that we read Irigaray's designation of woman as becoming as "the strategic gesture of a combatant" (285) designed to make a critical incursion into the intertwined ancient legacy of time and gender.

In the final chapter, Claudia Baracchi works to give voice to what has become "inaudible" in contemporary scholarly approaches to Aristotle: the primacy of *erōs* in matters both cosmic and human in that, for Aristotle, "everything...moves *for love* and *out of love*, stretching out in a desiring thrust" (289). Through a masterful reading of Aristotle's ambiguous assessment of Hesiod and Parmenides, Baracchi excavates an erotics at the heart of Aristotle's physics and follows it back to Plato's *Symposium*, where it operates as the deranging force that both creates and destroys worlds and that gives human beings the primary mandate to endure loss (of self, of other, of world) without ceasing to love. In such a physics (which is also an ethics and a metaphysics), androgyny emerges as a mode of being capable of responding to this mandate, as "the cipher of a completeness (at once accomplished and hyperbolical, because infinitely open) that can sustain any division, end, or loss" (302). To hear anything like this understanding of androgyny, we would have to look beyond the confines of traditional academic studies of ancient Greek thought to more poetic figurations, and Baracchi concludes with those Virginia Woolf employs in the praise of love she offers through the transformations of that all-too-human posthuman, Orlando.

WORKS CITED

Barad, Karen (2007) *Meeting the Universe Halfway: Quantum Physics and the Entanglement of Matter and Meaning*. Durham, NC.

Bell, Jeremy Randolph, and Michael Naas (eds) (2015) *Plato's Animals: Gadflies, Horses, Swans, and Other Philosophical Beasts*. Bloomington, IN.

Bénatouïl, Thomas (2003) "Deux usages du Stoïcisme: Deleuze, Foucault," in Frédéric Gros and Carlos Lévy (eds), *Foucault et la philosophie antique*. Paris: 17–49.

Bernal, Martin (1987) *Black Athena: The Afroasiatic Roots of Classical Civilization. Volume 1*. New Brunswick.

Bernal, Martin (1990) *Black Athena: The Afroasiatic Roots of Classical Civilization. Volume 2: The Archaeological and Documentary Evidence*. New Brunswick.

Berryman, Sylvia (2009) *The Mechanical Hypothesis in Ancient Greek Natural Philosophy*. Cambridge.

Bianchi, Emanuela (2014) *The Feminine Symptom: Aleatory Matter in the Aristotelian Cosmos*. New York.

Cavarero, Adriana (1995) *In Spite of Plato: A Feminist Rewriting of Ancient Philosophy*, trans. S. Anderlini-D'Onofrio and Aine O'Healy. New York.

Chesi, Giulia Maria, and Francesca Spiegel (eds) (Forthcoming) *Classical Literature and Posthumanism*. London.

Cixous, Hélène (1986) "Sorties: Out and Out: Attacks/Ways Out/Forays," in Hélène Cixous and Catherine Clément (eds), *The Newly Born Woman*, trans. Betsy Wing. Minneapolis: 163–32.

Clarke, Michael (1999) *Flesh and Spirit in the Songs of Homer: A Study of Words and Myths*. Oxford.

Dee, J. H. (2003–4) "Black Odysseus, White Caesar: When Did 'White People' Become 'White'?", *Classical Journal* 99: 157–67.

Deleuze, Gilles (1988) *Spinoza: Practical Philosophy*, trans. Robert Hurley. San Francisco.

Deleuze, Gilles (1990) *The Logic of Sense*, trans. Mark Lester with Charles Stivale. New York.
Deleuze, Gilles, and Félix Guattari (1983) *Anti-Oedipus: Capitalism and Schizophrenia*, trans. R. Hurley, M. Seem, and H. R. Lane. Minneapolis.
Derrida, Jacques (2008) *The Animal That Therefore I Am*, trans. David Wills. New York.
Descola, Philippe (2013a) *Beyond Nature and Culture*, trans. Janet Lloyd. Chicago.
Descola, Philippe (2013b) *The Ecology of Others*, trans. Genevieve Godbout and Benjamin P. Luley. Chicago.
duBois, Page (1994) "The Platonic Appropriation of Reproduction," in Nancy Tuana (ed.), *Feminist Interpretations of Aristotle*. University Park, PA: 139–56.
Fradenburg, Louise, and Carla Freccero (eds) (1996) *Premodern Sexualities*. New York.
Freeland, Cynthia (ed.) (1998) *Feminist Interpretations of Aristotle*. University Park, PA.
Goldberg, Jonathan, and Madhavi Menon (2005) "Queering History," *PMLA* 120: 1608–17.
Grafton, Anthony, and Lisa Jardine (1986) *From Humanism to the Humanities: Education and the Liberal Arts in Fifteenth- and Sixteenth-Century Europe*. London.
Greenstine, A. J., and R. J. Johnson (eds) (2017) *Contemporary Encounters with Ancient Metaphysics*. Edinburgh.
Grosz, Elizabeth (2017) *The Incorporeal: Ontology, Ethics, and the Limits of Materialism*. New York.
Halperin, David (1990) *One Hundred Years of Homosexuality: And Other Essays on Greek Love*. New York.
Halperin, David M. (2002) *How To Do the History of Homosexuality*. Chicago.
Harper, Kyle (2016) "The Environmental Fall of the Roman Empire," *Daedalus* 145: 101–11.
Holmes, Brooke (2012) *Gender: Antiquity and Its Legacy*. New York.
Hölderlin, Friedrich (2008) *The Death of Empedocles: A Mourning Play*, trans. David Farrell Krell. Albany, NY.
Honig, Bonnie (2013) *Antigone, Interrupted*. Cambridge.
Hutchins, Richard (2016) "Interspecies Ethics and Collaborative Survival in Lucretius' *De Rerum Natura*," in Schliephake (2016): 91–112.
Irigaray, Luce (1985) *Speculum of the Other Woman*, trans. Gillian C. Gill. Ithaca.
Isaac, Benjamin (2004) *The Invention of Racism in Classical Antiquity*. Princeton.
Johnson, R. J. (2017) "On the Surface: The Deleuze-Stoicism Encounter," in A. J. Greenstine and R. J. Johnson (2017).
Lloyd, Genevieve (1984) *The Man of Reason: "Male" and "Female" in Western Philosophy*. Minneapolis.
Lovejoy, Arthur O., and George Boas (1935) *Primitivism and Related Ideas in Antiquity*. Baltimore.
Marchand, Suzanne (2003) *Down from Olympus: Archaeology and Philhellenism in Germany, 1750–1970*. Princeton.
Matzner, Sebastian (2016) "Queer Unhistoricism: Scholars, Metalepsis, and Interventions of the Unruly Past," in Shane Butler (ed.), *Deep Classics: Rethinking Classical Reception*. London: 179–202.

McCoskey, Denise (2012) *Race: Antiquity and Its Legacy*. New York.
Mueller, Melissa (2016) *Objects as Actors: Props and the Poetics of Performance in Greek Tragedy*. Chicago.
Nietzsche, Friedrich (1954) *Thus Spoke Zarathustra. The Portable Nietzsche*, ed. and trans. Walter Kaufmann. New York: 112–439.
Nietzsche, Friedrich (1967) *The Birth of Tragedy and the Case of Wagner*, trans. Walter Kaufmann. New York.
Onians, R. B. (1951) *The Origins of European Thought about the Body, the Mind, the Soul, the World, Time, and Fate*. Cambridge.
Orrells, Daniel, Gurminder K. Bhambra, and Tessa Roynon (eds) (2011) *African Athena: New Agendas*. Oxford.
Padel, Ruth (1992) *In and Out of the Mind: Greek Images of the Tragic Self*. Princeton.
Payne, Mark (2010) *The Animal Part: Humans and Other Animals in the Poetic Imagination*. Chicago.
Payne, Mark (2016) "Teknomajikality and the Humanimal in Aristophanes' *Wasps*," in Philip Walsh (ed.), *Brill's Companion to the Reception of Aristophanes*. Leiden: 129–47.
Purves, Alex (2015) "Ajax and Other Objects: Homer's Vibrant Materialism," *Ramus* 44: 75–94.
Ramey, Joshua (2012) *The Hermetic Deleuze: Philosophy and Spiritual Ordeal*. Durham, NC.
Rankine, Patrice (2006) *Ulysses in Black: Ralph Ellison, Classicism, and African American Literature*. Madison.
Richlin, Amy (1993) "Not before Homosexuality: The Materiality of the Cinaedus and the Roman Law against Love between Men," *Journal of the History of Sexuality* 3: 523–73.
Roby, Courtney (2013) "*Natura machinata*: Artifacts and Nature as Reciprocal Models in Vitruvius," *Apeiron* 46: 419–45.
Saxonhouse, Arlene (1994) "The Philosopher and the Female in the Political Thought of Plato," in Nancy Tuana (ed.), *Feminist Interpretations of Aristotle*. University Park, PA: 67–86.
Schliephake, Christopher (ed.) (2016) *Ecocriticism, Ecology, and the Cultures of Antiquity*. Lanham, MD.
Sellars, John (2007) "*Aiôn* and *Chronos*: Deleuze and the Stoic Theory of Time," *Collapse* 3: 177–205.
Snowden, F. M. Jr. (1970) *Blacks in Antiquity: Ethiopians in the Greco-Roman Experience*. Cambridge, MA.
Snowden, F. M. Jr. (1983) *Before Color Prejudice: The Ancient View of Blacks*. Cambridge, MA.
Sorabji, Richard (1993) *Animal Minds and Human Morals: The Origins of the Western Debate*. London.
Taylor, Rabun (1997) "Two Pathic Subcultures in Ancient Rome," *Journal of the History of Homosexuality* 7: 319–71.

Telò, Mario, and Melissa Mueller (eds) (2018) *The Materialities of Greek Tragedy: Objects and Affect in Aeschylus, Sophocles, and Euripides*. London.

Traub, Valerie (2013) "The New Unhistoricism in Queer Studies," *PMLA* 128: 21–39.

Tuana, Nancy (1993) *The Less Noble Sex: Scientific, Religious, and Philosophical Conceptions of Woman's Nature*. Bloomington, IN.

Tuana, Nancy (ed.) (1994) *Feminist Interpretations of Plato*. University Park, PA.

Vernant, Jean-Pierre, and Pierre Vidal-Naquet (1988) *Myth and Tragedy in Ancient Greece*, trans. Janet Lloyd. New York.

Vidal-Naquet, Pierre (1986) "Land and Sacrifice in the *Odyssey*: A Study of Religious and Mythical Meanings" in Pierre Vidal-Naquet, *The Black Hunter: Forms of Thought and Forms of Society in the Greek World*, trans. Andrew Szegedy-Maszak. Baltimore: 15–38.

Winkler, J. J. (1989) *The Constraints of Desire: The Anthropology of Sex and Gender in Ancient Greece*. New York.

Wohl, Victoria (2005) "Beyond Sexual Difference: Becoming-Woman in Euripides' *Bacchae*," in Victoria Pedrick and Steven M. Oberhelman (eds), *The Soul of Tragedy: Essays on Athenian Drama*. Chicago: 137–54.

Part 1
Posthuman Antiquities?

2 The human reconceived

Back to Socrates with Arendt

Adriana Cavarero

"I have clearly joined the ranks of those who for some time now have been attempting to dismantle metaphysics,"[1] writes Hannah Arendt in her last work, *The Life of the Mind*, published posthumously. In the 1970s, at the time she makes this claim, the dismantlers of metaphysics are many and a diverse group, but share with her the conviction that the history of metaphysics begins with Plato. For Arendt, Martin Heidegger, her first and controversial teacher, as well as the philosopher that has developed the most thorough critique of metaphysics' Platonic paternity, takes up a prominent role among the various dismantlers. After all, starting with Nietzsche, and leaving aside the peculiar anti-metaphysical stance of analytic philosophy, one could even draw a relevant map of twentieth-century thought in light of the critical treatment of Plato by a variety of philosophers, Heidegger included, who identify Plato as the originator of the metaphysical tradition and, therefore, of the so-called destiny of the West. In this map, Arendt would appear in an original position, for at least two reasons. First, because for her, the Platonic inauguration of metaphysics takes the shape of a decisive turn from political thought that makes its belated effects still felt in the twentieth century. Second, because the Arendtian interpretation of Plato and of the Greek world in general, far from being in line with the theories of most interpreters, consistently and persistently seeks to address the tragic urgency of rethinking the human, and along with that, the political, after the age of totalitarian regimes and the horror of Auschwitz. This is the historical perspective—concretely rooted in the critique of the present—wherefrom Arendt looks at Plato. Even though there are many authors in the second half of the twentieth century that reread the Greeks starting from the challenges of their time, Arendt does so in a distinctive way and with a specific political intensity directly connected

---

[1] Arendt (1978) 212.

to the raw and unclassifiable reality of the totalitarian phenomenon, on which her entire work never stops reflecting.

One can never insist enough on the anomaly of Arendt's thought, notoriously problematic already at the level of the lexicon, because it is engaged in the radical redefinition of what is meant by "human condition" and by "politics." The perspective from which Arendt rereads Plato's texts not only follows chronologically her monumental work, *The Origins of Totalitarianism*, published in 1951, but is also rooted in the firm conviction that it is necessary to revisit the specific category of the human in light of the experience of mass totalitarian organizations, that is a perverse system of destruction, at the heart of the humanistic culture of Europe, that has sought and has been able to reduce men to "superfluous" beings, whose "murder is as impersonal as the squashing of a gnat."[2] It is therefore precisely European civilization, the Western civilization, rooted in the metaphysical tradition originating with Plato, that is to be put under investigation. In other words, when Arendt rethinks the human and revisits the conceptual developments since its Greek origins, she does so starting from the given of dehumanization produced by the infernal machine of the extermination camps. She does so starting from those living skeletons "brought down to the lowest common denominator of organic life itself"[3]—the inmates at Auschwitz that Levi calls "men in decay" and "mussulmans"[4]—that witness a "truth" about extermination that goes beyond the fabrication of living corpses on a large scale: "Perhaps what is behind it all is only that individual human beings did not kill other individual human beings for human reasons, but that an organized attempt was made to eradicate the concept of the human being."[5] In the horrific originality of the totalitarian system of which Auschwitz is the atrocious symbol, Arendt makes clear that "suffering, of which there has always been too much on earth, is not the issue, nor is the number of victims. Human nature as such is at stake."[6] That is to say, the erasure of the person's uniqueness is at stake, and therefore the will is one "of destroying spontaneity as an element of human behavior" in order to produce "a completely undistinguishable and undefinable specimen of the species homo sapiens."[7] Arendt specifies that, like Pavlov's dog, this too is a degenerated animal, produced in the lab. Something unheard of and without precedent in the history of humankind

---

[2] Arendt (1973) 443.   [3] Arendt (1994) 198.   [4] See Levi (1996) 89.
[5] So writes Arendt in a letter to Karl Jaspers dated December 17, 1946, in L. Kohler and H. Saner (1992) 69.
[6] Arendt (1973) 458–9.   [7] Arendt (1994) 304.

has come into being: by translating ideas into facts, the Nazi ideology, insisting on the natural difference between "subhuman and superhuman people,"[8] has produced a posthuman artifact. Even though the Arendtian vocabulary does not technically include this term, and the postmodern age is obviously not yet on the scene, it is nonetheless the case that Arendt makes available to us an unusual and particularly tragic twist of the posthuman which is worthy of our reflection.

In order to avoid misunderstandings, or falling prey to a facile power of suggestion, it is necessary to bring to the fore the radicality of Arendt's discourse. Far from simply being a useful category in deconstructing and bypassing the cage of humanism, the Arendtian version of the posthuman not only coincides with the historically perpetrated event of the tangible collapse of the various but monotonous definitions of "man" and of "humanity" crafted by the metaphysical tradition, but it also goes hand in hand with the strong suspicion that precisely this tradition, born with Plato, is in some way implicated in such a collapse. Not that there is a causal continuity between this tradition and the totalitarian catastrophe, instead there is a disconcerting break, so much so that in it "all traditional elements of our political and spiritual world were dissolved into a conglomeration where everything seems to have lost specific value, and has become unrecognizable for human comprehension."[9] However, in a famous letter to Jaspers, dated March 4th, 1951, speaking about "radical evil," which she discusses in *The Origins of Totalitarianism*, Arendt writes:

What radical evil really is I don't know, but it seems to me it somehow has to do with the following phenomenon: making human beings as human beings superfluous (not using them as means to an end, which leaves their essence as humans untouched and impinges only on their human dignity; rather, making them superfluous as human beings). This happens as soon as all unpredictability—which in human beings is the equivalent of spontaneity—is eliminated.... I suspect that philosophy is not altogether innocent in this fine how-do-you-do. Not, of course in the sense that Hitler had anything to do with Plato.... Instead, perhaps in the sense that Western philosophy has never had a pure [*reine*] concept of what constitutes the political, and couldn't have one, because, by necessity, it spoke of man the individual and dealt with the fact of plurality tangentially.[10]

---

[8] Arendt (1994) 199.
[9] Arendt, H. "Preface to the First Edition," in *The Origins of Totalitarianism*, viii.
[10] Kohler and Saner (1992) 166 (translation modified). In the English edition, "*reine*" is translated with "clear."

In addition to giving a synthetic definition of radical evil, this excerpt has the merit of illustrating succinctly the fundamental thesis, reaffirmed throughout all of Arendt's work, on the constitutive link between ontology and politics. For Arendt, it is the definition of the human, of the human condition, that determines the concept of politics. As she will argue with greater detail in her main work, *The Human Condition*, a "pure" concept of the political can come about only in the recognition of the ontological given of plurality: "the fact that men, not Man, live on the earth and inhabit the world..., that nobody is ever the same as anyone else who ever lived, lives, or will live... is specifically the condition—not only the *conditio sine qua non*, but the *conditio per quam*—of all political life."[11]

A text, of the same period as the letter to Jaspers, more synthetically, reads: "politics is based on the fact of human plurality."[12] The issue is precisely about the constitutive link between the human condition understood as a plurality of unique beings and the pure concept, that is genuinely Arendtian, of politics as shared space of interaction. After the production of the posthuman in the inferno of the Nazi extermination camps, Arendt writes: "human dignity needs a new guarantee which can be found only in a new political principle,"[13] namely, the principle of acting in concert as unique beings, freely and spontaneously on a horizontal plane, a principle that she never tires of illustrating. Symptomatically, in the letter quoted above, Arendt explicitly denies that there lies a direct relationship between philosophy and the extermination camps, between Plato and Hitler. In other words, she does not claim, as Popper will, that the model of Plato's *Republic* forewarns the twentieth-century totalitarian regimes.[14] By intersecting the history of ontology with the history of politics, she claims instead that there is a complicity between the horror of Auschwitz, as the laboratory for producing the degenerated Homo, and the metaphysical tradition's proclivity for the abstract category of Man, to the detriment of the "paradoxical condition of unique beings" that distinguishes human plurality. To ignore this condition means to neglect spontaneity, the capacity to begin anew and the capacity for freedom, and therefore, for Arendt, for political action as the activity "from which no human being can refrain and still be human."[15]

In this sense then, Plato is the noble father of a false ontology consisting of fictitious, generic, and universal entities such as "Man," and in the subsequent philosophical vocabulary, the "Individual" or the "Subject." It is an abstract ontology that, on the one hand, prevents the metaphysical tradition from thinking a "pure" concept of politics, and on

---

[11] Arendt (1958) 7–8. [12] Arendt (2005) 93. [13] Arendt (1973) ix.
[14] Popper (1966). [15] Arendt (1958) 176.

the other hand, precisely because of this, it is not able to oppose any theoretical resistance to the factual nullification of plurality perpetrated in the Nazi Lager. In other words, the atrocious historical production of the posthuman, carried out in the extermination camps, is facilitated, though not caused, according to Arendt, by an authoritative philosophical tradition that defines the human in an improper, if not dangerous way, insofar as the false ontology of this tradition is structurally already open to the material elimination of human plurality. One therefore can understand why the reduction of humans to absolutely superfluous beings—that is to say, precisely that which Arendt calls "radical evil" in the letter to Jaspers and in the writings of this period—can be compared to an ontological crime. In the Lager's infernal machine, it is the human condition itself, in its real plurality, that undergoes the terrible mutation that aims at eliminating every residual spontaneity in the inmates, by erasing their uniqueness and transforming them into identical specimens of the artificial species Man. After Auschwitz this is the posthuman with which we are confronted. If revisited through Arendtian eyes, the posthuman is not a category of critical thought, useful to dismantle the modern anthropocentric ostentation, but rather a material outcome of totalitarianism, an entirely new species artificially created in the Nazi laboratory, the horrendous product of a historical event, the extreme aberration of an age.

This is why the history of metaphysics, beginning with Plato, who designed its conceptual layout, may not be entirely innocent, nor clean from any stain, and therefore brings forth a serious indictment. Rereading Plato with Arendt means precisely to align oneself with the seriousness of this indictment, that is to say, to enter a path where, in the name of a suspicious complicity between the metaphysical errors in ontology and the abyss of totalitarian perversion, the human has to be rethought radically, and with it politics. In other words, the interrogation runs deep and it concerns precisely the beginning of philosophy where Plato established the theoretical foundations of the discipline and, by condemning the fact of human plurality to insignificance in the eternal world of ideas, breached an original abyss between philosophy and politics. Crucially, for Arendt, the opening of this abyss, never bridged, is also the gesture where Plato's betrayal of Socrates, his teacher, is consummated.

Starting from the 1950s and in all her subsequent work, Arendt's critique of Plato's "faults" is accompanied by highlighting Socrates' "merits." According to her, Socrates was an exemplary thinker, thanks to that possible friendship between philosophy and politics that the ensuing metaphysics, inaugurated by Plato, has liquidated. Significantly, the presupposition of this thesis is the clear distinction, if not the outright opposition, between the Socratic and the Platonic position, an operation that is always very difficult, and in philological and historical terms, very risky. Of course Arendt knows this, but her only goal, when she rereads the Platonic dialogues, is to work unscrupulously on the Socratic figure in order to deepen what lies close to her heart, namely, the analysis of the relationship between philosophy, politics, and human plurality after the totalitarian catastrophe. In other words, "it is not as a philosophy historian that Hannah Arendt is interested in Socrates; by releasing him from his age, she sees in him the example or the paradigm of a disposition in life and in thought that constitutes, in her view, the only effective antidote against the evil of the twentieth century, namely: 'total domination.'"[16] After all, for Arendt, the Greeks and Greek culture are never some archeological evidence to study and to classify, but a living training ground for thought, a theater where the origin and its deviations are imagined, on the backdrop of which she projects the tragic questions she raises in the Preface to the 1966 edition of her book on totalitarianism: "What happened? Why did it happen? How could it have happened?"[17] As a sort of positive split image of Plato's negativity, Socrates is singled out precisely in this context of interrogation about radical evil and then, later, about the banality of evil.

In the by now vast critical literature on and about Arendt, the relationship between the two concepts of evil represents a *vexata quaestio*, which is impossible to account for here. Moreover, in the 1960s Arendt herself reconsiders her lexicon and declares: "It is indeed my opinion that evil is never 'radical,' that it is only extreme and that it possesses neither depth nor any demonic dimension."[18] In order to grasp the relevance she attributes to the Socratic figure, even at the risk of simplification, it is worth trying to summarize the issue in its essential traits.

The concept of radical evil, elaborated at the time the book on totalitarianism was written, evokes the ontological crime of the artificial production of a posthuman species and calls directly into question the problem of the connection between ontology and politics. Established in detail at the time of Adolf Eichmann's trial—which Arendt attends and about which she writes a series of articles, culminating in a controversial book published in 1963—the concept of the banality of evil refers instead to the problem of the collaboration of the very large majority of German people in Nazi crimes, that is to say, of the astonishing phenomenon by which, not only particularly cruel or sadistic people, but absolutely

---

[16] Vallée (2006) 9.   [17] Arendt (1973) xxiv.   [18] Young-Bruehl (1982) 369.

normal individuals, devoted fathers interested in their own careers, whose behavior conformed to the Ten Commandments, put themselves suddenly in the service of extermination, or accepted becoming its accomplices. A banal bourgeois figure of the "average German," a gray and steadfast bureaucrat, not affected by any concealed wickedness, the perpetrator Adolf Eichmann embodies this typology in an emblematic way, characterized, according to Arendt, by a passive acceptance of the current moral standards, and therefore ready to go from the gospel's precepts to Hitler's orders in the name of a necessary obedience to the predominant rules of conduct, whatever they may be. In this sense, although his crimes are atrocious, Eichmann is not a monster, he is the mirror of a widespread ethical lethargy. Affected, as Arendt claims, by an extraordinary thoughtlessness and therefore by an inability to judge, he, along with many of his fellow countrymen, abandons his prior convictions without any resistance, in order to become a docile operator of the unprecedented production of the posthuman.

Therefore, to be precise, it is neither convictions nor rules of conduct that guide him, it is rather the egoistic principle of his own return that elects unconditional obedience to the dominant order as his sole criterion, in this particular case of a new "table of values" compiled by Hitler. In Arendt's terminology, if "radical evil" summons the theme of the relationship between ontology and politics, the "banality of evil" calls into question the moral issue and, more specifically, the issue of the relationship between the activity of thinking and the ability to judge the principles of one's own actions, instead of conforming to the order of the powerful. In conclusion, even though they are two distinct concepts, there is no incompatibility between radical evil, or extreme evil, and the banality of evil: both are necessary to the Nazi totalitarian machine. The former, which risks wrapping itself around the fascination of a satanic greatness, cannot be perpetrated without the collaboration of "mediocre demons,"[19] faint and anything but Satan-like, in which the latter materializes. Mediocre demons which, far from weakening the seriousness of the situation with their banality, make it even more atrocious and, in a way, are always incumbent upon us and upon our time.

It is precisely against this danger that Arendt warns us: "if it is true that in the final stages of totalitarianism, an absolute evil appears (absolute

---

[19] I borrow this effective expression from Simona Forti's book, *The New Demons: Rethinking Power and Evil Today* (2015); for a more thorough and well-argued analysis of the meaning of the banality of evil, see 189–97.

because it can no longer be deduced from humanly comprehensible motives),"[20] it is also true that under everyone's eyes it is still the archetype of the banality of evil, namely "the 'bourgeois' who only focuses on his own private existence and is a stranger to all civic virtue," the adaptable individual, driven by opportunistic motives, that a perverse turn of events can transform into a mass-man and make him the instrument of whatever folly and horror. In the so-called mass society that favors private egoistic motives, the bursting in of the posthuman is therefore always possible. By way of a formula, even if Auschwitz is a unicum in the history of mankind, the horror that has taken place there—if we do not address the issue of the banality of evil—can still present itself today in another form. Socrates' lesson, in Arendt's interpretation, works purposely as an antidote to this danger.

In a 1954 essay that functions as a bridge between her thinking about radical evil and her broader elaboration of the banality of evil, Arendt writes: "The gulf between philosophy and politics opened historically with the trial and condemnation of Socrates, which in the history of political thought plays the same role of a turning point that the trial and condemnation of Jesus plays in the history of religion."[21] Besides the comparison with Christ, the thesis is anything but new; on the contrary, at least starting with Hegel, it is commonplace in the critical literature on Plato. It is, however, new and unusual the way Arendt develops it, by identifying the decisive factor of the difference between Plato and Socrates, and therefore the turning point of political thought, in the different approaches to the given reality of human plurality in their philosophy. It is worth reaffirming that, for Arendt, human plurality is a real given, a hard fact, and the plurality of opinions (*doxai*) is a direct expression of that: "To Socrates, as to his fellow citizens, *doxa* was the formulation in speech of what *dokei moi*, that is, of 'what appears to me.'"[22] Human plurality, which entails the uniqueness of every human being and therefore a multi-perspectival vision of the world, is such that to everyone the world appears (*dokei*) from a different point of view: "the world opens up differently to every man according to his position in it."[23] Socrates, who lives and works in the *polis* among its citizens, is above all the philosopher who has the merit of comparing himself with the plurality of opinions, forcing every one of his interlocutors to give an account of their opinions, to examine them together, so that these *doxai* do not risk becoming crystallized in arbitrary truths and, in and through the dialogue, are instead put together and shared, albeit through a temporary

---

[20] Arendt (1973) viii–ix. [21] Arendt (2005) 6.
[22] Arendt (2005) 14. [23] Arendt (2005) 14.

and contingent agreement, one that is always open to revision. Since they cannot be constrained to agree, in opposition to truth that is one by definition, opinions remain always multiple, plural, because they are the expression of an originary plurality.

The sphere of "human affairs" as a genuine political sphere is characterized, according to Arendt, by contingency, mobility, and openness, which, as constituted by plurality, does not allow absolute criteria, but rather *doxai*, points of view, convictions that are more or less acritical, prejudices that are to be verified through dialogue in order to formulate a judgment. This examination—the Socratic elenchus—is, on one hand, an important exercise that awakens our ability to judge and, on the other hand, it attests to how thinking consists in an activity rather than in a baggage of objective knowledge. Regrettably, the Athenian court condemns Socrates to death, precisely because he refuses to give up this exercise. It is exactly from here that the Platonic turning point proceeds.

The sight of Socrates, who submits his own *doxa* to the irresponsible opinions of the Athenians and who is put to death by them—this is Arendt's general thesis—induces Plato to distrust the dialogical and refutational style of his teacher, as well as to despise the plurality of *doxai* and, above all, induces him to the speculatively fatal action of introducing "absolute standards into the realm of human affairs,"[24] that is, of using ideas as firm and objective principles to design and govern politics. This happens especially in the *Republic*, where the idea of the Good, principle of the unitary order of ideas, becomes the parameter upon which the philosopher draws the layout of the *kallipolis*. The eternal and static regime of truth or, as Arendt says, "the tyranny of truth" that preaches the law of one, imposes itself in an improper and surreptitious manner on the genuinely plural, contingent, and unpredictable sphere of politics as a space of interaction. The "pure" and still Socratic concept of the political as an interactive realm corresponding to the human condition of plurality is eclipsed and substituted by the Platonic conception of a politics understood instead as an order built on static and timeless principles that the philosopher discovers, sees (*theōrein*) in his solitary contemplation of the ideas. In short, the fact of human plurality, essential condition of politics, succumbs under the solitary noetic design of the philosopher who leaves the real world of men in order to live in the other world, and shapes the best *polis* according to it.

The door for this sensational exit from the real world is opened up by an experience of a particular kind, very dear to metaphysicians, that

---

[24] Arendt (2005) 8.

Arendt does not hesitate to define as shock, namely "the wonder at that which is as it is."[25] "Wonder (*to thaumazein*) is what the philosopher thrives on most; for there is no other beginning of philosophy than wonder,"[26] writes Arendt quoting a well-known passage from Plato's *Theaetetus* (155d). Paradigmatically, it is a silent wonder, a "speechless state," a mystical and mute experience that puts the philosopher directly into contact with truth, without any discursive mediation. From this comes the Platonic conviction, shared by Aristotle as well, that, even though wonder must be translated into words, "ultimate truth is beyond words."[27] Characterized by a pure, motionless, absorbing contemplation that carries the philosopher to the speechless world up there, noetic thought supplants Socrates' dialogical activity that grappled with the contingent plurality down here. It replaces the *politeuein* as living and operating in the *polis*, a realm marked by the risk of unpredictability and contingency that is typical of the sphere of "human affairs."

Notoriously, this is a decisive issue in the Arendtian reflection on Plato's metaphysical faults. Noetic thought, as speechless contemplation of the ideas, as knowledge of an orderly, static, unchanging cosmos, turns for Arendt into a real flight from politics: the pure concept of politics, still at work in the Socratic approach, is replaced by a "body politic" shaped after the stability and immutability of the ideas. Moreover, in knowledge as vision (*theōria*) of an organic whole that is eternal and perfect, what leaps out is a correspondence between Truth and Unity that replaces the plurality of the real world. This, after all, is Plato's most serious fault: he has sacrificed the plural world to the totalizing effect of the One, just as the totalitarian power has made plurality disappear "into One Man of gigantic dimension."[28] In Arendtian terms, the heart of the problem lurks exactly here: in the Platonic system, the correspondence of Being, Truth, and Unity speaks already the language of absolute domination.[29] This, Arendt argues, is completely consistent with Plato's decision to prolong indefinitely the speechless wonder that is at the beginning and at the end of philosophy, that is, of identifying the thinking activity itself with the traumatic instant that separates the philosopher in shock from the real world. Solitude, typical of thinking, becomes therefore isolation, estrangement. A fictitious world, dominated by the One, is imposed as the supreme object of knowledge: constructed on it, *bios theōretikos* reigns at the expense of that interacting plurality which characterizes the *politeuein* of *bios politikos* still practiced by Socrates.

---

[25] Arendt (2005) 38. [26] Arendt (2005) 32. [27] Arendt (2005) 33.
[28] Arendt (1973) 466. [29] See Forti (2006) 122-3.

A typical trait of Arendt's speculation, the method of exaggerating is particularly evident in her interpretation of Plato: to reduce his entire and complex discourse on thinking to the model of *theōria* doesn't work, really. As every good reader of Plato knows—Arendt included—the timeless instant of contemplation, the *exaiphnēs*, is indeed presented in the Platonic texts as the highest and most perfect form of thought, but not as the only one. Characterized by different stages and by internal articulations, the activity of thinking, as Plato presents it, admits of other forms, among them, in the first place, the discursive one, although still burdened by a soundless *logos* that consists in the silent dialogue of the soul with itself. In other words, next to the *noein* as pure *theōrein*, we find in the Platonic work a definition of thinking as dialogue with oneself that, although it maintains the speechless character of wonder, is not to be assimilated to the estranged and motionless state of *thaumazein*. The problem is that Arendt is inclined to attribute the latter meaning of thinking, that is, the discursive one she greatly appreciates, to Socrates rather than to Plato.

The definition appears in a well-known passage of the *Sophist*, where, by pointing out two modalities of expression of the *logos*, Plato writes that "thought and speech are the same; only the former, which is a silent inner conversation of the soul with itself, has been given the special name of thought ... But the stream that flows from the soul in vocal utterance through the mouth has the name of speech."[30] Internal to the soul and intangible, a pure mental activity, thinking is the inner dialogue that precedes and anchors speech, which is, so to speak, its simple vocal materialization. According to the critical literature it is therefore a genuine Platonic doctrine, not by chance situated in the so-called dialectical dialogues, that reflects Plato's position. Contrary to the common opinion, Arendt finds instead good reasons to assert that the thesis that thinking is an internal dialogue of the soul is originally that of Socrates, who then becomes the discoverer of a mental activity that implies the existence, if not of plurality, at least of the duality of the one who, dialoguing silently with oneself, is two-in-one because one questions and answers oneself. In a passage of the *Theaetetus*, we read that in the soul a dialogue takes place "not with someone else, nor yet aloud, but in silence with oneself," because the soul is inclined to speak and to listen to itself "asking itself questions and answering, affirming and denying."[31] It is precisely this disposition toward internal confrontation, toward examination of one's conduct and of one's own moral principles, uncovering

---

[30] Plato, *Sophist* 263e in Plato (trans. Fowler) 1921.
[31] Plato, *Theaetetus* 190a.

the duality of thinking, that in Arendt's view is the most valuable Socratic legacy against the banality of evil. It is, at the same time, and not by chance, the discovery of conscience as the effect of an activity that, precisely thanks to this internal questioning and answering, puts into question every cliché and reveals itself structurally to be anti-authoritarian and anti-conformist. "Could the activity of thinking as such...be among the conditions that make men abstain from evil-doing or even actually 'condition' them against it?"[32] asks Arendt in her last work, *The Life of the Mind*. This question, however, is already at work in her previous texts and it evokes Socrates' name, regularly.

Already in the final pages of *The Origins of Totalitarianism*, without Socrates being mentioned, Arendt observes that thinking is "the freest and purest of all human activities"[33] and that "all thinking, strictly speaking, is done in solitude and is a dialogue between me and myself; but this dialogue of the two-in-one does not lose contact with the world of my fellow-men because they are represented in the self with whom I lead the dialogue of thought."[34] In later writings, as Arendt's attention focuses on Socrates, this interior dialogue becomes more meaningful and solicits the figure of conscience, of which Socrates himself would be the discoverer. By quoting Socrates' well-known passage from Gorgias (482b–c), where he claims that "it would be better for me that my lyre or a chorus I directed should be out of tune and loud with discord, and that multitudes of men should disagree with me rather than that my single self should be out of harmony with myself and contradict me," Arendt highlights that "the Socratic agent, because he was capable of thought, carried within himself a witness from whom he could not escape; wherever he went and whatever he did, he had his audience, which, like any other audience, would automatically constitute itself into a court of justice, that is, into that tribunal which later ages have called conscience."[35] The duality inherent in the activity of thinking is not a lifeless representation of human plurality under a different mathematical quantity; rather it is a vigilant theater of comparison and interrogation that sees the I splitting and returning to itself. Solitary but not an estranged sphere, conscience is the secluded place where everyone, having left others and returned home to oneself, gives an account of oneself to oneself and, precisely in this active confrontation, in judging oneself, puts down one's roots. It is exactly this ability that Eichmann and Hitler's volunteers and accomplices lacked. Thoughtlessness, and therefore being without any roots, is the other side of that extreme evil,

---

[32] Arendt (1978) 5. [33] Arendt (1973) 473.
[34] Arendt (1973) 476. [35] Arendt (1990) 102.

that in the 1960s Arendt no longer wishes to call "radical" due to its lack of depth and roots, so as to avoid all misunderstanding. It is not simply a question of adjectives: the evil of posthuman production remains absolute and extreme, but density and depth are gone.

Socrates, the character upon whom Arendt projects her conception of the human and of politics after the catastrophe of the posthuman, works as a double antidote: against the radical evil and against the banality of evil, that are, after all, one the reverse of the other. But Socrates works also for other aspects that are equally important to Arendt. The teacher betrayed by Plato remains a constant interlocutor for Arendt and, as the questions she raises in *The Origins of Totalitarianism* gradually come to further maturation, the Socratic figure becomes more and more complex. By way of an outline, one can affirm that, in the development of Arendt's work, Socrates functions essentially as a model for two main spheres of human activity: acting and thinking, spheres that Arendt likes to distinguish and separate, but that she also tries to connect, although not always convincingly. Their connecting link is the category of plurality. Contrary to Plato, who despises and abandons the plural sphere of "human affairs" and takes refuge in pure contemplation, Socrates has for Arendt the merit, first of all, of doing philosophy by living among his peer citizens and by dialoguein with them. Socrates practices the *politeuein*: he lives and acts in the public sphere, the theater of plurality par excellence and, for Arendt, the synonym of politics. Furthermore, and in tune with his dialogical practice, he has the merit of discovering that the activity of thinking, as the seat of conscience, consists in a silent dialogue of the soul with itself, an activity that therefore attests to human plurality, in so far as, by questioning and answering itself, the one who thinks understands him- or herself to be two-in-one. In the first case, what comes to the fore is the Socratic example of a *vita activa*, of actions and words with direct interaction with other human beings and their tangible plurality; in the second case, it is instead the Socratic discovery of the experience of the solitary relationship of the I with itself, manifestation of human plurality in the form of duality.

Nevertheless, in my view, there appears to be a problem here, at least at the theoretical level, worth articulating: what kind of relationship do human plurality and the duality of conscience entertain? Bringing together the plurality of political action and the duality of thinking proves in fact to be rather problematic. Drawing a parallel between two structurally uneven planes gives rise to a number of perplexities, which, in truth, have to do with the Arendtian difficulty in reconciling the sphere of action and that of thinking, rather than with her interpretation of Socrates. In a programmatic piece that has the quality of being concise,

Arendt writes: "There exist two basic modes of being together: to be together with other men and with one's equals from which springs action, and to be together with one's self to which the activity of thinking corresponds."[36] This synthetic description casts a light on that which is perhaps the greatest intrinsic difficulty of Arendt's thesis, namely the transition from the external to the internal, from the public sphere of appearances to the private one of non-appearances that, in the case of thinking, as she never tires of repeating, is absolute invisibility. The first way of being together, that is, acting politically in a shared public sphere, is all external; it takes place on the outside, in the visible realm of appearances, which, for Arendt, is real precisely because it is guaranteed by a multitude of perspectives on what appears and shows itself. The second way of being together, that is, the silent dialogue of the I with itself, is instead all internal; it takes place inside the subject, in the invisible and speechless sphere of thought, where the phenomenon of appearing is structurally absent. It is worth adding that, in reference to Socrates, the type of relationship between the two ways of being-together is never sufficiently clarified by Arendt; she suggests, at least, that the internal duality of the two-in-one is a symptom of the external plurality of the shared world, as if the plural duality of thinking reflects, confirms, becomes evidence of the plural reality of action which functions as its premise and foundation. To put it in the form of a question: is there a sort of transition from the ontological given of the plural human condition to its manifestation in the duality of thinking, or is what is at stake a simple, though interesting, correspondence? Since we are dealing with the redefinition of the human after the catastrophe of the posthuman, the issue is not of little significance. It is perhaps worth recalling again the questions that Arendt poses in the Introduction to the *Origins of Totalitarianism*: "What happened? Why did it happen? How could it have happened?" to which we could add other questions different from these only in their formulation: how did it become possible, under the Nazi regime, to destroy the real, incontrovertible, visible, and apparent given of human plurality? How did the sudden transformation of ordinary people, whose conduct was rooted just in ordinary moral precepts, into accomplices of this ontological crime, become possible? Or, to put it in Arendtian language: how was radical evil possible? How was the banality of evil possible?

Plato, the father of metaphysics, and his fault of having sacrificed the fact of plurality to the speculative triumph of unity, helps to provide an

---

[36] Description of Proposal, Rockefeller Correspondence 013872. Document 3, December 1959, quoted by Margaret Canovan in Canovan (1995) 100–1.

answer to the first question about radical, or if we prefer, extreme evil. Socrates, the philosopher not listened to, at a time when philosophy could have taken a different turn, helps, above all, build a double alternative, both to absolute evil as well as to the banality of evil. With regard to the relationship between external plurality and internal duality, the problem nonetheless still remains. One has the impression that Arendt, for love of a forced parallelism, has sacrificed her intuition of the reality of the visible and incontrovertible, concrete and shared, external plurality to the notion—plausibly entirely Platonic—of a silent conscience that roots the I in the invisible internal duality of thinking.

Arendt's proposal of a new image of the human after the catastrophe of Auschwitz and her critique of the metaphysical conception of the human, turned complicit with the totalitarian production of the posthuman, can be summed up in the famous sentence worth citing here once again: "*men*, not *Man*, live on the earth and inhabit the world."[37] The opposition between plurality and the singular is clear and, above all, in the notebooks and journals where Arendt writes down her thoughts, it is continually employed and evidenced in shorthand through the article that precedes the nouns. These texts are written in German, a language that allows Arendt to provide the emphasis on the opposition between the plural and the singular through the use of the article. She stresses here that "the doctrine of philosophers about man in the singular and about the negligence of men in the plural, can make men in the plural superfluous in front of the monster of man conjugated as a singular hybrid."[38] Tellingly, not only does she call into question philosophy, but also the model of a universal history embraced by some historians; Arendt argues that, "it is the perspective of universal history that defines the concept we have of humanity: humanity as paradigm of man, but in such a way that it creates the illusion that to this abstract paradigm, a mere outcome of thought, corresponds actually a reality."[39] Even though without precedents, the posthuman produced in the laboratories of extermination is inscribed in human history, as it has been conceived in the Western tradition. To rethink humanity, or maybe to think humanity for the first time in its concrete traits, means therefore, to think against Plato and in Socrates' company, to mark plurality that makes every human being a unique being, different from any one else that "lived, lives or will live."

At the end, it is even possible to recover a positive variation of the posthuman meaning: every human in the name of the uniqueness that

---

[37] Arendt (1958) 7.   [38] Arendt (2003) 159.   [39] Arendt (2003) 304.

makes us human, that is to say, in the name of the fragility that makes us incomparable and unpredictable, comes after the humanism of the monster man conjugated already by Plato according to a singular hybrid, and it poses a strong resistance to the radical evil of human beings made absolutely superfluous. There is, at the beginning of Western history— Arendt seems to suggest—a correctly understood human, grasped by Socrates, but betrayed by Plato and by the humanisms inspired by the father of metaphysics. To return to Socrates after the catastrophe of the twentieth century therefore means to recover a figure of the human in which action and thought attest to plurality, the elimination of which consists in evil properly speaking, both radical evil and the banality of evil. "Could the activity of thinking as such... be among the conditions that make men abstain from evil-doing or even actually 'condition' them against it?"[40] as indeed Arendt asks in *The Life of the Mind*. The Socratic agent, because capable of thought, embodies a figure of the human that aspires to function as a possible answer, throughout Arendt's work.

WORKS CITED

Arendt, H. (1958) *The Human Condition*. Chicago.
Arendt, H. (1973) *The Origins of Totalitarianism*. New York.
Arendt, H. (1978) *The Life of the Mind, Volume One: Thinking*. New York.
Arendt, H. (1990) *On Revolution*. London.
Arendt, H. (1994) *Essays in Understanding 1930–1954*. Orlando.
Arendt, H. (2003) *Denktagenbuch 1950–1973*, Erster Band. Munich.
Arendt, H. (2005) *The Promise of Politics*. New York.
Canovan, M. (1995) *Hannah Arendt: A Reiterpretation of Her Political Thought*. Cambridge.
Forti, S. (2006) *Hannah Arendt fra filosofia e politica*. Milan.
Forti, S. (2015) *The New Demons: Rethinking Power and Evil Today*. Stanford.
Kohler, L., and H. Saner, eds (1992) *Correspondence 1926–1969: Hannah Arendt, Karl Jaspers*. Trans. R. and R. Kimber. New York.
Levi, P. (1996) *Survival in Auschwitz: The Nazi Assault on Humanity*. Trans. S. Woolf. New York.
Plato (1921) *Plato in Twelve Volumes*. Trans. Harold N. Fowler. Cambridge, MA.
Popper, K. (1966) *The Open Society and Its Enemies, Volume I: The Spell of Plato*. London.
Vallée, C. (2006) *Hannah Arendt: Socrate e la questione del totalitarismo*. Bari.
Young-Bruehl, E. (1982) *Hannah Arendt: For Love of the World*. New Haven.

---

[40] Arendt (1978) 5.

3 Hearing voices

The sounds in Socrates' head

Ramona Naddaff

> What does it mean for a being to be immersed entirely in listening, formed by listening or in listening, listening with all his being?
>
> Jean-Luc Nancy

> Socrates' *daimonion* was a single entity with a single nature, individual to him.
>
> Maximus (of Tyre)[1]

Socrates is not human: he may be mortal, he may be a man, but he is not a human among humans. Socrates is *atopos*: strange, unclassifiable, eccentric, "a being out of the way" of humanity.[2] Alcibiades says of Socrates at *Symposium* 221d that "He is like no other human being, living or dead." One among many features constitutes Socrates' peculiarity, which *Republic* 6. 496c tells us "has happened to few or none before me" (*tini allōi ē oudeni tōn emprosthen gegonen*): it is the *daimonion*, his divine sign, the divine thing that he hears on select and significant occasions. This *daimonion*, this supernatural thing, as Gregory Nagy translates it, not only makes Socrates into the alien being that is the philosopher, but it also transforms Socrates into a supernatural force disrupting ontologically the category of the human.[3] For Nietzsche, in *The Birth of Tragedy*, the fact that Socrates possessed, listened to, and

---

[1] Nancy (2007) 4. Maximus, "Socrates' *Daimonion*" in Trapp (1997) 73.

[2] See Destrée (2005) 64: "When they philosophically defend the assumption that the *daimonion* is a private thing or event proper to Socrates, interpreters are referring it to Socrates' *atopia*: Such a *daimonion* would be precisely one of the main features that make for such an *atopia*." See Plato, *Symposium* 175b, 221d and *Gorgias* 494d. See further Vlastos (1991) 1 on the significance of the term *atopia*. To date, *Socrates' Divine Sign* (Destrée and Smith (2005)) is the most compelling collection of essays on the subject of Socrates' *daimonion*. I am indebted to the authors for their keen insights and commentaries.

[3] Nagy (2013) 605: "In the usage of Plato's Socrates, as in Plato's *Republic* (6.496c), *daimonion* functions as the adjective of the neuter noun *sēmeion*, which is derived from another neuter noun, *sēma*...I propose to translate the expression *to daimonion sēmeion*, as we find it in the *Republic*, as "the superhuman signal." Elsewhere in the usage of Plato's Socrates, however, in Plato's *Apology of Socrates*, the expressions *to daimonion* and *sēmeion*

obeyed uncritically his *daimonion* accounts for Socrates' exceptional status as both human being and philosopher. Socrates' deviation from other humans results partially from the reversal of functions of instinct and consciousness once the divine sign manifests itself. The auricular intervention, an "abnormal" situation, creates an "abnormal" and exceptional being whose logical drive, overdeveloped and unwieldy, defers, only under extraordinary situations, to the "wisdom of instinct":

> Whenever it appears, this voice always *warns* him to *desist*. In this utterly abnormal nature the wisdom of instinct only manifests itself in order to *block* conscious understanding from time to time. Whereas in the case of all productive people instinct is precisely the creative-affirmative force and consciousness makes critical and warning gestures, in the case of Socrates, by contrast, instinct becomes the critic and consciousness the creator—a true monstrosity *per defectum*.[4]

"Whenever it appears"—Socrates' *daimonion* is not only a relatively infrequent visitor—it comes at the most morally urgent moments as well as the most trivial (*panu epi smikrois*, Plato, *Apology* 40a4). It is a "kind of voice" ("*phōnē tis*," Plato, *Apology* 31d) that Socrates listens to "with all his being," to borrow Jean-Luc Nancy's phrase (see the opening quotation of this chapter): "something divine and spiritual comes to me (*hoti moi theion ti kai daimonion gignetai phōnē*)... I've had this thing from my childhood; it is a sort of voice that comes to me (*phōnē tis gignomenē*). Whenever it happens, it always turns me away from whatever I'm about to do but never encourages me" (Plato, *Apology* 31d). First of all, the *daimonion* only appears as a voice pure and simple. Its content is never specified; as voice it seems to defy linguistic laws and limits. Anonymous, even disembodied, without particular tone, timbre, rhythm, or accent, this voice is a sudden occurrence that befalls Socrates, saying nothing but signifying lucidly to Socrates, who both listens and hears, its constant message and command: Do not speak. Do not act. Desist. Insofar is it signals what not to do, it specifies what must be done. Here are some examples:

> I just so happened to be sitting in the place where you saw me, in the undressing room, all alone. I was about to get up and go; but as I was about to do so, my divine signal appeared. So, I sat down again. (*Euthydemus*, 272e)[5]

---

are used separately as synonyms; in these cases, I will translate *to daimonion* as "the superhuman thing" and *to sēmeion* as "the signal."

[4] Nietzsche (1999) 66.

[5] See McPherran (2014) 202: "Another instance of daemonic activity is found at *Euthydemus* 272e–273a. There we find that Socrates had formed the intention to leave

When such men return and beg me, as they do, with wonderful eagerness to allow them to join me again, the divine signal that comes to me forbids me to associate with some of them but allows me to converse with others. (*Theaetetus* 151a)

Plato provides no explanation of what goes on in Socrates' mind as he interprets the "divine signal." Does he—or does he not—question the *daimonion*'s authority and knowledge, as he did in the *Apology*, the Delphic Oracle, poets, politicians, and sophists alike? If he does, we have neither clue of his internal elenchus nor evidence of his usual critical defiance. For example—perhaps the most famous of examples—in *Apology* 40a–b, the "customary signal" mysteriously provides "a serious indication" (*mega . . . tekmērion*) to Socrates that it is erroneous to assume that "death is an evil." Quite the contrary—Socrates concludes without offering evidence of his reasoning process—death must be met as "something good."[6] All that allows Socrates, we are led to believe, to reach this controversial conclusion is that he experienced no resistance. He did not hear a voice. All ears, he listened instead to silence, and understood what to do: "for the customary signal would surely have opposed me if what I was going to do was not something good" (40a–b). It may be that Socrates was at a loss for words to explain his radical decision and invented an excuse and argument or even experienced an auditory hallucination. Be this as it may, Socrates, at the moments when the divine signal intervenes, remains uncharacteristically silent: he listens receptively and uncritically.[7]

A listening rather than speaking subject, Socrates obeys a voice that need not defend itself or render transparent its assumptions and beliefs. Socrates opens himself up to an auditory force that reshapes identity. He engages in a form of listening that he, like other human beings, shares

---

his seat, but just as he was getting up the *daimonion* opposed him, and so he remained. In this case, Socrates exhibits no doubt that its warning is utterly reliable; rather, Socrates implicitly trusts the *daimonion*, although *how* or *why* it is that the result of his obedience will be good-producing is opaque to reasoned calculation. But this trust is in no way *irrational*."

[6] See Joyal (1997) for a careful analysis of Socrates' argument about death in this passage.

[7] It is tempting to claim that at these very moments, when listening to the *daimonion*, Socrates ceases to be himself, in the sense that he is metaphorically identified as an animal, the philosophical animal—the "gadfly." As Michael Naas (Naas (2015) 52) comments: "Hence Socrates is *like* a gadfly insofar as he stings individuals and arouses the sluggish city with his constant questioning . . . [he is as gadfly] the vigilant, self-sacrificing, knowing human gadfly who pricks and goads the city and its citizens *for their own good*." I am grateful to Sara Brill for suggesting Naas's essay as well as her questions regarding the definition of Socrates' "humanity" in the context of the *daimonion*. I have yet to answer her questions properly and hope to do so with further research.

with animals. Barthes explains well this type of listening in his essay, *Listening*. Such listening occurs when a

> living being orients its hearing (the exercise of its physiological faculty of hearing) to certain *indices*: on this level, nothing distinguishes animal from man: the wolf listens for a (possible) noise of its prey, the hare for a (possible) noise of its hunter, the child and the lover for the approaching footsteps which might be the mother's or the beloved's. This first listening might be called an *alert*.[8]

When his divine sign intrudes, Socrates is alerted of a potential or real danger: something is at stake that will affect his whole being. The anonymous voice that belongs to him but is not his voice does not need to reason with Socrates nor does Socrates need to test the *daimonion*'s reasoning, as he is wont to do on most occasions. Socrates, in Barthes's terms, does not decipher: "what the ear tries to intercept are certain *signs*. Here no doubt begins the human: I listen the way I read; i.e. according to certain codes."[9] If anyone deciphers the divine sign, it is Plato, who—we must note briefly here—listens to Socrates himself as some kind of hybrid being—a mixture of human and divine being; the ideal human and the atypical one. Barthes describes this third form of listening, "whose approach is entirely modern" thusly: "[it] does not aim at—or await—certain determined, classified sign: not what is said or emitted, *but who speaks, who emits*: such listening is supposed to develop in an inter-subjective space where 'I am listening' also means 'listen to me.'"[10]

For Gregory Vlastos, Socrates' relationship to the *daimonion*, his acceptance of it, was "so embarrassing to modern readers that a long line of Platonic scholarship has sought—[and] is still seeking—to explain it away."[11] My desire, in this essay, does not consist in this. Rather, I wish to explain the rhetorical and philosophical function of the *daimonion*, which commentators have understood as one of the most alien features of Socratic religion. The act of listening to the *daimonion* allowed Socrates a unique means to construct his identity as a philosopher who resists categorization as wholly and completely human—with all the limitations and capacities this implies. This "self-transforming, life-transforming askesis," to use Arnold Davidson's expression, the careful listening to a sound without apparent sense and meaning, becomes the

---

[8] Barthes (1991) 245.
[9] Barthes (1991) 245.
[10] Barthes (1991) 245–6, my emphasis. This form of listening may indeed be acousmatic: a sound is heard and the listener does not see the cause of the sound. I am grateful to Pauline LeVen for suggesting this connection.
[11] Vlastos (1991) 158.

means by which Socrates distinguishes himself from other humans and lays claim to a practice that is simultaneously both outside of and constitutive of the practice of philosophy.[12]

3.1. When he hears the divine thing

Over and again, scholars insist that Socrates' sign—at least in Plato—is apotreptic: it prevents him from doing and saying something; it diverts and hinders action and voice; it stops him from engaging in acts which, in hindsight, are morally deleterious. Socrates' *daimonion*, his "*daimonion sēmeion*," functions, in other words, as a moral conscience that directs Socrates from doing harm to himself and to others. It prohibits this philosopher from complete moral autonomy.[13] If, as in the example discussed earlier—and to which I shall return—Socrates had resisted death, thereby disobeying the *daimonion*'s dictates, he, sovereignly deciding and judging, would have been morally culpable. The ethical codes Socrates follows, when the divine sign occurs, are not the internalization of authoritative institutions, guardians, religion, or traditions. It is indeed an internalization but, as Gerd Van Riel writes, Socrates' "privatization of the divine...is not a matter of a 'private conception of the gods' (as Vlastos and others would have it)." Van Riel argues, instead, that it is a "conception of a private god, a matter of an internal relationship that remains mysterious but is nonetheless perceived as being part of the personality."[14] This private, supernatural force befalls Socrates and decides his destiny in relation to affairs, big and small. As *Apology* 31b tells us, since childhood—presumably prior to the time he was a philosopher—Socrates has needed guidance; human council was insufficient. Socrates is uniquely equipped with a *daimonion* answering to this lack. Why, one must ask, does he need such a voice? What precisely does Socrates lack or possess in excess? Why, when the *daimonion* comes and he obeys the voice, does he suspend the use of his critical faculties?

---

[12] Davidson (2005) 137.
[13] On the question of moral autonomy see Brisson (2005) 7–12, esp. 11–12.
[14] Van Riel (2005) 35. The *daimonion* is not Socrates' *daimōn*, the personal guardian allotted to everyone at birth, "an omnipresent, tutelary element throughout a person's life." Cf. Destrée (2005) 63: "Plato simply does not use the word 'daimon' to characterize what Socrates says occurs to him, we are not allowed to talk about the '*daimon* of Socrates.' Moreover, it is probably because they do not want to confuse this 'daimonic thing,' whatever it may be, with some traditional religious way of considering a *daimon* as a personal guardian or the destiny of a person, that they both intentionally avoided such appellation."

What, then, is this "privatization of the divine"? It is, first and foremost, the source of Socrates' criminality, his rejection of the religious rules, rites, and regulations of democratic Athens' religion. The charge directed against him, known all too well, is not only for corrupting the youth but also "for not believing in the gods of the state": "Socrates does criminal wrong (*adikei*) by not recognizing (*ou nomizōn*) the gods that the *polis* recognizes (*nomizei*) and furthermore by introducing new divinities (*daimonia*); and he does criminal wrong by corrupting (*diaphthairōn*) the youth (*neous*)."[15] Under the power of the divine sign, Socrates, as Hegel well understood, possesses an oracle that is a rival to the *polis*'s sacred oracles. Socrates' *daimonion* moves him to heed an interior power, one that is only present to him and speaks alone, and privately, to him. Or, more precisely, the *daimonion*, which is within Socrates, is simultaneously a "thing" alien to, outside of, Socrates.[16] Socrates recognizes that his identity is shaped by a "foreign power" which, when listened to, causes him to engage intentionally in behaviors that, if left to his own devices, he would not have willed for himself. In later dialogues, Plato will insist that *to logistikon* is the divine psychic part of human beings; the capacity to reason is that which draws the human closer to the gods, that accounts for the dwelling of the god within. Socrates, divinely rational, is also divinely gifted; his *daimonion* grants him access to truths, which are perhaps universal but most definitely perfectly tailored to address the situations he—and only he—directly confronts, be it facing death bravely or leaving or staying with interlocutors.

Socrates' *daimonion* knows what is best for Socrates and Socrates only has to listen attentively to its directions to craft himself as other than he may have if judging and deciding solitarily. The beauty, of course, of this attentiveness and receptivity is that in listening to the alien voice within, Socrates becomes more of what he is: a singular philosophical spirit. This is the case not only because the sign is divine but also because it sets Socrates, as a self-conscious being, apart from other citizens whose humanity is defined in relation to their submission to the state's conventional order. Again, no one but Socrates hears this voice, a voice ultimately allowing him to redefine what it means to be a citizen in the

---

[15] Diogenes Laertes 1.5.40 cited by Ober (2011) 139.
[16] It is tempting to think here of Freud's and Lacan's notion of "*la chose*" (*das Ding*), very roughly speaking, that which escapes, defies, representation. Jane Bennett, in *Vibrant Matter: A Political Economy of Things* (Bennett (2010) 17) offers another suggestive means to interpret this "thing," "this outside": "this out-side can operate at a distance from our bodies or it can operate as a foreign power internal to them, as when we feel the discomfort of nonidentity, hear the naysaying voice of Socrates' demon." I am grateful to James Porter for this citation.

city, to engage in innovative philosophical practices, and to establish a new relationship between Socrates and other citizens and non-citizens.[17] Equally significant, Socrates, affected by this voice, enters into a virtually unprecedented relationship with himself. He listens to that which is *a-logos*, a non-propositional, purely auditory, non-veridical logical event, and allows this voice to shape his identity in new and unexpected fashions.

Above all, the divine sign permits Socrates a new means to care for the self (*epimeleia heautou*), and to listen attentively to a non-human, non-discursive voice operating as that guide whom Foucault tells us is that "other" necessary to truly care for the self: "care for the self implies also a relationship to the other... in order to really care for self, one must listen to the teachings of a master. One needs a guide, a counselor, a friend— someone who will tell you the truth."[18] I do not want to concentrate here on what Foucault means by the "truth"—or the strange occurrence of such an idea in Foucault. Rather, I want to underscore how Plato—like Foucault—opens a new path to truth that does not emerge simply from knowledge of the self, by the self. It appears, at certain times, and in certain contexts, there exists an "other" who knows the truth of and for one. The divine voice seems, for example, to know, as Socrates does not, that he should *not* cross the stream until he acknowledges and atones for his offense (*Phaedrus* 242b–c). Only when Socrates listens to this voice, *the voice*, can he then present a "true" speech on *eros* and possess not only "objective" truth about *eros* but also the techniques and practices of the self that allow for authentic erotic experiences. The divine voice cares for Socrates and knows, to cite again *Apology* 40a, when to be silent, to not oppose Socrates, even if he seems to be caring little about his own life:

the divine voice did not oppose me either when I left my home in the morning, or when I came here to the court, or at any point of my speech, when I was going to say anything; and yet on other occasions it stopped me at many points in the midst of a speech; but now in this affair, it has not opposed me in anything I was doing or saying.

---

[17] See Destrée (2005) for arguments on the uniqueness of Socrates' *daimonion*. Destrée concentrates on Socrates, despite the uniqueness of his divine sign, as a paradigm of the perfect philosopher who should be imitated and emulated: "an exceptional human being since he has been 'elected'... by the gods to initiate such a new practice of philosophy as care of the soul. And he is an exceptional man since he is the very first philosopher to practice philosophy in such a way. But precisely as the very first and perfect one, he must be a paradigm we should imitate" (77).

[18] Foucault (1998) 287.

An authoritative voice, the divine sign proposes a set of laws, of ethical imperatives, created for Socrates and then appropriated by Socrates as his own. Socrates submits to this auditory order since, from childhood, the voice has proven itself to be a loyal companion that possesses a sort of divine wisdom surpassing that even of the divinely human, yet limited, wisdom of Socrates. In listening to the *daimonion*, Socrates simultaneously submits to an order of knowledge and truth that is imposed on him and creates, through the spiritual practice of listening to the divine voice, the truth about *himself* and for himself. Socrates constitutes his own relation to the truth. As Foucault explains in *Hermeneutics of the Subject*, to care for the self, to know what it is to care for the self, implies not only concern and rule of the self, but also of others:

> The care of myself must therefore be such that it also provides me with the art (the *technē*, the know-how) which will enable me to govern others well. In short, the succession of the two questions—what is the self and what is the care?—involves responding to one and the same demand: one's self and the care of the self must be given a definition from which we can derive the knowledge required for governing others.[19]

Insofar as Socrates truly cares for the self when, for example, he listens to the divine voice that tells him not to practice politics (*Apology* 31d), he aspires to care for the other. He is neither selfless nor practicing a masochistic, nor even perverse, form of altruism. He practices politics differently and uniquely. Socrates explicitly recognizes this ability at *Gorgias* 521d, an ability that emanates from his careful capacity to distinguish the good from the pleasant, to know their different ends and effects:

> I believe I'm one of a few Athenians—so as not to say I'm the only one, but the only one among our contemporaries—to take up the true political craft and practice the true politics. This is because the speeches I make on each occasion do not aim at gratification but at what's best. They don't aim at what's most pleasant.[20]

Socrates cares for and governs others through espousing a way of life that recognizes the human values governing everyday existence essentially oppose and conflict with the truly human values of the philosophical man who questions privately citizens about how they live. Socrates' divine voice stops him from doing politics to do philosophy—the act Foucault summarizes thus:

---

[19] Foucault (2005) 51–2.
[20] Plato, *Gorgias*, trans. Zeyl (1987). I am thankful to Sara Brill for encouraging me to review the *Gorgias*.

[Socrates] is the one who hails people in the street or young boys in the gymnasium, by saying to them: Are you concerned with yourself? A god has charged him with that. That is his mission and he will not abandon it, even at the moment when he is threatened by death. He is truly the man who cares for others. That is the particular position of the philosopher.[21]

To occupy this position, Socrates must heed the non-human voice "that comes to him" and commands him to transform into an exceptional human form that relies solely on rationality (understood as the marker of individual identity) and views the body as "limiting the scope of the mind."[22]

3.2. To care differently: the *daimonion*'s mission

Let me now turn to the actual details of what the *daimonion*, the disembodied voice that controls and commands him, does to Socrates and how it redirects his bodily and spiritual movements such that he cares for himself and others differently. Indeed, as we have already noted, the *daimonion* is but a voice, a speechless voice without *logos* that is nonetheless comprehensible to Socrates, the man who follows solely, unlike the vast majority of human beings, the dictates of reason. That Socrates was marked from childhood by a sound in his head, a sound that is not strange but familiar to him (*eiōthos*, *Apology* 40c2; *Phaedrus* 242b9), that only he could hear and interpret, comes really as no surprise given all the peculiar bodily powers he already possesses. Indeed, as the *Symposium* tells us, Socrates does not really resemble a man; he comes closer in image to a satyr, who—being half man and half donkey—blurs the distinction between human and animal. Socrates as satyr, as Silenus, goes even further: he confounds the boundaries between human, animal, and divine worlds.[23]

---

[21] Foucault (1998) 287.
[22] For a scholar such as Pramod K. Nayar (Nayar (2014) 6) this might make Socrates a "transhumanist", one who believes "in the perfectibility of the human, seeing the limitations of the human body (biology) as something that might be transcended through technology so that faster, more intelligent, less disease-prone, long-living human bodies might one day exist on Earth."
[23] As Daniel del Nido, "The Body of Socrates: Plato's Appropriation of Dionysian Mystery Religion in the *Symposium*," unpublished paper, p. 3, remarks: "Socrates blurs distinctions between animal and divine worlds. While outwardly comic and animalistic in his appearance, Alcibiades claims that Socrates keeps his *agalmata* 'hidden within' himself (*Symp*. 217a). Socrates' outer appearance is, as Hadot claims, a mask for something divine inside of him which he keeps hidden from the world."

The object of the gods' exceptional attention, Socrates shows no shame in discussing this acoustical event. Mentioned the most in the *Apology*, the sign appears first, as discussed earlier, as a prohibition against politics.[24] To have engaged in politics would have been to accept an early death or, even more importantly, to have deprived Socrates of caring for the city and himself: "This is what prevented me from taking part in public affairs, and I think it was quite right to prevent me. Be sure, men of Athens, that if I had long ago attempted to take part in politics, I should have died long ago, and benefited neither you nor myself" (*Apology* 31d5-e2).[25] Without explanation, the *daimonion* provides the evidence: to achieve the philosophical mission, it is mandatory to neglect politics. But one must ask: Why does Socrates need a divine sign to tell him this? Shouldn't this be obvious to him? He has already been in a political position and witnessed firsthand its limitations. Something more is at stake and the appearance of *to daimonion* signals this. Just as when Socrates' interlocutors tell the odd philosopher that they don't understand what he is saying when he adopts a counter-intuitive argument, so too does the divine sign mark those moments where Socrates proposes a controversial practice whose logic is anything but obvious. A "non-rational source of certain knowledge," the *daimonion* is more compelling, has greater motivational force, than reason. Socrates has more confidence in this voice than in elenchus. He questions not; he listens.

The divine voice demands Socrates abstain from politics. This demand, it goes without saying, runs counter to the traditional obligations required of the male citizen. Even though the voice does not encourage him to do anything specific, Socrates seems to understand where his ethical path leads him. The prohibition signifies implicitly an action, an activity: "Do not do politics" means "Do philosophy instead." To be a philosopher, "to intervene in other people's affairs to give... advice in private" (*Apology* 31c5-7), we learn earlier in the *Apology*, is to not be human. Socrates, in famous imagery, compares himself "absurdly" to a gadfly stinging a sluggish, noble and large horse: he is one who "attaches himself to the city as a gadfly to a horse" (*Apology* 30e3-4). To be a gadfly, as Socrates attests, is to be a "kind of gift from the god":

I have neglected all my own affairs and have been enduring the neglect of my concerns all these years, but I am always busy in your interest, coming to each

---

[24] In Plato's opus, the *daimonion* is mentioned at: *Alcibiades* 103a-b; *Apology* 31c-e, 40a, 40c, 41d; *Euthyphro* 272e; *Republic* 6.496c; *Phaedrus* 242b-c; *Theaetetus* 151a; *Theages* 128d-31a.
[25] Trans. Destrée (2005) 67.

one of you individually like a father, or an elder brother, and urging you to care for virtue; now, that is not like human conduct. (*Apology* 31b1–9, Loeb)

Socrates is a divine thing (a gift) who resembles an animal (gadfly) who resembles a human (father or brother) who performs an unnatural act (philosophy) that in harming the city (the horse) brings benefit to the people (they "care for virtue").[26] Socrates' divine sign requires this metamorphosis: becoming animal, Socrates will challenge conventional values that, in fact, render the citizens less human insofar as they do not live the examined life, the human life par excellence. The citizens need to become their own gadfly so as to be human and beyond human, the very ontological position the philosopher himself occupies.

When the *daimonion* is mentioned again explicitly in the *Apology*, it emits a voice that relates to the central practice of philosophy: becoming pure soul through death. To care for himself and for others, Socrates must listen to the supernatural force within and follow the rules and practices it stipulates eccentrically at the trial, which are transparent only to him. In maintaining silence, in prohibiting Socrates' silence and escape, the *daimonion* offers Socrates an alternative way of existing that he himself could not predict or account for rationally. It urges him to accept death as the greatest of goods; the sign's absence becomes for Socrates the "serious indication" justifying his aberrant actions. I quote, at length, the relevant passage where Socrates understands, on this very day, at this very moment, the new ethical order his obedience, his active subjugation to the *daimonion*, creates:

Yes, judges—and when I call you "judges," I am using the proper formula—something amazing happened to me. In fact, whereas the divinatory voice that is familiar to me (*hē gar eiōthuia moi mantikē*), that in which the divine sign consists (*hē tou daimoniou*), has never ceased manifesting itself until today (*en men tōi prosthen chronōi panti panu puknē aei ēn*) to prevent me (*enantioumenē*) even in matters of little importance (*kai panu epi smikrois*), from doing what I shouldn't do, today, as you can observe yourself, there occurred to me what could be thought the greatest evil (*oiētheiē . . . eschata kakōn einai*) and which is thought to be so (*kai nomizetai*). And yet, the divine sign (*to tou theou sēmeion*) did not hold me back (*ēnantiōthē*) either this morning, when I was leaving home, nor in the moment when here, before the tribunal, I was going up to the tribune, nor during my plea, to prevent me from saying anything. Quite often, in other circumstances, it has silenced me right in the middle of my speech (*kaitoi en allois logois pollachou dē me epesche legonta metaxu*). Today, on the contrary, in the course of this affair, it never prevented me from doing or saying anything. What reason explains this phenomenon? I will tell you. What is happening to me

---

[26] See Naas (2015) *passim*.

might well be a piece of good fortune for me, and we all—all of us who are present—are mistaken if we imagine that to die is an evil. A serious indication of this for me (*mega moi tekmērion*) is the following: for the customary signal (*to eiōthos sēmeion*) would surely have opposed me (*ouk ēnantiōthēan moi*) if what I was going to do was not something good (*egō agathon praksein*).[27]

The sign transmits to Socrates a message about how to behave such that he constitutes himself as an ethical subject who freely and sovereignly creates his own destiny: to not fear death, to not envision death as a danger, to risk speaking freely without self-censorship or fear of the consequences. Just as the voice commands him to pay attention to quotidian gestures that unwittingly shape his subjectivity and discourse—as I will discuss—so too it intervenes to transform radically Socrates' commitments and concerns. He chooses philosophy over life; to care more for his soul than his body; to listen to a voice that opposes general opinion and common sense. The *daimonion* thus forces Socrates to enter into a spiritual relationship with himself and with the city. Attending to silence, Socrates cares for himself and creates a new form of philosophical discourse and legal-political practice. The *daimonion* provides Socrates with the occasion to invent a non-familiar type of spiritual existence. If the Delphic oracle commands Socrates to "know thyself" (*gnōthi seauton*), the *daimonion* institutes the new orders of philosophy, which requires a radical reevaluation of what constitutes the self and how to care for that self in private life as well as in the *polis*.

3.3. Who cares for Socrates?

But what of the sign's manifestation at seemingly non-consequential moments? Is it not still "something amazing" (*thaumasion ti*)? What then becomes of Socrates when it "prevents [him] from doing or saying" something? To begin Socrates, as he is wont to do, listens to a voice that transmits a non-verbal message. He trusts the voice; he believes that something with meaning and meaningfulness is being said. This voice should and must be interpreted. Unlike his treatment of his interlocutors, Socrates does not second-guess the meaning of this non-linguistic sign. As we saw in the above quotation, Socrates even takes the sign as a "serious indication" that he would be mistaken in thinking death should be feared and is "not a good thing." Socrates listens because the

---

[27] Trans. Brisson (2005) 7. I have underlined my changes to this translation.

voice makes him aware that he has to be more, as it were, self-conscious about what he says, thinks, and does. Even in the "smallest matters," Socrates cannot act without thought—the *daimonion* guarantees that he self-reflects. To return to the example from *Euthydemus* 272e–273a cited before: when Socrates is prevented from "getting up and going" and made to "sit down again," the *daimonion* alerts Socrates to the fact that he is about to miss a philosophical opportunity if he doesn't stay still and think and engage his interlocutors in the transformative experience of philosophical discourse. Socrates heeds the *daimonion*'s call and hinders his own instinctive bodily movements. No one, nothing commands such respect: not even the Delphic Oracle whose pronouncement, as we all know, sends Socrates in the *Apology* on a quest that questions its authority and authoritative statements. The *daimonion*, to shift slightly the formula with which I have been working in this essay, cares for Socrates, even at the most inconsequential of moments.

Caring for Socrates, this divine sign makes recognizable a Socrates who needs care, who is susceptible to human error and convention. For example, in *Theaetetus* 151a, the appearance of the *daimonion* makes us aware that Socrates might not be able to discern best with whom he should converse. A sign is necessary to distinguish worthy and virtuous students from the wayward and wicked: "the *daimonion* that comes to me forbids me to associate with some of them, but allows me to converse with others." The *daimonion* happens to Socrates; it is not a voice Socrates intentionally calls on. He recognizes his own limits, his own ignorance. The divine intervention makes Socrates aware of his lack of epistemic certainty about what is the best path to take—a path we can only assume Socrates might not have taken if not for the vocal manifestation. It is not that Socrates is divinely inspired at these moments, nor that he is irrational, as some would argue. It is rather that he is shown to *not* be a sovereign subject, to *not* be master of himself. As such, he is not the *atopos* philosopher; he is rather very much a run-the-mill, ordinary human being who might do wrong, who might desire something other than the greatest good.

I end then with a claim much different from that with which I began. And yet, what I wish to insist upon is that the *daimonion* constitutes Socrates as both human and divine, human and animal. He is a dynamic hybrid, a composite, of ontologically different elements. This comes as no real surprise, since in dialogues such as the *Republic* and the *Phaedrus*, Socrates likens parts of the human soul to animals, lions, beasts, and horses. It is not just that these are those elements that must be ruled rather than rule. The animal parts within—just as that divine bit of us that reasons—make humans human and neither solely animals nor gods.

And yet Socrates has another part which others lack, which others have missed out on—that voice. What would Socrates have been without this voice, one that provided him with a specific and particular spiritual dimension, connected as it was to the practice of philosophy? Socrates would have been merely mortal, a human among humans. But he is anything but that. The sound in his head, the extra-rational voice he hears, sets him apart from his fellow creatures. It compels him to redefine himself as a philosopher who continued to live in the city among humans until the moment he could no longer live as a human among beings who heard nothing but the human, far too human, voices within.[28]

WORKS CITED

Barthes, R. (1991) "Listening," in *The Responsibility of Forms: Critical Essays on Music, Art and Representation*. Trans. R. Howard. Berkeley.

Bennett, J. (2010) *Vibrant Matter: A Political Economy of Things*. Durham, NC.

Brisson, L. (2005) "Socrates and the Divine Signal According to Plato's Testimony: Philosophical Practice as Rooted in Religious Tradition," in Destrée and Smith, 1–12.

Davidson, A. I. (2005) "Ethics as Ascetics: Foucault, the History of Ethics, and Ancient Thought," in G. Gutting (ed.), *The Cambridge Companion to Foucault*. Cambridge: 123–48.

Destrée, P. (2005) "The *Daimonion* and the Philosophical Mission: Should the Divine Sign Remain Unique to Socrates?" in Destrée and Smith, 63–80.

Destrée, P. and N. D. Smith, eds. (2005) *Socrates" Divine Sign: Religion, Practice and Value in Socratic Philosophy*. Kelowna, B.C.

Foucault, M. (1998) "The Ethics of the Concern of the Self as a Practice of Freedom," in P. Rabinow (ed.), *Ethics: Subjectivity and Truth (Essential Works of Foucault, 1954–1984, vol. 1)*. Trans. R. Hurley. New York.

Foucault, M. (2005) *The Hermeneutics of the Subject: Lectures at the College de France, 1981–1982*. Ed. F. Gros and trans. G. Burchell. New York.

Joyal, M. A. (1997) "The Divine Sign did not Oppose me," in M. Joyal (ed.), *Studies in Plato and the Platonic Tradition: Essays Presented to John Whittaker*. Aldershot: 43–58.

---

[28] I am grateful to Emanuela Bianchi, Sara Brill, and Brooke Holmes for organizing the "Posthuman Antiquities" conference. Sara Brill's comments on the final draft were especially helpful and necessary. Members in the audience and conference speakers provided me with much-appreciated feedback, as did the participants at the conference, "Haunting Antiquity," Shane Butler organized at Johns Hopkins. I thank Shane Butler, Judith Gurewich, James Porter, Peter Sahlins, Caroline Smith and Alyosha Zim for conversation, commentary, and care. The University of California, Berkeley, provided research funds that facilitated my scholarship.

McPherran, M. L. (2014) "Socrates and the Religious Dimension of Plato's Thought," in J. Hardy and G. Rudebusch (eds), *Ancient Ethics*. Göttingen: 197–212.

Naas, M. (2015) "American Gadfly: Plato and the Problem of Metaphor," in J. Bell and M. Naas (eds), *Plato's Animals: Gadflies, Horses, Swans, and Other Philosophical Beasts*. Bloomington, IN: 43–59.

Nagy, G. (2013) *The Ancient Greek Hero in 24 Hours*. Cambridge, MA.

Nancy, J.-L. (2007) *Listening*. Trans. C. Mandell. New York.

Nayar, P. K. (2014) *Posthumanism*. Cambridge.

Nietzsche, F. W. (1999) *The Birth of Tragedy and Other Writings*. Ed. R. Geuss and trans. R. Speirs. Cambridge.

Ober, J. (2011) "Socrates and Democratic Athens," in D. R. Morrison (ed.), *The Cambridge Companion to Socrates*. Cambridge: 138–78.

Trapp, M. B. (1997) *Maximus of Tyre. The Philosophical Orations*. Oxford.

Van Riel, G. (2005) "Socrates' Daemon: Internalisation of the Divine and Knowledge of the Self," in Destrée and Smith, 31–42.

Vlastos, G. (1991) *Socrates: Ironist and Moral Philosopher*. Ithaca, NY.

Zeyl, D. J. (1987) trans. *Plato, Gorgias*. Indianapolis, IN.

4 Song and dance man

Plato and the limits of the human

Michael Naas

In the *Laws*, Plato's Athenian distinguishes the human from all other animals by granting the former and denying the latter an attribute or capacity that is not among those commonly used by the philosophical tradition to draw a line between them. Indeed this capacity does not even figure in the long list drawn up by Jacques Derrida in *The Animal That Therefore I Am* of those capacities or qualities traditionally used by philosophy to mark a putatively single and indivisible line or limit between humans and all other animals.[1] For the Athenian there argues, in effect, that it is not so much living in cities, using tools, or wearing clothes, not laughing, crying, lying, mourning, dying, or philosophizing, that distinguishes the human from the animal, but, curiously, singing and dancing. Contrary to common sense and ordinary language, animals like the cockatiel may appear to sing and wolves may seem to dance but only the human can really do either. *Anthrōpos* would thus be not accidentally or occasionally but always and in his very being or essence not only a *zōion echon logon*, as Aristotle famously characterizes him in the *Nicomachean Ethics*, but a *zōion echon mousikēn* and a *zōion echon choreian*, in short, a song and dance man—a claim that no one who ever attended a philosophy conference would ever dare to advance, unless, of course, that conference was attended by the likes of Adriana Cavarero.

It is an amusing and rather surprising claim, so much so that one might be tempted to write it off as having been uttered in jest or with irony, especially since it appears in a passage where the Athenian is trying to defend the practice of drinking parties for the guardians of the state. But the justification that follows is wholly Platonic and is supported by passages in a host of other dialogues. In the final analysis,

---

[1] As Derrida argues, "*all* philosophers have judged that limit to be single and indivisible" (Derrida (2008) 40). Plato's Stranger seems to suggest at one point in the *Statesman* that this single and indivisible line is drawn out of a kind of narcissism or anthropocentrism and that if other animals that appear to think were to give names out of the same principle of self-pride, animals like the crane, for example, they would no doubt draw a line just as crudely and indiscriminately between themselves and all other animals (*Statesman* 263c).

it is because humans have or are able to develop reason or intelligence, *nous* or *phronēsis*, that they—and only they—are able to sing and dance. While every animal, including the human when it is young, is given to wild crying and leaping about, in other words, to "frenzy [*mainetai*]," to the uncontrolled emission of sounds and the unordered making of movements, only the human animal is able, through training and education, to develop his reason or intelligence so as to refrain from these disorderly sounds and movements and begin to cultivate orderly forms of both (*Laws* 672c).[2] While other animals emit sounds or make movements when compelled by external circumstances, only the human, the mature, adult human, is capable of checking the disorderly movements of his limbs and the unharmonious sounds of his tongue so as to make orderly or even, if he so chooses, disorderly forms of both. If gymnastics thus has its origin, as the Athenian argues, in the "natural tendency [*kata physin*]" of living creatures to leap about, and music in the natural propensity for them to cry out, these natural inclinations will have been transformed by humans, who alone have a "sense of order [*taxeōs*]," into rhythm and harmony, that is, into dance and song, "the combination of which is choristry [*choreia*]" (*Laws* 664e–665a; see 673c–d).

It is, therefore, the development of reason or intelligence that allows humans to sing and dance but then also, it seems, to perceive and appreciate the song and dance of others. As the Athenian argues earlier in the dialogue, only humans have a "perception [*aisthēsin*] of the various kinds of order and disorder in movement [*kinēsesi taxeōn oude ataxiōn*]," including, therefore, the kind of order in sound and bodily movements that makes for "rhythm and harmony [*rhythmos... harmonia*]" (*Laws* 653e). As a result, only humans can take pleasure in this perception, a pleasure that comes by perceiving the joys that—and this is significant—the gods themselves, says the Athenian, will have put into these orderly things.[3] It was in fact the Muses, along with Apollo and Dionysus, who first implanted in man rhythm and harmony. Indeed it was Dionysus himself who, instead of turning a sober and rational man

---

[2] I quote throughout this essay the Loeb Classical Library edition of Plato's dialogues, in particular, R. G. Bury's translation of *Laws* (1926) and Paul Shorey's translation of *Republic* (1989).

[3] A capacity for song and dance thus seems to require, on this account, both being able to make orderly movements and harmonious sounds and being able to perceive them in others. One could thus argue that if certain animals engage in orderly movements or harmonious sounds, they are not really dancing or singing because they themselves do not perceive the order of their own movements and do not take pleasure in them. They would simply be following or embodying an order that has been imposed upon them by nature, which would then explain why these orderly behaviors are limited and admit little variation.

into a frenzied one, as is often thought, actually helped humans to order their frenzied movements and put rhythm into their disorderly cries. As such, the gods are, in the words of the Athenian, our "fellows in the dance [*synchoreutas*]" (*Laws* 653e), the gods and not, obviously, animals of any other kind. The human and the human alone, then, is able, like a god, to perceive and take pleasure in the order that will have been put into orderly things by the gods themselves.

Now, I begin with this passage from the *Laws* and this radical claim about the centrality of the human in Plato because I think it is essential to our topic here. To begin to think anything like a posthuman antiquity, that is, as I understand the phrase, anything that would come before or after the human within antiquity, anything in antiquity, whether animal, plant, mineral, monster, or machine, that would oppose or resist the human from either outside or within, we must first take the full measure of the human within antiquity, the full measure, in this case, of what Plato, who is not just anyone within antiquity, thought the human to be. It is, in short, only when we have appreciated the full range and scope of this anthropocentrism within ancient Greek thought that we will be able to identify what resists it. For if the Greeks were in fact particularly attentive to what comes before or what lies beyond the human sphere, there is also, especially in Plato, an irrepressible confidence in the centrality of the human that cannot be ignored or underestimated. I thus begin with attributes or capacities of the human, namely song and dance, that are not usually considered among those that would distinguish humans from other animals in order to see just how far Plato's confidence in, and privileging of, the human goes and just how pervasive the logic that supports it runs. In an academic climate where the animal has become the new marginalized human, and the plant or even the stone is on its way to becoming the new animal, in other words, in an academic climate where our enthusiasm for the posthuman has caused us, and rightly so, to concentrate on all these non-human entities, it is important not to lose sight of the logic—call it anthropocentric, phantasmatic, or just narcissistic—that either denigrates these entities explicitly or else uses them in such a way as to place the human in an even more favorable light.

Plato's claim that only humans can sing and dance is thus not as surprising as all that. For if singing and dancing require the perception of order, and *phronēsis* or *nous* is required for that perception, then only the human—the only animal with *phronēsis* or *nous*—will be able to sing and dance, among many other things. And yet the examples of singing and dancing as activities made possible by the possession of *phronēsis* or *nous* are not two abilities among others in Plato. Both involve, as we will see, not only the perception of order but the calibration of that order upon the human, and, in an exemplary way, upon the human voice, that is, upon a voice that tends—and it is the work of Adriana Cavarero that I wish to pay tribute to in this essay by means of this hypothesis—to reduce or overcome its properly vocal aspect, which is to say its animal or childish aspect, its feminine aspect as well, in the name of a human, male, adult voice that ultimately becomes conflated with meaning and order themselves. It is this conflation of voice or sound with meaning, with *logos*, in short, this process by which, to quote Cavarero's *For More Than One Voice*, "logos lost its voice," that will ultimately allow Plato to calibrate or index not just all order upon human meaning but being itself.[4] It will be this ultimate indexing of being upon *logos*, being upon a human meaning that will be held to be universalizable if not universal (at least among the Greeks), that will allow Plato to adapt to his own philosophical purposes the dictum of Protagoras that "man is the measure of all things." While Plato's Socrates in the *Theaetetus* is able to reduce this dictum to absurdity, Plato himself seems to endorse a modified version of it throughout the dialogues. Though he will continue to reject the view that just any individual human being is or can be the measure of all things, though he will never cease to find such relativism anathema to philosophy, he will nonetheless accept the view that the reasonable or reasoning man is the measure of all things, that is, the educated and rational man, the one whose voice, whose speech or ordered words, are the measure of all things because those words take their own measure from the things themselves. If the animal or any other post-, pre-, or non-human antiquity thus comes to appear and find a place in Plato's dialogues, it is always, on this view, thanks to a *logos* that will have measured, that is, situated, ordered, relativized, and denigrated that animal or non-human thing in relation to the human from the very start.

The absence of *nous* or *phronēsis* in animals and their concomitant inability to perceive order means not only that animals cannot do philosophy or mathematics or even speak but that they cannot engage in any kind of ordered or law-governed activity at all, including singing and dancing.[5] To return to the *Laws* for a moment, the hierarchy

---

[4] See Cavarero (2005) 17–91. Cavarero writes, for example, "The devocalization of logos inaugurated by Plato above all tends to liberate speech from the corporeality of breath and the voice" (62). This means, of course, that *logos* is "liberated" from everything with which corporeality is typically identified—animals, children, women, slaves, and so on.

[5] The movement of stars presents an interesting case in the *Epinomis*, a dialogue that is almost certainly not Plato's but is almost just as certainly Plato-inspired. It is there argued that because the stars move always in the same way they must be possessed of *mind*, since what is intelligent "acts always in the same respects, in the same way, and

between humans and animals that is sketched out in that dialogue on the basis of *nous* or *phronēsis* is established in large part, as always in Plato, by means of analogy, for example, though this is in many ways the paradigm for all analogy, the analogy between humans and the gods. It is said in the *Laws* that Kronos, out of his "love of humanity," that is, out of his *"philanthropy,"*[6] set the gods, a nobler race, to rule over humans, just as we humans rule over oxen and goats (*Laws* 713d), an arrangement that, he says, is for the benefit of both the ruler and the ruled. It is the human's ability to rule over other animals and, in the *polis*, to rule over himself through laws, says the Athenian much later in the dialogue, that distinguishes man from the most savage of beasts and at once sets him above the beasts and likens him—or at least what is best and most noble in him—to the gods (*Laws* 874e).[7]

If animals often serve an important rhetorical role in Plato's dialogues, if they sometimes provide examples and analogies for understanding humans and human action, if they sometimes even function as models for human behavior or virtue, the human is always the exemplary example and his *logos* that which provides the analogies by which all these other animals are situated and understood.[8] This becomes particularly clear when one looks not just at Plato's understanding of the origins of song and dance, and thus at the human's exclusive claim to these activities, but at the criteria by which good song and dance are to be distinguished from bad. A work of music, says the Athenian, is considered successful *not* when it produces pleasure, when it panders, so to speak, to the tastes and expectations of its audience, but when it successfully imitates and represents some worthy thing or action. But that then depends upon *logos*, for an imitation or representation of some thing or action is best achieved only when it is put into the form of a meaningful

---

from the same causes" (*Epinomis* 982c–d). As a result, the stars dance an even more beautiful dance than man.

[6] This is, interestingly, a characteristic sometimes attributed to Socrates (see Plato, *Euthyphro* 3d).

[7] Earlier in the dialogue, the Athenian tells us that man is an animal, not a god, but a "tame" animal who turns out most tame and godlike when a happy nature is combined with right education. He is thus the "tamest" animal when properly educated and trained, the animal best suited, therefore, to rule over other animals, but, when poorly educated and trained, the "wildest of all earth's creatures" (*Laws* 766a).

[8] For example, the Athenian of the *Laws* says that women would do well to imitate birds when their offspring are attacked, for it would be disgraceful, he argues, if humans did not show themselves the equals or superiors of these animal models (*Laws* 650d; see also 814a for the image of the family as a flock of birds). In a couple of famous passages from the *Laws*, the Athenian argues against homosexuality by suggesting that humans, who are able to act contrary to nature and pursue unnatural pleasure, should in fact follow the example of nature and avoid such pleasures and behaviors (*Laws* 636b, 836d–e, 838e,840d–e, 841d).

logos. This becomes evident when the Athenian runs through a list of mistakes that humans—and not the Muses—commonly make in music, each of these mistakes being rooted in a form of disorder, that is, in the severing of sound from meaning, or in the mere reproduction of meaningless sounds, such as the sounds of animals. The Athenian thus speaks of incongruity (where the words, tunes, or gestures of a piece of music are out of harmony), of senselessness (where tunes and gestures are divorced from words), and of barbarousness (where the things represented are paltry or uncouth—for example animal sounds), and of virtuosity (where a performer makes a display of his control over his limbs and instruments to the detriment of what is being represented—a mistake or error that Aristotle will criticize in a similar fashion in the *Politics*) (*Laws* 669b–e). All these are mistakes from the point of view of the educated guardian or music warden who must thus condemn them because they are neither "correct" nor morally elevating.

Having enumerated these mistakes of composition, the Athenian goes on to claim that certain tunes, which always represent certain characters, are appropriate for certain individuals or classes and not for others. Hence tunes for women should never be assigned to songs for men, or those of slaves to freemen, and so on (*Laws* 669c). Moreover, says the Athenian, the Muses *would* never—and so the human songwriter *should* never—"combine in a single piece the cries of beasts and men, the clash of instruments, and noises of all kinds, by way of representing a single object" (*Laws* 669d). The reason for this, it might be thought, is that this multiplicity confuses the single human being or action being represented or portrayed. But soon thereafter it becomes clear that what the Athenian really condemns in animal cries and other non-human sounds is the fact that they are, precisely, "without words [*aneu rhēmatōn*]," making it thereby "almost impossible," says the Athenian, "to understand what is intended [*bouletai*] by this wordless rhythm and harmony, or what noteworthy original it represents" (*Laws* 669e). Though music obviously requires the elements of sound in addition to words, words—the meaning of words rather than their sound—appear to be the primary means of representation in music. Sound, inhuman sound, including the inhuman sounds within the human, would therefore be, on this account, a first pre- or posthuman antiquity.

The human or, more specifically, human speech, thus marks both what is represented and the means of representation. Much later in the *Laws*, the Athenian will go on to argue that the notes (*phthongoi*) of the lyre must be in *accord* with the notes of the voice and that a tune should have few notes and not be complicated and varied, since "the jarring of opposites with one another impedes easy learning," yet another indication, first, that the aim of music is not pleasure but education and, second, that the human voice, insofar as it is marked by an orderly *logos*, is the means to such education (*Laws* 812d). All this helps explain, of course, why, in the *Republic*, certain sounds and not others are to be banned from the state. In short, the further one gets away from the sounds of the reasonable man or the reasoning of man, the closer one comes to the gibberish of mad men or the *logos*-less sounds of children, animals, or nature, the less warrant there is for allowing something to enter into or to remain in the state. The argument in the *Republic* regarding why the guardians should not imitate unbecoming things is well known—the dangers, as Socrates puts it, of "imbibing the reality" of the shameful things one imitates, the tendency for these imitations to become habits, a kind of second nature, and so on.[9] But it is worth underscoring that the kinds of things one must refrain from imitating are those things that deviate from the ordered *logos* of the adult, male citizen: women arguing with their husbands, or defying heaven, or boasting, lamenting, or sick, in love or in labor, slaves or cowards or madmen, smiths and other craftsmen who demonstrate a certain slavishness in their repetitive movements, and, especially, the sounds of horses, bulls, rivers, the sea, thunder, and so on.[10] The explicit reason for the prohibition on these representations, namely, that the imitator may become like that which he imitates, seems to be subtended and supported by a sliding scale of coherent *logos* that runs from the full or meaningful speech of the adult male to the meaningless words of the woman or madman to, finally, the mere sounds of animals and natural phenomena (*Republic* 396a–b). Though one would not want to discount a certain humor or irony on Plato's part here, this list of censured sounds seems perfectly consistent with the view we just saw in the *Laws*, namely, that the further one slides down this scale of coherent *logos* the more difficult it becomes "to understand what is intended" and, as a result, the less reason there is for allowing such representations into the state (*Laws* 669e). One might thus be able to report on these things, to speak *of* them, but not *imitate* them. Only the most "debased [*phauloteros*]" individual, says Socrates, will imitate "in the presence of many" and in all "seriousness [*spoudēi*]"—since the

---

[9] The guardians should thus not become "clever at imitating" such things, "lest from the imitation they imbibe the reality," since "imitations, if continued from youth into life, settle down into habits and (second) nature in the body, the speech, and the thought" (*Republic* 395c–d).

[10] Hence the guardians must not, for example, "form the habit of likening themselves to madmen either in words nor yet in deeds [*en logois oud' en ergois*]. For while knowledge they must have both of mad and bad men and women, they must do and imitate nothing of this kind" (*Republic* 396a).

guardians might do so in jest or in the presence of few in order to teach a lesson—things such as thunder and hail or, says Socrates, the "cries of dogs, sheep, and birds" (*Republic* 397a). This argument regarding the accord of sound and sense in both the *content* and the *form* of music is subsequently reiterated and reinforced in the discussion of the *means* of representation, where a prohibition is placed on many-stringed and panharmonic instruments, that is, on those instruments that are the least able to accompany and be in accord with the human voice.[11]

Music must thus conform to speech (*Republic* 399e–400a), and not just any speech, not the speech of the woman, slave, or madman, but the speech of the good man, a speech that requires good character, which is itself attached to a certain "disposition of the soul [*psychēs ēthei*]" (*Republic* 400d). As Socrates argues: "Good speech [*eulogia*], then, good accord [*euarmostia*], and good grace [*euschēmosynē*], and good rhythm wait upon a good disposition [*euētheiai*], not that weakness of head which we euphemistically style goodness of heart [*euētheian*], but the truly [*alēthōs*] good and fair disposition of the character [*ēthos*] and the mind [*dianoian*]" (*Republic* 400d–e). Everything begins with a disposition of mind or character, with *dianoia* or *ēthos*, and good speech, diction, rhythm, and seemliness all emanate out from it. In order to cultivate this inner disposition, then, the guardians of the city must pursue orderliness and grace in everything outside themselves in the city, in music, as we have seen, but also in painting, weaving, embroidery, architecture, utensils, and in the natural bodies of plants and animals. It is the task of education, it seems, to teach the young to perceive and imitate the graceful and avoid the graceless in all these things. But, again, and already in *Republic* and not just the *Laws*, this grace is associated with human speech and is, in a sense, already indexed or measured by it. Socrates says that "gracelessness [*aschēmosynē*] and evil rhythm and disharmony are akin [*adelpha*] to evil speaking [*kakalogias*] and evil temper [*kakoētheias*], but the opposites are the symbols and kin of the opposites, the sober and good disposition" (*Republic* 401a). The relationship of kinship or the analogy is, again, more than a mere analogy. Gracelessness in architecture or embroidery or even in natural bodies is akin to evil speaking because of the disorder, the lack of sense or of

---

[11] Socrates says that they will "admit" into the city no triangles, or harps, or flutes or flute-makers. Thus only the lyre and cithera are left, these being "useful" in the city, while the piccolo [*syrinx*] will be left to the shepherds to use in the fields (399d). Socrates says that in making these distinctions they are favoring the instruments of Apollo over those of Marsyas. But the advantage of stringed over wind instruments is also, it seems, their clear, measurable proportions based on the lengths of their strings, proportions that would correspond to, and be the measure of, measured human speech.

meaning, within them. Human imitation of graceful or disgraceful things is first made possible, it seems, because of this kinship, as if graceful or disgraceful things were themselves, already in nature, indexed upon, or imitations of, human speech or meaning. It is, in short, as if nature itself were good or evil depending upon whether it corresponded or not to man's good disposition and good speech.

Socrates concludes in the *Republic* that not only the poets but the craftsmen must embody the "semblance [*eikona*] of the good character" and not represent "the evil disposition [*kakoēthes*], the licentious [*akolaston*], the illiberal [*aneleutheron*], the graceless [*aschēmon*], either in the likeness [*eikosi*] of living creatures or in buildings or in any other product of their art" (*Republic* 401b). The guardians must thus find craftsmen who have a natural sense for what is beautiful and graceful in nature, "those craftsmen who by the happy gift of nature are capable of following the trail of true beauty and grace [*euschēmenos physin*: natural grace, grace in nature]" (*Republic* 401b), that is, things that resemble human grace, so that they can represent them in all their works of art. As a result, the inhabitants of the city will be surrounded by images and objects of grace and beauty that "from earliest childhood insensibly [*lanthanēi*, that is, unawares] guide them to likeness [*homoiotēta*], to friendship [*philian*], to harmony [*xymphōnian*] with beautiful reason [*kalōi logōi*]"—that is, beautiful *logos* (*Republic* 401c–d). On the opposite side, the guardians must not be bred or raised around the "likenesses [*eikosi*] of evil," "as it were in a pasturage of poisonous herbs," says Socrates, for they might pick a little evil everyday and so build up "unawares ... a huge mass of evil in their souls" (*Republic* 395c–d). By being exposed, therefore, to beautiful and graceful things, the guardians will be led "unawares" to avoid being misled "unawares" by shameful or graceless things. Reason or ordered speech, *logos*, is thus the measure *of* all these things and the giver of measure *to* all things, to things both as they appear in nature and as they are represented in the *polis*.

This claim about the relationship between human speech and the things of the world that would *seem* to come before that speech is supported by arguments, images, and analogies from many other dialogues. Socrates famously argues at *Phaedrus* 264c, for example, that speech, a good speech, must be organized like a *zōion*, that is, like an organism or an animal body, with a head, torso, and limbs, an animal that, and this is hardly coincidental, is in no way incompatible with man. In the *Statesman*, the Stranger argues in a similar fashion that it is more appropriate to "portray any living being [*zōion*] by speech and argument [*lexei kai logōi*] than by painting or any handicraft whatsoever to persons who are able to follow argument," that is, to those humans who are most attuned to the essence of the human as a being endowed with *logos*, while "to others [that is, to those who have not fully developed this essence] it is better to do it by means of works of craftsmanship" (*Statesman* 277a–c).

Human speech must be organized like a living being, like an animal body, and, in the end, like the human body. But the corollary also seems true, namely, that bodies—for example, though, again, this is more than an example, the human body—are already organized like human speech, like a good *logos*, with a beginning, a head (which is higher than the rest, closest to the celestial bodies), middle parts, and an end. The things themselves, so to speak, seem to be organized like the verbal organisms that we might think simply represent them, and these things are divided up and related to one another as if they had already undergone the divisions of human speech. We see evidence of this in the way animals are divided up by classes during the Age of Kronos in the myth told in the *Statesman* (271d).[12] And we see this in a different though not unrelated way in the *Timaeus* where Timaeus says that there is a fit, a relation, a reflection, even, between various kinds of beings and the kinds of discourse that are appropriate to them, a likely account, a merely plausible *logos*, for visible things or things of becoming, such as the cosmos, a certain or truthful account for things that belong to being, and, finally, a bastard account for that third *genos* that goes by the name of *chōra* (*Timaeus* 29a–d). It is not just that certain forms of discourse or *logos* are appropriate to represent or to speak of certain things; it's that the things themselves appear already ordered by the form of human speech that would try to speak of or approach them.

Human speech, as the measure of all meaning, is thus, insofar as things correspond to this meaning, the measure of all things. The human is, then, in Plato, never just an example, that is, just one example among others, as every good example should be, but always the first example, the exemplary example, the one that usually comes first to mind and the one to which all things must ultimately conform. To return to the *Laws* for a moment, in the course of his argument that those in the state who judge the accuracy of visual representations, those who judge whether a work of art is beautiful or deficient, must know, as the Athenian says, the nature of the "bodies represented [*tōn memimēmenōn*]," the nature of the "animal being represented [*memimēmenon zōion*]"—its dimensions and the positions of its body parts, their number, order, color, shape, and so on—it is no coincidence that the body that is first introduced,

---

[12] I treat this theme at some length in the first chapter of my *Plato and the Invention of Life* (New York: Fordham University Press, 2018), 1–41.

apparently just as an example, is that of man (*Laws* 668d). After asking Clinias, "Do you suppose that anyone could possibly decide these points if he were totally ignorant as to what animal was being represented?" the Athenian answers his own question with another, "Suppose we should know that the object painted or molded is a man, and know that art has endowed him with all his proper parts, colors, and shapes..." (*Laws* 668e–669a). The Athenian goes on to conclude, on the basis of this example, that "in regard to every representation—whether in painting, music, or any other art—the judicious critic must possess...first, a knowledge of the nature of the original; next, a knowledge of the correctness of the copy; and thirdly, a knowledge of the excellence with which the copy is executed" (*Laws* 669a–b). The example of man is clearly more than a mere example. Everything begins here with the human body—the order, color, shape, of the human body—which is itself ultimately indexed or calibrated upon the order that is to be found in the human voice, or rather, in human speech. Though I cannot show it here, the priority of *eikastikē* over *phantastikē* in the *Sophist* would also seem to be based on the same relationship between an order of human speech that corresponds to the order of the things themselves and an order of mere semblance that simply appeals to the way things *seem* to man—the visual equivalent of pandering to public tastes in music rather than trying to represent things as they truly are.

Man, *anthrōpos*, is, then, never a mere example but the example that provides the rule and the measure. It is thus surely no coincidence either that, in the *Sophist*, the first example of a meaningful sentence involves man, the noun man, *anthrōpos*. The Stranger there argues that discourse, *logos*, requires not just a succession of either nouns or verbs but a combination of the two. For example, and the examples are, yet again, telling, verbs such as "walks," "runs," or "sleeps," whether singly or in conjunction, mean nothing without the addition of nouns, while nouns such as "lion," "stag," and "horse," whether singly or in conjunction, mean nothing without verbs. The first meaningful sentence, the first example of a genuine *logos* offered by the Stranger, is thus not, as the examples of nouns and verbs would have led us to expect, "a lion walks," a "stag runs," or "a horse sleeps," but, rather, "a man learns [*anthrōpos manthanei*]" (*Sophist* 262c; see *Theaetetus* 157b–c and *Parmenides* 130b–c for similar "examples"). The point of the Stranger's example is ultimately to show that ideas, like words, like letters, can mingle only with certain ideas and not others; that is, only certain ideas can be combined, just as only certain letters can combine to form words and only certain words, nouns with verbs, can mingle to make a *logos*. These ideas would thus be those that, precisely, "man learns," through, say, diairesis or dialectic. But the ideas themselves seem to have already been determined by that first sentence "man learns," determined already in advance by human speech and the laws of combination within it. If man's *body*, indexed upon the order of things which are themselves already ordered by *logos*, is the measure of all things in the visual arts, and his words, or, rather, the order and meaning of his words, are the measure of all things in music, his ideas—always related to his words and to his speech—are the measure of all things in the realm of ideas or the forms, that is, in a conceptual landscape that has itself already been organized like a living organism.

Plato thus rewrites in his own way and for his own purposes the Protagorean dictum that "man is the measure of all things"; it is not man's subjective opinion that serves as this measure but the nature of man or, rather, of the reasonable man, who is himself in conformity with what is. As such, the dictum is not at all in conflict with the claim found in the *Laws* that it is in fact God who is the measure of all things, since it is man and man alone who reads the order that God or the gods will have put into these things and so he alone who can become like and therefore dear to the gods. To return one last time to the *Laws*, when the Athenian asks what kind of conduct "is dear to God and [follows] in his steps [*philē kai akolouthos theōi*]," he himself answers after making reference to the Homeric proverb of "like to like":"In our eyes God will be 'the measure [*metron*] of all things' in the highest degree—a degree much higher than is any 'man' they talk of," that is, of course, any man Protagoras talks of (*Laws* 716c; cf. *Cratylus* 386a, *Theaetetus* 152a). God is thus the measure of all things, but then so too is the man who follows Him and thus becomes *like* Him. The one who becomes like God—and, as a result, dear to God—is thus temperate and just, and those who are intemperate and unjust become unlike God and so are not dear to Him, says the Athenian, by "parity of reasoning [*kata ton auton logon*]" (716d), that is, "according to the same *logos*." Man is therefore himself, insofar as he follows this God, an image and likeness of Him. And that's exactly what Socrates says in the *Republic* when he argues that in order for the guardians to sketch the figure of the constitution, of the *politeia*, they would need to:

glance [*apoblepoien*] frequently in either direction, at justice, beauty, sobriety, and the like as they are in the nature of things, and alternately at that which they were trying to reproduce [*empoioien*] in mankind, mingling and blending from various pursuits that hue of the flesh, so to speak, deriving their judgment from that likeness of humanity which Homer too called when it appeared in men the image and likeness of God.... And they would erase one touch or stroke and paint in another until in the measure of the possible they had made the characters of men pleasing and dear to God as may be.

(*Republic* 501b–c; see Homer, *Iliad* 1.13, *Odyssey* 3.416)

The nature of things—in this case the nature of justice, beauty, moderation, and so on—are thus used as the index for creating, for depicting or for painting, according to the analogy, a human form that would itself be the image and likeness of God. We can now see why, for Plato, the gods, rather than animals or anything else, are, as the *Laws* puts it, our "fellows in the dance," and why song and dance, in addition to *logos*, *phronēsis*, or *nous*, are what distinguish the human from the animal, and why they do so in such a consistent and insistent way.

Does that then mean that there are no posthuman antiquities in Plato? Nothing that, in the guise of the pre-, post-, or non-human, resists from within the Platonic text and the hierarchies it establishes between the human and its others? Not at all, it's just that these places of resistance will not be so easily locatable: they will not be found simply on the side of myth, for example, as if myth were a simple opposite to *logos*, since *logos* is everywhere, including in myth; and they will not be found in any straightforward way on the side of animals, in any of the examples, analogies, or models of animal life in the dialogues, since the human, as we have seen, is the measure of all things, including the animal. Posthuman antiquities will thus have to be located instead in the form of an excess or a remainder, in the meaningless sounds of children, animals, and madmen—though also in the meaningless sounds that make possible the meaningful *logos* of the rational man; they will be found not simply on one side or the other of the opposition but always in the place of transition, transfer, or translation, the place where, as with Derrida's archē-writing, the entire matrix of terms gets constituted, not only *logos* and *mythos* but all those other binaries we call Platonism, soul and body, being and becoming, the intelligible and the sensible, the invisible and the visible, though also speech and writing, sense and sound, the human and the animal. Posthuman antiquities would therefore be found, as their name suggests, in what follows the human or in what precedes or resists it from within, from the place, then, of an even more ancient or antique antiquity within antiquity itself, a place that had to be forgotten in order for *mythos* to be opposed to *logos*, or the animal to the human, a wholly other scene that had to be forgotten in order for the human—in the guise of Plato's song and dance man, for example—to come onto the stage and take a bow to his own applause.

WORKS CITED

Bury, R. G., trans. (1926) *Plato: Laws*. Cambridge, MA.
Cavarero, A. (2005) *For More Than One Voice*. Trans. P. A. Kottman. Stanford.
Derrida, J. (2008) *The Animal That Therefore I Am*. Trans. D. Wills. New York.
Fowler, H. N., trans. (1975) *Plato: Statesman*. Cambridge, MA.
Fowler, H. N., trans. (1977) *Plato: Sophist*. Cambridge, MA.
Lamb, W. R. M., trans. (1979) *Plato: Epinomis*. Cambridge, MA.
Naas, M. (2018) *Plato and the Invention of Life*. New York.
Shorey, P., trans. (1930) *Plato: Republic*. Cambridge, MA.

5 Precarious life

Tragedy and the posthuman

Miriam Leonard

5.1. Who invented the human?

In a recent article in the *Independent* and again in a lively discussion with Edith Hall on BBC Radio Three, Ian Jenkins made the claim that the "Greeks invented the human being."[1] Jenkins, the curator of Greco-Roman antiquities at the British Museum, was speaking in the context of its recently opened exhibition *Defining Beauty*. For him, the Greeks' intense appreciation of the human form manifested in their sculptures prefigures the modern understanding of the human: "We humans," he says, "are at the centre of the Greek universe. They are an anthropocentric tradition in the way that the great religions are not.... The Greeks imagined their gods in the image of mankind, not as fearsome, nebulous abstractions."[2] In this, Jenkins seems to suggest, the Greeks are the natural ancestors of modern secular humanism. But the same marble statues which inspired Jenkins to associate the Greeks with a recognizable and familiar concept of the "human" had a very different effect on E. R. Dodds. At the start of *The Greeks and the Irrational*, he speaks of his encounter with a fellow museum goer who remarked as he stood before the Parthenon sculptures: "I know it's an awful thing to confess, but this Greek stuff doesn't move me one bit."[3] For Dodds and his interlocutor, far from suggesting a communality, the cold, pristine marble instead spoke to the profound inaccessibility of the Greeks. This chance meeting would lead Dodds in a very different direction, one which would convey to future generations of classicists the strangeness, even the monstrosity, of Greek culture. For Dodds, it would seem, it made no sense to talk about "we humans" especially in the context of the Greeks and their religion.

---

[1] Ian Jenkins cited in article in the Independent, Montgomerie (2015). Many thanks to the editors of this volume as well as audiences at NYU and the Classical Association Annual Meeting in Bristol for their invaluable comments on this essay. Some passages expand and reformulate material first published in Leonard (2015).
[2] Montgomerie (2015).   [3] Dodds (1951) 1.

Writing a decade or so after Dodds, Michel Foucault would give a very different chronology to the invention of the human: "Man," he proclaimed in 1966,

is an invention of recent date. And one perhaps nearing its end. If those arrangements were to disappear as they appeared, if some event of which we can at the moment do no more than sense the possibility... were to cause them to crumble, as the ground of Classical thought did, at the end of the eighteenth century, then one can certainly wager that man would be erased, like a face drawn in sand at the edge of the sea.[4]

For Foucault, man is an invention explicitly of the *post*classical age—man coincides with the waning of the authority of antiquity at the end of the eighteenth century and the advent of modernity.[5]

We may hear echoes in Foucault's peroration of Cassandra, who in Aeschylus' *Agamemnon* imagines human life as a picture blotted out by "the dash of a wet sponge," but in predicting the end of man, Foucault was fully in tune with the apocalyptic melody of his own age. In the wake of the atom bomb, the specter of total annihilation hung over the globe. Foucault could also have been thinking as a Frenchman about the process of decolonization and the long overdue decentering of Europe which ensued. Each age has its own catastrophe. Our particular catastrophe is climate change: the realization that human beings are responsible for world destruction. We have, so the scientists tell us, been living in the era of the anthropocene, an era which dates roughly to the end of the so-called "Classical" epoch that Foucault invokes. The age of the anthropocene is the age of industrialization, it denotes a period where the human impact on the atmosphere, on land use, on ecosystems, biodiversity, and species extinction has grown exponentially. The notion of the anthropocene has thus paradoxically become the site both of man's greatest narcissism and of a critique of anthropocentrism. Man has simultaneously never been so aware of his/her power and so aware of his/her fragility. If nuclear war and decolonization provide the context for Foucault's *anti*-humanism, then climate change could explain the urgency of some of the debates within what has come to be known as *post*humanism. While Foucault provocatively and presciently imagined man being washed away by the forces of the rising oceans, posthumanism mobilizes objects, organisms, and animals to

---

[4] Foucault (2002) 422.
[5] While the *Order of Things* posits this divide between ancient and modern, it is significant that in the *History of Sexuality* Foucault's genealogy of the self has its genesis in antiquity.

relativize human experience. Both positions, it might be said, want to put us in our place.

As my juxtaposition of Dodds, Aeschylus, Foucault, and posthumanism implies, the temporalities of the discourses of the human are complex. While I have associated Foucault with antihumanism, others co-opt him into the posthuman canon. The force of the *post* in posthumanism has an interesting charge and can be interpreted in a number of different ways. At one level it is *post* because in the chronologies of criticism it comes after both the humanism of the Renaissance or the Enlightenment and the so-called anti-humanism of structuralism and post-structuralism. Its postness also reflects its emergence in a period which is particularly self-conscious about technological innovation and about the role that machines, computers, and prostheses have come to play in human experience. At another level, the preposition *post* is an alternative to the antagonism of the *anti*: it could potentially triangulate the binary between humanism and anti-humanism. Its postness suggest that we should move beyond this old tired debate. Alternatively, one could see posthumanism as an intensification of anti-humanism and in this sense it would act as a critique of the persistent anthropocentrism of even the most radical anti-humanisms. For all Foucault's emphasis on the contingency of man, even he never conceptualized the world from the perspective of the non-human. Yet another dimension is implied by Cary Wolfe in his introduction to the book *What is Posthumanism?*. There he specifies how his "posthumanism is...analogous to Jean-François Lyotard's paradoxical rendering of postmodern: [in that] it comes both before and after humanism."[6] This is where antiquity can and has played an important role. *Pace* Jenkins, premodern conceptualizations of life, human and otherwise, can act as a corrective to the universalist assumptions of the humanisms of modernity.

I want to look at one particular ancient contribution to this debate. Perhaps to an even greater extent than the Parthenon marbles, Greek tragedy has long played a role in modernity's investigation of humanism. In Hegel, it is Oedipus who in giving the solution "man" to the riddle of the Sphinx seals the association between tragedy and the human. From a posthumanist perspective, we might note that it is Oedipus' encounter with animality that presses him to "man" as the answer to the animal-riddle; in fact, it is the female animal—here in the form of the Sphinx—who calls man to his identity. More than a century after Hegel, Jacques

---

[6] Wolfe (2010) XV.

Lacan in the *Ethics of Psychoanalysis* now returns to Sophocles to question the association between tragedy and humanism:

> Some people have said... that Sophocles is a humanist. He is found to be human since he gives the idea of a properly human measure between a rootedness in archaic ideals represented by Aeschylus and a move toward bathos, sentimentality, criticism and sophistry that Aristotle had already reproached Euripides with. I don't disagree with the notion that Sophocles is in that median position, but as far as finding in him some relationship to humanism is concerned, that would be to give a wholly new meaning to the word. As for us we consider ourselves to be at the end of the vein of humanist thought.[7]

For too long, Lacan argues, we have found in Greek tragedy's conflicts between agency and finitude a reaffirmation of humanity. Lacan, by contrast, "sees himself at the end of [this] vein" and instead wants to enlist Sophocles to what he saw as his decidedly *anti*-humanist project. Can Lacan's avowed *anti*-humanist Sophocles offer us new insights into the question of the *post*-human? This paper takes the psychoanalytic reading of Greek tragedy as its focus and investigates ancient drama's own questioning of the human. If tragedy can challenge Jenkins's easy assimilation by showing us how we have *never* been human, does it also have the capacity to expose the limitations of the current posthuman turn?

5.2. Freud and the germ cell

In his *Introductory Lectures to Psychoanalysis* Freud talks about the three, so-called, "narcissistic wounds" that have been inflicted on humanity. The first blow to what Freud calls "the naïve self-love of men" was orchestrated by Copernicus, who made us realize that our earth "was not the centre of the universe but only a tiny fragment of a cosmic system of scarcely imaginable vastness."[8] The second blow came with Darwin, who destroyed "man's supposedly privileged place in creation." The third, and what Freud calls "most wounding," blow was dealt by Freud himself, who revealed how the "ego is not a master in his own home." These three narcissistic wounds, these three blows, rupture the transhistoricism of humanism, alienating us from our history, our sense of place in the world, and from the ancients so often taken to be our forebears.

But for all the stress he places on this succession of revelations, Freud's account in the *Introductory Lectures* is not predicated on a chasm

---

[7] Lacan (1997) 273.   [8] Freud SE XVI, 285.

between antiquity and modernity. Speaking of the cosmological blow, Freud claims, "this is associated in our minds with the name of Copernicus, though something similar had already been asserted by Alexandrian science."[9] In a later reworking of this passage Freud pushes the discovery back still further to the "Pythagoreans" and declares: "Even the great discovery of Copernicus, therefore, had already been made before him."[10] Freud folds the pre-existence of cosmological theories in antiquity back into his general thesis about the vulnerability of mankind's self-love. Copernicus was not a master in his own home and modernity, for all its rhetoric of progress, is not capable of keeping out the intrusion of antiquity.

Beyond the evident irony of Freud's statements about the demise of narcissism being expressed in a passage replete with his own narcissism, what interests me is the way that Freud shines a spotlight on the ability of ideas from the ancient world to unsettle an account of the human. Psychoanalysis, as the site of a certain *posthumanism*, thus finds its source for critique in antiquity. Indeed it would not be difficult to make the case for Freud's posthumanist credentials. His emphasis on sexuality presents man in his naked animality. More important still, in his foregrounding of the unconscious he threatened the site of human exceptionalism. In overthrowing the primacy of reason, Freud laid the ground for a different conception of life. Nowhere is this more evident than his discussion of the life and death instincts in *Beyond the Pleasure Principle*:

The instincts which watch over the destinies of these elementary organisms that survive the whole individual, which provide them with a safe shelter while they are defenceless against the stimuli of the external world, which bring about their meeting with other germ-cells, and so on—these constitute the sexual instincts. They are conservative in the same sense as the other instincts in that they bring back earlier states of living substance; but they are conservative to a higher degree in that they are particularly resistant to external influence; and they are conservative too in another sense in that they preserve life itself for a comparatively long period. They are the true life instincts. They operate against the purpose of the other instincts which, leads, by reason of their function, to death.[11]

Freud's fundamental insight into the dynamics of existence is no philosophical exposition on human finitude, but the exploration of the instincts of a "germ cell." In choosing the "germ cell" as the object of analysis, Freud decidedly threatens the priority of human life with a focus on life as such, what we would now call vitalism. Indeed by analogizing the experience of

---

[9] Freud SE XVI, 285. [10] Freud SE XVII, 140.
[11] Freud SE XVIII, 40.

human and primitive cellular life, Freud draws attention to what Jane Bennett has called the "vital materiality" of existence:

Vital materiality better captures an "alien" quality of our own flesh, and in so doing reminds humans of the very *radical* character of the (fractious) kinship between the human and the non-human. My "own" body is material, and yet this vital materiality is not fully or exclusively human. My flesh is populated and constituted by different swarms of foreigners. The crook of my elbow, for example, is "a special ecosystem, a bountiful home to no fewer than six tribes of bacteria" [Nicholas Wade]. The *its* outnumber the *mes*. In a world of vibrant matter, it is not enough to say that we are "embodied." We are, rather, *an array of bodies*, many different kinds of them in a nested set of microbiomes.[12]

Nevertheless, within several pages Freud's microbiome has ceded its place to a different account of vitality:

The germ-cells themselves would behave in a completely "narcissistic" fashion—to use a phrase that we are accustomed to use in neuroses to describe a whole individual who retains his libido in his ego and pays none of it out in object-cathexes. The germ-cells require their libido, the activity of their life instincts, for themselves, as a reserve against their later constructive activity.... In this way the libido of our sexual instincts would coincide with the Eros of the poets and the philosophers which holds all living things together.[13]

Changing the focus to the "whole individual," Freud ascribes narcissism to his cells. Despite the cosomological force of *Eros* in a figure like Empedocles, it seems to me that in his reference to poets, Freud further transfers the discussion to a human, if not to say, *humanist* plane. The instincts of biological organisms give way to the poetic vocabulary of *Eros*. As Freud would write elsewhere of his adoption of the language of *eros*: "Anyone who considers sex as something mortifying and humiliating to human nature is at liberty to make use of the more genteel expressions "Eros" and "erotic". I might have done so myself from the first and thus spared myself much opposition."[14] Freud's genteel Greek would seem to stand as the last defense of "the naïve self-love of man."

But there is more at stake in the classical reference than a concession to gentility. Freud's classical vocabulary gestures towards a longer intellectual history. For despite Freud's denial of influence, critics have detected a precursor to his life and death drives in another figure who would create his own posthuman antiquity:[15]

Their two deities of art, Apollo and Dionysos, provide the starting-point for our recognition that there exists in the world of the Greeks an enormous opposition,

---

[12] Bennett (2010) 112–13. [13] Freud SE XVIII, 50.
[14] Freud SE XVIII, 91. [15] See, in particular, Gordon (2001) 55–71.

both in origin and goals, between the Apolline image-maker or sculptor and the imageless art of music, which is that of Dionysos. These two very different drives (*Triebe*) exist side by side, mostly in open conflict, stimulating and provoking (*reizen*) one another to give birth to ever-new, more vigorous offspring in whom they perpetuate the conflict inherent in the opposition between them, an opposition only apparently bridged by the common term "art"—until eventually, by a metaphysical miracle of the Hellenic "Will", they appear paired and, in this pairing, finally engender a work of art which is Dionysiac and Apolline in equal measure: Attic tragedy.[16]

In designating the Apollonian and the Dionysian as *Triebe*, drives, Nietzsche lays the groundwork for *Beyond the Pleasure Principle*.[17] The resonance is perhaps at its strongest in Nietzsche's description of Apollo:

Thus in an eccentric sense, one could apply to Apollo what Schopenhauer says about human beings trapped in the veil of maya: "Just as the boatsman sits in his small boat, trusting his frail craft in a stormy sea that is boundless in every direction, rising and falling with the howling, mountainous waves, so in the midst of a world full of suffering and misery the individual man calmly sits supported by and trusting the *principium individuationis*." Indeed one could say that Apollo is the most sublime expression of imperturbable trust in this principle and of the calm sitting-there of the person trapped within it; one might even describe Apollo as the magnificent divine image (*Götterbild*) of the *principium individuationis*, whose gestures and gaze speak to us of all the intense pleasure, wisdom and beauty of "semblance."[18]

The image of Apollo calmly navigating the seas and preserving the individual from the onslaughts of the external world has a strong echo in Freud's discussion of "elementary organisms." In Freud's hands, the *principium individuationis*, which Nietzsche identified with Apollo, becomes the pleasure principle. It is the life instinct which preserves the individual by providing a safe shelter from the onslaughts of an outside world. But these life instincts also conserve the individual against its *internal* destruction through death. Nietzsche's Olympian duel between Apollo and Dionysus is transformed by Freud into a contest between *Eros* and *Thanatos*:

Our speculations have suggested that Eros operates from the beginning of life and appears as a "life instinct" in opposition to the "death instinct" which was brought into being by the coming to life of inorganic substance. These speculations

---

[16] Nietzsche (1999) 14.
[17] Freud notoriously denied the influence of Nietzsche on his thought. Both were influenced by Schopenhauer, whose tragic thought pervades both Nietzsche's *Birth of Tragedy* and Freud's *Beyond the Pleasure Principle*. On the relationship to Schopenhauer and Nietzsche and the wider context of Freud's "reluctant philosophy" see Tauber (2010).
[18] Nietzsche (1999) 16–17.

seek to solve the riddle of life by supposing that these two instincts were struggling with each other from the very first.[19]

In this conflict between different drives (*Triebe*), Freud envisions a bounded self in conflict not only with an external world but also with itself: "If we are to take it as a truth that knows no exception that everything dies for *internal* reasons—becomes inorganic once again—then we shall be compelled to say that '*the aim of all life is death*'."[20]

While Nietzsche populates his essay with Greeks, Freud's text teems with primitive organisms. And yet, Freud would soon give a social context to the discussion of the death drive. In *Civilization and its Discontents*, Freud projects the struggle between *Eros* and *Thanatos* onto the screen of culture. Its core thesis about the origins of civilization in the sublimation of aggression restages at the societal level the conflict we previously witnessed at the microbiological level. Art, literature, music, even political organization, emerge as the by-products of the clash between *Eros* and *Thanatos*. If "art" is the term that bridges the conflict between Nietzsche's Apollo and Dionysos, civilization is the remainder of the struggle between Freud's life and death instincts. But there is one cultural by-product that retains a special place in his narrative:

> The analogy between the process of civilisation and the path of the individual development may be extended in an important respect.... The super-ego of an epoch of civilisation has an origin similar to that of an individual. It is based on the impression left behind by personalities of great leaders—men of overwhelming force of mind or men in whom one of the human impulsions has found its strongest and purest, and therefore often its most one-sided, expression. In many instances the analogy goes still further, in that during their lifetime these figures were—often enough, even if not always—mocked and maltreated by others even despatched in cruel fashion. In the same way, indeed, that the primal father did not attain divinity until long after he had met his death by violence. The most arresting example of this fateful conjunction is to be seen in the figure of Jesus Christ—if, indeed, that figure is not a part of mythology, which called it into being from an obscure memory of that primal event.[21]

Tragedy is the art form that best expresses the "epoch's superego." In the constant *va et vient* of destructive aggression and instinctual renunciation, civilizations restage the drama of the primal horde. Although it is Jesus Christ who is named here, we know from *Totem and Taboo* that it is Oedipus who stands behind the mythology of the "primal event." The great leader and his inevitable fall models the dynamics of civilization.

---

[19] Freud SE XVIII, 61. [20] Freud SE XVIII, 38.
[21] Freud SE XXI, 141–2.

Oedipus is the figure in whom *eros* and *thanatos* conjoin in the most dramatic fashion.

5.3. **Oedipus and the death drive**

But while *Civilisation and its Discontents* tracks the tragic dynamic of culture modeled on Oedipus, it is Freud's self-appointed successor, Jacques Lacan, who will explicitly seal the relationship between Oedipus and the competing forces of the life and death drives.[22] For Lacan it is Oedipus' fate that illustrates how: "The human being himself is in part outside life, he partakes of the death instinct."[23] While Freud had focused his discussion of Oedipus on Sophocles' *Oedipus Tyrannus*, Lacan argues that "Oedipus's analysis is only completed at Colonus."[24] In his return to Freud, Lacan reminds us:

Don't forget that Oedipus's unconscious is in fact that fundamental discourse which accounts for the fact that Oedipus's history has for a long time, forever, been written, accounts for the fact that we know it, and for the fact that Oedipus is totally ignorant of it, despite his having been its plaything from the start.[25]

Oedipus' unconscious forms the central plank of Freud's decentering of the human subject. By showing how the ego is not master in his own home, Freud reveals the fragility of individual consciousness and upends the enlightenment vision of Oedipus. As Shoshana Felman has shown, Freud's Oedipus demonstrates to Lacan "that the unconscious is the discourse of the Other." For, as he goes on to argue, "the unconscious is the subject unknown to the self, misapprehended, misrecognised by the ego."[26] Lacan, however, reveals the centrality of death to Oedipus' unconscious: "when we come to talk of death again, I will perhaps try and explain to you the end of Oedipus' tragedy, as the great dramatists have portrayed it. You should read *Oedipus at Colonus*.... There you will discover that the final word of the relation of man to this discourse of which he is ignorant, is death."[27] Lacan turns to a particular passage in Sophocles' play to elucidate this declaration:

In *Oedipus at Colonus*, Oedipus says the following: *Am I made man in the moment when I cease to be?* That is the end of psychoanalysis—the psychoanalysis of

---

[22] See Razinksy (2013) 215. [23] Lacan (1988) 90.
[24] Lacan (1988) 214. [25] Lacan (1988) 209.
[26] Lacan (1988) 59, in Shoshana Felman's translation (1987) 129.
[27] Lacan (1988) 209.

Oedipus is only completed at Colonus, when he tears his face apart. That is the essential moment, which gives the story its meaning.[28]

Oedipus' question to Ismene, which might be translated more literally as "When I no longer exist, then I am a man?" (*Oedipus at Colonus* 393), unlocks the drama for Lacan.[29] In locating his identity as a man in the moment of his death, Oedipus reveals the identity of the subject in its own negation. Oedipus becomes in Lacan's terms "the subject beyond a subject."[30] The story of Oedipus' death at Colonus is exemplary for Lacan because it illustrates the entry of Oedipus into collective discourse *through his death*. This is the longer passage from the *Oedipus at Colonus* on which Lacan draws:

> OEDIPUS What, had you come to hope that the gods would ever have concern enough for me to give me rescue?
> ISMENE Yes, that is my hope, father, from the present oracles.
> OEDIPUS What are they? What has been prophesied, my child?
> ISMENE That you will be desired some day, in life and death, by the men of that land, for their safety's sake.
> OEDIPUS And who could profit from such a one as I?
> ISMENE Their power, it is said, proves to be in your hands.
> OEDIPUS When I no longer exist, then I am a man?
> ISMENE Yes, for the gods now raise you up; but before they worked your ruin. (trans. R. Jebb)
>
> Οἰδίπους: ἤδη γὰρ ἔσχες ἐλπίδ' ὡς ἐμοῦ θεοὺς
> ὥραν τιν' ἕξειν, ὥστε σωθῆναί ποτε;
> Ἰσμήνη: ἔγωγε τοῖς νῦν γ', ὦ πάτερ, μαντεύμασιν.
> Οἰδίπους: ποίοισι τούτοις; τί δὲ τεθέσπισται, τέκνον;
> Ἰσμήνη: σὲ τοῖς ἐκεῖ ζητητὸν ἀνθρώποις ποτὲ
> θανόντ' ἔσεσθαι ζῶντά τ' εὐσοίας χάριν.
> Οἰδίπους: τίς δ' ἂν τοιοῦδ' ὑπ' ἀνδρὸς εὖ πράξειεν ἄν;
> Ἰσμήνη: ἐν σοὶ τὰ κείνων φασὶ γίγνεσθαι κράτη.
> Οἰδίπους: ὅτ' οὐκέτ' εἰμί, τηνικαῦτ' ἄρ' εἴμ' ἀνήρ;
> Ἰσμήνη: νῦν γὰρ θεοί σ' ὀρθοῦσι, πρόσθε δ' ὤλλυσαν.
> (Sophocles, *Oedipus at Colonus*, 385-94)

Sophocles' *Oedipus at Colonus* recounts Oedipus' transition from transgressive individual and social pariah to symbol of collective safety. This

---

[28] Lacan (1988) 214.
[29] As Simon Goldhill points out to me, Lacan misses the irony, or even the sarcasm, of Sophocles' locution "ἄρ'"—"*So* when I'm dead, I finally get to be a mensch...".
[30] Lacan (1988) 210.

transition crucially takes place at the moment of his death. By narrating Oedipus' metamorphosis from man to myth, Sophocles also narrates Oedipus' entry into language. Lacan's aim in turning to Oedipus is to understand the relationship of the ego to discourse. The ego, he argues,

> is caught in a chain of symbols. It is an element indispensable to the insertion of the symbolic reality into the reality of the subject, it is tied to the primitive gap of the subject. On account of that, in its original sense, within the psychological life of the human subject it is what appears as closest to, as most intimate with, as on closest terms with death.[31]

For Lacan, the ego is close to death because it exists as a nodal point between "the common discourse, in which the subject finds himself caught, alienated, and his psychological reality."[32] Lacan describes the splitting of the self that occurs when one learns to use (an) other's language. The entry into language is experienced by the subject as a form of death. Oedipus' death is thus crucial to understanding the nature of his fractured identity and a myth through which to understand our own.

Within this context, it is notable that the famous description of the *fort-da* game that sets the scene for *Beyond the Pleasure Principle*—that is the game in which the young child repeatedly throws his toy to the edge of the cot only to reel if back again—is analogized by Freud to the creation of tragedy:

> Finally, a reminder may be added that the artistic play and artistic imitation carried out by adults, which, unlike children's, are aimed at an audience, do not spare the spectators (for instance, in tragedy) the most painful experiences and can yet be felt by them as highly enjoyable. This is convincing proof that, even under the dominance of the pleasure principle, there are ways and means enough of making what is in itself unpleasurable into a subject to be recollected and worked over in the mind. The consideration of these cases and situations, which have a yield of pleasure as their final outcome, should be undertaken by some system of aesthetics with an economic approach to its subject matter. They are of no use for *our* purposes, since they presuppose the existence and dominance of the pleasure principle; they give no evidence of the operation of tendencies beyond the pleasure principle, that is, of tendencies more primitive than it and independent of it.[33]

The "motive for play" that Freud identifies in his young grandson is paralleled by the urge for artistic imitation that persists into adulthood. Tragic poetry would in this sense be a form of repetition compulsion—or alternatively a therapeutic working through—which allowed the spectators to recuperate the "unpleasurable" content of the play in an act of

---

[31] Lacan (1988) 210. [32] Lacan (1988) 210. [33] Freud SE XVIII, 17.

pleasurable spectatorship. Tragedy on this analysis has nothing to do with the death drive because the painful experiences that the spectators witness are filtered through an Apollonian veil of aesthetic enjoyment. But as Lacan argues: "the significance of *Beyond the Pleasure Principle* is that that isn't enough":

> What Freud's primary masochism teaches us is that, when life has been dispossessed of its speech, its final word can only be the final malediction expressed at the end of *Oedipus at Colonus*. Life doesn't want to be healed. The negative therapeutic reaction is fundamental to it. Anyway, what is healing? The realisation of the subject through a speech which comes from elsewhere. This life we're captive of, this essentially alienated life, ex-sisting, this life in the other, is as such joined to death, it always returns to death.[34]

In turning to *Oedipus at Colonus*, Lacan questions Freud's understanding of tragedy. Analysing Oedipus through his end at Colonus reveals how tragedy cannot be contained by the pleasure principle. The real outcome of tragedy is not the life but the death instinct. As Shoshana Felman phrases it: "*Beyond the Pleasure Principle* stands to *The Interpretation of Dreams* (the work in which Freud narrates for the first time his discovery of the significance of *Oedipus the King*) in precisely the same relation in which *Oedipus at Colonus* stands to *Oedipus the King*."[35] In his recalibration of Freud, Lacan replaces the Oedipus of *eros* with the Oedipus of *thanatos*.

Nevertheless, while Lacan emphasizes the anti-humanism of tragedy by bringing the death drive to the fore, he obscures the posthumanist force of Freud's depersonalized drives. The death drive that Lacan envisions has a decidedly human form. Where Freud's discussion of drives derives some of its power from showing the human subject to extrahuman forces, Lacan in a sense repersonalizes these instincts in the move from *eros* to *thanatos*. In contradistinction to Freud, whose drives are common to all organisms from the germ cell upwards, so to speak, Lacan seems to assume that what is most human about us is our death. Indeed by aligning the divided subject of psychoanalysis to the death drive, does Lacan not run the risk of resurrecting a different kind of humanism?[36] Within contemporary theory, tragedy has repeatedly been invoked in the formulation of what Bonnie Honig has called a "mortalist humanism": "Humanism," she writes,

> has in recent years been making a comeback; not the rationalist universalist variety discredited by post-structuralism and the horrific events of the twentieth

---

[34] Lacan (1988) 232–3.   [35] Felman (1987) 138.   [36] Honig (2013) 38.

century, but a newer variant. This humanism asserts that what is in common to humans is not rationality but the ontological fact of mortality, not the capacity to reason, but the vulnerability to suffering.[37]

Should one understand Lacan as a mortalist humanist? Defined by our finitude and not by our desires, Lacan's humans could be seen as bearers of a rather conventional and common humanity. But he will insist otherwise:

That is what life is—a detour, a dogged detour, in itself transitory and precarious, and deprived of any significance. Why, in that of its manifestations called man, does something happen, which insists throughout this life, which is called meaning? We call it *human*, but are we so sure? Is this meaning as human as all that? A meaning is an order, that is to say, a sudden emergence. A meaning is an order which suddenly emerges. A life insists on entering into it, but it expresses something which is perhaps completely beyond this life, since when we get to the root of this life, behind the drama of the passage into existence, we find nothing beyond life conjoined to death.[38]

The *precarious life* that Lacan describes is a life without significance. This is a life that can only be betrayed and split and never fulfilled by entry into the symbolic and into the world of signification. It is not a life given meaning by virtue of its precarity, but a life whose potential for meaning is negated by its *telos* in death. "The drama of the passage into existence" is completely overshadowed by the tragedy of death. Moreover, where mortalist humanism emphasizes *communality* as an essential component of human loss, the relationship of Lacan's divided self to a community is much more circumspect. Nevertheless, both Lacan and Judith Butler, in her book *Precarious Life*, understand fragile lives as lives lived in common with others. For Lacan, as we saw, it is a subject's entry into collective language that constitutes both her identity as a subject and her orientation towards death. Butler's human vulnerability is a recognition of the necessity of intersubjectivity:

There is a more general conception of the human with which I am trying to work here, one in which we are, from the start, even prior to individuation itself and, by virtue of bodily requirements, given over to some set of primary others: this conception means that we are vulnerable to those we are too young to know and to judge and hence, vulnerable to violence; but also vulnerable to another range of touch, a range that includes the eradication of our being at the one end, and the physical support of our lives at the other.[39]

---

[37] Honig (2013) 17.   [38] Lacan (1988) 232.   [39] Butler (2004) 31.

Where Lacan emphasizes discourse as the site of primordial interdependence, Butler pays attention to the bodily needs which open us to others. Bonnie Honig has criticized Butler for failing to recognize a *third* possibility for human communality between "eradication" and "support." She posits collective action as an alternative to the violence of sovereignty that both Lacan and Butler reject for different reasons. "Action," Honig argues, "... is a non-sovereign performance that works to reconstitute communities and inaugurates new realities. Action exposes us to mortality, we may die in action, after all; but it is not about grievability."[40] By failing to recognize action, Butler, just like Lacan, subsumes "the drama of the passage into existence" to the tragedy of mourning. Yet, if both Lacan and Butler emphasize a life that "does not want to heal," Lacan nevertheless acknowledges some agency—one might even say, some action in concert—involved in living such a life: "Anyway, what is healing? The realization of the subject through a speech which comes from elsewhere."[41]

5.4. We have never been human

Tragedy, I want to argue, is this "speech which comes from elsewhere." In his essay "And say the animal responded?", Derrida takes Lacan to task for his failure to listen to a voice which comes from elsewhere—in this case the voice of the animal. Despite his desire to "subvert the subject," Derrida exposes Lacan's deafness to the language of what he calls the *ahuman*.[42] Language may come from the Other but this Other for Lacan is always an Other understood from the perspective of the human. Although Lacan thinks it is language as such that calls the human being into question, Derrida will argue that it his very emphasis on speech and language that is the site of Lacan's anthropocentrism. He sees this dynamic played out in a quotation from Lacan's "The Direction of Treatment": "It must be posited that, produced as it is by any animal at the mercy of language [*en proie au langage*], man's desire is the desire of the Other."[43] As Derrida reacts:

(This figure of prey symptomatically and recurrently characterizes "animal" obsession in Lacan at the very moment when he insists so strongly on dissociating the anthropological from the zoological; man is an animal but a speaking

---

[40] Honig (2013) 43–4; Honig also configures this debate in terms of a conflict between ethics and politics (17–35). See also Leonard (2005).
[41] Lacan (1988) 23. [42] Derrida (2003) 121. [43] Lacan (1977) 264.

one, and he is less a beast of prey than a beast that is prey to language.) There is no desire, and thus no unconscious, except for the human.[44]

Lacan's language may symptomatically fall prey to bestial figuration, but his theory of language nevertheless reaffirms the distinction *and* the hierarchy between human and animal. For Derrida, speech is what reintroduces the human back into Lacan's discourse. But does it matter what language Lacan speaks? When Lacan speaks Greek, when he speaks *tragic* Greek, is he speaking in a human language? In designating Greek tragedy as a "speech that comes from elsewhere," I want to argue that while Lacan himself seems to reinscribe the human, psychoanalysis in its engagement with tragedy could remain receptive if not to the animal, then, at least, to the posthuman. By this, I do not mean to imply that the Greeks were literally not humans, nor even that they did not have an interest in the human form: rather, I want to question what it is about the term human that supposedly gives us a connection to the Greeks? What, in other words, are the assumptions that lie behind Ian Jenkins's use of the phrase "we humans"? Far from investing in tragedy as a celebration of humanism, Freud and Lacan in their different ways turned to ancient drama to explore the problem of human life. Rather than finding a prototype for liberal individualism, modernity has uncovered in tragedy a model of radical intersubjectivity—an intersubjectivity that repeatedly calls the human subject into question.[45] While in Lacan, this questioning of the subject remains ultimately anthropocentric, in *Beyond the Pleasure Principle*, Freud juxtaposes his discussion of the life and death instincts in "elementary organisms" to the tragic drama he sees enacted in his grandson's *fort-da* game. By placing Greek tragedy's confrontation with the death drive on a continuum with the instincts of a "germ-cell," Freud's text, and psychoanalysis more generally, offers a model for understanding antiquity's contribution to posthumanism. In Freud's reading of Greek tragedy the temporal dislocation of antiquity converges with a structural decentering of the human to deliver a wounding blow to the self-love of man.

But if tragedy, as I have implied, can show us how we have never been human, can it also expose some of the limitations of the posthuman as it is presently conceptualized? And if it is right to think of posthumanism as a reaction to the threat of climate change, can antiquity provide a resource which amounts to more than a nostalgic yearning for a preindustrial age? Posthumanism in its current guise seems to be beholden to a certain

---

[44] Derrida (2003) 122–3.
[45] See also Benjamin (2010) for a similar argument about the role of ancient tragedy and philosophy in continental philosophy.

scientificity. It envisages our own culture as exceptional in its technological innovation and presents science in some senses as both the problem and the solution to the problem. Posthuman theorists thus waver between rethinking the human as either an animal or a cyborg—that is as either what lies outside or beyond the human in the natural world or as the product of human over-inventiveness. Greek tragedy, on the other hand, rejects the either/or logic of modernity and positions its human protagonists on a spectrum of sub- and supra-human possibility. In Vernant's famous reading, Oedipus is *both* a *pharmakos*—a sacrificial animal—and a *tyrannos*—a divine king.[46] Contra Hegel, Oedipus, for Vernant, is never simply "man," he is always at the same time more and less than human. But while there is, for sure, a hierarchy implied in this "more" and "less," there is also a focus on the interconnectedness of these states of being. From the perspective of the gods, human life is no more exulted than animal life—indeed, Oedipus is destined to experience his life as if he were a beast. In fact, tragedy shows us that it is precisely when we think we are a god—or even a man—that we are exposed as a beast. The solution that tragedy suggests is not to go beyond man nor to double down on man but to hold on to all the human and non-human dimensions that tragedy risked exploring. The current posthuman turn is enthralled to science and its promise of rescue, but perhaps it can itself be rescued by this almost lost history of man—a history which sees man on a spectrum from the animal to the monstrous. This tragic history is available to be excavated from beneath the ongoing humanism of one posthumanist after another including Freud and Lacan. On this reading, Foucault may be right to say that "man is an invention of recent date." For even if all those years ago Oedipus offered "man" as his answer to the riddle of the Sphinx, we all know how far that got him! Perhaps Sophocles is telling us that if we think man is the answer to the question of the animal, perhaps the animal is also part of the answer to the question of man.

WORKS CITED

Benjamin, A. (2010) *Place, Commonality and Judgement: Continental Philosophy and the Ancient Greeks*. London.
Bennett, J. (2010) *Vibrant Matter: A Political Ecology of Things*. Durham, NC.
Butler, J. (2004) *Precarious Life: The Powers of Mourning and Violence*. London.

[46] Vernant (1988).

Derrida, J. (2003) "And Say the Animal Responded," in C. Woolfe (ed.), *Zoontologies: The Question of the Animal*. Minneapolis: 121–46.
Dodds, E. R. (1951) *The Greeks and the Irrational*. Berkeley.
Felman, S. (1987) *Jacques Lacan and the Adventures of Insight: Pyschoanalysis in Contemporary Culture*. Cambridge, MA.
Foucault, M. (2002) *The Order of Things: Archaeology of the Human Sciences*. London.
Freud, S. (1953–74) *The Standard Edition of the Complete Psychological Works of Sigmund Freud* [SE]. Ed. and trans. J. Strachey et al. London.
Gordon, P. (2001) *Tragedy after Nietzsche: Rapturous Superabundance*. Urbana, IL.
Honig, B. (2010) "Antigone's Two Laws: Greek Tragedy and the Politics of Humanism," *New Literary History* 41: 1–33.
Honig, B. (2013) *Antigone, Interrupted*. Cambridge.
Jebb, R. C. (1899) *Sophocles: The Plays and Fragments, with Critical Notes, Commentary, and Translation in English Prose. Part II: The Oedipus Coloneus*. Cambridge.
Lacan, J. (1977) *Écrits: A Selection*. Trans. Alan Sheridan. New York.
Lacan, J. (1988) *The Seminar of Jacques Lacan, Book II: The Ego in Freud's Theory and in the Technique of Psychoanalysis*. Trans. S. Tomaselli. Cambridge.
Lacan, J. (1997) *The Ethics of Psychoanalysis*. Trans. D. Potter. London.
Leonard, M. (2005) *Athens in Paris: Ancient Greece and the Political in Post-War French Thought*. Oxford.
Leonard, Miriam (2015) *Tragic Modernities*. Cambridge, MA.
Montgomerie, H. (2015) "Defining Beauty: The Body in Ancient Greek Art at the British Museum Gives Visitors Quite an Eyeful." *The Independent*, March 21, viewed June 15, 2017 <http://www.independent.co.uk/arts-entertainment/art/features/defining-beauty-the-body-in-ancient-greek-art-at-the-british-museum-gives-visitors-quite-an-eyeful-10123257.html>.
Nietzsche, F. (1999) *The Birth of Tragedy and Other Writings*. Ed. R. Geuss and R. Speirs, trans. R. Speirs. Cambridge.
Razinsky, L. (2013) *Freud, Psychoanalysis and Death*. Cambridge.
Tauber, A. I. (2010) *Freud, the Reluctant Philosopher*. Princeton.
Vernant, Jean-Pierre (1988) "Ambiguity and Reversal: On the Enigmatic Structure of *Oedipus Rex*", in Jean-Pierre Vernant and Pierre Vidal-Naquet, *Myth and Tragedy in Ancient Greece*. Trans. Janet Lloyd. New York: 113–40.
Wolfe, C. (2010) *What is Posthumanism?* Minneapolis.

Part 2
Alternate Zoologies

6 Aristotle's meta-zoology

Shared life and human animality in the *Politics*

Sara Brill

Near the end of the first episode of his *Suppliants*, Aeschylus composes a question about public space that is vital to the life of any democracy. The question is asked by the leader of the Chorus, a group of women who have fled Egypt to the city of Argos seeking protection from forced marriage to their cousins, and it is addressed to Pelasgus, king of the Argives. The stakes of this request for protection are high. The unwanted suitors are on their way, heavily armed and ready to take what they see as theirs by force if necessary. Unwilling to exercise his power as king without the consent of his people, Pelasgus sends the women's father, Danaus, to supplicate the gods of Argos and agrees to attempt to persuade the people himself. While this is happening, he asks the women to move from the altar of Zeus, where they have assembled in the traditional gestures of supplication, to an open grove. This requested move from divinely protected, sacred space to public, shared space prompts the Chorus Leader to ask, "How can a space that is open to all protect me?" (498).[1]

The women are right to be concerned. Within the power structure from which they are fleeing, a space open to all is a space in which all have access to each, a space of danger for some and an arena for the exercise of the power to seize for others. And it is freedom from seizure that the Danaids seek. But the Danaids themselves are deeply overdetermined characters. Much of the dramatic tension of the play stems from the Danaids' claim not only to the right of the suppliant, protected by Zeus, but also to a right of citizenry, to a right to Argive soil and protection on the basis of their genealogical connection with the Argive maiden Io. Thus, the Danaids claim the right of protection both as strangers supplicating Argos, and as of Argive stock, a contradiction embodied, pleading, immediate, and wringing from Pelasgus the *hapax*

[1] Burian (1991) translation.

legomenon designation of *astoxenon*, "citizen strangers" or "native strangers" or even "kin strangers." Pelasgus' resolution to the Danaids' request provides Aeschylus with the opportunity to celebrate a fundamental institution of shared rule, which the playwright describes in terms that illuminate the nature of ancient investment in the practice: "Argos voted as one man, and bolted it clear through, like a hull, to hold it fast. This is not something scratched on tablets or sealed in scrolls; it is the plain speech of a free tongue" (965–68).[2]

But the Chorus Leader's question—"How can a space that is open to all protect me?"—lays bare the conditions of democracy in an even more profound way. We can hear in it a deep awareness of the relation between how humans bear the weight of symbolic life and the fragility of embodied existence. Will we be safe here, in this shared and open space created by human agreement? For Aristotle too this question is foundational to political life, and he will spend quite a bit of thought and concern on the manner in which political community is constituted by the intimacies that arise from living together and sharing space. In a particularly dramatic moment in his *Politics*, for instance, Aristotle describes in some detail the systematic erosion of trust, friendship, frank speech, and economic security that characterizes a tyranny, and the fear, isolation, paranoia, and poverty that replace them (5.11). In Aristotle's analysis, a tyranny thrives off of the dismantling of social bonds, i.e. the institutions and qualities that allow humans to share their lives with one another. It is this very aspect that assures the instability of the tyranny, and that marks out in negative form what is essential to a recognizably human life. For while the division of labor secures human survival, it is the ability and desire to perform our most cherished tasks with one another, to share these aspects of our lives, that is essential for the living well at which political life aims.

Aristotle designates this sharing of life with the word *syzēn*, formed from the verb *syzaō*, "to live with or together." *Syzēn* appears frequently in his ethical and political works to indicate the forms of intimacy (*synētheia*) that arise from the possession of *logos* and the capacity for choice. Aristotle often uses it to help explicate the active state of human *philia* (friendship), which he will describe in the *Politics* as "the choice of living together" (1280b38–39).[3] In his ethical texts, shared life indicates an active awareness of one's being that is made possible by living with others (see e.g. *Nicomachean Ethics* 1171b32–1172a8). At its most vivid

---

[2] Burian (1991).
[3] ἡ γὰρ τοῦ συζῆν προαίρεσις φιλία. The Greek text is that of Ross (1964). Unless otherwise noted, all translations of Aristotle are my own.

it includes three aspects that prove useful in describing more specific features of *philia* as well, and whose designation also employs *sy(n)*-constructions; first, the sharing in joy and sadness, and more broadly feeling-with (*synkhairein, synalgein, synēdesthai, synakhthesthai, synōdos, syllypeisthai*), that is especially vivid in the relationship between mothers and their children and also exhibited in non-human animals like birds (e.g. *Eudemian Ethics* 1240a35); second, the shared perception (*synaisthēsis*) of justice and injustice that forms the basis of political community (*Politics* 1253a15); and third, the sharing in understanding (*syngnōrizein, Eudemian Ethics* 1244b26) and contemplation (*syntheōrein, Eudemian Ethics* 1245b4) that emerge from philosophizing together (*symphilosophein, Nichomachean Ethics* 1172a5, see also *Eudemian Ethics* 1245a22).[4]

In contemporary theoretical engagement with Aristotle's political thought, little attention has been given to what we learn about *zōē* from the fact that it can be shared, nor to the significance the possibility of sharing in *zōē* has for our understanding of the relationship between *zōē*, *bios*, and political life.[5] This is especially the case for those thinkers working with Giorgio Agamben's alignment of *zōē* with the material, "inarticulate," "mute," and "private" against the purported discursive, symbolic, "articulate," and "political" character of *bios*.[6] In its affiliation with *philia*, the concept of shared life permeates Aristotle's conception of human political life in such a way as to inscribe *zōē* in the most fundamental of political phenomena and to render inadequate any such distinction between *zōē* and *bios* along the lines of the biological as opposed to the political.[7] The centrality that the sharing of life plays in Aristotle's understanding of human political life requires us to reconsider the roles of *zōē* and *bios* in Aristotle's political thought.

Moreover, the concept of shared life is uniquely positioned to illuminate the connection between the zoological, ethical, and political lenses through which Aristotle pursues his investigation of human political life. Because, for Aristotle, *syzēn* includes a robust capacity to share affect that

---

[4] Several of these forms resonate with the Stoic conception of sympathy Holmes discusses in her contribution to this volume.
[5] Dubreuil (2006) is an exception to this trend.
[6] Agamben (1998) 187–8. Agamben himself will make brief reference to *syzēn* in his study of monastic life (Agamben, 2013) but does not develop the significance of this term for his earlier formulation of the difference between *zōē* and *bios*.
[7] The present essay aims to lay the foundation for an exploration of the challenge the concept of *syzēn* makes to Agamben's formulation of the *zōē/bios* distinction, and in this contributes to the larger criticism of Agamben's reading of Aristotle, see e.g. Derrida (2009), Dubreuil (2006), and Finlayson (2010). For a more comprehensive critique of Agamben in the context of a study of the concept of *syzēn* in Aristotle's ethical and political thought, see Brill (forthcoming a).

is held across a broad spectrum of living beings as well as a specific dynamics of attachment (to material things, ideas, and other living beings), it serves not only to mark out what Aristotle thinks is distinct about human life but also to discern how even these distinctions fall into place in a larger vision of living being.[8] A comprehensive study of the relationality it illuminates tells us something essential about Aristotle's approach to human political phenomena; namely, that they arise as forms of intimacy whose political character can only be seen when measured on a zoological scale, where they emerge not as categorically distinct from animal sociality, but as intensifications of it.[9]

In this chapter I sketch the implications of a study of *syzēn* for our understanding of Aristotle's political thought by focusing on the reconceptualization of the scope of the zoological perspective informing Aristotle's *Politics* that the sharing of *zōē* invites. For while scholars have noted parallelisms between Aristotle's treatment of political and zoological phenomena, the tendency has been to isolate the explanatory force of the zoological lens to the "anthropological" dimension of the *Politics*, relegating its role in his political science to the generation of metaphors with varying degrees of heuristic value.[10] I argue, on the

---

[8] In this, a study of *syzēn* contributes to the long-running debate about the degree of continuity between humans and non-human animals in Aristotle's thought. For the primary ethical stakes in this debate, see especially Sorabji (1995), Nussbaum (2001), and Osborne (2007).

[9] As DePew (1995) has observed, both Kullmann (1991) and Cooper (1990) offer forms of an intensification thesis grounded in the possession of *logos*, Kullmann that the possession of *logos* intensifies animal sociality and Cooper that it allows for more sophisticated forms of the division of labor. Here I extend Kullmann's analysis of the zoological character of Aristotle's anthropology, as it is given in the *Politics*, to Aristotle's *polis* analysis as well. I take his reasons for not doing so to hinge upon the assumed division between "the biological" and "the rational" in Aristotle's thought. Kullmann's subsequent alignments of the political with the biological and *logos* with the rational obscure the political basis of *logos* and result in the conclusion that the human is a more political animal than others because of some *extra-political* capacity, as Güremen (2018) astutely observes. A more expansive sense of both *logos* (like that called for in Frank 2015) and *zōion* would permit a clearer view of the political function of *logos* and would also bring *logos* under the purview of *zōē*, which, I will argue, is more in line with Aristotle's thinking across his ethics and politics, as becomes evident if we focus on the use of *logos* to enshrine the attachment created by a shared perception of just and unjust within *polis* institutions via the forms of *politeia*.

[10] This is particularly clear in Kullman (1991), with the distinction between Aristotle's treatment of the nature of human beings (which, he finds, is firmly rooted within a zoological context) and his treatment of the *polis* (the quasi-organismic character of which, Kullmann argues, must be read as an analogic or heuristic extension), but is evident in varying degrees throughout recent studies of the "biological" dimension of Aristotle's *Politics*, see e.g. Pellegrin (2015), DePew (1995), Lord (1991), Cooper (1984/2004), see also Mulgan (1974). Here I am working against the grain of this distinction, bearing in mind that where we mark the limit of Aristotle's zoological perspective must take into account his expansive sense of the phenomena that constitute it. Kullmann (1991) will go on to argue

contrary, that a comprehensive understanding of the approach to human political phenomena Aristotle takes in his *Politics* requires us to acknowledge that Aristotle's zoological perspective extends beyond his characterization of human beings to his understanding of the *polis* itself. The *polis* need not be a living being in order to be meaningfully (and essentially, as opposed to analogically or heuristically) understood within a broader investigation of living beings; even if this perspective is not sufficient, it is nevertheless necessary. Put differently, organisms are not the only entity usefully explicated by a zoological perspective (even if they are the most significant such entity); in order to understand them, if we are to follow Aristotle's account, something else must be understood as well, namely, the milieu in which they thrive, the set of environmental factors that support them and shape them as, for instance, land-dwellers or water dwellers, what Pierre Pellegrin calls the "situation" of animals.[11] As the horizon toward which human life aims and the milieu in which it unfolds, the human political community operates in its relation to its constituents as an amplification of the relation between any living being and its environment.[12]

Indeed, I argue, it is only with this context in mind that we can fully appreciate what is unique about the *polis*, namely, the degree to which it is shaped by the entities whom it shapes, a reciprocity illuminated by an analysis of what Aristotle calls the *bios* of the *polis*—the *politeia* (*Politics* 1295a40–b1)—insofar as it highlights not only the exchange between persons and structure, but the status of institutional structures themselves as traces of shared human perception of the just and the unjust. Because of the intensity and endurance of human interactions granted by

---

that for Aristotle *polis* itself is neither living nor a substance, and suggests that we should read Aristotle's attribution of a *bios* (1295a40, 1327b4 and 5), *ergon* (1326a13), *aretē* (1253a38), and political character (*politikon*: 1327b5) to the city as analogical and heuristic. For the debate about whether the *polis* is an *ousia* see, for example Barker (1959) 221, 276–7; Clark (1975) 102–4; Reidel (1975) 76–7; Kamp (1985) 116, 106–7; and Mogens (2013) 22–3 for arguments in the affirmative and Höffe (1987) 269–70, Kullmann (1991), Yack (1993) 92, and Pellegrin (2015) for the negative.

[11] Pellegrin (2015) 40.

[12] "Constituents" rather than "inhabitants" because for Aristotle not all people residing within the boundaries of a *polis* are fully enfranchised citizens—in fact, most are not. Whatever else may and should be said about Aristotle's account of the so-called natural slave, it makes clear that his ideal of citizen life is parasitic on the labor of others. Conceiving of the *polis* in ecological terms has the added value of drawing out this parasitic character more clearly and problematizing the sense of the "natural" with which Aristotle is operating at this juncture of the *Politics*. On the role of *physis* in Aristotle's political thought Miller (1997) remains canonical; for more recent work, see Trott (2013) and Riesbach (2016).

the use of *logos*, the *polis* is an unstable environment, one requiring a mode of analysis—an ecology—that Aristotle does not extend to other animal habitats. And because the human capacity for viciousness is more pervasive in political life than the rare cases of human completion, Aristotle's focus on the human, at least in the *Politics*, is more alarmist than celebratory; his anthropocentrism here should not be confused for a humanism, at least as it is traditionally conceived.[13]

In order to make good on these claims, I begin by sketching the stakes of a renewed consideration of the zoological dimension of Aristotle's *Politics*. I then turn to frame this dimension within the relationship between *zōion* and *topos* that is illuminated in Aristotle's ecological account of animal *bioi* in the *History of Animals*. Finally, I return to the *Politics* to consider, in light of Aristotle's account of *bios*, what it would mean to call the *politeia* the *bios* of the *polis*.

6.1. Political animals

In the first Book of his *Politics*, Aristotle offers the following list of human ways of life (*bioi*): the nomad, the farmer, the pirate, the fisher, the hunter, and those who live pleasantly by combining several of these (1256a40–b4). This list is based upon differences with respect to sustenance (*trophē*) that leans heavily upon the similarity between humans and other animals. Aristotle observes that such differences have made the ways of life of all animals distinct. Some live in herds and others are scattered, depending upon whether they are carnivorous, herbivorous, or omnivorous. And because even within these groups what is naturally pleasant to one is not so to the other, the ways of life amongst the carnivorous themselves, for instance, differ. "The same is the case for human beings as well; for there are many differences with respect to their ways of life" (1.8.1256a29–30).[14]

We would do well in our understanding of Aristotle's political thought to consider how this list—nomad, farmer, pirate, fisher, hunter, and their combination—stands with respect to the two candidates for most choiceworthy human *bios* that Aristotle discusses in Book 7, the political and

---

[13] See Johnson (2006) on the challenge that Aristotle's teleology presents to the anthropocentrism of many of his contemporaries. On how Aristotle's anthropocentrism might stand with respect to the "mortalist" humanism Bonnie Honig (2013) criticizes see below pp. 117–118.

[14] ὁμοίως δὲ καὶ τῶν ἀνθρώπων. πολὺ γὰρ διαφέρουσιν οἱ τούτων βίοι.

the philosophic.[15] At first pass, these two lists seem to require that a philosophic analysis of human political phenomena straddle two worlds, as it were: the realm of physical necessity—in which human life is defined by its need for sustenance—and the realm of produced meaning, in which human life takes its shape from collective deliberation about attaining the highest end and for which *bios* and *zōē* are objects of choice.[16] But, I submit, Aristotle's *Politics* as a whole requires something more radical of us, namely, that we set aside this distinction and look instead at the manner in which political phenomena mark out precisely the intersection of matter and meaning, that we see the *polis* as the site in which all dimensions of human embodiment are engaged and come to light—the desire for companionship, the assessment of one's own worth and the worth of others, the capacities for collective action, deliberation, and thought, to be sure, but also the need for sustenance and the very structure of one's organs. Doing so requires us to sort through the conceptual perspectives that inform Aristotle's approach to human political phenomena, and to revisit the question of the scope of influence of a zoological perspective in Aristotle's *Politics*.

At stake in this question is nothing less than how we read Aristotle's claims that the human is a political animal. In particular, at stake is the status of a reading, to be found in a significant strand of contemporary thought from Martin Heidegger to Hannah Arendt to Agamben, that takes this to mean that "political" names the essence of the human. And yet, if we follow Aristotle's specification of the political in the *History of Animals*—those animals are *politika* which have some one common activity (*History of Animals* 488a8–9)—this cannot be the case because: (1) some animals other than human are really political and not just metaphorically political, i.e. some non-human animals (e.g. bees, wasps, ants, and cranes) also pursue a common task; and (2) because human beings, like a few other kinds of animals, are dualizers, and specifically dualize between gregarious and solitary (*History of Animals* 488a7), humans may reject collective life, and this possibility is part of what it means to be human.[17] As such, a divergence from the trajectory toward

---

[15] This list contains two of the traditional three lives discussed in the *Nicomachean Ethics*, the life of pleasure, the political life, and the contemplative life (1.5.1095b17). On the history of the three-life trope, see Lockwood (2014).

[16] And two unequal worlds at that, as Aristotle will claim that it is primarily in hunting for virtue that different forms of *bios* and *politeia* emerge, see *Politics* 7.8.1328b.

[17] As Cooper (1990) and Lord (1991) observe, there is some ambiguity in this passage as to whether the human dualizes between gregarious and solitary or between political and scattered; however, I am convinced by Depew (1995), against Lord and others, that the former makes the most sense of Aristotle's writing about the full range of human possibilities (as Cooper (1990) argues as well). For my purposes, nothing is riding on the

community is always within the human horizon. And so, while Aristotle will describe the one who is no part of a city as "either a beast or a god" (*Politics* 1253a28),[18] that there are "beastly" humans Aristotle does concede, and sees their existence as an indication of the need humans have for practitioners of the political art.[19] For while there is in all humans an impulse toward political partnership, yet, "the one who first constituted a city is responsible for the greatest goods" (1253a29–31).[20] Aristotle continues, "for just as a human being is the best of the animals when completed, when separated from law and adjudication it is the worst of all" (1253a33–34).[21] Whatever Aristotle means when he claims that humans are political animals, he cannot mean that humans are exclusively political.

This is in no way to deny that, for Aristotle, human life is fundamentally political; rather, it is to assert that what is essentially human is not politics per se, but how humans "do" politics. To be sure, Aristotle is clear that humans are exemplary political animals (*Politics* 1253a7–9), and this suggests that what Aristotle claims makes them so at this juncture of the *Politics*—the possession of *logos*—must also be examined in light of his larger zoological interests.[22] That is, we must return to the question of how the possession of *logos*, as well as human political phenomena more generally, stand with respect to human animality.[23]

One long-standing way of answering this question, made perhaps most explicit by Arendt but present also in David Keyt's and Terrence Irwin's treatment of the *zōion politikon*,[24] is that Aristotle aligns the animal with the "biological" and rejects this biological dimension as outside the scope of political phenomena, that is, as an aspect that is best understood as defining daily needs and thus as best addressed in the

---

distinction, as the failure at collective life I am speaking of here would be demonstrated in either case, even granting with Cooper (1990) that this failure is the exception to normal human behavior.

[18] ὥστε ἢ θηρίον ἢ θεός.
[19] See e.g. *Nicomachean Ethics* 1118b5 and the discussion of *thēriotēs* in Book 7.
[20] ὁ δὲ πρῶτος συστήσας μεγίστων ἀγαθῶν αἴτιος.
[21] ὥσπερ γὰρ καὶ τελεωθεὶς βέλτιστον τῶν ζῴων ἄνθρωπός ἐστιν, οὕτω καὶ χωρισθεὶς νόμου καὶ δίκης χείριστον πάντων.
[22] Aristotle is equally clear that only human beings deliberate (*History of Animals* 488b25). While there are important differences between the possession of *logos* and the capacity for deliberation, for the purposes of this paper what is said above about the former could also be said of the latter.
[23] An effort greatly aided by Frank (2015) and Aygün (2017).
[24] To the extent that both Keyt (1991) and Irwin (1988) take the extension of *politikē* to non-human animals as mainly metaphorical. For discussion of the similarity here, see DePew (1995) 162.

household and decidedly not in the *polis*.²⁵ This reading, in turn, lends itself to the conclusion that human animality has no place in a true *polis* so far as Aristotle is concerned.²⁶ But this is so only if we assume in advance that Aristotle is operating with an *ontological* divide between humans and non-human animals and that an unproblematic correlate to the "biological" exists in Aristotle's thought. If I am right, both are an anachronism. As a *zōion ekhon logon*, the human possession of *logos* is bound to human animality. For Aristotle, having *logos* may mark humans as unique animals, but it does not mark humans as not animal.

I thus aim, over the next few pages, to challenge an assumption about the nature of human being embedded in a now entrenched reading of Aristotle's claim that the human is a *zōion politikon* by considering his analysis of the *polis* in the context of his larger examination of living beings. I am not arguing that political science is really theoretical rather than practical, nor collapsing the distinction between political science and zoology.²⁷ I *am* arguing that Aristotle's tendency to view human political phenomena through a zoological lens extends to his conception of what the *polis* is, what it does, and how it does it. This tendency

---

²⁵ To be sure, there are grounds for this elision even in Aristotle's zoological work, so much of which is shaped by consideration of animal nutrition. However, Aristotle's account of non-human animal character in Book 8 of the *History of Animals* makes clear that we cannot reduce all non-human animal behavior to "the biological" any more than we can human behavior.

²⁶ See Arendt (1958) 27; see also 36–7, and, for a discussion of Arendt's reading of nature and the household in Aristotle and Agamben's appropriation of this discussion see Finlayson (2010). Depew (1995) 162 attributes Arendt's constructions here as (like Strauss, and ultimately Heidegger) stemming from a mis-reading of the claim that human is a political animal. See also the critique of Heidegger in Kullmann (1991) 107, as well as that of Bein (1973) 123 n. 27, who objected that *zōion* doesn't mean beast in pejorative sense but rather "animated being" or "living creature."

²⁷ That is, I agree that the main thrust of the *Politics* is in recognizing and aiding the work of the statesman, work that is made possible by the open-endedness of human political life. But implicit in its study of this work is a theoretically informed study of the *polis*; this is particularly evident in the investigation of the forms of *politeiai* in Books 4–6. As Kullmann (1991) 108 observes, Aristotle's collection and account of various forms of *politeia* invites comparison with the study of salient animal differences in his zoological work (especially, I add, differences with respect to animal *bios*), even as this *politeia*-analysis serves the ultimate purpose of advising the statesman in how to preserve them. Such a study affords a glimpse of the forms of life to which a *polis* gives rise and informs one's sense of whether these forms will stabilize the *polis* or destabilize it. After all, Aristotle's *politeia* analysis is also in part an exercise in discerning the history and processes of what he will characterize as an error with respect to the shared perception of just and unjust, and this returns us to the work of the statesman. Kullmann's designation of the work of the political expert, the one with *politikē epistēmē*, as pertaining not to a different object than zoology but to drawing finer distinctions about one kind of political animal, the human, seems to me both right and to be pushing against the border between the theoretical and the practical; see Kullmann (1991) 114. See Johnson (2015) for another account of the theoretical aspect of political science.

requires us to resist the temptation to read a more contemporary denial of human animality into Aristotle's texts, even if that denial attempts to anchor itself within Aristotle's thought.[28] If I am right about Aristotle's thinking about living beings, then the conception of human being held by inheritors of the reading of Aristotle criticized here (and its effects on political thought) is in need of a "re-animalization," and of the ecological conception of human political relations that accompanies it.[29]

Without doubt, when Aristotle claims, for instance, that slaves and animals do not have a *polis* (1280a33), he draws a very sharp divide between some humans and other animals. Aristotle is equally clear in his claims that only humans deliberate and have recollection (*History of Animals* 488b25). There can be no denying that there is an exceptionalism at work here. But exceptionalism of what sort? After all, Aristotle is also perfectly comfortable treating human beings as examples of two-legged, warm-blooded animals (see, for example, *History of Animals* 489a31–490a27) whose capacities in some cases exceed and in others fall short of other animals, a fact that is not always well marked by interpreters of Aristotle's political thought.

In the case of Arendt, as Adriana Cavarero makes clear in her contribution to this volume, her concern lies in using ancient Greek thought in order to analyze totalitarianism, rather than the other way around, and as Aristotle himself points out, no one seeks absolute political power for the sake of creature comforts alone, that is, "no one becomes a tyrant in order to get in out of the cold" (1267a13).[30] Nevertheless, if we construe too quickly the difference between human and animal, we risk overlooking something essential about Aristotle's thinking not only about the *polis* and the entire field of political phenomena, human and otherwise, but also about *zōē* itself. For while Aristotle's low opinion of cattle, for instance, is clear, if we assume the same general attitude toward all living things we miss the broader scope of his thinking about *zōion* as such. This is, after all, a category that includes not only cattle and wild beasts and humans but also the divine (*Metaphysics* 1072b26).[31] Far from operating as the "mute" representative of materiality, *zōē* figures,

---

[28] As Kullmann (1991) 107 suggests, this form of the human/animal divide is more characteristic of early Christian thought.

[29] Here I am appropriating and repurposing a term used by Alan Bloom, for whom, in a clear example of the kind of thinking about animality I aim to rebut, it is intended as a criticism. I do so in a manner closely related to the movement toward re-naturalization argued most extensively by Elizabeth Grosz, with significant elaboration by Hasana Sharp. See especially Grosz (1994), (2005), and Sharp (2011).

[30] οἷον τυραννοῦσιν οὐχ ἵνα μὴ ῥιγῶσιν. Here I follow Lord's (1984) translation.

[31] καὶ ζωὴ δέ γε ὑπάρχει· ἡ γὰρ νοῦ ἐνέργεια ζωή, ἐκεῖνος δὲ ἡ ἐνέργεια· ἐνέργεια δὲ ἡ καθ'αὑτὴν ἐκείνου ζωὴ ἀρίστη καὶ ἀΐδιος.

essentially, into Aristotle's most speculative thinking about the nature of divine and human intellectual capacities.[32] The perceiving and thinking that are particularly revelatory of certain living beings are themselves explicitly treated by Aristotle not as standing outside the realm of *zōē* but precisely as expressions of *zōē*, indeed as the most vivid expressions belonging to this particular kind of living being (*Eudemian Ethics* 1244b25).

Thus, to return to the question posed above about human animality, to elide the animal with the need for sustenance is to be at odds with Aristotle's own sense of what constitutes "living." When Aristotle asserts that the one who is without a city is either a beast or a god he is not making use of a distinction between animal and divine; rather, he is marking out two extreme poles of animality, the beastly [*to thērion*] and the divine [*ho theos*].[33] Further, to say that human political life does not have to be concerned with the dimensions of life like sustenance or that the city is not concerned with human animality but rather human rationality or ethical agency, is to determine in advance what remains to be seen, namely, the range and horizons of animality as such. Rather than assume an ontological distinction between human and animal, we need to construe the field of living beings as, in some instances, including rationality, and watch how distinctions between humans and other animals emerge. The challenge, in other words, is to view the human possession of *logos* as an expression of *zōē*.[34] Taking up this challenge is especially important for an engagement with Aristotle's *Politics*, as it is in the *Politics* that human animality and human exceptionality collide.

What is required, then, in order to understand Aristotle's treatment of the human possession of *logos* in the *Politics* is a broad sense of human

---

[32] See, for instance, *Eudemian Ethics* 1244b29: "living is a kind of knowing" [τὸ γὰρ ζῆν δεῖ τιθέναι γνῶσιν τινά].

[33] Contra a strand of reading, exemplified in Keyt (1989) 18, which distinguishes between divine and animal in order to discern a split between human animal nature and human divine nature.

[34] With respect to our intellectual capacities, Aristotle's treatment of perception and thought as expressions of *zōē* indicates that in speaking of the human capacity for thought we are not speaking of something that stands outside of the realm of animality but rather of something that marks humans as unusual animals (see *Eudemian Ethics* 1244b23–25). On natural virtues, see e.g. Lennox (1999), Lloyd (2013), and Leunissen (2010), (2012), and (2013). Of course, this is not to deny Aristotle's insistence that habits do not come to us by nature and that it is by habit that virtues of character develop, nor what Pellegrin (2015) 46 calls the "entire machinery of deliberation and choice" as decisive for human life. My point is simply that these are present as potency in children and that their expression occurs via a process of maturation, of "growth" that may, like any other animals, be interrupted or twisted. Pellegrin's invocation of the machine seems meant to combat the image of the organism, but this already concedes conceptual pride of place to the organism and betrays an anxiety that Aristotle may simply not have had.

qua *zōion*, qua living being. In the growth of plants, the perceptual capacities and movement of animals, and the impulse that animates thinking, speaking, and deliberating Aristotle sees the working of a single complex activity, living (*to zēn*), come to expression in an array of forms of life (*bioi*), and it is in these, if anywhere, that one could find the resources needed for a philosophic account of the nature of life as such (*zōē*). And, while it is commonplace to refer to Aristotle's biology, or to describe an aspect of his ethics or politics as biological, the infelicities in doing so—especially given the connotation of determinism the "biological" carries for contemporary ears, and the accompanying tendency to meld the "biological" with the material—has not gone unremarked by scholars.[35] There is no ancient Greek word or phrase that could be easily translated by "biological," nor does a *logos* of *bios* map easily on to what we would call a biological account. It is worth bearing in mind David Balme's reminder that for Aristotle, "matter qua matter is not a thing but a role played by things."[36] The logic of embodiment that emerges from out of Aristotle's zoological work is a regional logic, one that may have cosmic aspirations but that unfolds in very earthly realities and struggles to accommodate itself to what Emanuela Bianchi calls the aleatory character of materiality.[37] To speak of Aristotle's zoology, then, is to speak of a broad inquiry into the nature of living beings, an inquiry aimed at discerning the very terms of living embodiment itself. It is this broader context that forms what I am calling his zoological perspective, and, I submit, it is within this broader context that we should locate Aristotle's analysis of human political life.

I will take as my point of entry, and the horizon within which the remainder of this inquiry develops, an explication of the claim that the

---

[35] e.g. Gotthelf and Lennox (1987) 5, Balme (1987a), and Pellegrin (2015) 31. Nevertheless, these cautionary observations have not changed the broad scholarly tendency to characterize Aristotle's work in this way and Pellegrin (2015), Cooper (1982/2004), Depew (1995), Kullmann (1991), and Lord (1991), for instance, all observe what they call the biological character of Aristotle's *Politics*. I am in strong agreement with Sophia Connell's (2001) call to read Aristotle's studies of animals as philosophical in their own right, and add that in doing so we are well served by setting aside the designation of "biological." To the extent that it is useful to consider these texts as a category of Aristotle's thought, it is safer to remain within a more direct equivalent to Aristotle's own description and refer to them as zoological.

[36] Balme (1990) 49. Ebrey (2015) 66 offers a nearly identical formulation of matter, and Code (2015) section 2 assumes such a formulation.

[37] See Bianchi (2014) and Balme (1987b). See also Ebrey (2015) on the inaccuracy of referring to "material necessity" in Aristotle and Gelber's (2015b) argument against treating facts about matter as primitive. I take Johnson's (2006) 4 alignment of Aristotelian explanation with biological theories of evolutionary adaptation as strategic, designed mainly to distinguish it from natural theology.

politeia is the *bios* of the *polis* by focusing on the two terms of this equation, *bios* and *politeia*.

6.2. Bio-logy in the *History of Animals*

If we evaluate Aristotle's zoological writing with a positivist commitment to the absolute priority of perception, we have little to prevent us from using our relatively greater sophistication of perception, our ability to see more of the parts of animals than Aristotle can, to conclude that he has little to tell us about animals' lives and bodies. But this assumes that in looking at these animals we see the same things, just better, as though our seeing were not already informed by certain sensibilities pertaining to what is to be seen. I think it wise not to take for granted that we and Aristotle have identical things in mind when we talk about animal parts, organs, movements, etc.[38] In evaluating Aristotle's zoological writings, it is worth making a concerted effort to recover some sense of what Aristotle saw when he looked at animals.

If we pursue this question from the perspective of the *Metaphysics*, in which living being plays such a powerful role in elucidating substance, it appears that Aristotle sees unities, held together over time with the cooperation of more or less tight collections of more or less sophisticated capacities for temperature regulation, movement, nutrition, reproduction, perception, and, in some cases, thought. If we move to the zoological works, it is clear that Aristotle takes as his field of inquiry the array of similarities and differences by which one is confronted in the realm of living beings. For Aristotle this array requires us to treat an investigation of organic unity as going hand in hand with an investigation of biodiversity, and, if we are to take the *History of Animals* in particular as an indication, this endeavor takes place not through a system of classification but through a science of differences. Of the differentiae that Aristotle claims divide animals into kinds—parts (*moria*), manner of life (*bios*), character (*ēthos*) and action (*praxis*) (*History of Animals* 487a10)—parts are the most vivid of differentiators (*History of Animals* 491a15–16) and are treated in the greatest detail. But the other differentiae have their day as well, and Aristotle will spend some time detailing, for instance, the actions that indicate that an animal has the *bios* of a land-dweller or a

---

[38] As Kuriyama (2002) on anatomical seeing makes clear, programmatic claims about the self-evidence and vividness of animal parts often mask the historical and cultural contingency of a kind of seeing.

water-dweller, or of a carnivore or a herbivore, as well as the complex forms of character to be seen in the animal realm. Some are intelligent (*phronimos*), ingenious (*tekhnikos*), scheming (*epiboula*), resourceful, gentle or spirited, fearful or courageous, jealous or loving, caring or indifferent.[39] Signs of these qualities are often written onto the body of the animal, in the shape of the eyebrows (491b15), the color, size (492a1), and nick of the eye (491b25), etc.

While accounts of both animal unity and animal difference are necessary, we cannot lose sight of yet another feature that Aristotle attributes to living being qua living: its display of modes of power and hierarchy. For if living being is a paradigm of substance, it is also a paradigm of rule: "an animal is the first thing composed of soul and body, of which the one is the ruling element by nature, the other the ruled" (*Politics* 1254a34–36).[40] For the vast majority of animals, this relationship between soul and body takes the form of mastery.[41] What is true of the power relation within the individual animal is also true of the relation between animals and so we read that for those animals competing for food, there is a perpetual state of war (*polemos*),[42] marked, at least in the case of one conflict, by the turn of fortune, *peripeteia*, familiar to the audience of tragedy: the crayfish, master of most of its opponents, is so afraid of the octopus that when caught in a net with this enemy it has been known to die of fear.[43] Because the forms of rule are written into organic life, the student of rule would be well served to take a broad view of its workings in the animal realm. The student of *politikē* must, then, be a student of *zōē*. Far from asserting a division between embodiment and the symbolic, these descriptions, and Aristotle's zoological studies as whole, assert rather their intertwining. That is, they assert that *zōē grants* meaning.

Any explanation of the unity that arises out of this complexity would be incomplete without an account of the *topos* in which the living being

---

[39] Phronimos: 488b15, 612a4, 614b18; *dianoian syneseos*: 588a23; *dianoias*, 612b21; *tekhnikos*: 616a5: ingenuity; 620b11; 622b24; scheming (*epiboula*): 488b18; resourceful: 616b19: *biomekhanos* "resourceful in way of life" and 21: "in intelligence it is resourceful in getting a living" (*tēn de dianoian eumekhanos pros ton bion*), see also 616b28; gentle or spirited, fearful or courageous, jealous (488b24) or loving, caring or indifferent. Labarrière (1990) remains the most comprehensive study of both the similarities and differences between humans and other animals with respect to *phronēsis*.

[40] τὸ δὲ ζῷον πρῶτον συνέστηκεν ἐκ ψυχῆς καὶ σώματος, ὧν τὸ μὲν ἄρχον ἐστὶ φύσει τὸ δ' ἀρχόμενον.

[41] Political rule can be seen in those animals that possess intellect as well as appetite, as this is the means by which the former rules the latter (*Politics* 1254b4–6).

[42] See *History of Animals* 608b19–31 and 610a5.

[43] *History of Animals* 590b14.

conducts its living. When Aristotle explains why plants do not emit a waste product, for example—that the warmth of the earth in which they are rooted concocts their food for them, serving as an "external stomach" (*Parts of Animals* 650a20–25)—he makes of this earth an instrument, an "organ" vital for the plant's survival. While the plant is an extreme case, it is so as a particularly vivid example of the intimacy that obtains between place and living being for all animals, which are divided, "according to the places" [*kata tous topous*] (*History of Animals* 589a11), whose lives depend upon the place in which their sustenance is "housed" (see *Politics* 1256b9–23), and whose matter "is of the same nature as the region in which they exist."[44] Or, as Jessica Gelber puts it, for Aristotle habitat "is already included in what it is to be an animal of [a particular] kind."[45]

The unity that is the living being, then, is maintained only to the extent that it navigates the fluidity and porosity of embodiment, with its demands that the living being take in and expel what is outside of it; its character as a substance emerges from its ability to hold itself together in the performance of these negotiations. Thus, its body is organized around the passageways, fissures, apertures, openings that connect the internal with external and *zōion* with *topos*. And while a sophisticated account of the relation between parts, capacities, and ends is necessary to understanding animal life, these on their own do not amount to an account of the living being without also a subtle account of the interaction between *zōion* and *topos*, precisely because of the intimacy of their interaction and the extent to which nature "supplies" the animal with what it needs in order to live in a particular place (*Politics* 1256b5–23). If one is to understand with any specificity the unity and diversity of living beings, one must develop as subtle a conceptual vocabulary as possible for the interaction between *zōion* and *topos*.

It is in the context of this aspiration that we should locate Aristotle's analysis of animal *bios*, as it is *bios* that, following Lennox, "accounts for the unity that integrates the many parts of an animal's body and the many different activities those parts perform."[46] And the most general forms of *bios* that are mentioned in the *History of Animals* distinguish

---

[44] *On Respiration* 477b30, Ross translation. Aristotle will go on to say that the conditions of their bodies might be contrary to their environment; e.g. they could feel cold while residing in a hot place or vice versa. Nevertheless, "while states of the body can be opposed in character to the environment, the material of which it is composed can never be so" (478a5).

[45] Gelber (2015a) 279. Gelber provides a careful and convincing account of the intimacy between *topos* and *zōion* in Aristotle's zoological work, and briefly gestures toward the *polis* as the proper habitat for the human (see 289–90). See also Gotthelf (1997) 91, (2012) 192, and Lennox (2009) and (2010).

[46] Lennox (2010) 350.

between animals on the basis of the *topos* in which they do their living: land animals and water animals.[47] This reliance on *topos* has important implications for what an analysis of *bios* tells us. For, whatever teleology an account of *bios* may serve, it is, as Ross observes, an immanent teleology precisely because of the extent to which it is shaped by the animal's *topos*.[48] *Bios* names the relationship between parts and functions that enables the living being to successfully interact with its *topos*; it is thus contingent on *topos*, and if one were to ask what its end is, it would seem that any particular *bios* has its end in living (*to zēn*). In nonhuman animals, differences with respect to achieving this end are marked by the condition of *eubiotos*, in humans with that of *eu zēn*.[49] That this integration can be more or less successful, that an animal may *eubiotos* or *kakobios*, should remind us that we are not dealing with a strict environmental determinism here, but rather marking out the horizon within which and to which morphology responds to greater and lesser degrees of success.

What, then, does a *logos* of *bios* provide that a careful analysis of parts and functions does not? Or, more simply, what do we know when we know an animal's *bios*? We know the manner in which the animal's

---

[47] See *History of Animals* 589a11: "they have been divided according to the places: for some are land animals and others are water animals."

[48] Ross (1923) 129. See also Johnson (2006). It is constructive to consider what an ancient account of *bios* that does support a more universalist anthropocentric teleological framework would look like and here we have Plato's *Timaeus* (wherein Timaeus claims that women and non-human animals exist because of the moral failings of the human prototype; see Brill (2015)) and his *Phaedrus* (in which kinds of *bioi*, like that of the farmer or the poet or the philosopher, are a function of the proximity to truth one's soul attained prior to embodiment, see Brill (forthcoming b)) as examples.

[49] *History of Animals* 609b20; see also also at 615a17, 615a28 and 34 with *euētheis* "goodnatured," 616b10, 14, 24, and 31, 619b24, 620a22: *eubiotatoi*. Balme (227) notes that: "*eubiotos*... seems to denote more than an easy food-supply: it suggests that the bird lives successfully in its surroundings. The opposite is not *dusbiotos* (living in hardship) but *kakobios* (living poorly, 616b31, 619a2)"; see also 601a23: *euemerousi*; 601b9: *euthenei*; 602a16: *eustheneian*, in claiming that, "places help each kind to thrive" and then just below at 19: "But there are also certain places peculiar to each kind, where they thrive [*euthenousin*]." On the role of *topos*, see also 605b23: "In general the animals differ according to localities" and just below, "not thrive" is *ouk euemerei* and 607a9: "Localities also produce differences in character"). While it is important to mark this difference in terminology, it is also necessary to avoid reading more into it than Aristotle's text warrants. I will discuss this a bit further in the conclusion, but for now observe that Aristotle may be marking a distinction between the forms of *failure* to flourish available to non-human animals and to humans. For non-human animals there can be a success or failure to flourish with respect to their manner of life, that is, with respect to their integration of capacities for the purpose of thriving in a particular place. The human, on the other hand—the suicidal animal—can fail with respect to living itself in the sense that it can fail not only in the *integration* of capacities marked by *bios*, but also in the *exercise* and *maintenance* of capacities, that is, it can starve itself, blind itself, deafen itself, refuse to speak or think, etc.

parts, actions, and character are integrated into a single way of taking up the task of living, a manner that is not reducible to the parts themselves nor their functions and which, rather, is what explains why the animal has the parts and functions it does. Or, as Lennox puts it, "it is by grasping an animal's way of life that we grasp the underlying unity in organic complexity."[50] *Bios*, then, names how the animal reacts to and is composed within certain limits established by its *topos*. Consequently, neither animal unity nor animal difference can be understood without understanding the animal's *topos* and its role in shaping the essential features of the animal.

To anticipate the coming argument, an extension of this understanding of *bios* to the claim that the *politeia* is the *bios* of the *polis* requires us to consider the *polis* less as an organism itself than as the *topos* of a particular kind of organism. In this formulation, the *polis* refers not to the animal that has a *bios* but to the *topos* to which the *bios* suits the animal. That is, the pressing question to which Aristotle's *Politics* responds is not, "is the *polis* a substance?" but rather, "to what forms of living does a *polis* give rise?" But this is more complex than it seems, as this *topos* is made up not of the preponderance of an element, but of the traces, presences, and absences of other people. It is a human environment.[51] What takes on the determining role of land or water, in the human context, is other human beings, both in the presence of other people with whom to share power, resources, and life, but also in the traces of others, their affect, values, judgments of the just and unjust, that are memorialized in laws, structures, and institutions. In the *polis*, we are surrounded by what Plato's Diotima would call the psychic "children" of others.

In order to see this more clearly, however, we need to take a closer look at the way in which *politeia* operates in the *Politics*. If the *politeia* provides the *bios* of the *polis*, this is so because it describes the integration of parts and capacities possessed by its citizens to which individual *poleis* give rise and from which they attain their character; that is, it explains why this particular *polis* has these particular citizens. Does Aristotle's treatment of *politeia* operate in this way in the *Politics*? I believe that it does, provided we take the complexity of the term, the range of meanings it embraces, into account.

---

[50] Lennox (2010) 352.
[51] To be sure, these affects, values, judgments, etc. interact with geographical features. But they cannot be reduced to these features. Here Arendt's work on the human character of political community seems to me to be written very much within an Aristotelian vein.

6.3. *Politeia* in the *Politics*

Aristotle devotes much of *Politics* 5 to identifying the forms of estrangement that threaten the human capacity to share life. That is, he turns in this book to the tragedy of political life, to identifying the error (*hamartia*) with respect to justice out of which many regimes come to be, an error that stems from a misunderstanding of oneself and one's place in the political community (1301a26–40). His analysis of the minutiae of political life, of the scorned feelings of former lovers or the humiliation of a failed bid for marriage, and his tracing of the manner in which small matters come to take on larger and larger proportions (5.4) are aimed at discerning to the finest degree possible the scene of political life, the actions, passions, and system of meanings that determine one's position in the *polis* and the extent to which one is able to judge one's worth accurately (a capacity, Aristotle points out, of which humans are notoriously short, 3.9.1280a14).

Throughout Book 5's analysis of political instability, we find Aristotle straining to discern the character and quality of life within the city, objects which defy reduction to single causes and which must be taken as irreducibly many and seen in their complex dynamic. Indeed, Aristotle's assertion of the heterogeneous nature of power structures the entirety of his *Politics*. Because the forms of rule are irreducibly many, it is incumbent upon the political analyst to attend to the unique features of each form. We can see this discernment at work, for instance, in the list he offers of the factors that can foment revolution and destruction of a particular *politeia*. People are goaded to revolt by unrest over their allotment in the city, that is, by how the city conceives of and administers justice. They are galvanized by an array of what we would call psychological, demographic, and broadly behavioral factors: humans, "are stirred up against one another [*paroxynontai pros allēlous*]" (1302b39) by seeing others aggrandize themselves as well as, "by arrogance, by fear, by preeminence, by contempt, by disproportionate growth, and further, though in another manner, by electioneering, by underestimation, by [neglect of] small things, and by dissimilarity" (1302b2–5).[52]

The object whose analysis permits access to this set of factors is the *politeia*. This is to say, an analysis of *politeia* is the site in which Aristotle conducts his psychopathology of political life; it is where he develops his interest in tracing the way in which desire, self-assessment, recognition,

---

[52] ἔτι διὰ ὕβριν, διὰ φόβον, διὰ ὑπεροχήν, διὰ καταφρόνησιν, διὰ αὔξησιν τὴν παρὰ τὸ ἀνάλογον· ἔτι δὲ ἄλλον τρόπον δι' ἐριθείαν, δι' ὀλιγωρίαν, διὰ μικρότητα, διὰ ἀνομοιότητα.

and honor adhere to structures and institutions, animating, preserving, and destroying them. When Aristotle describes the *politeia* as the *bios* of the city he highlights precisely this promise of a study of *politeia*—its ability to illuminate the contingent and volatile forms of life that emerge within the city."[53]

Attaining this perspective on *politeia* requires that we view political structures and institutions as codified perceptions of advantage and disadvantage, just and unjust. That is, as ossified forms of *logos* which are perpetually reanimated by the citizen body and which may at any point succumb to a refusal on the part of this body to perform this reanimation. The particular instability that attends the properly human *topos* is thus clearly an effect of that which makes humans especially political. However, it is not the *possession* of *logos* that requires a political analysis distinct from a zoological analysis. *Logos* too admits of a zoological account. If Pellegrin is right that Aristotle offers in his *Politics* the same zoological analysis for language that he offers for political character, we can read the *Politics* as an extension of the concern that animates the *History of Animals*, namely, to identify and describe the most salient differentiae of living beings.[54] Throughout the *Politics,* the operation of *logos* to enable the perception of just and unjust serves to mark the comparatively greater political character of one kind of animal. The possession of *logos* thus functions as an essential facet of human animality, one to which human bodies have been suited by the form of the human tongue, for instance, or the thinness of human skin (see *Parts of Animals* 2.16.659b33–660a13). In this, the *having* of *logos* does not sever the political from the animal, nor a study of politics from a study of zoology.

---

[53] Unfortunately, this sense of *politeia*, as conveying the ways of life that the *polis* fosters, is obscured if we translate *politeia* solely or even primarily as "constitution." Of the meanings alive to Aristotle that J. J. Mulhern (2015) catalogues—citizenship, citizen body, constitution or arrangement of offices, and regime—half of them are insufficiently present to the reader if this course of translation is adopted. This runs the risk of overlooking Aristotle's acute awareness of the relationship between individual and structure, and of his efforts to highlight the manner in which institutions are animated by their citizens, defined by the delineation of the citizen body and preserved and destroyed by the partnership in power-sharing and the individual's sense of place within that partnership. Strauss (1959) 33–4 also emphasizes this sense, as Mulhern observes. But this is not an exclusively Straussian insight; see, for instance, Robinson (1995) xvi–xvii, who observes that "a constitution tends to be laws to us, but men to [Aristotle]." It is their interpenetration that an analysis of *politeia* provides. Frank (2005) provides an especially lucid account of the interaction between individual and institution in Aristotle's political theory; Saxonhouse (2015) offers an equally illuminating discussion of the relationship between *poleis*.

[54] Pellegrin (2015) 43.

To be sure, that Aristotle bothered to compose work devoted to human political life tells us that the particular and contingent *use* of *logos* in the formation and maintenance of *poleis* transforms every facet of human life and requires its own focused and nuanced analysis. But, as we follow the *Politics*, this is because, far from marking a departure from other forms of political life, the possession of *logos* creates the conditions for an intensification of the political bond, an intensification that comes with some ambivalence.[55] What such a study tells us is that it is other people, along with the artifacts of their collective deliberation, that provide the landscape to which human morphology responds and by which it is nourished.[56] Because the *polis* is founded upon the accretions of deliberation and opinion that constitute its *politeia*, which, in turn, provide it with its identity and life, the *polis* is subject to the tenuousness and instability of human shared perception of what is just and unjust. For this reason, Aristotle takes himself to be in need of conceptual resources beyond what he uses in the zoological texts by means of which he can give an account of this fragility, to describe it, diagnose its particularly pathological forms, and outline some treatment for them. We should read Aristotle's analysis of pathological political conditions as resulting from the particular vulnerability that attends the possession of *logos*, the human tendency to miscalculate, to mistake one's worth and the worth of others, to draw false distinctions, to insult, to wound, to be in error—a condition, Aristotle claims, in which humans spend most of their lives.[57] Thus, the *Politics* does not constitute a break with the study of animality so much as a recognition of the unique fragility of the properly human *topos*.[58] While the intimacy *logos* provides opens up possibilities for pleasures and community that appeared to him to be more vivid than any he found elsewhere in the animal world, so too, of necessity, it opens up possibilities of wounding and estrangement.

---

[55] See, for instance, Aristotle's justification for banishing "foul speech" (*aischrologia*) from the city, "for by speaking readily about some foul matter one comes closer to doing it" (7.17.1336b4, compare with the critique of mimesis in the *Republic*) and the discussion of Aristotle's critique of empty talk (*kenologia*) in Kelsey (2015).

[56] Aristotle presents the familial location of the earliest scenes of this intimacy in a zoological vein. It is those animals who have memory and thus maintain long-term relations with their offspring who are more political (*History of Animals* 588b28–589a). It is amongst these animals that intergenerational shared endeavors are made, and such an endeavor the *polis* must of necessity be.

[57] See e.g. *De anima* 427a29–b2.

[58] For one, this situation must be accomplished, rather than given. As Aristotle writes, while the *polis* is an end toward which humans tend by nature, still, particularly blessed is the human who founds a *polis* (1253a29–31).

6.4. Conclusion

For Aristotle, political life is a life in which we constantly encounter, in forms both intimate and estranging, near and distant, the lives of those who have gone before us and the lives of those who will come after through the memorializations of their affect, judgment, thought, and action by which a *polis* is structured and its *politeia* determined. That is to say, political life is haunted life. Perhaps it is *zōē* that bears the character of these hauntings, while *bios* emerges as signifying the effort to mark out one's own place amidst this sea. But if this is so, it is a limited place and one that also has been occupied by others and will be so again after one is gone. What, if anything, endures is the arrangement, and this too is subject to radical change and destruction.

Tracing the zoological dimensions of Aristotle's approach to the *polis* in the *Politics* highlights that it is the possibilities of interaction between individuals, the intensity of intimacy and endurance of these interactions—the manner in which they can become externalized and take on a life of their own—that proves to deeply and profoundly differentiate the character of human political life. That is, the zoological perspective with which Aristotle operates throughout the *Politics* suggests that humans are distinct in the *degree* to which they can share their lives with one another and that this capacity for sharing life colors all aspects of human life, not simply with respect to deliberation and the division of labor, but also in perceiving and eating and reproducing, in the most intimate terms of human embodiment. The thinness of human skin, for instance, goes under-employed when its perceptions are not submitted to collective interpretation and analysis and, in turn, the fineness of human distinctions, whether about the advantageous, the just, the fair, etc. is directly related to the thinness of human skin. Human bodies need not only mind, but the forms of dialogue and collective deliberation that can only be provided by other minds if their capacities are to be fully realized.

While Aristotle's ethico-political works explore this intimacy, as it is realized in the form of friendship, to some depth, they are also interested in the other side of the coin, in the forms of alienation that are opened precisely by this capacity for intimacy and sharing, the ways in which humans fail to properly value one another, and the effects of the perception (real or imagined) of this failure. What the Danaids know all too well, to return to Aeschylus' *Suppliants* for a moment, is that the success of their request for asylum hinges on the degree of attachment the Argives have to them, and they will use whatever forms of connection at their disposal (piety to Zeus, care for kin) to create this attachment. As the *topos* of shared perception, the *polis* reveals human being in its need for recognition, in its craving for intimacy, in its sense of placeless-ness and exile without them. Viewing these phenomena in the context of Aristotle's larger exploration of life and living beings allows us to see more clearly the effects of pathological political communities and invites us to appreciate the ecological character of Aristotle's *polis*-analysis. While the fragility of the human environment requires other considerations than Aristotle felt it necessary to include in his zoological works, this is not because these other habitats are invulnerable, but rather because they cannot operate differently than they do.[59]

The peculiarity of the human habitat lies not in its rejection of animality, then, but in its intensification of animal sociality, such that this sociality serves an ambient function, forming the features of the human landscape. Of course the other environmental aspects of the human landscape matter to Aristotle—oligarchies are most likely to flourish where the land is able to support horses (1321a8–9), for instance—but the interpenetration of these features is striking, at least to eyes trained to divide the human from the animal. That human relations come to take on these larger proportions, enduring beyond the lives of particular individuals, tells us something important about human political life, to be sure, but also tells us about how this life fits in to a larger vision of the cosmos. Its vulnerability, its potential to be tyrannized by the intensity of its intimacies and estrangements, to be blinded by its inability to judge its own worth and determine its standing amongst others, to misuse its possession of *logos* and its capacity for choice, locate the human political animal by reference to its precarity, its fragility, its potential for viciousness, and thus to its need for attention. In this, the anthropocentrism of Aristotle's *Politics* operates beyond any celebratory humanism.[60]

WORKS CITED

Agamben, G. (1998) *Homo Sacer: Sovereign Power and Bare Life*. Trans. D. Heller-Roazen. Stanford.
Agamben, G. (2013) *The Highest Poverty: Monastic Rules and Form-of-Life*. Trans. A. Kotsko. Stanford.
Arendt, H. (1958) *The Human Condition*. Chicago.

---

[59] See Pellegrin (2015) 41.
[60] Although it comes much closer to the mortal humanism Honig (2013) critiques and Leonard discusses in her contribution to this volume.

Aygün, Ö. (2017) *The Middle Included: Logos in Aristotle*. Evanston, IL.
Balme, D. (1987a) "The Place of Biology in Aristotle's Philosophy," in Gotthelf and Lennox (1987): 9–20.
Balme, D. (1987b) "Aristotle's Biology Was Not Essentialist," in Gotthelf and Lennox (1987): 291–312.
Balme, D. (1990) "Matter in the Definition: A Reply to G. E. R. Lloyd," in D. Devereux and P. Pellegrin (eds), *Biologie, Logique et Metaphysique chez Aristoteles*. Paris: 49–54.
Barker, E. (1959) *The Political Thought of Plato and Aristotle*. New York.
Bien, G. (1973) *Die Grundlegung der Politischen Philosophie bei Aristoteles*. Munich.
Bianchi, E. (2014) *The Feminine Symptom: Aleatory Matter in the Aristotelian Cosmos*. New York.
Brill, S. (2015) "Animality and Sexual Difference in the *Timaeus*," in J. Bell and M. Naas (eds), *Plato's Animals*. Bloomington, IN: 161–78.
Brill, S. (forthcoming a) *Aristotle on the Concept of Shared Life*. Oxford.
Brill, S. (forthcoming b) "Between Biography and Biology: Bios and Self-Knowledge in Plato's *Republic* and *Phaedrus*," in J. Ambury and A. German (eds), *Knowledge and Ignorance of Self in Platonic Philosophy*. Cambridge: 113–131.
Burian, P. (1991) *Aeschylus*: The Suppliants. Princeton.
Clark, S. (1975) *Aristotle's Man*. Oxford.
Code, A. (2015) "The 'Matter' of Sleep," in Ebrey (2015): 11–45.
Connell, S. (2001) "Toward an Integrated Approach to Aristotle as a Biological Philosopher," *The Review of Metaphysics* 55.2: 297–322.
Cooper, J. (1982) "Aristotle on Natural Teleology," in M. Schofield and M. Nussbaum (eds), *Language and Logos*. Cambridge: 197–222; repr. in J. Cooper (2004).
Cooper, J. (1990) "Political Animals and Civic Friendship," in Gunter Patzig (ed.), *Aristoteles Politik: Akten des XI. Symposium Aristotelicum*. Gottingen: 221–41.
Cooper, J. (2004) *Knowledge, Nature and the Good: Essays on Ancient Philosophy*. Princeton: 107–29.
Dubreuil, L. (2006) "Leaving Politics: *Bios*, *Zōē*, Life," *Diacritics* 36: 83–98.
DePew, D. (1995) "Humans and Other Political Animals in Aristotle's 'History of Animals.'" *Phronesis* 40.2: 156–81.
Derrida, J. (2009) *The Beast and the Sovereign, Volume 1*. Ed. M. Lisse, M.-L. Mallet, and G. Michaud, trans. G. Bennington. Chicago.
Ebrey, D. (ed.) (2015) *Theory and Practice in Aristotle's Natural Science*. Cambridge.
Finlayson, J. (2010) "Bare Life and Politics in Agamben's Reading of Aristotle." *The Review of Politics* 72.1: 97–126.
Föllinger, S. (ed.) (2009) *Was ist "Leben"? Aristoteles' Anschauungen zur Entstehungsweise und Funktion von Leben*. Stuttgart.
Frank, J. (2005) *A Democracy of Distinction: Aristotle and the Work of Politics*. Chicago.
Frank, J. (2015) "On *logos* and Politics in Aristotle," in Lockwood and Samaras (2015): 10–30.
Gelber, J. (2015a) "Aristotle on Essence and Habitat." *Oxford Studies in Ancient Philosophy* 48: 267–91.

Gelber, J. (2015b) "Are Facts about Matter Primitive?" in Ebrey (2015): 46–60.
Gotthelf, A. (1997) "The Elephant's Nose: Further Reflections on the Axiomatic Structure of Biological Explanation in Aristotle," in W. Kullmann and S. Föllinger (eds), *Aristotelische Biologie: Intentionen, Methoden, Ergebnisse*. Stuttgart: 85–96; repr. in Gotthelf (2012): 186–96.
Gotthelf, A. (2012) *Teleology, First Principles, and Scientific Method in Aristotle's Biology*. Oxford.
Gotthelf, A., and J. Lennox (eds) (1987) *Philosophical Issues in Aristotle's Biology*. Cambridge.
Grosz, E. (1994) *Volatile Bodies: Toward a Corporeal Feminism*. Bloomington, IN.
Grosz, E. (2005) *Time Travels: Feminism, Nature, Power*. Chapel Hill, NC.
Güremen, R. (2018) "In What Sense Exactly Are Human Beings More Political according to Aristotle?" *Philosophy and Society* 29.2 170–81.
Höffe, O. (1987) *Politische Gerechtigkeit*. Frankfurt.
Honig, B. (2013) *Antigone Interrupted*. Cambridge.
Irwin, T. (1988) *Aristotle's First Principles*. Oxford.
Johnson, M. R. (2006) *Aristotle on Teleology*. Oxford.
Johnson, M. R. (2015) "Aristotle's Architectonic Sciences," in Ebrey (2015): 163–86.
Kamp, A. (1985) *Die Politische Philosophie des Aristoteles und ihre Metaphysischen Grundlagen*. Freiburg.
Kelsey, S. (2015) "Empty Words," in Ebrey (2015): 199–216.
Keyt, D. (1989) "The Meaning of BIOS in Aristotle's *Ethics* and *Politics*." *Ancient Philosophy* 9: 15–21.
Keyt, D. (1991) "Three Basic Theorems in Aristotle's Politics," in Keyt and Miller (1991): 60–123.
Keyt, D., and F. Miller (eds) (1991) *A Companion to Aristotle's* Politics. Oxford.
Kullman, W. (1991) "Man as a Political Animal in Aristotle," in Keyt and Miller (1991): 94–117.
Kuriyama, S. (2002) *The Expressiveness of the Body and the Divergence of Greek and Chinese Medicine*. New York.
Labarrière, J-L. (1990) "De la Phronesis Animale," in D. Devereux and P. Pellegrin (eds), *Biologie, Logique et Métaphysique chez Aristoteles*. Paris: CNRS, 405–28.
Lennox, J. (1999) "Aristotle on the Biological Roots of Virtue: The Natural History of Natural Virtue," in J. Maienschein and M. Ruse (eds), *Biology and the Foundation of Ethics*. Cambridge.
Lennox, J. (2009) "*Bios, Praxis* and the Unity of Life," in Föllinger (2009): 000–000.
Lennox, J. (2010) "*Bios* and Explanatory Unity in Aristotle's Biology," in D. Charles (ed.), *Definition in Greek Philosophy*. Oxford: 329–55.
Leunissen, M. (2010) *Explanation and Teleology in Aristotle's Science of Nature*. Cambridge.
Leunissen, M. (2012) "Aristotle on Natural Character and Its Implications for Moral Development." *Journal of the History of Philosophy* 50: 507–30.

Leunissen, M. (2013) "'Becoming Good Starts with Nature': Aristotle on the Moral Advantages and the Heritability of Good Natural Character." *Oxford Studies in Ancient Philosophy* 44: 99–127.

Lloyd, G. (2013) "Aristotle on the Natural Sociability, Skills and Intelligence of Animals," in V. Harte and M. Lane (eds), *Politeia in Greek and Roman Philosophy*. Cambridge: 277–93.

Lockwood, T. (2014) "Competing Ways of Life and Ring Composition (NE x 6–8)," in R. Polansky (ed.), *The Cambridge Companion to Aristotle's Nichomachean Ethics*. Cambridge: 350–69.

Lockwood, T., and T. Samaras (eds) (2015) *Aristotle's Politics: A Critical Guide*. Cambridge.

Lord, C., trans. (1984) *Aristotle's Politics*. Chicago.

Lord, C. (1991) "Aristotle's Anthropology," in C. Lord and D. O'Connor (eds), *Essays on the Foundations of Aristotelian Political Science*. Berkeley: 49–73.

Miller, F. (1997) *Nature, Justice, and Rights in Aristotle's Politics*. Oxford.

Mogens, H. H. (2013) *Reflections on Aristotle's Politics*. Copenhagen.

Mulgan, R. (1974) "Aristotle's Doctrine That Man Is a Political Animal." *Hermes* 102.3: 438–45.

Mulhern, J. (2015) "*Politeia* in Greek Literature and Inscriptions and in Aristotle's *Politics*: Reflections on Translation and Interpretation," in Lockwood and Samaras (2015): 98–119.

Nussbaum, M. (2001) *Upheavals of Thought: The Intelligence of Emotions*. Cambridge.

Osborne, C. (2007) *Dumb Beasts and Dead Philosophers: Humanity and the Humane in Ancient Philosophy and Literature*. Oxford.

Pellegrin, P. (2015) "Is Politics a Natural Science?" in Lockwood and Samaras 2015): 27–45.

Riedel, M. (1975) *Metaphysik und Metapolitik, Studien zu Aristoteles und zur politischen Sprache der neuzeitlichen Philosophie*. Frankfurt.

Riesbach, D. (2016) *Aristotle on Political Community*. Cambridge.

Robinson, R. (1995) *Aristotle Politics: Books III and IV*. Oxford.

Ross, W. D. (1923) *Aristotle*. London.

Ross, W. D. (1964; orig. edn 1957) *Aristotelis politica*. Oxford: 1–269 (1252a1–1342b34).

Saxonhouse, A. (2015) "Aristotle on the Corruption of Regimes: Resentment and Justice," in Lockwood and Samaras (2015): 215–37.

Sharp, H. (2011) *Spinoza and the Politics of Renaturalization*. Chicago.

Sorabji, R. (1995) *Animal Minds and Human Morals: The Origins of the Western Debate*. Ithaca, NY.

Strauss, L. (1959) "What Is Political Philosophy?" in L. Strauss, *What Is Political Philosophy and Other Studies*. Glencoe, IL: 9–55.

Trott, A. (2013) *Aristotle on the Nature of Community*. Cambridge.

Yack, B. (1993) *The Problems of a Political Animal*. Berkeley.

Sounds of subjectivity or resonances of something other

Kristin Sampson

To speak in one's own voice is often considered as speaking with authenticity and autonomy.[1] It is associated with expressing one's true self and giving sound to the real identity of one's being. Such a notion of giving voice to one's true self—or subjectivity—by speaking autonomously in one's own voice and words is not new. It can be found in ancient Greece, for instance in Plato. However, how is the voice understood if the notion of an autonomous self has not yet been conceived? If there is no firmly established subjectivity to be found, how then is speaking and giving voice to words and sounds perceived? Moving back in time from Plato it is possible to find an understanding of the voice that differs from what can be read out of his dialogues. This chapter investigates an hypothesis that the voice carries different meanings in early Greek conceptions of corporeality, such as can be found for example in Homer, compared to what emerges later in antiquity, for instance in Plato. This postulation rests on certain assumptions about identity, which again relates to the body and soul.

Arriving at the time of Plato both the body and the soul have been conceived as components of a living human being. This makes possible a notion of identity where the voice, or speaking in one's own voice, can be regarded as related to the autonomy of the subject speaking. Moving a few centuries back in time, to the Homeric texts, a different picture appears. Neither the body nor the soul is conceptualized in relation to the living human being in the same way as can be found later, for instance in classical Athens. Instead we find what I call a *corporeality without body*. The question considered here thus concerns how this

---

[1] The paper on which this chapter is based was presented at the conference *Posthuman Antiquities* at New York University in November 2014. I would like to thank the audience there for helpful comments and suggestions, and also especially Sara Brill, Stein Arnold Hevrøy, and two anonymous readers for their valuable and fruitful comments to earlier drafts.

corporeality without body relates to conceptions of voice in the *Iliad* and the *Odyssey*: How is the voice comprehended if the body and the soul are not established as entities that can function as a ground for an autonomous identity? Is the voice then expressive at all, or does it resonate with something other?

The argument of this chapter places itself within a theoretical tradition that problematizes conceptions of the voice as a source of true self or an underlying identity of a subject. Jacques Derrida famously argues that the voice in the Western metaphysical tradition is posited as a source of self or identity. This is achieved within what he characterizes, and criticizes, as a "logocentrism which is also a phonocentrism: absolute proximity of voice and being."[2] Judith Butler, following Derrida's critical discussion of the conception of identity understood as a metaphysical substance or essence, develops a critique of gendered identity, including feminist projects working towards creating spaces for women to speak in their own authentic voice, thereby expressing their own true self.[3] The trouble with such projects is that they easily end up establishing a universalized gendered identity that participate in the tradition of Western phonocentrism. The arguments of both Derrida and Butler concerning voice have in recent years received critique. Adriana Cavarero questions Derrida's reading of the Western metaphysical tradition as phonocentric. Turning to history, Cavarero "reads the history of metaphysics as a devocalization of logos, instead of as a triumph of phonocentrism."[4] She endeavors "to theoretically redeem the *phone*."[5] Following Cavarero's discussion of Derrida, Annette Schlichter offers a similar argument against Butler. While she acknowledges Butler's criticism of representational feminism, where the voice is constructed as the representation of a true self, Schlichter contends that not only does Butler "miss out on theorizing the voice, she eventually presents us with voiceless bodies."[6] Both Cavarero and Schlichter argue in favor of a renewal of interest in, and new perspectives on, the voice. I will not go further into these theories in the present context. Cavarero's work resonates with my argument, for instance when she traces the "devocalization of logos" and the "subordination of speaking to thinking" back to Plato.[7] My aim, however, is to move further back in time within the context of Greek antiquity, to the Pre-Platonic context of Homer, in order to find a way of perceiving the world that is previous to a conception of voice as expressive of an underlying identity.

---

[2] Derrida (2016) 12.
[3] Butler (1990) 33–4.
[4] Cavarero (2005) 215.
[5] Cavarero (2005) 214.
[6] Schlichter (2011) 32.
[7] Cavarero (2005) 42–7.

First I will consider examples of voices in Homer. Then I will move on to the notion of corporeality without body, and show how this differs from notions of corporeality, identity, and voice in Plato, using examples from the *Protagoras*. Hopefully this will make some of the strange and foreign features of the voices in Homer resound.

7.1. Voices in Homer

There is a lot of literature from the past century that has studied speech in Homer.[8] This is not surprising, since there is a lot of speech in the *Iliad* and the *Odyssey*. Most of these commentaries examine questions concerning how the heroes in Homer are portrayed through their speech, looking, for example, at the relation between the speech of Achilles and the personality expressed.[9] My aim is another. In part I propose a critical look at assumptions that it is valid to depict the voice in Homer as expressive of a form of identity in a manner that is so obvious to our contemporary conceptions of self. Instead of looking at the words and speeches made for instance by Achilles, Agamemnon, or Odysseus, I consider mainly the most common word for the voice—*phōnē*—and examine how this is used in the *Iliad* and the *Odyssey*, and attributed not merely to human mortals, but also to gods and animals. As will be shown, the voice in Homer flows between all these, and also even further, sounding through nature, beyond the realm of the purely human.

According to Aristotle in *De anima*, several hundred years after Homer, it is only animate living beings that can possess a voice.[10] He relates this to the breath and the ability to breathe as a condition of having a voice. In the instances where the flow of the voice is said to be stopped at death, such a connection between being alive and having a voice seems plausible. Nonetheless, as we shall see, in Homer the voice (*phōnē*) is portrayed in a variety of guises, some of which may not fit into

---

[8] In speaking of Homer, I'm referring to the *Iliad* and the *Odyssey*. The complicated questions concerning authorship of these texts I will not go into in this article. For a discussion of the problems embraced by the so-called "Homeric question" see for example Richard Rutherford's book *Homer* (1996). Written about 800–700 BCE, these texts are here mainly studied as expressions of conceptions from this period. My perspective arises from an interest in questions concerning what the *Iliad* and the *Odyssey* can be said to reveal—not least through the language and words used—about the world of thought into which they were composed and written.
[9] e.g. Parry (1956); Cramer (1976); Friedrich and Redfield (1978); Griffin (1986); Villela-Petit and Gage (1998); Lardinois (2003).
[10] Aristotle, *De anima* 2.8.420b5–6.

this Aristotelian understanding of the voice. This becomes even more evident if we also consider Aristotle's claim that the voice is "a sound that means something (*psophos semantikos*)," as distinct from, for example, a cough.[11] Let me return to this after considering a few prominent aspects of the voice in Homer.

Phōnē is not the only word for the voice in the classical Greek language. There are other words that also denominate the voice both directly and in more indirectly related ways. In addition to *phōnē* there is for instance the poetical noun *ops*, which can be used of the voice in speaking, shouting, and lamenting, for example of the voice of the Sirens (*Odyssey* 12.192) or of Circe (*Odyssey* 10.221), and also of the song of the cicadas, and the voice of the lambs or of flutes. *Glōssa*, which is the word for the tongue, can also signify the words of the tongue or the words of the mouth, that is, language or speech. Another highly interesting word is *kleos*, renown or fame, which is created by the sonorous voice. The poetical expression *phthongē* (poetical for *phthongos*) indicates a clear sound, such as the voice, and is used of the voice of, for instance, the goddess Iris (*Iliad* 2.791), and also of humans, and animals. Interestingly, *legō* (say, speak) is never used in *Homer*, but only first in *Hesiod*.[12] Unfortunately there is not room to consider all these words in this present context. *Phōnē* is both the most common word for the voice in the classical Greek language and there are numerous examples of this word to be found in Homer, and in part for these reasons this chapter focuses mainly on this word.

Several aspects appear through the word *phōnē* in the *Iliad* and the *Odyssey*, of which several relate to the fluid character of the voice. The following three characteristics will be emphasized here: the flow of the voice, the voice as disguise, and fluid boundaries.

The first aspect of the voice in Homer that I would like to draw attention to is the flow of the voice. In Homer the voice of mortals is often described as flowing through them or from them. Death, sorrow, or strong emotions can stop the flow of the voice. When, for example, Athena in wrath kills Admetus' son Eumelus, his voice is said to be checked (*escheto phōnē*, *Iliad* 23.397).[13] Sorrow also curbs the voice of Antilochus when Menelaus tells him about the death of Patroclus: Antilochus' eyes are filled with tears, and the flow of his voice (*phōnē*)

---

[11] Aristotle, *De anima* 2.8.420b27–9. See also Svenbro (1993) 139.
[12] See e.g. Liddell and Scott, *Greek–English Lexicon*, on *legō*.
[13] Homer, *Iliad* 23.397: "Eumelus himself was hurled from out the car beside the wheel, and from his elbows and his mouth and nose the skin was stripped, and his forehead above his brows was bruised; and both his eyes were filled with tears and the flow of his voice (*phōnē*) was checked."

is checked (*Iliad* 17.696).[14] In the *Odyssey* as well, we hear how the voice of Penelope is stopped in sorrow when she learns (from Medon) that Telemachus has gone after his father.[15] Another example of the voice being stopped in the *Odyssey* is when the old woman recognizes Odysseus. This time it is the combination of joy and grief—that together constitute a strong emotional mixture—that checks the flow of her voice (*Odyssey* 19.472).[16] In all of these examples the voice is described as flowing in a stream that can be stopped, either temporarily by strong emotions, or permanently, at death. These examples also seem to be in accordance with the definition Aristotle gives of the voice as conditioned on belonging to an animate living being with the ability to breathe. It is not difficult to imagine the grief suddenly imposed upon Antilochus, and Penelope, as something that suddenly pauses their breath and consequently silences their voices. And when Eumelus' voice is said to be checked when he dies, he obviously also stops breathing.

So far voice, breath, and being alive appear to be woven together in accordance with the way Aristotle defines the voice. Neither are these examples necessarily at odds with a notion of the voice as an expression of subjectivity, and an autonomous, authentic form of identity. There are, however, other instances in Homer that complicate this picture. Let us turn to some examples that may illustrate the second aspect of the voice in Homer I would like to highlight: the voice as a disguise.

In Homer there are a number of descriptions of what may be called vocal disguises. Furthermore, these instances where the voice is used as a concealment are not presented as problematical. There does not seem to be an emphasis put upon the importance of speaking in one's own voice here, and neither is giving voice to an authentic and autonomous form of subjectivity presented as significant, and as something which consequently could make these vocal disguises appear as questionable. There is an important difference between Homer and Plato at this point. Turning to consider voice in Plato below, we will see that using the voice as a disguise in the way that can be found in Homer is described as a far more dubious affair.

---

[14] Homer, *Iliad* 17.696: "So spake he [Menelaus], and Antilochus had horror, as he heard that word. Long time was he speechless, and both his eyes were filled with tears, and the flow of his voice (*phōnē*) was checked." Throughout, citations use Murray's translations for the Loeb Classical Library.

[15] Homer, *Odyssey* 4.703–5: "So he spoke, and her knees were loosened where she sat, and her heart melted. Long time she was speechless, and both her eyes were filled with tears, and the flow of her voice (*phōnē*) was checked."

[16] Homer, *Odyssey* 19.472: "Then upon her soul came joy and grief in one moment, and both her eyes were filled with tears and the flow of her voice (*phōnē*) was checked."

Nonetheless, also in Homer the voice is presented as part of the appearance that makes someone recognizable. For example, in the *Odyssey*, when the old woman in his house in Ithaca is on the verge of recognizing Odysseus, she says: "Many sore-tired strangers have come hither, but I declare that never yet have I seen any man so like another as thou in form, and in voice (*phōnēn*), and in feet art like Odysseus" (*Odyssey* 19.381). However, even if the voice can make someone recognizable, it does not thereby follow that it is expressive of an inner or underlying substance or foundation. In Homer there is no equivalent to the emphasis that can be found later, for instance in Plato, on the importance of speaking in one's own voice. On the contrary, speaking in the voice of another is not necessarily portrayed negatively in Homer. Rather, it is displayed several times as an ingenious exertion. One famous example is when Menelaus in the *Odyssey* speaks to Helen about how she, when the Trojan horse came to Troy with all of the Danaans inside, tried to lure them out by speaking in the voices of the wives of the chieftains hiding within (*Odyssey* 4.279).[17] Helen is not criticized for her ingenuity in trying to lure the chieftains out. Quite the reverse, Menelaus tells her how it almost worked.[18]

Furthermore, to disguise oneself in the voice of another is not reserved for Helen or the mortals. The Greek gods are typically portrayed in the guise of various appearances—of both form and voice—in Homer. They frequently clothe themselves in the voices of mortals. Just to mention a few examples: Poseidon comes "forth from the deep sea, in the likeness of the Argive seer Calchas, both in form and untiring voice (*phōnēn*)" (*Iliad* 13.45). Athena appears in the form and voice of Phoenix, son of Amyntor (*Iliad* 17.555).[19] Apollo dresses himself in the voice of a mortal when he comes forward sounding as Lycaon, son of Priam (*Iliad* 20.81).[20] In these examples the voice emerges as related to a manner of appearance, not to the expression of some sort of true identity or subjectivity. When

---

[17] Homer, *Odyssey* 4.279: "Thrice didst thou go about the hollow ambush, trying it with thy touch, and thou didst name aloud the chieftains of the Danaans by their names, likening thy voice (*phōnēn*) to the voices of the wives of all the Argives."

[18] And, in fact she is not blamed for siding with Priam either, as this is put down to the influence of some divinity.

[19] Homer, *Iliad* 17.555: "Athene...enwrapping herself in a lurid cloud, entered the throng of the Danaans, and urged on each man. First to hearten him she spake to Atreus' son, valiant Menelaus, for he was nigh to her, likening herself to Phoenix, in form and untiring voice (*phōnēn*)."

[20] Homer, *Iliad* 20.81: "he likened his own voice (*phōnēn*) to that of Lycaon, son of Priam. In his likeness spake unto Aeneas the son of Zeus, Apollo." And Athena again (*Iliad* 22.27) approaches Hector "in the likeness of Deiphobus both in form and untiring voice (*phōnēn*)."

for example Athena appears as Phoenix she neither looks nor sounds as herself, but is explicitly said to come into sight and sound in a specific form, namely that of Phoenix. All of these three Olympian gods appear and speak in the guise of some mortal.

It is hardly a form of authenticity that is expressed in these examples. In the vocal disguises the point is not that the voice indicates a form of genuine or underlying identity. What matters is to give an impression on the listener that achieves a specific goal or promotes a certain action. The voice is thus inscribed within a different purpose and infused with another meaning than to give sound to a subjectivity. Furthermore, to use the voice as a disguise is not portrayed as problematic or despicable. It is not depicted as threatening towards an autonomous self that somehow lies beneath or behind the disguise. The reason for this, as I will argue, is that the conception of such an underlying form of identity is not yet conceived in Homer.

The voice as a disguise does not necessarily stand in contrast to Aristotle's definition of *phōnē* as belonging to animate beings in possession of breath. Examples can, however, be found in Homer, where not only mortal humans and gods are portrayed as speaking, but also animals and even entities that do not fall into an Aristotelian understanding of what counts as animate being. With this we have arrived at the third characteristic of the voices in Homer which this chapter considers: fluid boundaries.

The fluidity of the boundaries between different entities within the world of Homer is expressed in various way. The border between the immortal divinities and the mortals, which include not only humans but even animals, is in a certain way traversed through the manifestations of the undying divinities within the fleeting realm of transience where the lives of the mortals are unfolded.[21] The immortal gods enter into and interfere with the lives of the mortals, and they are not even invulnerable to attacks from them. They may be wounded by strikes and weapons, such as for example both Aphrodite and Ares are injured by the mortal hero Diomedes (*Iliad* Book 5). Moreover, the divine gods of Olympus do not merely disguise themselves as mortal men and women. They can also appear in the guise of animals, such as Athena and Apollo did, when they sat themselves in a lofty oak in the likeness of two birds to watch the fight between Hector and Ajax (*Iliad* 7.25–62). This shows that the boundaries

---

[21] A typical characterization of humans in Homer is as mortals: *broteios*. The main distinction between gods and humans is connected to mortality. But humans are of course not the only transient beings. Everything that lives will perish.

between not only gods and humans, but also between gods and animals are in a certain sense fluid.

When it comes to carrying a voice—*phōnē*—this is not reserved for gods and mortal humans in Homer. Also animals, monsters, and even meat and natural phenomena are attributed with voice. In the *Iliad* (*Iliad* 17.111) there is a description of the voices of dogs and men in an attack at the battle field, where both "dogs and men drive from a fold with spears and shouting [voices] (*phōnē*)." In the *Odyssey* the sorceress Circe changes the men into pigs, giving them not only the visual appearance of swine, but also the voices (*phōnēn*) of these animals (*Odyssey* 10.239).[22] Also in the *Odyssey*, the voice of the terrible monster Scylla is described as the voice (*phōnē*) of a new-born whelp (*Odyssey* 12.86).[23] She herself is a terrible monster, but her voice comes out—deceptively—as the voice of a puppy. That is to say, the impression Scylla gives through her audible resonance differs from the horrible, dangerous creature that she is. *Phōnē* is even used of the screams from roasting meat. When Odysseus and his men steal and cook the cows of Helius, "the hides crawled, the flesh, both roast and raw, bellowed upon the spits, and there was a lowing as of kine (*boōn d' hōs gigneto phōnē*)" (*Odyssey* 12.396). The word used of the screaming meat, which is attributed with voice, is *phōnē*. With this example, we are moving away from Aristotle's definition of the voice as something belonging to living beings in possession of breath.

Even natural phenomena, such as the waves of the sea, the blazing of a fire, or the roaring of the wind, are said to resound with voices akin to those of men raging into battle:

> Not so loudly bellows the wave of the sea upon the shore, driven up from the deep by the dread blast of the North Wind, nor so loud is the roar of blazing fire in the glades of a mountain when it leapeth to burn the forest, nor doth the wind shriek so loud amid the high crests of the oaks—the wind that roareth the loudest in its rage—as then was the cry of Trojans and Achaeans, shouting in terrible wise (*phōnē deinon*) as they leapt upon each other. (*Iliad* 14.400)

The sound of waves, the wind, and the fire are here likened to the terrible sound of the voices of warriors screaming in battle. An even more literal and striking example in Homer of voice being ascribed to what in a contemporary context would be considered a natural entity is the river

---

[22] Homer, *Odyssey* 10.239: "Now when she had given them the potion, and they had drunk it off, then she presently smote them with her wand, and penned them in the sties. And they had the heads, and voice (*phōnēn*), and bristles, and shape of swine."

[23] Homer, *Odyssey* 12.86: "Therein dwells Scylla, yelping terribly. Her voice is indeed but as the voice (*phōnē*) of a new-born whelp, but she herself is an evil monster, nor would anyone be glad at sight of her, no, not though it were a god that met her."

Scamander. In Book 21 of the *Iliad*, Achilles battles with the river Scamander, also called Xanthus. Achilles is nearly defeated by the river and has to be saved due to the interference by Hera, Athena, and Hephaestus. Scamander rises up and, enraged, chases after Achilles following the hero's slaying of Asteropaeus, who is a son of Pelegon, whose father is the wide-flowing Axius, another river. The river is said to send forth "a voice from out the deep eddy (*chōsamenos prosephe potamos bathydinēs*)" (*Iliad* 21.212). Although *phōnē* is not used at this point in the text, Scamander most assuredly possesses a voice with which he exchanges words with Achilles over several pages in Book 21.

Several of these examples complicate Aristotle's characterization of the voice—*phōnē*—as specific to animate living beings who breathe and as "a sound that means something." Neither the roasting meat, the waves of the sea, the blazing fire, the roaring wind, or the river can be said to possess living breath. Nor do all of these voices constitute what he calls a sound that means something. In the examples with the voices of animals, as well—the new-born whelp and the swine—they can hardly be said to speak meaningful words. In Homer *phōnē* embraces sound more broadly, as it appears, in that it is attributed both to entities devoid of breath and to sounds that do not express meaning.

Or, perhaps, this should rather be considered the other way around. It could be that, in Homer, animals, wind, fire, the sea, and even roasting meat are not devoid of breath and meaning. Instead the world may be depicted through the Homeric poems as living in a broad sense, breathing and full of voice. Conceivably, animals, divinities, what we would call forces of nature, in addition to human mortals, all speak and express sounds that mean something. The personified portrayal of the river Scamander could then be considered as a demonstration of such a world where even what for us—and Aristotle—would be a non-living entity is given a voice with which to speak words that carry some form of meaningfulness.

Moreover, these voices that resound through the *Iliad* and the *Odyssey* are hard to inscribe into a strict understanding of speech and voice as something belonging to a subjectivity that expresses its autonomy or authenticity through words said. The river Scamander, for instance, is not easily identified as just a particular river. On the one hand he is the concrete and specific river flowing near Troy, but on the other he is also a river god less specifically connected to this distinct river. The river exchanging words with Achilles in Book 21 of the *Iliad* is not even called by a single name, but two—Scamander and Xanthus—and these names are used interchangeably. This talking river may stand as an image of the three aspects of voice in Homer that are emphasized in this chapter, namely the flow of the voice, vocal disguises, and fluid boundaries. As river Scamander is, literally, a floating speaker of a stream of words, giving voice with a fluid, floating voice. In order to speak the river has to adorn himself "in the semblance of a man (*aneri eisamenos*)" (*Iliad* 21.213). Still, even in the resemblance of a man Scamander is nonetheless a river speaking and raging against Achilles. In the battle between the two Scamander fights with water and torrents, as a mighty river of raging streams flooding beyond the riverbanks and onto the plain. In the very combination of speaking in the semblance of a man and raging as a river with gushing waters in the battle Scamander reveals the fluid boundaries between man and nature in a forceful way.

The aim of drawing attention to these three aspects—the flow of the voice, the voice as a disguise, and the fluid boundaries that the voices in Homer indicate—is to argue that *phōnē* in Homer gives sound to something other than a subjectivity. In order to clarify this let us consider the form of corporeality to which the voice in Homer belongs, namely what I call a corporeality without body.

7.2. Corporeality without body

It can be argued that the *Iliad* and the *Odyssey* belong to a time that is prior to the physical body.[24] The very words for "the body" and "the soul," used as a description of a living human being, do not yet exist in Homer in the way they later can be found, for example in Plato. One of the first to point this out was Bruno Snell in his book *The Discovery of the Mind: The Greek Origins of European Thought* (*Die Entdeckung des Geistes*) first published in 1946 and first translated to English in 1953. Snell's seminal work has been extensively discussed since it was published. I agree with those who consider Snell's contribution significant and valuable.[25] According to Hermann Fränkel, there is yet no clear distinction between the corporeal and the spiritual and emotional aspects of the living human being in Homer: "[t]here are no boundaries, there is no cleavage between feeling and the corporeal situation."[26] As James M. Redfield claims: "Homer is pre-Cartesian and, for that matter, pre-

---

[24] Previously I have presented a similar argument in two articles: "*Sōma, technē* and the Somatechnics of Sexual Difference" (2013) and "Beyond the Subject: Early Greek Conceptions of Corporeality" (2015).
[25] Such as for example E. R. Dodds (1951), Hermann Fränkel (1975), James M. Redfield (1975), Michael Clarke (1999), and Brooke Holmes (2010).
[26] Fränkel (1975) 79.

Socratic. He does not make a sharp distinction between body and soul."[27] Or, as Michael Clarke writes: "Homeric man does not *have* a mind, rather his thoughts and consciousness are as inseparable a part of his bodily life as are movement and metabolism... [B]y the same token he will not *have* a body."[28] As Brooke Holmes puts it: "[t]he physical body is something new in the late archaic and classical periods."[29] Furthermore, this physical body is something that has become so entrenched in modern Western culture, as she points out, "that it is difficult to conceive of its absence."[30] What we would call a living body today, and consequently can regard as an entity, is not even gathered together by a single name in Homer.

This lack of a conception of an underlying entity within the living human being makes it difficult to postulate a subject. The Homeric conception of corporeality thus points to what lies outside of and is previous to an understanding of corporeality where the living body is conceived as *sōma*, that is to say, as a separate and generalized entity that can be grasped as an object. It is previous to a corporeality with a body. Instead this view opens itself up to a comprehension of variety and difference without an underlying substance or being. It represents a conception of a human existence that is beyond the distinction between body and soul, and thus also beyond the subject. Instead of a human being with a body and a soul that expresses itself in some form or fashion, we thus find in Homer a corporeality without body.[31] The concept of corporeality without body expresses a corporeality without an underlying entity or substance that persists through change or that binds together the various ways of perceiving, moving, and acting. The way in which this corporeality is expressed in Homer resides beyond a dualistic conception of body and soul. It is oriented toward concrete ways of being in the world, is inherently embedded in individual situations, and is expressed through a wealth of concrete symbols, as for instance Snell points out.[32] This is the corporeality in terms of which the voice in Homer should be understood.

The conception of corporeality in Homer is in a historical sense previous to a dualistic conception of body and soul. This should not, however, be understood in terms of postulating a progress from what

---

[27] Redfield (1975) 175.   [28] Clarke (1999) 115.   [29] Holmes (2010) xi.
[30] Holmes (2010) 4.
[31] This notion is in part inspired what Mario Perniola (2001) in *Ritual Thinking: Sexuality, Death, World* terms *ritual without myth*, which is meant to point to the demystification of myth typical of Roman religion. I describe this inspiration in the (2015) article "Beyond the Subject: Early Greek Conceptions of Corporeality."
[32] Snell (1982) 1 writes that in Homer "[a]bstractions are as yet undeveloped, while immediate sense perceptions furnish it with a wealth of concrete symbols."

could be described as a more primitive to a more sophisticated conception of corporeality. The point is rather that a conception of a corporeality without body differs from a conception of corporeality where the body is seen as a separate and generalized entity. Going back in time to Homer thus opens up a different way of understanding corporeality, namely one that is beyond a dualistic conception of body and soul. This does not necessarily mean that a conception of corporeality without body is forever lost to us. Revisiting the conceptual world of Homer may hopefully, by representing a sort of outside to conceptions of selfhood, subjectivity, and body that belong to our time, contribute to open up possibilities for new and fruitful ways of conceptualizing corporeality beyond or without a body.

In order to further illuminate the Homeric conception of voice and the corporeality to which it belongs, it can be contrasted with conceptions of the voice later in antiquity, for instance in Plato. At the time of Plato, the distinction between body and soul as separate and underlying entities that belongs to the living human being, and the notion of the soul as a separate entity within the living body, are firmly established. The emergence of the subject is conditioned on the materialization of the physical body, and the physical body can be seen to be materialized both within the thinking of the Presocratic philosophers (and their inquiry into nature) and within the development of classical Greek medicine.[33] Both these areas of inquiry can be located after Homer (around the fifth century BCE). This makes possible a new conception of the self as a separate, internal entity that is seen as an underlying foundation for the identity of the living person. It makes possible the conception of a subject.

One of the implications of the late archaic and classical conceptions of the self, is the notion that the voice can express such an underlying identity. In Plato, for example, we find the voice—*phōnē*—depicted as an expression of what might be called a subjectivity or an autonomous self. This is an understanding of the voice that differs significantly from what can be found in the Homeric texts. To illustrate this claim, let us consider briefly just one passage from one of Plato's dialogues, namely the *Protagoras*.

At *Protagoras* 347c–348a Socrates describes the difference between the ones who speak in their own voices and the ones who do not, quite explicitly. In this quite short passage the word *phōnē* is, strikingly, used five times.[34] According to the view expressed by Socrates, to be a citizen

---

[33] See e.g. Holmes (2010) 4.
[34] This is the passage in Plato's *Protagoras* (347c–348a) where *phōnē* is used five times: "For it seems to me that arguing about poetry is comparable to the wine-parties of common

involves the ability to speak in one's own voice. As Charles Griswold puts it, "Socrates here sketches an ideal and tells us to model ourselves on it. The ideal is that of a person who relies on his or her own voice."[35] This involves speaking on behalf of oneself, and in this sense giving voice to one's own true self, which in turn implies that such a true self—or identity—is established. The voice is thus conceived as something that can express an underlying or internal entity: a subjectivity that ideally should be authentic and autonomous. Again, as Griswold claims: "We may say that Socrates is recommending the virtues of autonomy."[36] Being able to speak on behalf of oneself—autonomously—was crucial for a political citizen in the Athenian democracy. One could argue that the ideal of the Athenian man is portrayed in the *Protagoras* as being autonomous with a voice that expresses the true self of the speaker. He is *autophonous*.[37]

Those placed in opposition to this autophonous Athenian man open themselves up to listening to for instance "the extraneous voice (*allotrian phōnēn*) of the flute" played by the flute-girl (*Protagoras* 347d). The sound of the voice of the flute—and also the harp, as well as the girls playing and dancing—will not, however, be present among the true gentlemen who speak in their own voices. These other, extraneous voices, as well as femininity, personified through the playing and dancing girls, have, as it appears, no place among the autophonous men who give voice to their own true self.

---

market-folk. These people, owing to their inability to carry on a familiar conversation over their wine by means of their own voices (*tēs heautōn phōnēs*) and discussions—such is their lack of education—put a premium on flute-girls by hiring the extraneous voice (*allotrian phōnēn*) of the flute at a high price, and carry on their intercourse by means of its utterance (*tēs ekeinōn phōnēs*). But where the party consists of thorough gentlemen who have had a proper education, you will see neither flute-girls nor dancing-girls nor harp-girls, but only the company contenting themselves with their own conversation (*tēs hautōn phōnēs*), and none of these fooleries and frolics—each speaking and listening decently in his turn, even though they may drink a great deal of wine. And so a gathering like this of ours, when it includes such men as most of us claim to be, requires no extraneous voices (*allotrias phōnēs*), not even of the poets, whom one cannot question on the sense of what they say; when they are adduced in discussion we are generally told by some that the poet thought so and so, and by others, something different, and they go on arguing about a matter which they are powerless to determine. No, this sort of meeting is avoided by men of culture, who prefer to converse directly with each other, and to use their own way of speech (*en tois heautōn logois*) in putting one another by turns to the test."

[35] Griswold (1999) 288.
[36] Griswold (1999) 303. In a note to this page Griswold argues against Gregory Vlastos and claims that the concept of autonomy is not post-Platonic.
[37] Marco V. Garcia Quintela (2009) 258 in his article "The Phonological Politics of Plato and the Myth of *Protagoras*" uses the expression "the autophonous" of these men who express their own true self authentically.

In the *Protagoras* the famous sophists visiting as guests at the house of Callias are marked as foreign and different from the autonomous Athenian man in part by the sound of their voices: their *phōnai*. It is not, however, the content of their words that is described but the more purely auditory, phonetic aspects of their voices. We are told how Protagoras is enchanting his listeners with his voice (*kēlōn tēi phōnēi*) like Orpheus, and hear of the booming voice (*phōnēs bombos*) of Prodicus (*Protagoras* 315a, 316a).[38] In a way, what is accentuated in these descriptions is what Cavarero calls the imperfection or dead weight of the voice, something which in turn would further distance the sophists from "the realm of truth."[39] The sound of their enchanting and booming voices is emphasized, and also their foreignness in terms of their non-Attic dialects: Hippias with his Elean dialect, Prodicus with his central Ionic dialect, and Protagoras with his eastern Ionic dialect. The word *phōnē* can in fact also mean "dialect."[40] Understood as dialect the voice functions as an indicator of political identity, and in the *Protagoras* several delineations are marked by the phonetic sound of the voice or dialect. There is the one between Greeks and the non-Greek barbarians. This would be what some have called the Panhellenic scope of normal, or traditional, Greek perception. At *Protagoras* 341c the expression "barbaric dialect (*phōnēi barbarōi*)" is used, and this is in accordance with a common Greek way of delineating themselves from non-Greeks, namely by reference to language, or to put it in a different way: by indication of their manner of speech or voice: *phōnē*. The phonetic differences of the dialects— *phōnai*—used by the sophists present in the house of Callias mainly marks a demarcation between Athenians and non-Athenians.[41] The sophists differ from the autonomous autophonous Athenian citizen who speaks authentically and on behalf of himself in other ways, as well. They notoriously lend their voices to the views and words of others, for money, and they can give voice to many different and differing arguments. Instead of autonomous and autophonous, the sophists are rather heteronomous and allophonous.[42] As such they appear as feminine to a certain extent, more like women, or even prostitutes.[43]

---

[38] I've previously written about these audible characteristics in the *Protagoras* in the (2017) article "Visible and Audible Movement in the *Protagoras*."
[39] Cavarero (2005) 42.
[40] At *Protagoras* 341b, for instance, there is mention of the dialect—*phōnēn*—of Simonides; at *Protagoras* 341c-e there is mention of the Lesbian Pittacus' foreign dialect (*phōnēn*); and at *Protagoras* 346d-e there is mention of Mytilean dialect (*phōnēi*).
[41] See e.g. Quintela (2009) 255 and 256.
[42] Griswold (1999) 303 explicitly calls the sophists heteronomous.
[43] Quintela (2009) 258 indicates the distinction between autophony and allophony in terms of another distinction, namely one between humans—*anthrōpoi*—and men: *andres*.

This portrayal in Plato's *Protagoras* of the difference between the autonomous, autophonous Athenian man who expresses his own true self through his voice and the sophists who lend their voices to express the interests of others, illustrates a difference compared to what can be found in Homer. When we arrive at the time of Plato the conception of an autonomous self exists. Rather than a corporeality without body, such as can be found in Homer, in Plato the distinction between body and soul is thought, also for the living human being. Corporeality in Plato can be expressed as a body (*sōma*) and as something that is distinct from the soul (*psychē*). The notion of the soul as a form of inner core, self, or subjectivity, that can be expressed through the voice in an autophonous way, expressing the true self of the speaker, thus can be found in Plato in a way that it cannot in Homer.

7.3. Concluding remarks

This chapter endeavors to display how the voice—*phōnē*—appears differently in the pre-Platonic context of Homer compared to how it does a few centuries later, for instance in Plato. This relates to how, at the time of Plato, a new conception of an autonomous self—or subject—that can be expressed through an autophonous voice, has been conceptualized. Both these notions—of an autonomous subjectivity and an autophonous voice expressing such a self—are absent from the Homeric texts. Instead in Homer flowing voices run through the speakers like rivers of breath that, at least for the living, can be stopped at death. To speak in the voice of another is not portrayed as dishonourable. There is a heterophony of voices resounding from mortals and immortals, animals, and even natural forces. In the impersonal voices of the bellowing waves of the sea, the roar of a blazing forest-fire, and the howling wind there is not much personal autonomy being expressed.

What, then, is the sound of the voice previous to the conception of a subject that can express an autonomous self through the voice? Something other than subjectivity resonates through the voices in Homer. This something other emerges in a variety of concrete manifestations that make me hesitate to pin them down to a specific thing or force, with

---

Humans—*anthrōpoi*—are clearly inferior, "both vulgar and common. They are incapable of being authentically themselves." These are the allophones, and they are "occasionally women, prostitutes or slaves." In the *Protagoras* the sophists, who appear as allophones, are thus implicitly compared to women, slaves, and prostitutes.

a suspicion that this would take away some of the valuable foreign and strange aspects of these ancient texts. The aim is not to argue that we should start thinking like the Homeric Greeks. That would, of course, be an impossible task and a futile mission. However, in relation to a project that aims to create new ways of thinking about subjectivity, identity, masculinity, femininity, and the human, there is a need to find an outside to the conceptions that are all too familiarly embedded within our own times and cultures. What I do propose is that listening to the foreignness of the voices as they resound in Homer can make us both hear our own voices more clearly, and also—perhaps—help us to create new ways of making our voices flow.

WORKS CITED

Aristotle (1957) *On the Soul. Parva Naturalia. On Breath*. Trans. W. S. Hett. Loeb Classical Library. Cambridge, MA.
Butler, J. (1990) *Gender Trouble*. New York.
Cavarero, A. (2005) *For More Than One Voice: Toward a Philosophy of Vocal Expression*. Stanford.
Clarke, M. (1999) *Flesh and Spirit in the Songs of Homer: A Study of Words and Myths*. Oxford.
Cramer, O. C. (1976) "Speech and Silence in the *Iliad*," *The Classical Journal* 71: 300–4.
Derrida, J. (2016) *Of Grammatology*. Baltimore.
Dodds, E. R. (1951) *The Greeks and the Irrational*. Berkeley.
Fränkel, H. (1975) *Early Greek Poetry and Philosophy: A History of Greek Epic, Lyric, and Prose to the Middle of the Fifth Century*. Oxford.
Friedrich, P., and J. Redfield. (1978) "Speech as a Personality Symbol: The Case of Achilleus," *Language* 54: 263–88.
Griffin, J. (1986) "Homeric Words and Speakers," *The Journal of Hellenic Studies* 106: 36–57.
Griswold, C. L. Jr (1999) "Relying on Your Own Voice: An Unsettled Rivalry of Moral Ideals in Plato's *Protagoras*," *The Review of Metaphysics* 53: 283–307.
Holmes, B. (2010) *The Symptom and the Subject: The Emergence of the Physical Body in Ancient Greece*. Princeton.
Homer (1995) *Odyssey, Volumes I and II*. Trans. A. T. Murray, rev. G. E. Dimock. Loeb Classical Library. Cambridge, MA.
Homer. (1985) *Iliad, Volume II*. Trans. A. T. Murray. Loeb Classical Library. Cambridge, MA.
Homer. (1988) *Iliad, Volume I*. Trans. A. T. Murray. Loeb Classical Library. Cambridge, MA.
Lardinois, A. P. M. H. (2003) "The Wrath of Hesiod: Angry Homeric Speeches and the Structure of Hesiod's *Works and Days*," *Arethusa* 36: 1–20.

Liddell, H. G., and R. Scott. (1996) *Greek–English Lexicon*. Oxford.
Parry, A. (1956) "The Language of Achilles," *Transactions and Proceedings of the American Philological Association* 84: 124–34.
Perniola, M. (2001) *Ritual Thinking: Sexuality, Death, World*. New York.
Plato. (1990) *Laches, Protagoras, Meno, Euthydemus*. Trans. W. R. M. Lamb. Loeb Classical Library. Cambridge, MA.
Quintela, M. V. G. (2009) "The Phonological Politics of Plato and the Myth of *Protagoras*," *Metis* 7: 247–76.
Redfield, J. M. (1975) *Nature and Culture in the* Iliad: *the Tragedy of Hector*. Chicago.
Rutherford, R. (1996) *Homer*. Cambridge.
Sampson, K. (2013) "*Sōma, technē* and the Somatechnics of Sexual Difference," *Somatechnics* 3: 233–49.
Sampson, K. (2015) "Beyond the Subject: Early Greek Conceptions of Corporeality," *Ágalma* 30: 58–65.
Sampson, K. (2017) "Visible and Audible Movement in the Protagoras," in O. Pettersson and V. Songe-Møller (eds), *Plato's Protagoras: Essays on the Confrontation of Philosophy and Sophistry. Philosophical Studies Series*. Cham, Switzerland: 199–213.
Schlichter, A. (2011) "Do Voices Matter? Vocality, Materiality, Gender Performativity," *Body & Society* 17.1: 31–5.
Snell, B. (1982) *The Discovery of the Mind in Greek Philosophy and Literature*. New York.
Svenbro, J. (1993) *Phrasikleia: An Anthropology of Reading in Ancient Greece*. Ithaca, NY.
Villela-Petit, M., and J. C. Gage (1998) "The Might of Words: A Philosophical Reflection on 'The Strange Death of Patroklos,'" *Diogenes* 46: 101–13.

8 Shared life as chorality in Schiller, Hölderlin, and Hellenistic poetry

Mark Payne

This paper identifies a form of relationality with non-human life that I call chorality as it is staged in the theoretical poetics of Schiller, Hölderlin's novel *Hyperion*, and the three major Hellenistic poets. Chorality describes the sense that human beings have of belonging to organismic life as a whole by virtue of the way in which other life forms engage their sense of being subjects of life through a mode of interpellation: how they feel called upon to recognize themselves as beings at the center of a life world in which they participate by virtue of their organismic life, and how this participation has the form of participation in a chorus.

Schiller and Hölderlin make the recovery of chorality a central task of sentimental poetry, and it is the contours of a shared project with the Hellenistic poets that I want to trace. Schiller points to the Hellenistic period as a moment in the history of poetics in which the apprehension of a loss of naturalness in human sociality impels its poets to adopt the roles of "nature's *witnesses* and *avengers*" for their contemporaries,[1] and this, he argues, is the central task of the sentimental poet in any period. What, then, can Schiller's poetics tell us about Hellenistic poetry, what in Hellenistic poetry seems, after Schiller, commensurate with our own post-natural condition, and what can we learn from the means by which Schiller, Hölderlin, and the Hellenistic poets seek to stage chorality for their readers?

Schiller's essay "On Naïve and Sentimental Poetry" begins with a reflection on the relictualized forms of life that tantalize a modern European:

There are moments in our lives when we extend a kind of love and tender respect toward nature in plants, minerals, animals, and landscapes, as well as to human nature in children, in the customs of country folk and the primitive world. We do this, not because it makes us feel good and not even because it satisfies our intellect and taste (in both cases the reverse can often occur), but merely *because*

---

[1] Schiller (1998) 193–6. Emphasis original.

it is nature. Every more refined human being not utterly devoid of feeling experiences this when he wanders about in the open, when he resides in the country or lingers at the monuments of ancient times, in short, whenever in the midst of man-made contexts and situations he is taken aback by the sight of nature in its simplicity. It is this interest, often elevated to a need, that lies at the bottom of our many fondnesses for flowers and animals, for simple gardens, for walks, for the land and its inhabitants, for many an artifact of remote antiquity, and the like.[2]

This opening is a translation of the experience of walking into the form of an essay, much as Schiller's poem "Der Spaziergang" is the translation of the experience of walking into the form of a loco-descriptive poem. The subject of Schiller's essay is accustomed to leave his own place and wander in the open air, where he lingers among the relics of ancient times, whether ontogenetic (childhood) or phylogenetic (country people and the monuments of antiquity). What he is looking for in these relics is a naturalness in shared life that is no longer present in contemporary forms of human sociality. But if such subjects of modernity as the person of the essay are to emerge from their errancy, so that they might not merely attest to the naturalness of others, but have naturalness be a possibility of their own form of life, they must emulate the Greeks by not merely going into Nature, but by allowing beings as a whole to surround them once they are there:

> Let nature surround you like a lovely idyll [*Sie umgebe dich wie eine liebliche Idylle*], in which again and again you find the way back to yourself from the aberrations of art and gather courage and new confidence about the course of life, so that the flame of the ideal, so easily extinguished in life's storms, is rekindled in your heart. Recall the beauty of nature surrounding the ancient Greeks [*Wenn man sich der schönen Natur erinnert, welche die alten Griechen umgab*...]. Consider how confidently this people was able, under its serendipitous sky, to live with free nature; consider how very much nearer to the simplicity of nature lay its manner of thinking, its way of feeling, its mores, and what a faithful copy of this is provided by the works of its poets.[3]

Adopting a disposition to be surrounded is the first step in the recovery of naturalness, and what it affords is the opportunity to experience shared life with beings as a whole in precisely the way that it is afforded by the pastoral idyll. It is a gateway to the form of being surrounded that I have called chorality insofar as it allows human beings to understand their relationship to beings as a whole as participation in the larger

---

[2] Schiller (1998) 179. Emphasis original.
[3] Schiller (1998) 193. Translation slightly adapted.

community of subjects of life, which is what the naturalness of Greek sociality consisted in. It is an orienting experience of shared life that contrasts with a labyrinthine errancy in merely human sociality. Being surrounded by Nature is how you find your way back to yourself from the aberrations of an artificial form of life such that naturalness might take hold of you, and repossess you as a subject of life in the plural.

Later in the essay, Schiller regrets that the pastoral idyll typically places behind human beings the goal of naturalness toward which it is supposed to lead them, and so inspires the sad feeling of loss, rather than the joyous feeling of hope.[4] This is its risk, and, as we shall see, it is exactly the risk that, as Schiller argues, the Greeks themselves took, when feeling themselves cut off from the ground of their own sociality, they turned back to the past with forms of theoretical *poiēsis* whose aim was to contact what was lost and see what of it could be made to enliven the present once again. While the shared life with beings as a whole enacted in the pastoral idyll as a form of theoretical *poiēsis* may be set outside culture, or prior to its beginning, it guides us backward in a theoretical sense, to an apprehension of the difference between merely human sociality and the possibilities for a larger horizon of shared life that inhere in us as subjects of life.

How, then, do other life forms supervene upon the disposition to be surrounded by beings as a whole for which Schiller calls so as to enact the appeal of second-person subjectivity in interpellation? Recovering their active intervention in the process of self-formation is at the heart of Hölderlin's loco-descriptive poems of the late 1790s, such as "The Neckar" and "The Main." In these poems, a river is remembered to have addressed the poet as the agent of his emergence into second-person relationality, such that its appeal constituted a requirement for reciprocity that is answered by the gift of the poem. It is just such an experience that is articulated as the retrospective acknowledgment of obligation in Wordsworth's recollection of the River Derwent having spoken to him in his cradle, an interpellation into shared life with beings as a whole to which "The Prelude" is a response:

> —Was it for this
> That one, the fairest of all Rivers, lov'd
> To blend his murmurs with my Nurse's song,
> And from his alder shades and rocky falls,
> And from his fords and shallows, sent a voice
> That flow'd along my dreams? For this, didst Thou,
> O Derwent! travelling over the green Plains

---

[4] Schiller (1998) 228–9.

> Near my "sweet Birthplace", didst thou, beauteous Stream
> Make ceaseless music through the night and day
> Which with its steady cadence, tempering
> Our human waywardness, compos'd my thoughts
> To more than infant softness, giving me,
> Among the fretful dwellings of mankind,
> A knowledge, a dim earnest, of the calm
> That Nature breathes among the hills and groves.[5]

Wordsworth's sense of obligation is futural and self-grounding: the perdurance of his self-experience requires that he answer the gift of the river with the counter-gift of song. So, too, in "The Neckar," Hölderlin's self-constitution in the apostrophe of the poem's present looks back to his emergence into self experience when he was addressed by the river: "*In deinen Tälern wachte mein Herz mir auf | Zum Leben, deine Wellen umspielten mich.*" The apostrophe is a responsive call back to what constituted the self as a self; what woke it to and for itself in second-person relationality. Poetic responsiveness is the acknowledgment of that originary self-constitution in the second person. For Hölderlin and Wordsworth, the question is not whether beings as a whole might intervene in human subject formation, but rather how different kinds of living beings—rivers, mountains, trees, the sun—might enact this formation in different ways.

The poetry of Hölderlin and Wordsworth recalls a singular lyric subject's interpellation by a singular non-human being. In Hölderlin's *Hyperion*, however, the perspectivism of fiction allows for the staging of interpellation in the plural—the differential outcomes of interpellation by different kinds of living beings for more than a single subject. On Hyperion's first visit to the island of Calauria, Nature surrounds him like a lovely idyll, as human beings are folded into an experience of shared life granted by the mothering southern air:

As when a mother cajolingly asks where her dearest pet has got to, and all her children come rushing to her lap and even the littlest reaches out its arms from the cradle, so every life flew and leaped and struggled out into the divine air, and beetles and swallows and doves and storks circled together in joyous confusion in its depths and heights, and the steps of all that were earthbound became flight, the horse charged over the furrows and the deer over the hedges, the fish came up from the bottom of the sea and leaped over the surface. The motherly air affected the hearts of all, uplifted them and drew them to her. And men came out of their doors, and wonderfully did they feel the ethereal breeze as it lightly moved the

---

[5] Book 1.274–88 (1805 version).

fine hairs over their foreheads, as it cooled the sun's ray, and happily they loosed their garments to receive it upon their chests, and breathed more sweetly, felt more gently touched by the light, cool, soothing sea in which they lived and breathed and had their being.[6]

Hyperion is disposed to chorality in the present by his understanding of Greece in antiquity as a place where "the Sun God lived, amid the divine festivals at which all Greece shone round him like a sky of golden clouds" (9). All his experiences of intersubjectivity, including his human friendships, are patterned after this conception of the foundational role of non-human subjects in the shared life of the Greeks. When he meets his friend Alabanda after the failure of their nationalist ambitions, he describes how his "large, ever-animated eye shone upon me from his faded face like the midday sun from a pallid heaven" (87). Alabanda's effect upon Hyperion is to recall Hyperion to himself, and to provide his life with an organizing center, like the foundational role of the sun in gathering ancient Greek life around itself.

The form of Hyperion's disposition to chorality seems to pre-date his meeting with his lover Diotima, and his figuration of the shared life of chorality in foundational terms is very much his own. Diotima's image of relationality is a household, in which "each member, without exactly thinking about it, adapts himself to all the others," and "all live pleasing and rejoicing one another simply because that is what springs from their hearts." This labile, multi-relational conception of the household embraces, most immediately, the "kindly trees" around her house (46). In their presence, she imagines herself as "a blossom among the blossoms," and in the company of "trusted confidants" who nod to her as a friend (121).

These two versions of the shared life of chorality resonate with one another throughout the novel, both as ways of imagining forms of sociality that include non-human lives, and as ways of thinking about intersubjectivity within that expanded sociality. Diotima understands living with non-human life forms as a process of mutual understanding that, like confidential friendship, unfolds over time. This understanding contrasts with Hyperion's experience of chorality as a decisive foundational orientation enacted through the supervening agency of natural entities, and especially the sun. The contrast is never disharmonious, but Diotima does interrogate Hyperion's belief that his experience of chorality in the present can be a gateway to the experience of antiquity as a form of life that is still living in its relics.

---

[6] Hölderlin (1990) 39.

When Diotima asks Hyperion about chorality as an experience of shared life with beings as a whole that is continuous with that of the Greeks, he reiterates an earlier expression of his belief that the centering of Greek life in Nature by Nature can be re-experienced in the present by a sudden, decisive restructuring of second-person relationality that is in the giving of the Greek landscape (14):

Even as the Sun in the heavens found itself again in the thousand changes of light that the Earth sent back to him, so my spirit recognized itself in the fullness of life that was all about it, that beset it from every side.[7]

The messaging between subjects in the cosmos as a whole is reenacted within the individual human being, and the micro-chorality of the individual's relationship to Nature is the ground of the macro-chorality of the group.

The alternation between errancy and being at the center is both ontogenetic and phylogenetic, and is figured in contrasting mythological spaces: on the one hand, the labyrinth in which one wanders without the guidance of light (29), on the other, Delos' place at the center of the Cycladic islands. In "The standpoint from which we should consider antiquity," a short unpublished text from the same period (1799), the emergence of the island of Rhodes in Pindar's seventh *Olympian* ode is the image that lies behind the self-grounding emergence of reflective consciousness in history, but in *Hyperion*, Rhodes and Delos are overlaid. As Hyperion and his companions undergo the centering agency of Greek Nature, he senses that "the life in us was like the life of a newborn ocean island, with its first spring just beginning" (63); the Delos-like self that has become the middle point of Nature has a Rhodes-like newness of life to it.

The possibilities for shared life that Hyperion apprehends are almost overwhelming. Excess being besets him on every side, and self-experience would be overwhelmed by phenomenality were it not for the intervention of the sun in which foundational chorality appears as the possibility for the reenactment of a historical form of life.[8] But such reenactment cannot be sustained by a singular being, and of the two versions of shared life in the novel, it will be Diotima's that survives. By

---

[7] Cf. "Remind me not of time!...It was a divine life and in it man was the center of Nature [*es war ein göttlich Leben und der Mensch war da der Mittelpunkt der Natur*]" (69). Lowth (1998) 107 notes that Hölderlin consistently renders ὀμφαλός—the Greek "navel," often used of Delphi as what centered the Panhellenic sociality of the Greeks—as *Mittelpunct* in his Pindar translations.

[8] I discuss this overwhelming by phenomenality that Schiller theorizes in the *Letters on Aesthetic Education* under the rubric of the "realm of the Titans," in Payne (2016).

the end of the novel, Alabanda is no longer the orienting figure of the sun. He is a tree once firm and slender, but now moldering, whose fragments boys will gather to make a "merry fire" (127). The tree that has outlived its beauty and is now ready for the fire recalls Pindar's image of Oedipus in the fourth Pythian Ode as a disfigured trunk whose last relation to human life consists in its being used as firewood, and this image is followed by Hyperion's comparison of his voyage to Germany with blind Oedipus' journey to the gates of Athens.

In Germany, Hyperion becomes like Diotima as he is included in a confidential relationship with its trees. He recalls that, in his state of desolation, he "lived with the blooming trees as with geniuses, and the clear brooks that flowed under them whispered the care from my breast like divine voices" (131). The foundational relationality enacted by the intervention of natural entities of the highest ontic prestige is replaced by the friendship of more modest life forms with which his own subjection to life is more nearly akin. The consolation that the trees afford is not simply the common mortality of their rotten fruit, but a shared life in which death is only one of the commonalities. Shared nutrition, and shared delight in the sky as the ultimate source of maternal care, recall the "motherly air" of Calaurea, and build towards the novel's radiant final image of the tree of blood inside the human body (133):

Like lovers' quarrels are the dissonances of the world. Reconciliation is there, even in the midst of strife, and all things that are parted find one another again. The arteries separate and return to the heart and all is one eternal glowing life.

The dissonance between Hyperion and Diotima's versions of chorality never becomes a quarrel, but the two strands do remain apart from one another, like veins and arteries, or the co-presence of Sapphic and Pindaric poetology in Hölderlin's late work.[9] The relationship between the two versions of chorality is not resolved, except insofar as the retrospective character of the narration can be said to have afforded Hyperion an opportunity to bring Diotima's version to light as the recuperation of a mode of idyllic experience that was not available to him at the time of his lived experience of it. This is a modality of reflection that Hyperion calls "gleaning," *Ährenlesen*: the search for a salvific remainder in a prior constellation of experience that is made available for reflective consciousness in the present in a way that would not have been possible for the original agents themselves. It is the term that Hyperion uses for reflection on his own past and on the past of the Greeks, and the point is not so much that

---

[9] See Menninghaus (2005).

ontogeny recapitulates phylogeny as that what is lost to understanding in both these developmental processes can be recovered by this kind of retrospective, reparative reflection.

The epistolary form of *Hyperion*, in which Hyperion recalls his interpellation by Greek Nature retrospectively in response to the call of a friend, gives an explicitly second-person appeal to its fictional world as the sharing of a project of reparative knowing. A sentimental consciousness moves over its naïve remainders, on the lookout for what could not have been recognized as decisive in the original constellation of experience. The form of the work enacts the relay of interpellation that is essential to the project of theoretical *poiēsis* if the poetic work is to serve as a proxy for Nature, as Schiller understands it:

> By virtue of the very notion of a poet, poets are everywhere the *guardians* of nature. Where they can no longer completely be this, and where they have already experienced within themselves the destructive influence of arbitrary and artificial forms or have had to contend with them, they will appear as nature's *witnesses* and *avengers*. They will either *be* nature or *seek* the lost nature.[10]

This understanding of the task of the post-natural, sentimental poet as a quasi-legal representation of Nature's forgotten claims upon human beings as subjects of life literalizes the legalism of Fichte's account of the human being's normative emergence into second-person relationality as a kind of summons or interpellation, and extends the range of possibilities for what can configure a human subject to the life world as whole.[11] The idea would prove attractive to poets in the century to come. Shelley's famous claim, in "A Defence of Poetry," that poets are "the unacknowledged legislators of the world," is grounded in the belief that it is their representation of Nature that gives their work its proto-institutional character as an adumbration of "the gigantic shadows which futurity casts upon the present."[12] The lost naturalness of shared

---

[10] Schiller (1998) 193–6. Emphasis original.
[11] Fichte's term in *Foundations of Natural Right* (1796), and *System of Ethics* (1798), is *Aufforderung* whose "normative felicity conditions" as second-person address in a juridical imaginary are explicated by Darwall (2006) 254–6: "There are two assumptions that any attempt to address someone second-personally is committed to making. The first is that the addresser and the addressee share an equal authority to make claims of one another as free and rational. And the second is that they share a freedom to act on claims that are rooted in this authority." In the *Foundations of Natural Right*, Fichte briefly acknowledges the possibility that interpellation might be addressed to a human being by a non-human entity (Fichte (2000) 35–8) only to dismiss this possibility out of hand in the *System of Ethics* (Fichte (2005) 209). The possibility is, however, central to Romanticism's thinking about the personhood of the non-human, as the poems of Wordsworth and Hölderlin have shown.
[12] Shelley (2003) 677, 682, 699–701. Compare Hölderlin's claim in "Andenken": "Was bleibet aber, stiften die Dichter."

life with beings as a whole to which poetic witnessing attests is the promise of a form of life to come, and when this witnessing is imagined in legal terms, the full array of juridical modes of interpellation becomes available to poets. Shelley does not simply repeat the conflation of juridical roles in Schiller's conception of poets as "nature's witnesses and avengers." Poets, he claims, "usurp and unite" in their own persons "the incompatible characters of accuser, witness, judge, and executioner."[13]

Schiller suggests that it is in the Hellenistic period that Greek sociality loses the naturalness with respect to beings as a whole that had characterized it as a historical form of life in the past, and that poets in this period begin to adopt quasi-juridical functions on Nature's behalf.[14] We can go further than Schiller, in fact, and assert that here too, a theoretical *poiēsis* that sought to recover the historical form of life of chorality for reflective understanding in the present was enacted as the assumption by poets of a variety of roles that afford quasi-legalistic representation to the claims of lost Nature as the form of its second-person relationality. Each of the major Hellenistic poets enacts these juridical roles differently, but the *Hymns* of Callimachus exhibit a special fascination with the relationship between errancy and being at the center as this is figured through a quasi-legal imaginary of interpellation.

In the "Hymn to Delos," Callimachus emphasizes the inverse correlation between the island's topographic poverty and its choral authority. Its initial appearance is an austere reduction of the shared life of chorality: because the sea revolves around it so forcefully, only fishermen, a byword for poverty, have made it their home, and it is more of a circuit for sea birds than for horses. Nonetheless, when the other islands congregate to make their way to Ocean and the Titan Tethys, it is Delos who leads the way (1–18).

Delos owes her preeminence to the love of Apollo, the guardian who circles her about. Since so many songs revolve around her in consequence of this love, Callimachus wonders how he is to entwine her with a garland of song in his turn, and he settles on the story of how Delos came to be an island fixed in one place. Delos was once a nymph who had the name Asteria because she leapt from the heavens into the ocean like a star (*astēr*) to escape the advances of Zeus. She then wandered over the surface of the ocean like a stalk of asphodel until, volunteering herself as the birthplace of Apollo, she "set the roots of her feet in the Aegean sea" and was no longer inconspicuous (*adēlos*) (17–37, 193–208). She ceases her wanderings and grounds herself as Delos, a choral center around

---

[13] Shelley (2003) 699.   [14] Schiller (1998) 196.

which swans circle to honor Apollo's birth (249–50), and the other Aegean islands take their place around her in choral formation (300–1):

Ἀστερίη θυόεσσα, σὲ μὲν περί τ' ἀμφί τε νῆσοι
κύκλον ἐποιήσαντο καὶ ὡς χορὸν ἀμφεβάλοντο.

Fragrant Asteria, around and about you the islands made themselves into a circle and set themselves into a chorus.

This choral formation has its anti-image in the "twisted foundation of the Minotaur's coiling labyrinth,"[15] and Theseus, when he escapes from it, leads circular dances around the altar of Delos, just as present day mariners do not pass by the island without participating in a curious dance in which they are beaten as they too circle around its great altar (311–23). What is crucial is not made explicit: Theseus and his men adopt the behavior of the islands in forming a circle around Delos, but they do not do so deliberately. Their unreflective *mimēsis* is a mark of the naturalness with which they participate in the shared life of beings as a whole and which it is the task of theoretical *poiēsis* to recover as reparative knowing in the present.

The agency of the islands themselves in the constitution of Delos as a choral center distinguishes Callimachus' version of the story from the Homeric "Hymn to Delian Apollo." It is not just that Asteria stops moving of her own accord, but that the other islands take up a position around her as a center from which their circle derives. The agency of the islands in constituting themselves as a choral group after whose activity human beings model their own practice of shared life is in keeping with the literalization of Delos as a surrogate parent in Callimachus' poem. While islands and rivers had been caregivers (*kourotrophoi*) before Callimachus,[16] Delos bathes and swaddles the infant Apollo, and Callimachus describes his own activity in the poem as "acknowledging [Apollo's] beloved wet nurse" (10). Delos intervenes as kindly Nature to foster the development of both gods and men, and Callimachus' role as poet is to witness and attest to that intervention.

For all of its own inventiveness, none of this is in the Homeric Hymn, where the emphasis is upon Apollo's delight in the lands that belong to him by right, rather than the form of relationality in which such claims of mutual belonging are enacted. Moreover, while Delos in the Homeric

---

[15] Stephens (2015) 230 notes that Callimachus is the first to apply the term to the Minotaur's lair on Crete.
[16] See Holmes (2015) 49 on Scamander as *kourotrophos* in Book 21 of the *Iliad*, who, as a river, "participates in a network of social and affective relationships that cross the human and non-human worlds."

Hymn fears that her poverty may scare Apollo away when he sees it (64–88), this poverty is a thing of the past for the poem's moment of narration, whereas, for Callimachus, the poverty of the island in the present is what calls forth his own retrospective *poiēsis*. The poverty of the island stands for the neediness of the present; it is what inspires the going over of the past for the foundational agency of Nature, the salvific remainder ungarnered in the original constellation of experience.

Callimachus' "Hymn to Delos" is about the foundation of chorality; his "Hymn to Demeter" is about its loss. The poem tells the story of Erysichthon, a figure from the heroic age, who one day gathers his gigantic henchmen about him and sets off to cut down a poplar tree in a grove that the goddess Demeter loves. In this grove, fruit trees and wild trees grow together in a primeval forest so dense you can hardly shoot an arrow between their trunks (31–6). The tree that Erysichthon chooses to fell is so tall it reaches to the sky, and, when struck with the ax, it cries aloud. Demeter hears, and hurries to the scene in disguise, but Erysichthon will not heed her warnings. He threatens to cut her down too, as he is intent on making a mead hall for his comrades, and at this point Demeter manifests her divinity. Her feet remain rooted to the ground, but her head, like the top of her tree, reaches all the way to Olympus. She lets Erysichthon finish his work but punishes him with insatiable hunger.

The poem now changes character. We leave behind the world of primeval forests, magical trees, and half-human giant men, for Erysichthon's home, which is where his punishment is enacted. Callers come to seek him out for civic and social events, and his parents experience an all too human embarrassment in the face of his hunger. The excuses with which they try to conceal it (and him) from visitors—he can't come to a party, for example, because "he fell out of his chariot" (86)—map a human world whose forms of relationality are drastically curtailed in comparison to the scene of Erysichthon's crime. As Erysichthon's body withers away in hunger, the horizon of shared life in the poem contracts to human beings alone, and their relationships with one another are stultifying and claustrophobic in comparison to the open horizons of relationality in which his story began.

Erysichthon is punished for harming what is sacred to a god, but it is the form of his punishment that reveals why what he harmed was sacred to a god in the first place. He eats all his family's domestic animals, which include mules they keep for transportation, an ox awaiting sacrifice, horses for racing and for war, and a cat for catching mice. These animals are at hand for him to eat because they have already been instrumentalized for human use, and their distribution throughout the household—apart from one another in places assigned to them according to their operationalization by human intelligence—contrasts with the shared life of the fruit trees and wild trees in Demeter's grove. Growing together and at random, the trees are interesting to the goddess as entities that live together in self-care, and it is as such that Erysichthon's victim is allowed to fall: the goddess warns, but she does not intervene, for to intervene would be to domesticate the trees, to own them like the animals of a human household. Demeter, we might say, intervenes only to the extent that she can do so without compromising the sovereign existence of her tree and of Erysichthon, whose common mode of *physis* is to emerge untrammeled and unconstrained into the scene of their own being.

In the scene of interpellation, Demeter hails Erysichthon as "my child" three times in succession (6.46–7), inviting him to recognize that his participation in shared life with beings as a whole has the same form of relationality as his participation in human sociality.[17] Having failed to acknowledge the silent interpellation of Demeter's tree, Erysichthon gets three more chances from Demeter herself to recognize that he is in the presence of another free subject of life. Not heeding the goddess's interpellation, he looks at her "more fiercely than a lioness in the mountains of Tmarus looks at a hunter when she has just given birth" (50–2), and this nonverbal expression of ferocity is his last act before he becomes completely dependent on others as a result of Demeter's punishment. The insatiable hunger that requires non-stop devotion to the task of feeding him on the part of his household is a hypertrophic condition of dependence that ends only when he is finally ejected from his house to become a homeless beggar in the streets, outside all forms of relationality other than momentary occasions of charity.

In Erysichthon's Gregor Samsa story, it is the failure to recognize what exists through self-care that exposes the emptiness of need-based forms of relationality: the use relations with domestic animals that are immediately fungible as food, and the mutual dependence of the human household, whose care is exhausted with the food supply. What is talionic about Erysichthon's punishment is not simply that it is a life for a life, but that it obliges him to recognize that, in the extremity of his suffering, he too is a being who exists through self-care, and who may or may not be of interest to others as such.

Erysichthon's story is framed by a ritual celebration of Demeter as an agricultural deity. Erysichthon appears as a kind of culture hero in negative: he is punished for the harm he does to primordial nature, but on the other side of his crime lie the normative relations to non-human

---

[17] τέκνον: "A common word of kindly address to a younger person," as Hopkinson (1984) 122 puts it.

life forms in the society within which Callimachus is telling his story. It is only by restaging his ancient crime that access is possible to the more expansive forms of relationality that were available in his world.

True to what Bruno Snell calls his "post-philosophical" style,[18] Callimachus offers no explanation of his fable, explicit or otherwise. Erysichthon makes his fatal misstep when the friendly *daimōn* that had guided his family simply withdraws, without their being aware of it. The unrecognized ground of their fortunate life disappears and cannot be acknowledged by him. For it is a condition of Erysichthon's naturalness that it is enacted as a lack of the reflective consciousness about his being in Nature that would have allowed him to understand his own place in it. He is a child who "looks simply at the need and at the means closest to hand for satisfying it," as Schiller characterizes this form of naturalness.[19] Demeter in disguise pleads with him to desist, but she does not stay his hand. In her kindly instantiation as Nature's witness, she cannot help him transition from unreflective being in Nature to reflection on his being in relation to Nature, and she assumes the role of Nature's avenger instead, afflicting him with insatiability as the punishment that fits his crime. In the place of explanation, we have the narrator's disavowal of Erysichthon in the frame drama: "May I not share a wall with someone Demeter hates; I hate bad neighbors" (116–17).

Erysichthon, as bad neighbor, is the figure of the failure of shared life, just as, in Sophocles' "Ode to Man," the uncanniness of human mastery over Nature culminates in the figure of the corrupted neighbor at the center of the concentric circles of human life around the hearth and the city, who spurns the laws of the earth through of an excess of daring.[20] The "Hymn to Demeter" compresses epochs of human relationality to Nature into the story of a singular human life, and it divides these epochs by a single, punctual moment in this life, such that the story of Erysichthon mirrors the poem's formal articulation as an embedded narrative of primordial relationality surrounded by a frame drama set within the world of normative human relations to beings as a whole that have supplanted this primordial relationality.

Sophocles' *Philoctetes* offers a narrative template for the project of Hellenistic poetry in this regard. Philoctetes is removed from the ordinary forms of human sociality when he is abandoned on Lemnos by the

---

[18] Snell (1953) 266–7, 274–9.   [19] Schiller (1998) 186.
[20] Cf. Heidegger (1996) 51–97, which concludes with a discussion of the concentric circles of human life around the hearth and the city as this image appears in the chorus's rejection of whoever abuses technics in defiance of the regulations (νόμους) of the earth in Sophocles, *Antigone* 370–5.

Greek army that is on its way to Troy, and on this island, which Sophocles imagines as uninhabited by human beings, he is integrated into new forms of shared life with beings as a whole, only to be offered the chance to rejoin history and human culture when Odysseus and his men come back to collect him. The play stages the crossing of the threshold between a larger horizon of shared life and a more limited form of human sociality as a possibility that might be enacted within a single human life, and represents the farewell look that Nature gives to human beings as subjects of shared life as a glance directed at a singular human being who is leaving it behind. Callimachus' hymn develops this possibility as theoretical *poiēsis* by making the relay of interpellation more explicit in the poem's formal structure. The embedded story of Erysichthon is addressed to an internal audience who may or may not be interested in it, such that the possibility of reenacting the shared life of chorality in the present is seen to depend upon the actualization of a disposition towards second-person relationality with beings as a whole that itself must become an object of appeal.

A similar constellation of Demeter worship, hubristic violence, and access to the primordial appears in the complex structure of Theocritus' *Idyll* 7. Simichidas, the poet's proxy in the pastoral world of the poem,[21] ends his journey through the landscape of Cos at a festival of agricultural Demeter. In this poem, her festival is again a gateway to the ancient spirit of the wild. While drinking her wine, the poet is surrounded by the voices of poplar and elm, insects, frogs, and birds that mingle with the sound of holy water, and he wonders whether he might be drinking such liquor as the centaur Chiron once served to Heracles in the cave of Pholus, or that made the Cyclops Polyphemus dance among his mountain stock pens: preludes to scenes of mythic violence between primordial non-human life forms and their human antagonists (135–53).[22]

What happens in *Idyll* 7 is more than just Siegfried drinking the dragon's blood. As the grove of "The Hymn to Demeter" is what allows the before and after picture of Erysichthon to be understood as a double portrait of two distinct forms of human life, so interpellation by idyllic, surrounding nature in *Idyll* 7 is what affords imaginative access to the shared life of primordial humanity with beings as a whole. The centaurs and Cyclops of *Idyll* 7 are an evanescent glimpse of that early life, the

---

[21] Cf. Parry (1989) 35: "Nineteenth-century English nature poetry presents an idealized *nature* (and calls it that) with which the poet would like to identify himself, but cannot. Greek pastoral presents an idyllic nature in which the poet can move by proxy, and with which he is content." Emphasis original.

[22] As Fantuzzi (1995) 28 observes.

visionary fulfillment of a poem that ends by asking Demeter for a repetition of its own conditions of possibility.

These Hellenistic poems imagine a primordial way of being together with non-human life from which human beings have emerged into the form of shared life in the present through the violence occasioned by what lives though self-care. In some primordial beforetime, human beings lived alongside non-human life in relationships that were not predicated upon the binary of the wild and the domesticated, but the very indefiniteness of the human vis-à-vis the non-human in this primordial time provoked the violence towards non-human life that brought the era of open relationality to an end.[23]

And it is in the relationship between textual practice and the intimacy of reading that these Hellenistic poems stage the discoverability of chorality as a primordial form of shared life, and so constitute themselves as a proxy of Nature for a theoretical *poiēsis*. In *Idyll* 7, the wandering voice of the ur-goatherd Comatas lies at the heart of multiple layers of narrative embedding as the form of life that the poem around it wants us to reach. The reader is on the outside, trying to get in, and these multiple framings call forth the work of gleaning. Multiple layers of exclusion invite us to pursue an evanescent experience of relationality, such that we are guided backward in a theoretical sense. Our externality to another form of life becomes the condition of the recovery of a different form of self-experience, of reorientation, and a return from errancy. Plotinus, in "On Beauty," suggests that "the good holds beauty before it like a shield" (*Ennead* 1.6.9), and these poems enact this possibility as the relationship between surroundedness as a form of shared life in Nature and surroundedness as literary form in which we apprehend our shared life in Nature by finding our way through the layers of its form—a kind of mimetic materiality.[24]

In his expression of hope that the literary idyll might do common work with Nature itself, chorality is minimally expressed by Schiller in the verb (*sich*) *umgeben*, "surround (yourself)." If one kind of ecological poetics is synecdochic enactment of the kinds of vitality to which the

---

[23] As Apollonius figures the end of this era in the *Argonautica*, Heracles' killing of the chthonic serpent Ladon, who kept watch over the garden of the Hesperides, is a poignant marker of the difference between the early world that existed "until yesterday," and historical life as such, which is about to begin as the time of the poem comes to an end (4.1397). There is a pun here on χθόνιος, "of the earth," and χθιζόν, "yesterday," that I have not been able to reproduce.

[24] I borrow the term "mimetic materiality" from Victoria Saramago's forthcoming book project, *Environmental Fictions and Fictional Environments: Mimesis and Deforestation in Latin America*, where it refers to the material qualities of the representing object: text length, page size, lineation, and so forth.

poetic work attests—translating the form of our relationality with what else in the world is alive into metamorphoses of literary form so that we might apprehend it anew—literary chorality as a version of this project can be understood as the textual enactment of the interpellation of beings as a whole such that it relays this experience of surroundedness as an interpellation to the reader. If it works like Nature, writing can constitute itself as a proxy of Nature, and it works like Nature by affording the reader the opportunity to experience the intimate provocation of second-person relationality with beings as a whole as the operationalization of the textual possibilities of mimetic materiality.

From this perspective, we can hear the *immer wieder* of Schiller's textual chorality after Plotinus as the repeated practice of a reparative project: "Let Nature surround you like a lovely idyll, in which *again and again* you find the way back to yourself from the aberrations of art and gather courage and new confidence about the course of life." To get back behind the subject whose understanding of the possibilities of shared life has been constituted through particular cultural formations is work that has constantly to be begun again, because what is gained by it is always lost again, almost at once.

WORKS CITED

Darwall, S. (2006) *The Second-Person Standpoint: Morality, Respect, and Accountability*. Cambridge, MA.

Fantuzzi, M. (1995) "Mythological Paradigms in the Bucolic Poetry of Theocritus," *Proceedings of the Cambridge Philological Society* 41: 16–35.

Fichte, J. G. (2000) *Foundations of Natural Right (Cambridge Texts in the History of Philosophy)*. Ed. F. Neuhouser, trans. M. Baur. Cambridge.

Fichte, J. G. (2005) *The System of Ethics (Cambridge Texts in the History of Philosophy)*. Ed. and trans. D. Breazeale and G. Zöller. Cambridge.

Heidegger, M. (1996) *Hölderlin's Hymn "The Ister."* Trans. W. McNeill and J. Davis. Bloomington, IN.

Hölderlin, F. (1990) *Hyperion and Selected Poems*. Trans. W. R. Trask, adapted by D. Schwarz. New York.

Holmes, B. (2015) "Situating Scamander: 'Natureculture' in the *Iliad*," *Ramus* 44: 29–51.

Hopkinson, N. (ed.) (1984) *Callimachus: Hymn to Demeter*. Cambridge.

Lowth, C. (1998) *Hölderlin and the Dynamics of Translation (Legenda: Studies in Comparative Literature 2)*. Oxford.

Menninghaus, W. (2005) *Hälfte des Lebens: Versuch über Hölderlins Poetik*. Frankfurt.

Parry, A. M. (1989) "Landscape in Greek Poetry," in *The Language of Achilles and Other Papers*. Oxford: 8–35.

Payne, M. (2016) "*Aetna* and Aetnaism: Schiller, Vibrant Matter, and the Phenomenal Regimes of Ancient Poetry," *Helios* 43: 1–20.

Saramago, V. Forthcoming. *Environmental Fictions and Fictional Environments: Mimesis and Deforestation in Latin America*.

Schiller, F. (1967) *On the Aesthetic Education of Man*. Trans. E. M. Wilkinson and L. A. Willoughby. Oxford.

Schiller, F. (1998) *Essays*. Trans. D. O. Dahlstrom. New York.

Shelley, P. B. (2003) *The Major Works*. Oxford.

Snell, B. (1953) *The Discovery of the Mind*. New York.

Stephens, S. (ed.) (2015) *Callimachus: The Hymns*. Oxford.

9 Apples and poplars, nuts and bulls

The poetic biosphere of Ovid's *Metamorphoses*

Giulia Sissa

Ovid's *Metamorphoses* is a story of new bodies.
 The world emerged from a rough, undifferentiated mass, thanks to a god and a "better nature."[1] Jupiter destroyed it, in anger. Later, a divine collective decision brought it back into being. Finally, Phaeton, the unwary child of another god, the Sun, almost reduced the universe to ashes. The gods live in a beautiful town, a celestial Rome. They are over-occupied and worried for all human affairs: they help, advise, punish, and reward. They love, suffer, get angry, and take revenge. Bending people's will, directing their agency, and manufacturing events are, for them, an incessant activity. The gods care for the cosmos. Their truly favorite occupation, however, is the transformation of human beings into non-human, or at least non-anthropomorphic creatures. They can never stop reshaping women and men into other animals, plants, stars, or springs. These are hybrids: not quite the same as they were before, but not completely different either. Together with an unexpected corporeal *figura*, an old identity remains.
 New bodies are new configurations of embodiment.
 A poetic metaphysics runs through the *Metamorphoses*. At the end of the poem, a philosophical commentator, Pythagoras of Samos, delivers a lecture on its principles.[2] His long and famous speech, uttered in Book 15, has provoked many conflicting interpretations.[3] I shall suggest my own. In doing so I hope to be able to demonstrate two things.

---

[1] Ovid, *Metamorphoses* 1.5–25.
[2] On Book 15 and on Pythagoras' speech we now dispose of an extensive, excellent commentary: Hardie and Chiarini (2015).
[3] The most significant matter of dispute is the connection of the speech with the poem. Among the scholars who adamantly despise Pythagoras' intervention, and thus keep it separate from the rest (on account of irony, pompousness, mediocrity, or length), we should mention Douglas Little, Charles Segal, Karl Galinsky, Robert Coleman, John Miller, Stephen Wheeler, and Helen van Noorden. In contrast Luigi Alfonsi, Simone Viarre,

Firstly, Pythagoras offers a synoptic theory of change that subsumes what occurs in the *Metamorphoses*.[4] Change makes the world, and it does so quite well. *Cuncta fluunt*, all things are in flux, Pythagoras says, and yet the stream of becoming allows for moments of relatively lasting stability.[5] Without being eternal, concrete inanimate objects and complex living beings come into existence—and then subsist for a while. Pythagoras himself personifies this experience. He has enjoyed many different lives. He can remember the successive identities he took over time. Likewise, the *nova corpora* we encounter in the poem come to be, become what they now are—and are there to stay. What is more, these animal, vegetal, or mineral new beings know who they were, and still are anyhow, notwithstanding what they have also become. Their memory is their awareness of a transition from being shaped and equipped in a visibly human fashion, to being differently incorporated into the world. This point is hardly new, but its importance deserves to be emphasized once again, because it is precisely this *particular kind of becoming*— creative, rather than destructive; vital rather than deadly; cumulative rather than annihilating; partial rather than total—that explains the metamorphoses in the poem as well as Pythagoras' vision of changeability. The cosmos of the poem is posthuman for we could be recycled in an instant into other kinds of beings, but it is paradoxically anthropocentric because this plasticity affects *us*—and *we* are still there.[6]

Brooks Otis, Aldo Setaioli, Philip Hardie, K. Sara Myers, Norah Franklin, and Matthew McGowan have offered interpretations that take the speech seriously, and then try to make sense of its very presence in Book 15, at the end of the Roman/Augustan narrative.

See, in chronological order: Alfonsi (1958), Viarre (1964), Otis ([1966] 2010) 296–305, Segal (1969), Little (1970), Coleman (1971), Galinsky (1975) 104–7, Setaioli (1988), Myers (1994), Miller (1994), Hardie (1995), Wheeler (2000) 107–27, Wheeler (2009) 156–7, Segal (2001), Tillette (2009), van Noorden (2015) 261–4, and McGowan (2016). Barchiesi (2006) stands apart, for he does not approach the speech in order to decide whether Pythagoras is or is not Ovid's "mouth-piece." He rather frames his reading in terms of "narrative instances," as we will see in a moment. Fabre-Serris (2018) argues that the speech responds to Vergil. This is not incompatible with the interpretation I am offering in this paper.

The book of M. M. Colavito, *The Pythagorean Intertext in Ovid's Metamorphoses: A New Interpretation* (Colavito (1989)), stands apart, as an attempt to find proper Pythagorean ideas in the poem.

[4] The understanding of the speech as an organic part and even a "recapitulation" of the poem has become prevalent in recent scholarship on the *Metamorphoses*. See in particular the detailed arguments by Myers (1994) 133, 135. On this same point, see Franklin (2005) 65–73. I am arguing here that both metamorphosis and metempsychosis shape a very special kind of world, in which human beings are constantly at risk of misrecognizing their fellows, and might even eat them. Vegetarianism is a form of corporeal skepticism. It prevents tragic errors. This is the crucial point.

[5] Ovid, *Metamorphoses* 15.201.

[6] On similar textual situations, see Campana and Maisano (2016).

Secondly, Pythagoras sets up a taxonomy that separates humans, non-human animals, and plants. On the one hand, this taxonomy is porous on account of the liquid ontology that keeps together the world. "All things are in flux" means that immortal souls transmigrate from human to non-human beings. Fluidity blurs the lines of demarcation. But, on the other hand, it also creates perceptive uncertainty about the potential humanity of beings that do not look anthropomorphic. This is particularly disconcerting when it concerns food. By mistake, we might eat semi-human flesh. Precisely because humanity is diluted across the ecosphere, therefore, Pythagoras' taxonomy has to respect alimentary distinctions. Differences matter from the standpoint of what we, as human beings, may or may not eat. Once again, we are the protagonists. We must abstain from eating meat. We are permitted to consume only vegetables and fruits. This classification of food groups (edible versus inedible) fits perfectly Pythagoras' own conception of metempsychosis, a crucial component of his general theory of universal mutability. It is also consistent with the poetic and narrative thinking of the *Metamorphoses*.

Such a thinking deserves to be taken seriously, for the poem is not merely a masterful exemplar of a literary genre, epic poetry. The poem creates a "possible world," defined by a range of "modalities"—what must, should, might, or can happen.[7] All these necessities and possibilities may well be incompatible with the expectations of a Roman of the first century BCE, in their daily life. Metamorphosis itself is a miracle. And yet a consistent line of thought runs through this marvellous universe.

Metamorphosis brings about all kinds of animals—wild, domestic, unappetizing, or good to eat. We have to abstain from all of them, Pythagoras warns, lest we ingest potentially human flesh. We must all be vegetarians. In the same poetic biosphere, however, there exist also massive trees, colorful flowers, or aromatic herbs that either grow in the wilderness or can be cultivated. Metamorphosis gives rise to some of them. A question then arises. Since it is the transformation of humans into all sorts of non-anthropomorphic beings that creates the risk of anthropophagy, can vegetarianism protect us from eating a human transformed into a plant? The answer is yes. Metamorphosis generates no vegetables destined for culinary use. Only inedible plants are metamorphic. All farm or garden products that are comestible are "safe" to eat. These plants have always existed as such, unscathed by any human pedigree. No cannibalism is in sight, therefore, for a vegetarian. Far from being a foil or a fad, vegetarianism operates in the text itself. By crafting a

---

[7] On the concept of "possible world," in philosophy and literary theory, see Eco (1979).

consistent set of distinctive traits, Ovid makes sure that the poem agrees with Pythagoras' vegetarian ethics, and yet takes the liberty to recount the life of half-human plants. These vegetal hybrids may well bleed or speak, but nobody would dream of tasting them. They are not foodstuff. The cosmos of the poem respects a vegetarian *contrainte*, which is logical, structural, and literary.

To see this we have to take a glimpse at what the anthropologists of ancient societies call "ethnographic context," namely the cultural representations that lie in the background of Ovid's imaginary nature.[8] The poem is indeed "a tale of wonders," but, like science-fiction or fantasy, it abides by its internal rules. And such rules are both idiosyncratic and culturally meaningful. I agree, therefore, with Alessandro Barchiesi that Pythagoras' speech is a "hyperdidactic"—and yet failed—attempt to instill a non-violent philosophy into the life of people who readily enjoyed red meat and bloody sacrifice.[9] There is indeed a deeply ironic discrepancy between Roman culture and Pythagoras' mission. But such dissonance, I would add, extends to the possible world of the poem itself, for that world is ready-made for vegetarians. In the *Metamorphoses*, it is advisable to abstain from eating *all* animal flesh, for it is *possible* for *all* animals to derive from human beings. In contrast, *not-all* plants might be the product of transformation, therefore it is permissible to eat vegetables, but only *some* vegetables. This is the major point on which I intend to insist. Once we become aware of this compelling pattern, the entire poem, as the narrative creation of a metamorphic cosmos, flows seamlessly into its Pythagorean finale.

9.1. A non-nihilistic poem

Pythagoras clarifies in a generalizing and didactic argument the liquid ontology that underpins the poem's intricate storylines. Rather than providing a pedantic recapitulation, or simply claiming that change is pervasive in the world, the speech explains what particular kind of change has been operating in the *Metamorphoses*, and what specific kind of anthropological coherence keeps together its cosmos. Pythagoras utters a general premise that was known as a motto by Heraclitus: "*panta*

---

[8] For a synthetic overview of the methodological arguments of Claude Lèvy-Strauss, Marcel Detienne, and Jean-Pierre Vernant, see Zaidman and Pantel (1991). See also Branham et al. (1997): 167–71 (G. Sissa, "Philology, Anthropology, Comparison: The French Experience").

[9] Barchiesi (2006) 300–1.

rhei" (*cuncta fluunt*). He then glosses this universal assertoric proposition by adding that the same souls migrate into different bodies, resettle into "new homes" (*novae domus*), and "hide" (*condi*) in those new abodes.[10] Thanks to these transfers, psychosomatic hybrids take shape, which may well be mortal, but will enjoy a certain lifespan. When we disappear in our non-anthropomorphic residences, we may dwell there for years. All things come to be over time, therefore, and stay there for a while. This means that although all things ebb and flow, they are not in a state of *total* and *incessant* becoming. This is the twofold idea that runs deep through the poem: change is neither complete, nor is it continuous.[11]

Change is partial. Before the transit of a certain soul into a particular body, there was someone else, certainly, but that previous incarnation of the wandering soul was not entirely different. Fluidity, therefore, does not produce complete dissimilarity but *coexistence* of old and new, an interbreeding of same and different, in a creature that will be able to say "*egō*," and be *ipse*, without being *idem*. Pythagoras speaks as the testimonial, in the first person, of this conscious experience. He insists on the memory he has of his own life, through so many bodies. He remembers himself (*ipse egō*), when he was a warrior who died on the plain of Troy; he has just recognized (*nuper*) the shield he carried in those days, among the offerings that are now in the temple of Juno at Argos.[12] This incomplete transformation fits a universe in which we encounter a bear who can still think about herself and feel sorry for her own destiny, while now emitting only inhuman sounds; a stream that/who never stops crying; a cow who/that moos instead of speaking, but who can write. This cow, moreover, may even return to the previous version of herself. There is someone,

---

[10] *Cuncta fluunt*: Metamorphoses 15.201; *novae domus*: Metamorphoses 15.159.

[11] On this particular point, I disagree with Philip Hardie's otherwise inspiring interpretation of the speech. See Hardie and Chiarini (2015). In Hardie (1995), Philip Hardie argues that Pythagoras negotiates the transition of the narrative from Greece to Rome, and thus places Ovid himself at the culmination of the entire epic tradition. Further, Pythagoras lends himself to the role of a master of thought for Ovid, by analogy and in contrast with Epicurus, who plays the same role for Lucretius, in *De rerum natura*. This highly influential study situates Pythagoras within the poem, on account of the cultural memory that a native of Samos could bring to Crotone, and then to Roman culture, in his trans-historical existence. Mindful of his numerous consecutive lives, from the time of the Trojan War to present, Pythagoras personifies the Greco-Roman *longue durée* of which Ovid casts himself as the final interpreter. I will add that Pythagoras has yet another crucial, and unique, responsibility at the end of the poem: that of setting out in a retroactive, authoritative, didactic mode, the very peculiar kind of liquid ontology that explains why we must abstain from eating certain living beings.

[12] Ovid, *Metamorphoses* 15.160–70. Another character who recounts his biography through different identities is Hippolytus, who died but came back to life, thanks to Apollo. "You will be surprised," he says, "and I will hardly be able to prove it, but nonetheless I am that one" (*mirabere, vixque probabo, sed tamen ille egō sum*: Metamorphoses 15.499–500).

surviving and remembering, throughout a metamorphosis: a subject—*egō, illa, ille*—for whom various *figurae* will take over. Hybridization—that is to say a partial and cumulative change—, lies at the heart of the poem and, of course, of Pythagoras' speech.[13] Metamorphosis does not necessarily reveal, or clarify a previous identity; but it always creates hybrids. A human subject outlives her/his dehumanization.

Change is discontinuous. Pythagoras defuses even the slightest hint of fixity a reader might erroneously project onto a metamorphic world. He helps us avoid the blind spot of those theories of becoming which freeze change in a permanent alteration, and a constant translation. This kind of change would be always the same. Change would be always changing, and nothing else. Things would experience nothing but transiency. Reality would be nothingness in perpetual motion.[14] This is not what Pythagoras argues for, because his overarching point is that flux brings objects and people into existence. There are seasons, but they extend over months. There are ages, but they go on for years. This is not what the poem is about either, since it speaks about *nova corpora*, new bodies, namely living objects that suddenly come to life to be there, in time and in the world. Attention, readers! The *carmen perpetuum* has recounted so far the transformative fate of the ecosphere. But make no mistake! This is no invariable variation. It is, rather, a productive becoming that makes things come to be, albeit for a limited period of time. New bodies, once again, are now there. Old souls will inhabit them for a while. Life is frozen, stretched, displaced, relocated. Nothing is purely and simply annihilated, nobody dies entirely.[15]

To do justice to the poem in its entirety, we have to resist the temptation of a compartmentalized reading. Such reading might start from the premise that Pythagoras' vision of universal, natural, systematic

---

[13] On transformation as a systematic creation of hybrids, see Casanova-Robin (2009). On Ovid's aesthetics of hybridity, the beauty of metamorphic compounds and poetic forms that bridge genres, see Galand-Halyn (1994) 190-232.

[14] Plato and Lucretius attributed such vision of change to Heraclitus and his followers. Plato, *Cratylus* 402a: "all things move and nothing stays still" (πάντα χωρεῖ καὶ οὐδὲν μένει); *Theaetetus* 160d, 180b, and 181c (πάντα κινεῖται). See also *Theaetetus* 152d-e, 157a-d: "And so as a consequence of all this, as we said in the beginning, nothing is one, itself by itself, but everything is always becoming in relation to something, and 'to be' should be altogether abolished, though we have often (and even just now) been compelled by habit and lack of knowledge, to use that word" (trans. Harold N. Fowler, modified).

Lucretius (*De rerum natura* 1.670-74) criticizes Heraclitus' conception of change on account of its nihilistic implications. See also *De rerum natura* 1.790-94, for a similar argument about Empedocles. Ovid rethinks change, against Lucretius. His knowledge of Heraclitus might have been filtered through *De rerum natura*, which would explain why Heraclitus could not possibly figure in the *Metamorphoses*. Pythagoras acts as his "vitalist" surrogate.

[15] Setaioli (1988). Cf. Setaioli (1988) 489-90: "Endless mutation does not imply annihilation at all (*Il continuo mutare non comporta in nessun caso un annientamento*)." On a different kind of presence in stones, see Barolsky (2005).

mutability has nothing to do with the serendipitous, surprising, and divinely triggered events that befall humans and, occasionally, inanimate things. It would also insist on the difference between the dualistic opposition of body and soul implied in Pythagoras' language about metempsychosis, and the corporeal, material metamorphosis that occurs in the poem. Ovid's "very physical view of the body," Charles Segal argued in an influential paper, is allegedly not compatible with the "transcendence" of an immortal soul.[16] The poem speaks for itself, I will counter-argue. The modifications of humans and their adjustments to their *nova corpora* affect the whole hylomorphic complex that is in transition. A relocated soul has to set in motion, put to use, and become aware of, its altered anatomical equipment. That assemblage of organs, sensations, and abilities has to serve a newly enfleshed, human soul. An undying, alive, sentient, and intentional self infuses, imbues, animates the experience of a new "body." This is true both in metempsychosis and in metamorphosis. If my neighbour were to be reincarnated as an ox, "he" would be present in "his" bovine complexion, and this is why I must not eat "his" meat, according to Pythagoras. If a god were unexpectedly to transform a woman into a cow, that beefy creature would still carry "her" humanity through every beastly bit of her newly en-mattered self. The physicality of a metamorphically modified human such as Io, the cow-girl, has everything to do with her disfigured yet persistent humanity, and her brilliant ingenuity in coping with what, for her, is a sudden disability.[17] She is now differently able.

Io is a perfect example of a human-nonhuman re-embodiment. She is well aware of what has happened to her. She suffers and, more importantly, she struggles with the inarticulate voice, the cumbersome carcass, the unfamiliar range of motion she is now confined to. This is what she *is* now, but is also what *she* does not want to be, because *she* misses her previous self. That self was embodied differently. She misses, therefore, her ability to be in the world as before: to speak an articulated language, to walk on her two feet, to throw her arms in sign of affection, to express her feelings in words, and above all to be recognized as Io. Her new situation reveals a presence, a memory, a consciousness, an intentionality that transcends her recently acquired, uncomfortable, alien anatomy.[18] Notwithstanding her dismorphic prosthesis, however, Io tries to find a

---

[16] Segal (2001) 67.
[17] Io finds a way of using writing as a surrogate for speaking, exactly like Philomela, who, made mute after her tongue has been cut out, embroiders the tale of her rape on a piece of cloth (Ovid, *Metamorphoses* 6.412–674).
[18] On the outcome of metamorphosis as presence/absence, see Hardie (2002).

way of signifying who she still is. She succeeds in putting her bovine resources to work, in a typically human and highly civilized gesture: writing. *She* traces words on the ground, using her hoofs. She makes do with what replaces her hands, and reinvents herself as a cyborg: a writing cow. Then her father finally recognizes this prodigy as his own beloved daughter *and* a heifer. She is Io, and yet she will have to marry a bull.[19]

To be sure, the narrative account of this conflicted subjectivity complicates Pythagoras' metaphor of the soul "hiding" (*condi*), or lodging in new bodies, as "homes" (*domus*).[20] Taken at face value, this dichotomic, spatial language might seem to mean that a body is just like a building; a soul may take quarters in it. Should we start from this premise, in order to fit the template of metempsychosis, the *nova corpora* of the poem should be just thingy containers, in which intact human souls would settle and resettle. But beyond a deceptively simple "domiciliary" metaphor, the very logic of transmigration entails the idea that a human soul has to *adapt* to a non-human body. Metamorphosis supposes the same kind of adaptation. Ovid's poetry brings into light experiences of embattled *embodiment*. This complication produces a refined phenomenology.[21]

In the poem, new intertwinements of body and soul may well be fluid, fragmented, fumbling, inadequate, out of sync, but they are always an attempt to overcome the sheer impotence of a sudden deprivation of humanity. Episode after episode, and especially in a few hyper-detailed ekphrastic tableaux, Ovid experiments with the dilemmas of a sentient, intelligent, willing mind, *mens*, now in charge of a semi-automatic, half-manageable body that, for all its subhuman clumsiness, may be ingeniously retrained to do human things, more or less as before. Anatomy is a challenge, not a destiny. The new body, not just the old soul, has to live up to its transformations. The new body is new *for* someone: for the person who is fitfully trying to make the best of a crippling novelty. "To have a 'body' like mine, or to 'have' a body as I have one," writes Stanley Cavell, in his meditations on what it would mean for us to be a machine, "is to be subjected to it, to be the subject of it."[22] Ovidian hybrids are subjected to their new bodies, indeed, but their subjection is creative:

---

[19] Ovid, *Metamorphoses* 1.568–663, for the first section of the episode; 650–59, for Ianchus' consternation.

[20] Ovid, *Metamorphoses* 15.456–8.

[21] We should read the *Metamorphoses* with the help of the classics of phenomenology, such as Maurice Merleau-Ponty. For the body as a situation, not a thing, see the recent synthetical meditation by Romano (2013).

[22] Cavell (1979) 414. Cavell questions our ability to know other people's minds, through a thought experiment: what if a frog were a Prince (395–415).

they are super-efficient animals, so much so that a cow can write with no hands. The hoof will do.

Of course, all this is absurd, as Aristotle argued against Pythagoras' theory of metempsychosis. "Aristotle could not admit the possibility of a soul entering into a body of which it is not the *entelēcheia*," writes Gabriele Cornelli, "as would happen in the case of the transmigration of a human soul into an inferior animal body."[23] But this very possibility, that of coming to terms with the parts of an animal one was not meant to be, sustains the narrative thinking that runs through the poem. Pythagoras' insistence on the inventive, innovative, imaginative outcomes of change correlates with the actual storytelling about spiders, wolves, stars, streams, pigs, cows, and deer. For better or worse, as a reward or as a punishment, change brings a profusion of newly embodied creatures to life, be it in the frantic animation of a deer, the motionless existence of a weeping rock, or that of a sparkling constellation. Survival in a new-fangled corporeal situation counteracts nothingness, as well as human death.

This is the point of metamorphosis. Change is vital.

Change can be, however, treacherous. This too is the point of metamorphosis. The conversion into a new body means the loss of one's familiar aspect. Human beings cease to look human, and become unrecognizable for others.[24] Now, voluntary shape-shifting is typical of deities. A god such as Jupiter can morph from his divine appearance into theriomorphic or inanimate beings, as well as from one anthropomorphic shape to another—and back to his Olympian form. Think of his visit to Lycaon's house or his call, together with Mercury, to Baucis and Philemon's hut, as we will see in a moment. Human beings, such as Cephalus when he tries to test the faithfulness of his wife, Procris, can also play with their outward

---

[23] Aristotle, *De anima* 407b 12–17, 20–6. See Cornelli (2016) 15. An enlightening comment on Aristotle's argument can be found in Aquinas (1951), *lectio* 8, 131: "Indeed, we may associate their thesis (Aristotle goes on to say) with the Pythagorean fable that any soul can enter any body; the soul of a fly for instance might perchance enter the body of an elephant. This cannot in fact happen; for the body of each particular thing, and especially of living things, has its own form and species and type of movement: hence there are great differences between the bodies of a worm, a dog, an elephant and a gnat. When they say that any soul can enter any body, it is as if one were to say that the art of weaving could enter flutes, or that the art of the coppersmith could enter a weaver's loom. If it was in the power of these arts to enter bodies or instruments they would not do so indiscriminately, but the art of playing the flute would enter flutes, and not lyres, while the art of playing stringed instruments would enter stringed instruments and not flutes. In the same way, if there is a body for every soul, any soul does not enter any body; rather the soul shapes the body fit for itself; it does not enter a ready-made body. Plato and the others who speak only about the soul are too superficial; they fail to define which body answers to which soul, and the precise mode of existence of each in union with the other."

[24] On the frightening situation of having become unrecognizable, potential food see Riddehough (1959) 206.

show. This is why the arrival of a stranger at your door is always a challenge: who might this be? Hospitality is a prudent way of handling such uncertainty. But whenever a human being finds himself or herself translated into a morphologically new body, they move out of sight. *They* become invisible. The more ekphrastically flamboyant a new identity appears, the more visually confusing it is for an observer. Think of Io, the heifer, gesturing toward her father. Think of Acteon, reembodied in a timid cervide: he is still there, hopelessly undetectable in the eyes of his own dogs.[25] Ultimately the core of human subjectivity that adapts to new frames, limbs, skins, features, movements, sounds, and manners gives the poem not a euphoric tone, but a disturbing flavor. What if we failed to recognize a person, whose outer shell is not anthropo*morphic* any longer? What if we mistook somebody's presence under cover? Tragedy lurks.

In the end, Pythagoras invites Ovid's readers to meditate on the generative and vital outcomes of metamorphosis, but also on its deeply troubling effects. Since *cuncta fluunt*, as he diligently lectures us, a plethora of new bodies come into existence, but, for the same reason, our (Roman) eating habits become problematic. A piece of meat might, also, be a woman's flesh. It is advisable not to sink our teeth into it. Vegetarianism is epistemic precaution, in an ontologically tricky world.

9.2. Thyestean feasts

To do justice to vegetarianism in a metamorphic universe, we have to question the deceptively simple experience of food.

Food is dangerous. To eat is to grind, ingest, and digest—therefore to take into our own mouth, stomach and bowels—stuff that derives from more or less traceable sources. Culinary techniques transform the ingredients by drying, mincing, slicing, searing, stewing, charring, or broiling. Sauces and condiments may modify dramatically the aspect of the original foodstuff. On the one hand, nutrition is incorporation, so that something that used to be alive, as a plant or an animal, is now included in our own bodies and will become a part of our own flesh. Food fuses with us. On the other, cuisine itself is nothing else than a form of murderous processing. Food is but dead tissues. Cuisine, therefore, is a humanly contrived metamorphosis that destroys and disfigures pre-existing living beings, and may contaminate us with their death.

---

[25] Feldherr (1997). In this paper I will not discuss the problem of bloody sacrifice, which is also one of Ovid's major concerns, in regard to violence and food. See Barchiesi (2006).

As a humanly possible metamorphosis, the art of cookery creates situations of trompe-l'oeil. Meat is especially deceptive. Once the face is set aside, human flesh will look just like ordinary beef—ready to eat. Ovid explores precisely this potential of animal food to mislead us. Three gory tales fit the template of this misleading transformation. At the beginning of the *Metamorphoses*, Lycaon, the tyrant of Arcadia, kills a Molossian prisoner, cooks his limbs, and serves them on a dish to Zeus, who is visiting him in disguise. He wants to put to the test, beyond reasonable doubt, the god's divinity.[26] Zeus is not a dupe. He transforms the tyrant into a wolf, who "retains the vestiges of the ancient shape. The greyness is the same, the violence (*violentia*) of the face is the same, the same eyes shine, the image of ferocity (*ferocitatis imago*) is the same."[27] In his feral reincarnation, Lycaon will remain faithful to himself, and will enjoy the taste of blood. His will to know goes with cannibalism. In Book 6, two sweet sisters, Procne and Philomela, dismember a young boy, Itys, in order to roast and boil his body parts (minus the face), and to offer them for dinner to the youth's own father, Tereus, another tyrant who is guilty of raping Philomela, his sister-in-law. Tereus greedily amasses his own flesh (*sua viscera*) in his own belly (*in suam alvum*). He is transformed into a hoopoe.[28] In the *Fasti*, together with Philomela and Procne, Ovid also mentions Atreus and Thyestes.[29] Thyestes unwittingly devours his own beloved children whom his own brother, Atreus, has presented to him, artfully arranged on a plate. The same passage of the *Fasti* also alludes to Medea, culpable of murdering her own sons, and Ino, who plotted the immolation of her step-child to Apollo, by "toasting the seeds," thus provoking a famine for which a human sacrifice was supposed to be the remedy. All these characters must stay away from the celebration of the *Caristia*, a festival in honor of family concord.[30]

By operating on a human corpse through carving, seasoning, roasting, or boiling, Ovid's homicidal cooks perform, in their own maladroit way, a transfiguration that is meant to create confusion in the beholder. Whereas the gods make creative alterations, therefore, human beings such as Lycaon, Procne, Philomela, or Atreus kill for the sake of killing,

---

[26] Ovid, *Metamorphoses* 1.163–239. I have discussed this passage in Sissa (2016).
[27] Ovid, *Metamorphoses* 1.237–9 (*fit lupus et veteris servat vestigia formae. Canities eadem est, eadem violentia vultus, idem oculi lucent, eadem feritatis imago est*).
[28] Ovid, *Metamorphoses* 6.412–674. Gildenhard and Zissos (2007).
[29] On the parallel between the cannibalism of Atreus/Thyestes and that of Tereus, see Schiesaro (2003) ch. 3.
[30] Ovid, *Fasti* 2.627–30, *Tantalidae fratres absint et Iasonis uxor, | et quae ruricolis semina tosta dedit, | et soror et Procne Tereusque duabus iniquus | et quicumque suas per scelus auget opes*.

and convert their victims into what seems to be banal food, to be offered to a particular eater. They want to entomb a human corpse in the bowels of a guest, or a dear one. The culinary version of metamorphosis is murder. A misperception about food may result in cannibalism.

9.3. Tragic possibilities

In Ovid's world, anthropophagy is an ever-threatening possibility. Human flesh may look like red meat. The *Metamorphoses* and the *Fasti* explore this possibility, by narrating extreme cases of malignant revenge. Pythagoras makes this perilous event into a daily nightmare. More precisely, Pythagoras claims that tragic meals are not an exception, but the *paradigm* of what it means to indulge in the ordinary consumption of dead animals. We are all at risk of becoming Thyestes. The reason, he explains, is the fluidity of the cosmos. Since everything changes, and since we too are liable to (*possumus*) change—more precisely since our "winged souls" (*volucres animae*) "may enter into beastly homes and even be concealed in the bodies of cattle" (*inque ferinas possumus ire domos pecudumque in corpora condi*)—we should abstain from eating those bodies. They *may* contain the souls of human beings like us, even those perhaps of our own parents, brothers, children. "Let us not fill up our belly with Thyestean feasts! (*neve Thyestis cumulemus viscera mensis*)."[31]

In Pythagoras' own words, Thyestes' infamous name conjures up a suggestive cultural memory, in which the act of consuming human flesh reverts to the most intimate form of internecine violence. Chewing on your own people, enjoying their flavor, and digesting the substance of their bodies amount to an impermissible transgression, into which the perpetrator has been deceitfully forced. Consanguinity makes shedding blood a horrifying slaughter. But what Pythagoras reveals is that *any* succulent piece of steak *might* be a "Thyestean feast." *Any* appetizing stew ought to be looked at, through the metaphorical prism of those repulsive suppers. *Any* cut of beef, pork, or lamb should be treated as if it were—who knows?—the result of manslaughter, not just butchery. This is the scope of vegetarianism. Vegetarianism is neither a fad nor a matter of open-ended empathy: it is a means of pre-empting tragedy.

---

[31] Ovid, *Metamorphoses* 15.459–62.

Anthropophagy is the danger. And even more tragically, consanguinity makes that danger really terrifying. Fully to appreciate the pertinence of the tragic paradigm, we should notice that Pythagoras does not appeal to compassion for "living beings" as a vast group of creatures, equally worthy of respect, or able to feel pain. The vegetarian imperative does not derive from a descriptive syllogism: as a general principle, we must respect the sanctity of life, or the sentiency of living beings; animals are sentient living beings; therefore we must not hurt them. According to Pythagoras, we must abstain from meat on account of a probabilistic calculus that takes into consideration a modality, namely the hypothesis of what could possibly happen to us. Following the major premise that our souls transmigrate, a particular animal, taken individually, *might* host a human soul and, worse, the soul of one of our kinsmen. Its meat *might* be human flesh not only generically, but also specifically. It could be the flesh of a parent, a brother, an ally, or at the very least—for sure, any way (*certe*)—that of a man. Since we may all (*possumus*) settle in the body of a cow, let us not run the risk! Let us make sure that things are "safe and honorable" (*tuta esse ac honesta sinamus*), in order to avoid gorging our entrails at the table of Thyestes! The hazard is to eat a cut of meat that may contain "human blood," *cruor humanus*—our very blood. Blood creates identity. Like Thyestes, but also like Tereus, we might be engulfing our own flesh (*viscera*) into our own belly (*alvus*). We would be devouring ourselves. This is what might happen in the possible world of the *Metamorphoses*—a world in which the fragility of the human form, constantly exposed to transformation, require a cautious care of the human self. Vegetarianism is profoundly anthropocentric.

What matters is the uncertainty about whose life we might be taking. What is frightening is the distinct probability of devouring someone like us. This is indeed the domain of tragedy, a dramatic and philosophical genre where violence always strikes the wrong person: somebody who is too close. In the Greco-Roman theatrical tradition, to kill a member of one's own kin involuntarily is a canonical error. To ingest that same body, however, would be to take one step further into the horrendous. Imagine Oedipus slaying his father in ignorance and in self-defence, and, on top of that, being conned into eating Laius' flesh. Think of Thyestes himself, in Aeschylus' *Agamemnon*, or in the hyperbolically vilified version of the character contrived by Seneca, who was a playwright, but also a Stoic philosopher and a self-confessed vegetarian.[32] Pythagoras cannot ask us to renounce violence against animals once and for all, but

---

[32] Seneca, *Letters to Lucilius* 108, 18–19. See Sissa (2016).

he does require that we stop incorporating their meat in our own body—just in case. It is a principle of precaution, within a consequentialist morality. It is a sort of Pascalian wager. Better safe than sorry! In this logic, we are allowed to destroy or hunt animals that are our enemies, and we may have to do so in order to defend ourselves, exactly as we must fight fellow human beings who wage war against us. But we are prohibited from bringing the victims of our punishment to our lips. It is the contact of animal flesh with our own body—our mouth, and our bowels—that matters.[33] Not even the corpses of our enemies deserve to be swallowed. Potential cannibalism is a crime we are able to avoid. We must limit ourselves to nice foods that are certified (*tuta*), literally, as being "meek" (*mitia*).

All the conceptual threads relying the episodes of Lycaon and Tereus are reframed here, in Pythagoras' normative meditation. Pythagoras lingers on the suffering of edible animals while they are being immolated to a divinity, in a bloody sacrifice. The calf cries like a baby. Itys' desperate appeals to his infanticide mother, Procne, resonate in our memory.[34] But beyond the intratextual echoes, a genuine theory operates in the poem. The question is: what is the distance between this routine butchery and full-fledged murder (*plenus facinus*)?[35] And, as a consequence, are not we all none other than cannibals, simply by being carnivorous?

Firstly, let me insist, accidental anthropophagy is likely to occur because red meat, poultry, game, or fish, once sliced, chopped, minced, cooked, and exhibited on a dish, become indistinguishable from human flesh. The trompe-l'oeil of a cannibalistic dinner can only work because human and nonhuman bodies belong to the same family. Aesthetically, blood and muscles look alike. Once you remove the head, as Procne does, cuisine performs a deceptive disfiguration. This is why a father can be tricked into ingesting his children, not knowing who is actually lying, mangled and covered in sauce, on his plate. His genuine blindness parallels that of Acteon's faithful dogs, salivating after their beloved master who now looks like an appetizing deer. Acteon has become food for them. Once again, cuisine is deadly, deceptive metamorphosis.

Secondly, systemic anthropophagy is the unavoidable, structural risk of any meaty diet because any animal, no matter what its body may look like, is probably a human transformed. There are no completely nonhuman animals. But the deceptiveness of bodies, Pythagoras argues, creates a permanent threat. All living beings are to be regarded as your

---

[33] Ovid, *Metamorphoses* 15.463 (*viscera*), 478 (*ora*).
[34] Ovid, *Metamorphoses* 6.639–40. See also Tantalus and Pelops (6.403–11).
[35] Ovid, *Metamorphoses* 15.463-7.

own family, because any of them might be, at the very least, partially human. Any time, at every meal, daily life could turn to tragedy. This hypothesis is the major premise of Pythagoras' vegetarian syllogism. A deer, a bird, a fish, one of your timid, woolly sheep, and your industrious, helpful, patient cow might be members of your family, close or larger. Someone might be "concealed" (*condi*) in any of those creatures, whose appearance is non-human, but who are possibly, probably, invisibly human.

Whereas Io's story shows us the *potential* for such a dreadful mistake, Tereus' dinner *enacts* a culinary tragedy. A father blindly savors his own child's soft tissues. So be advised: when presented with a casserole, think twice! What if your own handsome son, your beautiful daughter were there? This terrifying hypothesis justifies Pythagoras' entire speech.

9.4. Apples and poplars

The poem alerts us to the provenance of seemingly non-human beings, therefore to their partial, hybrid, grafted, dissimulated humanity. The poem sharpens our semiotic ability to perceive vestigial traces of human characters. The poem invites us to a cautious skepticism. So does, more pedantically, Pythagoras by theorizing the ever-lurking *possibility* of scavenging on consanguineous new bodies. In the *Metamorphoses*, therefore, Pythagoras plays a role befitting its reputation, a role he plays well and that, in addition, gives full weight to his epilogue/comment. Vegetarianism is the high point of his speech.

Now, the modal logic of vegetarianism does not remain confined in Book 15. If we read carefully the fourteen books that precede Pythagoras' speech, it appears that the *Metamorphoses* respect a vegetarian *contrainte*.[36]

In the universe of the poem, the fauna derived from metamorphosis includes animals that are eatable, such as bovines and pigs, as well as inedible creatures, like spiders or wolves. All species may stem from human beings, including those that are usually consumed and even sacrificed to the gods, as it is the case for Io, the gorgeous cow. This is consistent with Pythagoras' prohibition against feeding on the entire genus of animals: *all* animals are forbidden. Meat is bad. Conversely, this explains the generic scope of vegetarianism: plants are good.

---

[36] On botanic taxonomies in ancient cultures, see Hautana (2014). See in particular 272–3, on the "reinvention of nature," through the creation of taxonomies. This is exactly what Ovid does, in the marvelous cosmos of the *Metamorphoses*.

The flora, however, is organized differently. Some species are transhuman, so to speak. Not all plants are good to eat.

Let us look at the menu of the vegetables that originate from a human body:

Daphne is transformed into the laurel tree (1.452–7).
Syrinx, into bamboo reeds (1.691–712).
The Heliades, into poplars, dripping amber (2.344–66).
Narcissus dies, and the narcissus blooms (3.344–413).
Crocus gives birth to the crocus (4.274–316).
Leucothoe becomes the tree that exudes frankincense (4.243–55).
Clytia is changed into a sunflower (4.257–70).
Philemon and Baucis become an oak and a linden intertwined (8.612–728).
Lotis first, and then Dryope, become the lotus (9.554–61).
Attis becomes the pine tree (10.103–5).
Cyparissus is changed into the cypress tree (10.134–42).
Hyacinthus dies, and his blood generates the hyacinth (10.162–219).
Myrrha morphs into the myrrh tree (10.488–502).
Adonis shifts into the windflower (10.725–39).
Minta becomes mint (10.728–30).
Ajax's blood soaks the ground, and a purple hyacinth is born (13.394–8).
An Apulian shepherd is transformed into the wild olive tree (14.512–26).

This catalog conveys an elegant taxonomy: metamorphosis affects only inedible plants. The poem encodes its botanical content along a neat line of demarcation: what is usually eaten *versus* what is not. The former vegetables are metamorphosis-free; the latter happen to contain traces of humanity. Once we perceive the consistency of this classification, everything falls into place—including Pythagoras' last words.

Ovid's categorization ought to surprise us for being so brilliantly obvious. Since metamorphosis is the master-plot of the poem, and since Ovid is fabricating a fictional world, it is only natural that metamorphosis should operate not merely as a literary device, but also as an organizing principle of this poetic cosmos. Metamorphosis brings about all sorts of animals (which calls for vegetarianism), but it happens to generate only plants that are unpalatable anyway. When human beings are transformed into vegetation, therefore, they become florae that are simply not part of Roman cuisine, raw or cooked. They become decorative flowers, useful herbs, or massive trees rather than juicy apples, figs, grapes, cereals, berries, or cabbage. The gastronomic unfitness of humanly generated plants is so evident, that a formal prohibition is not even necessary. Pythagoras preaches vegetarianism at large, without having to specify that plants are "safe" *except* for a few vegetally transformed humans.

Potential exceptions are strategically reabsorbed into the rule.

On the one hand, fruit that could have a human pedigree in different mythological sources are carefully described as immune from metamorphosis. According to Servius, the apple used to be a young man called Melus.[37] We cannot be sure whether Ovid deliberately omitted this story, or if he simply ignored its existence, but it is a matter of textual fact that, in his *Metamorphoses*, apples and cognate fruit exist in nature, with no human past. In the poem, mulberries were originally white, but have acquired a dark red color when Pyramus killed himself near a mulberry tree, and his blood first gushed onto the fruit, then reached the roots. Only the hue of the berries comes from human blood, not their pulp.[38] The narrator tries to make the sanguineous contamination of the berries both permanent and yet superficial enough, so that they can remain safely comestible. They are forever dyed. Only the color remains in the fruit (*nam color in pomo est*). Compare and contrast this purely chromatic alteration of a fruit that already existed as a fruit, with the transformation of Hyacinthus' and Ajax's blood into a full-bodied purple flower.[39] Compare and contrast it also with the blooming of the anemone out of a bubble of Adonis' blood, mixed with nectar. An entire flower comes to life. Its color is brilliant. "The flower grows of the same color as blood."[40] It is as brightly red as the interior of a pomegranate.[41] In the generation of these floral plants, blood is not merely a colorant, but fuses with the soil, and acts as a "seminal" substance. These flowers are made of blood.

Consistently, comestible fruit may well grow miraculously out of inanimate objects, but they are not the reincarnation of a previously anthropomorphic creature. Clusters of succulent grapes suddenly appear to crown Dionysus' head (*ipse racemiferis frontem circumdatus uvis*).[42]

On the other hand, whenever the destination of metamorphic plants might be uncertain, the text highlights ostentatiously their non-culinary

---

[37] Servius, comment to Vergil, *Eclogue* 8.37. See Littlewood (1968) (where another variant of human metamorphosis, from a young woman, is also discussed).

[38] Ovid, *Metamorphoses* 4.122–27. See Anderson (1996) 425: "The narrator, in her fussiness, proceeds in 126 to correct the impression of a definitive metamorphosis.... she now implies that the blood only temporarily stained the mulberries, and she resorts to pseudo-botanical lore to suggest that the tree roots were also soaked in gore." See Barolsky (2003) and Rhorer (1980).

[39] Ovid, *Metamorphoses* 10.162–219: Hyacinthus; 13.394–8: Ajax.

[40] Ovid, *Metamorphoses* 10.735: *flos de sanguine concolor ortus*.

[41] Ovid, *Metamorphoses* 10.736–7.

[42] Ovid, *Metamorphoses* 3.662–6. Ivy (*hederae*) may creep around the oars of a ship, and adorn the sails with their ivy-berries.

use. The laurel, a vegetal reincarnation of Daphne, will become an ornament in Apollo's rituals. As Christopher Francese rightly argues,

> The laurel is not just the plant which Daphne became, and the metamorphosis doesn't just add another species to the world. Rather, Ovid uses the aetiological aspect of the story to evoke impressions: the glamour of Greek athletics, the majesty of the Roman triumph, the dignity of Apolline cult and art, and the imposing presence of Augustus. This is the secret of aetiology's appeal to Ovid in this poem. It taps the meaningful potential of objects in the minds of the audience.[43]

All these culturally coded impressions, I will add, preclude any possible association of ideas with a well-appointed pantry, or a fragrant kitchen. The same can be said of the oleaster. The text places a heavy-handed accent on the bitter taste of its notoriously unpalatable olives (*bacis amaris*).[44] Even more ingenious is the diverted utility of mint leaves. As a fleeting allusion, the poem mentions a woman, Minta, who is changed into the homonymous aromatic herb.[45] Baucis, in turn, uses a bunch of fresh mint not as a condiment—cabbage *à la menthe*, why not—but as a handy tool to polish furniture.[46]

9.5. Nuts and bulls

The *Metamorphoses* is indeed a vegetarian poem. Not because it represents a world full of observant veggies, but because the narrative itself rules out the possibility that botanical foodstuff might have a human provenance. In the taxonomic biosphere of the poem, conventionally edible plants are guaranteed to contain zero percent of a metamorphic presence. By restricting your diet to them you cannot go wrong. You cannot run the risk of inadvertently ingesting your "own" flesh, or of hurting a human *Egō* who might suffer and wail.

---

[43] Francese (2004) 156. See also Barkan (1986) 85, Feeney (1988) 71–4, Flory (1995), Wheeler (1999) 202, Miller (2004–5), and Putnam (2004–5). All these studies insist on Daphne becoming not only Apollo's, but also Augustus' sacred plant—a long way from the kitchen.
[44] Ovid, *Metamorphoses* 14.525–6. See Pliny, *Naturalis historia* 15.5–7, on the repellent taste of the fruit yielded by the oleaster. These olives are improper to consumption, except for pharmaceutical preparations. A literary memory is also relevant in Ovid's unsavory connotation of the wild olive tree. In Vergil, *Aeneid* 12.766–90, Aeneas throws a spear into a wild olive tree, sacred to Faunus. The tree is characterized by the bitterness of its leaves (*forte sacer Fauno foliis oleaster amaris*). No blood is shed, but the god accepts Turnus' prayer, and refuses to let Aeneas extract the weapon from its very hard wood. Venus will succeed in so doing. On the significance of this episode, in the larger context of Vergil's meditation on "tree violation" and sacrificial imagery, see Dyson (2001).
[45] Ovid, *Metamorphoses* 10.728–30.   [46] Ovid, *Metamorphoses* 8.666.

Two sets of episodes prove these correlations. On the one hand, we encounter edible vegetables that are a cultural super-food; on the other we learn about inedible plants that might start bleeding.

A couple of exceptionally wise figures, Philemon and Baucis offer a paradigm of sophisticated simplicity, and an affectionate life-style.[47] When a pair of gods in disguise, Jupiter and Mercury, come and visit their modest hut, they show not merely a keen sense of hospitality, but an extraordinarily pious generosity. The meal they serve to the gods is the centerpiece of this metamorphic tale. The menu includes vegetables, fruits, wine, cheese, and eggs. The only meaty component is a tiny bit (*exiguam partem*) of bacon, presented as hors-d'oeuvre and, potentially, a roast.[48] When Baucis and Philemon realize that their guests might be superhuman (since wine starts to flow inexhaustibly), they feel compelled to add a special treat: a goose. The gods themselves, however, "prohibit the killing" (*superi vetuere necari*).[49]

Emily Gowers has analyzed the "arboreal" logic of this entire episode showing how Ovid's choice of details, ingredients, and words prepares the final transformation of the old couple into a block of intertwined trees, an oak and a linden. The emphatic focus on a quasi-vegetarian meal plays a crucial role in this crescendo.

> The simple meal laid out on the table (664–78) is unabashedly Roman and rustic in style.... Hors d'oeuvres of olives, preserved cornel cherries, endive, radish, cheese, and eggs are followed by a main course of boiled cabbage and bacon. Then comes dessert: nuts, figs, dates, plums, apples, grapes, and honey. The simplicity is deceptive.... The dinner seems to come from some pre-cereal era (there is no bread) and possibly a pre-sacrificial one (the gods stop the couple from slaughtering their household goose), but still it requires preparation, domesticating, laying down; a kind of civilizing process is involved and positively stressed (compare the gods' final decree: "Those who have cherished are cherished themselves" (*qui coluere coluntur*: 724).[50]

I could not agree more, and I will add that the accent placed on the homeopathic quantity of bacon, and the averted slaughter of a precious bird contribute to showcase Ovid's complicated negotiations with Roman culinary mores. The poem is not a piece of Pythagorean

---

[47] Ovid, *Metamorphoses* 8.612–728. See Hallett (2000), Fabre-Serris (2009).
[48] Ovid, *Metamorphoses* 8.649–50.
[49] Ovid, *Metamorphoses* 8.691–6.
[50] Gowers (2005) 341. See also Galinsky (1975) 197–204, on humor and literary stylization superseding myth. The emphasis on both the small portions of ham and the maladroit chase of the goose, Galinsky argues, are touches of humor that convey the viewpoint of an urban Roman man, looking at a bucolic, idyllic countryside. I will add that they also express connotations of minimized meat-eating.

fundamentalism. The poem settles for an approximate preference for meek food. A connotation of praise/blame colors different characters, on a spectrum from despicable cannibalism to perfect purity. Baucis and Philemon behave as anti-Lycaons.[51] Pomona, by cultivating her virginal orchard, does even better.[52] For these (quasi-) vegetarians, eating is an occasion to display civility. They appreciate a variety of wild or cultivated plants and fruit that can be enjoyed guiltlessly. And, once again, these nutritious and tasty produces exist in nature all by themselves, without metamorphosis.

By contrast quite a number of inedible vegetables ooze bodily fluids that prolong the human life of a pre-existing creature, now engrafted in their trunks, stalks, shafts, branches, and blossoms. Once made into poplars, the daughters of the Sun, the Heliades, never stop mourning their brother fallen from the sky, Phaeton. They are always weeping.[53] The lacrimous tree in which Myrrha, an incestuous daughter, is now alive—and prey to eternal regret—keeps leaking a precious perfume. "She cries however, and lukewarm droplets trickle from the tree. There is honor to the tears, and a stillicidium of myrrha flows from the hardwood" (*flet tamen, et tepidae manant ex arbore guttae. | Est honor et lacrimis, stillataque ex robore murra*).[54]

Dryope, a young mother, during a pastoral promenade with her little boy, stops in front of a pond where lotus is in full bloom.[55] She plucks some flowers for her small child to play with. Drops of blood fall from the fractured blossom (*guttas e flore cruentas decidere*).[56] The branches tremble in horror (*tremulo ramos horrore moveri*).[57] And then, in slow motion, the lotus starts to incorporate Dryope herself, who now becomes a tree. Dryope did not commit a voluntary crime: she was merely unaware

---

[51] Fabre-Serris (2009).
[52] Ovid, *Metamorphoses* 14.623–35.
[53] Ovid, *Metamorphoses* 2.340–66. The Heliades are paradigmatic of Ovid's transformations of humans into trees. See Perutelli (1985). Perutelli compares the Ovidian narration of their change while it is occurring with Vergil's descriptions of the final outcome of change. He then places these comments in a general perspective on the *Metamorphoses*. Ovid's descriptive storytelling emphasizes the *crossing* of *different* realms of nature (human/animal/vegetal/mineral). The concreteness of the language conveys a realistic rationalization of such process, as if the causes explained the effects. On the "congruence" of women and trees in this exemplary metamorphosis, see H. Casanova-Robin, "Dendrophories d'Ovide à Pontano: la nécessité de l'hypotypose," in Casanova-Robin (2009). On the sensitivity and sensibility of these plants, and more generally on metamorphosis as a "preservative event," see Zatta (2016). Ovid, *Metamorphoses* 2.340–66.
[54] Ovid, *Metamorphoses* 10.501–2.
[55] Ovid, *Metamorphoses* 9.340–93. On the narrative montage of Dryope's metamorphosis, see Fantham (2004) 68–9. On Dryope and other bleeding plants, Draskoczi (2010).
[56] Ovid, *Metamorphoses* 9.344.   [57] Ovid, *Metamorphoses* 9.345.

of the true identity of what appeared to be a splendid flower. She did not know that the lotus was an incarnation of Lotis, a young woman pursued by Priapus' obscene assaults. Again, she was not enough of a skeptic.

Erysichthon is an arrogant man who fails to pay respect to a monumental oak, sacred to Demeter. The goddess herself lies under the tree. He has the oak attacked with an ax. The tree bemoans and grows pale. Blood gushes from the wound (*vulnus*), as if it were a sacrificial victim.

> Blood flowed from the shattered bark, not differently from the blood that is usually shed from a broken neck, in front of the altars where, as a large victim, a bull falls to earth.[58]

Erysichthon is a killer. He does not hesitate to behead a devoted man who recoils from attacking the sacred oak. He challenges Demeter. In retribution, the goddess will inflict on him an inexhaustible hunger. The analogy with Lycaon (who cooks a Molossian slave, tricks Jupiter, and ends up in a state of ravenous appetite) is evident. The contrast with Philemon and Baucis (who are content with a frugal quasi-vegetarian regime, and will be transformed into an oak and a linden) is also clear. These are both intra-textual echoes and the marks of a structural pattern. Erysichthon's ferocious assault aligns metaphorically with bloody sacrifice. His "immolation" of a blood-shedding tree resonates with cannibalistic cuisine. Lycaon's unruly treatment of food as well as Erysichthon's impious aggression result in famine.

These sad stories offer elaborate variations on a pathetic theme, that of the wounded, bleeding, lamenting, weeping plant.[59] They fit an overarching narrative that presupposes what we could call a poetic biosphere. In this environment everything has its place. Nature and cuisine conform to a taxonomic order. Edible greens, roots, and fruits escape metamorphic hybridization. Like Pomona, Baucis, and Philemon, we can freely help ourselves to apples, berries, figs, grapes, honey, and plenty of common vegetables.[60] Like our blissful ancestors living in the golden age, we can

---

[58] Ovid, *Metamorphoses* 8.764–7: *cuius ut in trunco fecit manus impia vulnus, | haud aliter fluxit discusso cortice sanguis, | quam solet, ante aras ingens ubi victima Taurus | concidit, abrupta cruor e cervice profundi.*

[59] Vergil's depiction of the bleeding and speaking bush in which Hecuba's beloved son Polydorus survives is probably in the background of this recurring theme (*Aeneid* 3.28–9). Ovid displaces its pathos onto different vegetative transformations, be it that of Erysichthon or the Heliades. For a discussion of these intertextual resonances, see Smith (1997) 104–15. See also Casali (2007). I will add that there is a fleeting allusion to the myrtle, i.e. the bush from which Vergil's Polydorus emits his poignant lament: "*Egō sum*...", in Dryope's episode.

[60] Segal (1969) argued that since plants are permissible for Pythagoras, and since the poem contains numerous humans-into-plants transformations, vegetarianism proved to be not only irrelevant, but also insufficiently thought through. On account of metamorphosis,

gather arbute fruits, wild strawberries, and blackberries; we can collect "the sweet acorns fallen on the ground from Jupiter's large tree" (*et quae deciderant patula Iovis arbore glandes*).[61] Since the silver age, nutritious cereals have been available.[62] This mythologized periodization of natural history agrees with Pythagoras' appeal to the memory of a pre-carnivorous past: once upon a time, in that age we call "golden" fruit and herbs were our only source of livelihood, and we "never would pollute the mouth with blood." Back then birds, fish, and feeble animals were not afraid of us. "All things were safe from insidious wiles, fearing no deception. All things were filled with peace (*cuncta sine insidiis nullamque timentia fraudem plenaque pacis erant*)."[63]

To taste this kind of produce is safe and easy. Happily for us, metamorphosis brings about either utterly inedible plants, or trees such as the oak, the fruit of which come lose from the branches spontaneously, and can thus be picked up without any violence. Vegetarians do the same with the products of animal bodies, such as honey, eggs, and milk. Metamorphic species are not likely to bleed beneath the teeth of a cannibal despite himself, because the Romans abstain from eating wood, bark, incense, and flowers *anyway*. Who would think of chewing on a mouthful of timber, or an anemone?

9.6. Conclusion

According to Pythagoras in Book 15 of the *Metamorphoses*, the relocation of souls in disparate new bodies affects our being in the world. Since we *may* (*possumus*) change into other creatures, we must be careful in how we relate to them. It is a matter of knowledge, of knowing who they

---

one should not merely limit her diet to plants: one should starve. Pythagoras' speech, therefore, has allegedly nothing to do with the *Metamorphoses*. Charles Segal's charge of "illogicality," however, only reveals his failure to appreciate Ovid's nutritional rationality, which I hope to have demonstrated in sufficient detail.

[61] Ovid, *Metamorphoses* 1.102–6. On the connection between the golden age and alimentary non-violence, between Vergil and Ovid, see Habinek (1990). The detail about acorns being picked up from the ground is pertinent. These nuts come from a divine tree, the one Erysichthon slaughters and into which Philemon (or Baucis) is transformed. See Pliny the Elder, *Naturalis historia* 16.7: acorns are default ingredients for the confection of a surrogate bread, used in times of scarcity. They are collected. The XII Tables permit the collection of glands fallen on a neighbor's field (*ut glandem in alienum fundum procidentem colligere*).

[62] Ovid, *Metamorphoses* 1.123–4.

[63] Ovid, *Metamorphoses* 15.96–103.

are, but, because we have an alimentary relation with some of those creatures, doubts about their identity must modify, out of precaution, our eating habits. In the magic world of the poem, cyber-metamorphosis creates the distinct probability that an animal might be much more familiar than it looks or, at least, more human than its theriomorphic appearance would make us believe. The poem itself, as a sequence of metamorphic narratives, offers a virtually infinite instantiation of that very possibility. The *carmen perpetuum* could go on and on, to showcase the open-ended potential of that: "we may" (*possumus*). Io, the lovely cow; Acteon, the swift deer; Circe's pigs, and birds and fish and frogs are what they are, because they have changed, literally, beyond recognition. The children of Thyestes and Tereus, once processed and beheaded in a human kitchen, have also changed beyond recognition. We may fail to recognize them for who they also are in/beyond/notwithstanding/ through their *figura, imago, effigies, corpus*. Misrecognition is the stuff of tragedy. And we, readers of the *Fasti*, and the *Metamorphoses* up to the Pythagorean finale, have now learned that, for us too, in our daily life, to enjoy animal food may be a tragic mistake.

Pythagoras' vegetarianism finds its reason not in an imperative of respect for non-human animals as sentient, vulnerable, intelligent, and dignified living beings, worthy of care and regard, but rather in a risk we incur—we, civilized humans. This risk is anthropophagy. We must be vegetarian for our own sake, not in order to protect animal life. A carnivore runs the risk of becoming a cannibal. By eating what appears to be ordinary meat, we might inadvertently take into our mouth the flesh of a woman or a man, transformed and yet invisibly present in a new anatomy. A cow might be what it looks like, but it might also be a young woman, now converted into a bulky, speechless bovine, and yet still there—thoughtful, smart, and self-conscious.

Faithful to the same logic, the poem shows that plants, on the contrary, will be good to eat. But not any plant: only those the origin of which could not possibly be a person. In the ecosystem of the poem, we can see a familiar distinction at work, between the fruits and vegetables that are edible, on the one hand, and those that are not, on the other. But this commonplace antithesis (edible/inedible) overlaps with another one, which is idiosyncratic to an epic about "new bodies." Metamorphosis is, after all, the commanding design of the poem. The dichotomy of metamorphic versus non-metamorphic plants is the binary opposition that Ovid weaves into his narrative. In this possible world, therefore, metamorphosis creates no produce destined to culinary accommodation.

Pythagoras, I hope to have demonstrated, offers a retrospective comment on Ovid's vegetarian poem. The poem is posthuman, insofar as a metamorphic fluidity undermines the idea that humans might hold a specific and special place, among, and above, living beings. The poem is paradoxically anthropocentric, insofar as *our* terror of chewing, ingesting, and digesting *human* flesh, swollen with human blood, is the principle that orders its taxonomy.

WORKS CITED

Alfonsi, L. (1958) "L'inquadramento filosofico delle *Metamorfosi* ovidiane," in N. I. Herescu (ed.), *Ovidiana: Recherches sur Ovide*. Paris: 265–72.
Anderson, W. S. (ed.) (1996) *Ovid*: Metamorphoses, *Books 1–5*. Norman, OK.
Aquinas, T. (1951) *Commentary On Aristotle's* De Anima. Trans. K. Foster and S. Humphries. New Haven.
Barchiesi, A. (2006) "Voices and Narrative Instances in the *Metamorphoses*," in P. E. Knox (ed.), *Oxford Readings in Ovid*. Oxford: 273–319.
Barkan, L. (1986) *The Gods Made Flesh: Metamorphosis and the Pursuit of Paganism*. New Haven.
Barolsky, P. (2003) "Ovid's Colors," *Arion* 10: 51–6.
Barolsky, P. (2005) "Ovid, Bernini, and the Art of Petrification," *Arion* 13: 149–62.
Branham, R. B., G. Most, R. Hexter, G. Sissa, D. Selden, P. duBois, and W. R. Johnson (1997) "Panel Discussion: Classics and Comparative Literature: Agenda for the '90s," *Classical Philology* 92.2: 153–88.
Bruit Zaidman, L., and P. Schmitt Pantel (1991) *La religion grecque dans les cités à l'époque classique*. Paris.
Campana, J., and S. Maisano, S. (eds) (2016) *Posthuman Renaissance*. New York.
Casali, S. (2007) "Correcting Aeneas's Voyage: Ovid's Commentary on *Aeneid* 3," *Transactions of the American Philological Association* 137: 181–210.
Casanova-Robin, H. (ed.) (2009) *Ovide, figures de l'hybride: illustrations littéraires et figurées de l'esthétique ovidienne à travers les âges*. Paris.
Cavell, S. (1979) *The Claim of Reason: Wittgenstein, Skepticism, Morality and Tragedy*. Oxford.
Colavito, M. M. (1989) *The Pythagorean Intertext in Ovid's Metamorphoses: A New Interpretation*. Lewiston, NY.
Coleman, R. (1971) "Structure and Intention in the *Metamorphoses*," *The Classical Quarterly* 21: 461–77.
Cornelli, G. (2016) "Aristotle and the Pythagorean Myths of Metempsychosis," *Metexis* 28: 1–16.
Draskoczi, E. (2010) "'Come pintor che con essempro pinga': l'influenza ovidiana sulle metamorfosi vegetali nella *Commedia*," in E. Szkárosi and J. Nagy (eds), *Dal testo alla rete: letteratura, arte, cultura e storia in nuove prospettive*. Budapest: 13–28.

Dyson, J. T. (2001) *King of the Wood: The Sacrificial Victor in Virgil's* Aeneid. Norman, OK.

Eco, U. (1979) Lector in fabula: *la cooperazione interpretativa nei testi narrativi.* Milan.

Fabre-Serris, J. (2009) "Constructing a Narrative of *mira deum*: The Story of Philemon and Baucis (Ovid, *Metamorphoses* 8)," in P. Hardie (ed.), *Paradox and the Marvellous in Augustan Literature and Culture.* Oxford: 231–47.

Fabre-Serris, J. (2018) "Enjeux moraux et idéologiques des usages d'Empédocle au livre XV des *Métamorphoses*: une réponse d'Ovide à Virgile (*Enéide* VI et VIII)," in S. Franchet d'Espèrey and C. Lévy (eds), *Les Présocratiques à Rome.* Paris, 303–19.

Fantham, E. (2004) *Ovid's* Metamorphoses. Oxford.

Feeney, D. (1988) *Literature and Religion in Rome: Cultures, Contexts, and Beliefs.* Cambridge.

Feldherr, A. (1997) "Metamorphosis and Sacrifice in Ovid's Theban Narrative," *Materiali e discussioni per l'analisi dei testi classici* 38: 25–55.

Flory, M. B. (1995) "The Symbolism of Laurel in Cameo Portraits of Livia," *Memoirs of the American Academy in Rome* 40: 43–68.

Francese, C. (2004) "Daphne, Honor, and Aetiological Action in Ovid's *Metamorphoses*," *The Classical World* 97: 153–7.

Franklin, N. (2005) "'Unless All That The Poets Sing Is False': The Role Of Pythagoras' Speech In Ovid's *Metamorphoses*," *Hirundo: The McGill Journal of Classical Studies* 3: 65–73.

Galand-Halyn, P. (1994) *Le reflet des fleurs: description et métalangage poétique d'Homère à la Renaissance.* Geneva.

Galinsky, K. (1975) *Ovid's* Metamorphoses: *An Introduction to the Basic Aspects.* Berkeley.

Gildenhard, I., and A. Zissos (2007) "Barbarian Variations: Tereus, Procne and Philomela in Ovid (*Met.* 6.412–674) and Beyond," *Dictynna* 4: 1–25.

Gowers, E. (2005) "Talking Trees: Philemon and Baucis Revisited," *Arethusa* 38: 331–65.

Habinek, T. (1990) "Sacrifice, Society, and Vergil's Ox-Born Bees," in M. Griffith and D. J. Mastronarde (eds), *Cabinet of the Muses: Essays on Classical and Comparative Literature in Honor of Thomas G. Rosenmeyer.* Atlanta: 209–23.

Hallett, J. P. (2000) "Mortal and Immortal: Animal, Vegetable, and Mineral: Equality and Change in Ovid's Baucis and Philemon Episode (*Met.* 8.616–724)," in S. K. Dickison and J. P. Hallett (eds), *Rome and Her Monuments: Essays on the City and Literature of Rome in Honor of Katherine A. Geffcken.* Wauconda, IL: 545–61.

Hardie, P. (1995) "The Speech of Pythagoras in Ovid Metamorphoses 15: Empedoclean Epos," *The Classical Quarterly* 45: 204–14.

Hardie, P. (2002) *Ovid's Poetics of Illusion.* Cambridge.

Hardie, P., and G. Chiarini (eds) (2015) *Ovidio: Metamorfosi, Volume VI: Libri XIII–XV. Scrittori greci e latini.* Milan.

Hautana, S. (2014) "Piante," in M. Bettini and W. Short (eds), *Con i Romani: un'antropologia della cultura antica*. Bologna: 269–86.
Little, D. (1970) "The Speech of Pythagoras in *Metamorphoses* 15 and the Structure of the *Metamorphoses*," *Hermes* 98: 340–60.
Littlewood, A. R. (1968) "The Symbolism of the Apple in Greek and Roman Literature," *Harvard Studies in Classical Philology* 72: 147–81.
McGowan, M. (2016) "Pythagoras and Numa in Ovid: Exile and Immortality at Rome," in P. Mitsis and I. Ziogas (eds), *Wordplay and Powerplay in Latin Poetry*. Berlin: 241–58.
Miller, J. (1994) "The Memories of Ovid's Pythagoras," *Mnemosyne* 47: 473–87.
Miller, J. (2004–2005) "Ovid and Augustan Apollo," *Hermathena* 177/8: 165–80.
Myers, K. S. (1994) *Ovid's Causes: Cosmogony and Aetiology in the* Metamorphoses. Ann Arbor.
Otis, B. ([1966] 2010) *Ovid as an Epic Poet*. Cambridge.
Perutelli, A. (1985) "I '*bracchia*' degli alberi. Designazione tecnica e immagine poetica," *Materiali e discussioni per l'analisi dei testi classici* 15: 9–48.
Putnam, M. C. J. (2004–2005) "Daphne's Roots: In memoriam Charles Segal," *Hermathena* 177/8: 71–89.
Rhorer, C. C. (1980) "Red and White in Ovid's *Metamorphoses*: The Mulberry Tree in the Tale of Pyramus and Thisbe," *Ramus* 9: 79–88.
Riddehough, G. B. (1959) "Man-into-Beast Changes in Ovid," *Phoenix* 13: 201–9.
Romano, C. (2013) "Après la chair," *Journal of French and Francophone Philosophy* 21: 1–29.
Schiesaro, A. (2003) *The Passions in Play: On the Dynamics of Senecan Drama*. Cambridge.
Segal, C. (1969) "Myth and Philosophy in the *Metamorphoses*: Ovid's Augustanism and the Augustan Conclusion of Book XV," *The American Journal of Philology* 90: 257–92.
Segal, C. (2001) "Intertextuality and Immortality: Ovid, Pythagoras and Lucretius in *Metamorphoses* 15," *Materiali e discussioni per l'analisi dei testi classici* 46: 63–101.
Setaioli, A. (1988) "L'impostazione letteraria del discorso di Pitagora nel XV libro delle *Metamorfosi*," in W. Schubert (ed.), *Ovid Werk und Wirkung*. Bern: 487–514.
Sissa, G. (2016) "Promethean Tricks and Thyestean Feasts: Bloody Sacrifice and Vegetarianism in Ancient Cultures," in G. Dierckxsens, R. Bijlsma, M. Begun, and T. Kiefer (eds), *The Animal Inside: Essays at the Intersection of Philosophical Anthropology and Animal Studies*. London: 11–28.
Smith, A. (1997) *Poetic Allusion and Poetic Embrace in Virgil and Ovid*. Ann Arbor.
Tillette, J.-Y. (2009) "Ovide et son 'moralisateur' au miroir de Pythagore: figure(s) de l'auteur dans le livre XV de l' *Ovide moralisé*," in M. Szkilnik, L. Harf-Lancner, and L. Mathey Maille (eds), *Ovide métamorphosé: les lecteurs médiévaux d'Ovide*. Paris: 201–22.

van Noorden, H. (2015) *Playing Hesiod: The "Myth of the Races" in Classical Antiquity*. Cambridge.
Viarre, S. (1964) *L'image et la pensée dans les Métamorphoses d'Ovide*. Paris.
Wheeler, S. (1999) *A Discourse of Wonders: Audience and Performance in Ovid's Metamorphoses*. Philadelphia.
Wheeler, S. (2000) *Narrative Dynamics in Ovid's* Metamorphoses. Tübingen.
Wheeler, S. (2009) "Into New Bodies: The Incipit of Ovid's *Metamorphoses* as Intertext in Imperial Latin," *Materiali e discussioni per l'analisi dei testi classici* 61, *Callida Musa*: Papers on Latin Literature: In Honor of R. Elaine Fantham: 147–60.
Zatta, C. (2016) "Plants' Interconnected Lives: From Ovid's Myths to Presocratic Thought and Beyond," *Arion* 24.2: 101–26.

Part 3
Anthro-Excentric

10 Hyperobjects, OOO, and the eruptive classics—field notes of an accidental tourist

James I. Porter

> If mankind, or the thinking and contemplative beings which comprise it, were banished from the surface of the earth, the moving and sublime spectacle of nature that we know would be nothing more than a scene of desolation and silence. The universe would be mute; stillness and night would take possession of it. Everything would be transformed into a vast emptiness where unremarked phenomena would occur, dimly and unheard.... Once my existence and the happiness of my peers is abstracted from the world, what does the rest of nature matter to me?
>
> Diderot, "Encyclopédie"[1]

Object-oriented ontology (OOO), along with its doublet, speculative realism (also sometimes called speculative materialism), is a branch of theory that sits at one end of a broad spectrum known as "the new materialisms," which is perhaps best known through the writings of Bill Brown ("Thing Theory"), Karen Barad (*Meeting the Universe Halfway*), and Jane Bennett (*Vibrant Matter*).[2] Each of these approaches is an extension of the posthumanist turn in recent science studies, led by Michel Serres, Donna Haraway, Bruno Latour, Isabel Stengers, Cary Wolfe, and Michael Marder, among others, and together they mark a further development of poststructuralist critiques of humanism in the wake of Nietzsche, from Derrida to Foucault. Classical studies are just now catching up with these most recent trends. New and developing work in affect, object, and thing theory in Classics—in archaeology, literature, and philosophy—is at the vanguard of the field's latest turn to theory, while science studies are just now getting off the ground there as well.[3]

---

[1] Diderot (1992) 25; trans. adapted and supplemented.
[2] Brown (2004), Barad (2007), Bennett (2010).
[3] Archaeology: Knappett (2005), Olsen (2010), Hodder (2012), Smith (2015); literature: Mueller (2016), Telò (2016), Mueller and Telò (2018); philosophy and science studies: Kennedy (2002); Holmes (forthcoming).

Launched in a conference at Goldsmith's in 2007,[4] the philosophies associated with the "speculative turn" are less well known and understood, no doubt because this area of the new materialisms is both formidably difficult and inherently resistible: it runs directly, and aggressively, counter to the spirit of the humanities as these have traditionally been conceived, in line with another trend that is gaining traction in contemporary theory, namely posthumanism, which has provided the immediate provocation for this volume. The major players here include less familiar names: Graham Harman, Ray Brassier, Quentin Meillassoux, Iain Hamilton Grant, Levi Bryant, Steven Shaviro, and Timothy Morton.[5] While speculative realism and OOO are moved by a number of impulses, they could hardly be called a movement: they are more of a moving front that is trying to figure out where its own boundaries lie. Its exponents would all broadly identify themselves as speculative realists. Some of these (Harman, Bryant, and Morton) are more invested in the formal status of objects as metaphysically real entities, while others are more invested in speculative, open-ended possibilities that seek to circumscribe in thought the absolute facticity of the world as materially real without conferring on this reality the status of a metaphysical absolute.[6] With these caveats in mind, I will use the terms "speculative realism" and OOO more or less interchangeably, giving preference to the latter where the focus is being placed on the status of objects rather than on the status of reality. And although speculative realist thinking can be frustratingly difficult to pin down, whether singly or in its variety, the turn marked by this assemblage of theories has a number of welcome and attractive aspects, many of which can bear fruitfully on a reconceived postclassicist and posthumanist Classics, which in turn would have much to say in reply.[7] But before considering the question of the possible relevance of speculative realism and its congeners to the world of Classics and vice versa, let me first give a very quick sketch of the contemporary theoretical terrain as I understand it.

One of the unifying aims of speculative realism is its assault on the very idea of humanism—not simply with the purpose of stretching the

---

[4] See Brassier et al. (2007).   [5] See Bryant, Srnicek, and Harman (2011).
[6] Meillasoux's project, to be discussed momentarily, is virtually a transcendental argument about *"pure possibility"* (Meillassoux (2008) 62; emphasis in original). Given his commitment to "speculative materialism" (Meillassoux (2008) 121), we might call Meillassoux a transcendental materialist. Harman, by contrast, is reverting to a kind of metaphysical substance-formalism that is in part modeled on Aristotle (Harman (2012b) 199), but that conceives itself as hostile to materialism, which it takes to be a form of idealism in disguise (Harman (2011b) 40). I leave aside the strand in speculative realism that identifies with Whitehead's process philosophy (principally, Shaviro).
[7] The Postclassicisms Collective (forthcoming).

idea of the human in new directions, but with the express goal of eliminating its relevance altogether. The strategy here is to use metaphysics in a highly speculative and greatly hedged fashion in order to undermine correlationism—which, as Morton explains, is

> the spell that descended on philosophy since the Romantic period,... [viz.,] the notion [of] the human–world correlate: meaning is only possible between a human mind and what it thinks, its "objects," flimsy and tenuous as they are. The problem as correlationism sees it is, is the light on in the fridge when you close the door?"[8]

Speculative realists would reply, "Ask the light." Then they would add, "Ask the light if it cares." The primary appeal of speculative realism lies in its basic thrust, which is both threatening and liberating in intent: its exponents seek to displace a human-based theory of reality with an object-oriented one. There is something magnificently humiliating in such a stance, hard as it may be to hold it in any consistent fashion, or even to envision, let alone experience, its implications.

Working against Kant and Enlightenment philosophical ideology, speculative realism/OOO seeks to discredit the first-person, anthropocentric perspective on reality by turning reality into a world unto itself, one of whose minority members happens to be the human species. On this flipped version of things, the world is not reducible to the way it appears to the human eye or mind. Instead, humans are inhabited by the world as one more object among others—or one less. Donna Haraway's opening gambit in *When Species Meet* brings out this last implication beautifully:

> I love the fact that human genomes can be found in only about 10 percent of all the cells that occupy the mundane space I call my body; the other 90 percent of the cells are filled with the genomes of bacteria, fungi, protists, and such, some of which play in a symphony necessary to my being alive at all, and some of which are hitching a ride and doing the rest of me, of us, no harm. I am vastly outnumbered by my tiny companions; better put, I become an adult human being in company with these tiny messmates. To be one is always to *become with* many.[9]

This remark comes by way of an introduction that leads to Section I of her book, which is entitled: "We Have Never Been Human." If you ever wondered whether we have ever or never been modern, as Bruno Latour's challenging thesis runs, the stakes here look to be on a different order of magnitude altogether.

Speculative realism and OOO are more strident than Haraway in their attack on the exceptionalism of the human, never mind the humanistic—a

---

[8] Morton (2013) 9. [9] Haraway (2008) 4.

topic that instantly pales and shrivels by comparison. Nevertheless, the stances of the speculative realists and of Haraway originate in a similar impulse. Here is Harman:

> The ontological structure of the world does not evolve or undergo revolutions, which is precisely what makes it an ontological structure. Only objects undergo revolutions—and human beings make up just a few billion objects among others, and are not special guests at the table of Being whose absence would simplify the universe immeasurably.... It makes no difference to Being itself whether humans die off or not; the axes of the world will continue their strife long after we have all succeeded in murdering each other.[10]

From these few quotes I think we can get a sense of what it means to orient reality towards the object-world, but also why taking up this posture is so difficult to perform or to accept: the theory is literally inconceivable. It postulates a world to which we have no legitimate access, conceptual or other. A question to ask is why one might even wish to entertain such a theory at all. But before attempting an answer, let us proceed a bit further with an examination of speculative realism's most basic propositions.

The philosophy of speculative realism is *realist* in its defense of "a mind-independent reality,"[11] which the theory insists is always at-hand but forever inaccessible to the senses, being prior to and inexhaustible by its relations (hence non-relational and non-correlational), not made of eternal substances but of "mortal, ever-changing" objects "built from swarms of subcomponents," and highly resistant to "causal or cognitive mastery" (so Harman; "mortal" does not mean materially "perishable" but rather ontologically transient).[12] It is *speculative* in its adherence to a metaphysical model or ontology—a non-traditional and somewhat "bizarre" metaphysical ontology, to be sure—that can only speculate on its component entities.[13] To allow that the world exists in this form is to take up an *object-oriented* stance, but also to condemn oneself to a non-privileged place in the world. One becomes an accidental tourist, at best, of the essentially withdrawn Real in which a "democracy of objects" reigns: "no object can be treated as constructed by another object" in such a "flat" ontology.[14] Each object belongs to an assemblage, or a series of assemblages, to which they each contribute and which gives them their local, momentary nature; "no object... is the ground of all the others."[15] Objects do not so much exist as they simply occur, more like the event of

---

[10] Harman (2005) 244.
[11] Harman (2012b) 184.
[12] Harman (2012b) 188.
[13] Harman (2005) 78; Harman (2011a) 24.
[14] Bryant (2011) 19.
[15] Bryant (2011) 19.

their own (withheld) reality than like substantial things, irreducible to any and all relations, ungrounded by any principles that we can make out, and operating at every scale of reality.[16] Nature here is denaturalized ("unnatural"), made to be populated not by natural objects with phenomenal traits (relabeled "routes of access") but by unnatural objects with no obvious but only a vicarious (sensual) access, swarming and interacting but never encountering one another directly: they merely subsist, "weirdly," in a vital plethora (Harman speaks of "the smoldering volcanic core of things," an image that runs through a good deal of OOO as it happens)[17] that gives rise to ever-new and ever-surprising (and surprisingly sensuous) phenomena which cannot in turn be reduced back either to these objects or to their phenomena: objects are constitutively at war with, which is to say autonomous from, their own properties.[18]

Of course, simply to say anything about objects, so construed, is to involve oneself in a potential contradiction. How do we know what they are or what they do? This flirtation with illicit knowledge and hence too with contradiction is a trait that runs through all of speculative realism and that is dealt with differently in different theories. In Harman's case, vicarious sensual access to the "molten core" of the volcano of things allows him to revive phenomenology and extend its "theater of carnality" into the object-oriented world: "the world is dense with sensual or elemental relations between things: a form of realism far more enticing than the tedious kind repeatedly denounced or evaded by human-centered philosophy."[19] The challenge of speculative realism is to grant to objects a basic autonomy from determination but also from philosophical appropriation: phenomenalism, historicism, idealism, empiricism, and eliminative materialism are unable to exhaust the primary richness of objects. "A rock is neither downwardly reducible to quarks and electrons nor upwardly reducible to its role in stoning the Interior Ministry. The rock has rock properties not found in its tiny inner components, and also has rock properties not exhausted by its uses." Its reality exceeds all of its possible or actual relations—this is the purely speculative hypothesis of Harman's realism.[20]

In another, more extreme formulation, that of Quentin Meillassoux, what speculative realism insists on is what might be called the hyper-reality of reality, or what Meillassoux calls ancestral reality: "I will call

---

[16] Harman (2005) 85–6; Shaviro (2011) 284.
[17] Harman (2005) 251; 204; 197; 130; 171, etc. Harman (2012b) 188.
[18] Harman (2005) 18; 19: objects "withdraw even from the brute relational system of nature."
[19] Harman (2005) 171.   [20] Harman (2012b) 196, 199.

'ancestral' any reality anterior to the emergence of the human species—or even anterior to every recognized form of life on earth."[21] The point is not simply to predate the world prior to the advent of the human. It is to remove the thought of the world from the fact of the world itself. Reality, one has to say, is ancestral to the human even now, at this very present moment: "To think ancestrality is to think a world without thought—a world without the givenness of the world. It is therefore incumbent upon us to break with the ontological requisite of the moderns, according to which to be is to be a correlate."[22] The assault is on the coherence of thought, and then on the possessor of thought—on humanity itself: "Humanity becomes unable to invest the world with meaning that had hitherto allowed it to inhabit its environment."[23] In this scenario, the subject retreats, excluded from the world (and not just defeated by it), while the world persists—in a form that we can no longer say is as we once thought it to be.

I am less interested in the metaphysical commitments of speculative realism or the logical coherence of any of its claims, both of which are the source of much controversy at the moment, than in the conceptual work it promises to do. Though bizarre in many ways, and though its proponents would undoubtedly wish to deny this, speculative realism is no less bizarre, and no more verifiable, than many of its competitors (Anaxagorean pluralism, Democritean atomism, Aristotelian substance theory, Spinozan monism, Kantian transcendental critique, and so on). I think it's pretty obvious that all such metaphysical schemes have a performative value that outruns their truth value. Harman calls OOO not a method but a "counter-method."[24] Its virtues lie in its powers of theoretical resistance, its capacity to conjure not an "other" to the subject (objects are this too), but the ultimate frailty and falsehood of "the subject" as a category of thought or of experience. OOO also challenges our customary sense of what an object is. "Objects are not confined to one level of reality, but *exist in all sizes and in all natural and unnatural places.*"[25] Objects are irreducible to their contexts. They are not in principle unlocatable—quite the contrary—though one of their essential properties, to the extent that they have any at all, is to be "nonlocal" (Morton). Locating objects depends on where we locate them contextually. And to speak of "contexts" is merely to "open a space where *certain* interactions and effects can take place and not others."[26] That's why

---

[21] Meillassoux (2008) 10.
[22] Meillassoux (2008) 28. Harman's critique (Harman (2011a) 145) misses this.
[23] Meillassoux (2008) 136 n. 1.   [24] Harman (2012a) 16.
[25] Harman (2005) 86; emphasis added.   [26] Harman (2012b) 191.

when Harman speaks of "rock properties" he is bracketing a context, not describing an essence. Rocks also contain non-rock properties, for example, those that make up its inner components, or *their* inner components, ad infinitum: to pick these out is to take another slice of reality, to account for another context, to grab hold of another object.[27] The world becomes a scintillating cosmos of objects arrayed along an endlessly sliding scale without any determinable magnitude. OOO is in this sense a cosmology.

Enter the hyperobject. A hyperobject, a tool of ecocriticism, is described by Morton as any object that is "massively distributed in time and space relative to humans," the primary features of which include vastness, intensity, nonlocality (irreducibility to any given locale), and a spectral luminosity that borders on irreality.[28] Examples include a black hole, the Lago Agrio oil field in Ecuador, the biosphere, the Solar System, and so on, but these are only emblematic instances of an underlying phenomenon. Hyperobjects are not defined by any absolute magnitude. Rather, they are objects in their hyper-proximity to us: they are the threat of our being engulfed by the world of objects and by the absorptive reality of their ontology. Faced with a hyperobject, we are dwarfed and virtually incorporated by it: "*we are always inside an object*."[29] To stand before a hyperobject, which is to say, before the hyperreality of objects, is to surrender a (large) bit of one's self. It is to suffer existential and metaphysical humiliation. And it is to open a space where interactions and effects take place on a level not previously seen. Hyperobjects give us a glimpse of a posthumanistic world. A question to ask at this point is whether the idea of the hyperobject is a novelty or whether it has any known predecessors. Is its theory a telling product of our hypermodernity alone, or is it an idea that could have been embraced prior to 2011? Diderot reminds us in the opening quotation of this chapter that the thought of the world absent all human protagonists was at least conceivable in 1751, even if he produced the thought only to outlaw it. What about classical antiquity?

It is here that we can begin to take stock of contemporary object-oriented speculative thinking and attempt to orient it towards Classics. In what follows, I will suggest that close relatives, if not exact predecessors, to the hyperobject can be found in ancient philosophies of nature, nor were these imagined for the sole purpose of denouncing them. Quite the contrary. Taking our cue from Morton, and then more broadly from

---

[27] Harman (2012b) 199; Harman (2005) 85, 159. Components are not physical constituents for Harman. They are metaphysical trap doors.
[28] Morton (2013) 1. [29] Morton (2013) 17; emphasis in original.

other theorists of posthumanism, we can engage with the ancient materials in three ways. First, we can look at Greek and Roman conceptions of nature as ecologies of nature that were imagined in a hyperobjective mode. Secondly, we can hypothesize what options were available for conceiving materiality without ultimate matter (nonreductive materialism) in antiquity. More generally, we can investigate, with a certain license, whether there were any possibilities for object-oriented views of the world in antiquity, views that were unburdened by subject-oriented phenomenologies, but which nevertheless had the capacity to burden and thereby unsettle such phenomenologies.[30]

In response to this quick research agenda, three areas on which to concentrate spring to mind: (i) certain views of nature which turn nature into a kind of hyperobject (for instance as found in a Latin poem today called the *Aetna*, which is a hymn to a volcano dating from the mid-first century CE; its author is unknown); (ii) certain materialist and sensualist stances, wherein objects take on an independent existence that no longer seems beholden to human phenomenology—however briefly and possibly illusorily (atomism would be a prime candidate here, but there are tendencies even among poets that give objects and sensuous surfaces a life and vitality of their own); and (iii) self-destituting philosophies of nature, which is to say natural philosophies that turn mankind into one more object among others (Empedocles, atomism (again), Seneca and other Roman Stoic moralists). These three areas tend to converge, as a few brief examples will demonstrate. I will run through these in reverse order.

10.1. Destituted selves

Let's begin with a quotation from one of Seneca's *Dialogues*:

What is man? A vessel that the slightest shaking, the slightest buffet, will break.... A weak and fragile body, naked, in its natural state without defence, in need of another's assistance, exposed to all the insults of Fortune, and, once it has given its muscles a good exercise, food for the wild beast, prey to everyone; a patchwork of feeble and fluid elements that pleases the eye only in its external features,... doomed to decay,... a flawed and useless thing. (6.11.3)[31]

---

[30] Bennett (2010) likewise views ancient atomism as a conceptual resource and ally for rethinking the object-world. See Cole (2013) for a parallel if more wary inquiry into the relevance of OOO to another pre-modern field, that of medieval studies. Less warily: Petropunk Collective (2013). Meillassoux (2008) 113–14 strangely denies all candidates from antiquity.

[31] Seneca (2008); trans. slightly adapted.

Seneca repeats some of the phrasing and all of the thought in a meditation on earthquakes:

> If you want to be afraid of nothing, regard everything as something to be afraid of. Look around and see what trivial things can destroy us: not even food, not liquid, not waking, not sleeping, is beneficial except in moderation. Now you will realize that we are mere bodies, insignificant and frail, fleeting, destined to be destroyed with no great exertion. Without doubt this is the only danger we face, that the earth quakes, that it is suddenly shattered and drags down the things on its surface! (*Natural Questions* 6.2.3)[32]

Earthquakes have this kind of effect on the (self-)conception of subjects. To contain the force, as it were, of the earth's quaking by relegating it to the status of a mere geophysical disaster located in some time and place, as an exponent of OOO might try to do,[33] would be to misread, I believe, the force of Seneca's thought. The fact that the earth trembles so violently is a symptom of an underlying instability within the very heart of the Real. It is a sign that, in Morton's words, there is "something ontologically scary about our world." The world, on Seneca's view, just is the equivalent *of* an earthquake. Earthquakes are a hyperobject that deprives us of privilege and makes us into another object in the world—less a diminutive one than conceived as belonging to a system of (hyper-)objects. The destitution of the self that Seneca is pointing to in both of these passages can be achieved in countless ways beyond squaring oneself up to a concrete threat of nature in its sheer and brutal objectality. One of these ways, perhaps the most common if the least recognized, is the confrontation of a subject with some form of an abyss. The confrontation here is not with material objects, as old and new materialists would have it, but with their utter negation. Let's call this an "abyssal object."

Seneca knows this experience too. He arrives at it the way many other ancients do, by inquiring into, or rather picturing, time in its most unfathomable dimension. The trigger to this chain of reflections is the phrase (or the idea) "just now":

> I seem to have just lost you, for what is not "just now" (*modo*) when you are remembering? Just now I sat as a boy before Sotion the philosopher, I began to plead cases just now, I stopped wanting to plead just now, I stopped being able to plead just now.

---

[32] Hine (2010) 90.
[33] And as Morton appears to do in *Hyperobjects*: "such disasters take place against a stable background" ((2013) 15). He replaces this background with the hyperobject of "global warming," which "means something ontologically scary about our world" ((2013) 48). Seneca's example is meant to be no less "ontologically scary" than global warming is for us today.

But what is this "just now"? It is a point on the edge of an abyss. Thinking of this "now," and the "now" that follows, and the "now" that "just" was, leads to a greater reflection, and a greater imponderability:

> The speed of time is infinite, something more obvious to those looking back. For it slips by those preoccupied with present problems: the passing of its headlong flight is so gentle. You ask the reason for this? Whatever time has passed is in the same condition: it is observed in the same way and buried together: everything falls into the same abyss. And yet there cannot be long lapses of time in a business that is altogether short. We live for only a point in time, and so much less than a point, but nature has mocked even this tiniest thing with the appearance of a longer period [from infancy to youth to old age itself]. How many stages it has placed in such a cramped entity! It is just now that I escorted you on your departure, and yet this "just now" is a good portion of our life, such that we should reflect that its brevity will one day run out. Time used not to seem so swift to me: now its pace seems unbelievable, whether this is because I feel the deadlines being brought closer, or because I have begun to pay attention and calculate my losses. (*Letter* 49.2–4)[34]

In another letter Seneca notes how staring blank death in the face makes one wince with vertigo: even the bravest of men will "be blind with dizziness as he looks down on an immense depth when standing on the brink" (57.4)—namely, the brink of life, which so cast begins to resemble the brink of nothingness, which may be the greatest hyperobject there is. Hyperobjects are objects that cannot be objectified. The attempt to do so shatters the very logic of subjects and objects. To quote one last time from Morton, "The abyss in front of things is *interobjective*," while the intersubjective realm of you and me "is a small region of a much larger interobjective configuration space."[35] We are forever perched on the edge of the abyss of this interobjectivity, which leads to a radical dethroning of the human point of view.

There's only more point that needs to be made about Seneca's insight into this abyss: destitution of the self is not an aberration: it is one of the commonest ways in which subjects are formed in antiquity.[36] Self-destitution, paradoxically, is a finely honed technique of the self, a *practice* that produces, indeed *constitutes*, the self—not as the measure of things, but as one more (or less) thing among other things. This strategy

---

[34] Fantham (2010) 74–5. [35] Morton (2013) 81.
[36] Cf. Marcus Aurelius, *Meditations* 8.38, trans. Hard: "You are nothing but the stink of decay and a sackful of gore"; 4.41: "You are a little soul carrying a corpse around, as Epictetus used to say." And compare Morton (2013) 31: "Every subject is formed at the expense of some viscous, slightly poisoned substance, possibly teeming with bacteria, rank with stomach acid. The parent scoops up the mucky milk in a tissue and flushes the wadded package down the toilet.... In effect, the entire Earth is a wadded tissue of vomited milk."

is widespread: it can be found in writers from Heraclitus and Plato to Marcus Aurelius and Augustine. Unfortunately, it is not the kind of technique that is cataloged or even envisaged in Foucault's project on the hermeneutics of the self (which tracks not deformations, but only formations, of the self) or on any other theory of the emergence of the subject in Greece or Rome known to me. Part of Foucault's problem is that he takes for granted that selves exist in some stable state, whether at the starting point or at the end-point of the self-fashioning process, when in fact what I believe we find in the ancient literature, in a majority of cases, is an attempt to acknowledge and cultivate a sense of precarity at the heart of what it is to be a self, or if one prefers, to be human.[37] Only, on this view, the human is always deformed by its relation to the inhuman. This position brings us closer to the contemporary notion of the posthuman.

Consider Heraclitus' famous dictum, "I went in search of myself" (fr. 101 DK). What he says is that he "went in search of," not that he ever found what he was looking for. In another fragment, we can see why: "You would not find out the boundaries of soul, even by travelling along every path: so deep a measure does it have" (fr. 45 DK).[38] Clearly the self for Heraclitus is in a very real sense not only unbounded, because it is actually *abyssal*. But in what sense is it this? On the standard reading, the object of the trajectory of Heraclitus' search and his plunge into the abyss (the "solution" to this problem of the self) is said to lie not in the individual self, which is in radical flux, but in the identity of the cosmos as a whole, which (it is thought) does have a stable identity (that of being self-identical, a property not available to individual constituents of the world). I am not at all convinced by this argument. The identity of the universe is far from being determinate for Heraclitus, and it is far from being stable either. The "universe" (or "world") is in ways merely a rubric—a mental parenthesis—that is put around the endless cycle of activity, of radical transformative change, that takes place in reality, which in turn is at once both absolute and contingent.[39] If we were to put enough pressure on these two last terms we might want to say, adopting language that is closer to Meillassoux's, that the Heraclitean universe is absolutely contingent but also contingently absolute.

Meillassoux insists that the universe, conceived in rigorously speculative terms, must be both absolutely contingent (it could always be other

---

[37] See Porter (forthcoming). [38] Kirk, Raven, and Schofield (1983) 203.
[39] Cf. Heraclitus fr. 52 DK: "The everlasting is a child at play, playing draughts" (trans. Hussey (1999) 107)—not in the name of probability (see Meillassoux (2008) 96–108), but in the name of hazarding Being.

than it is now) and not dogmatically absolute (it is not reducible to a rational concept). But even in Meillassoux's rigorously logical construct, as with the Stoics and Heraclitus before him, the concept of "world" is as ineliminable as it is provisional. It is an ontological postulate (insofar is it sums up the "fact" or "facticity" of the world, which is to say the ineliminability of existence as such); and it is in all likelihood a falsification of reality whenever we try to picture it. Thus, Meillassoux repeatedly resorts to the postulate of "the (acausal) universe" or "world."[40] Objects may be erratic, but they are still objects. Reality (the world) *is*, and it is real.[41] Even the "hyper-Chaos" that Meillassoux claims "underlies" reality does nothing to eliminate reality's existence: chaos is just a view from which reality in its utter contingency appears most repugnant to rational thought; it is a subjective characterization of a third-personal view from nowhere. But that view does nothing to eliminate the absolute "necessity" of "*what is*," "of the 'there is.'"[42] In point of fact, the entirety of Meillassoux's project is premised on the proposition that "I am perfectly *incapable of thinking the abolition of existence....I can[not] conceive of the non-being of existence as such.*"[43] Reality may be irreducible to thought, but it is not irreducible to itself: such is the wager of speculative realism. Likewise, Harman is happy to contest the naturalizing premise of the independent physical existence of objects, but he cannot contemplate the non-existence of objects in general.[44]

But there is something more to be said about their positions. Both Meillassoux and Harmon may offer us a view from nowhere, or else the *idea* of such a view, since a view from nowhere is illicit. But the view they offer is decidedly a view of *something*.[45] Thus, the claim about facticity, about "the 'there is,'" is a claim that "there is something rather than nothing."[46] This is the frank realism that the two philosophers share. But what does it tell us? Is the claim a statement of a preference or does it

---

[40] Meillassoux (2008) 9, 15, 64, 92, etc.
[41] Meillassoux (2008) 85, and *passim*. Cf. ibid., 53: "the world *is*," albeit "without reason."
[42] Meillassoux (2008) 64, 66, 83, 80, 42, etc. The necessity of existence is implicit in—we might even say, smuggled into—contingency: "Contingency is such that anything might happen, even nothing at all, *so that what is, remains as it is*" (63; emphasis added). There are two applications of necessity, then: the necessity of contingency, and the necessity of existence: the universe can always be other than it is, but it can never not be at all.
[43] Meillassoux (2008) 76; emphasis added.
[44] Harman (2005) 31; 152 ("the sheer existence of objects"); 79 (opposing the inexhaustible reality of objects to nihilism), etc.
[45] The claim about "the 'there is'" is a preferential claim, evidently endorsed by Meillassoux, that "there is something rather than nothing" (Meillassoux (2008) 80).
[46] Meillassoux (2008) 71, 76, 80.

have deeper motivations? Meillassoux's remark that "I am perfectly incapable of thinking the abolition of existence" suggests an incapacity rather than a mere preference. And though both Meillassoux and Harman would contest this reading, I want to suggest that the concept of the world is for them, and possibly in general, a necessary appurtenance of human thought. Just try to imagine away the world, never mind the thought of the world. As Nietzsche once pointed out not so long ago, "A representing agency cannot 'not represent' itself, cannot represent itself away." This is tied to the corollary, "Not-being is unthinkable."[47] This did not prevent Nietzsche from experimenting with bizarrely imagined ontological scenarios that, much like those of the speculative realists, had the potential to eliminate the world as it was intuitively understood, apart from this one catch. I think that the power of both the ancient and modern theories considered so far derives from the fundamental conceptual instability (or regret) that they all bring to the fore, which rivets self to world at a point where each of the terms and their mutual relations become a vexing problem. The self is brought to the brink of a kind of posthumanism, at a thrilling limit, and then gently walked back. To the extent that speculative realists insist on this reciprocal problematization of self and world, they are travelling the same path as the ancient cosmologies. One salient difference is to be found in the fact that the ancient cosmogonies and their cosmological offshoots are forthrightly designed as *ethical* projects. Their aim is not to undermine objects in the name of some reassuring underlying metaphysical principle,[48] but to undermine *subjects* in the name of ethical considerations. Cosmogony and cosmology on the ancient view are meant as "a blow to humanity's narcissism" (Freud). They create a wedge, imagined *ex hypothesi*, that drives a gap into the very conception of the human by decentering it from itself, first by removing humanity from the world through the predication of a primal scene (an elemental "first cause" like water, air, the infinite, fire, or a primordial act of separation produced through a cosmic vortex or rotation) and then by reinserting the human back into that framework, which, ever indifferent to "us," continues to generate effects in all of its elemental ferocity. Ontology here creates an ethical problem for the self that is asked to imagine and then to inhabit, strangely and uncertainly, a strange and uncertain world.

---

[47] Nietzsche (1988) 7:575 (26[11]), from 1873. The latter claim is a repeated refrain in Nietzsche (1988) 7:84 (3[91]), and 7:543 (23[12]). Cf. further the last lines of *On the Genealogy of Morals* III:28.
[48] *Pace* Harman in The Petropunk Collective (2013) 233.

The same paradigm is developed in the *Meditations* of Marcus Aurelius, who gives us a good illustration of the way in which the destitution of the self is the principle aim, or at least the premise, of all technologies of the self in Roman thinking in its most radical and perilous moments. We might say that these technologies illustrate not "the art of life," but "the art of living on the edge." Let's take a quick look.

Marcus is normally viewed as the author of the idea that the self is an impregnable "inner citadel," but this is hardly the full story. It's true that he *does* at times appear to recognize a kind of interiority and a kind of autonomy of the self that can be the object of self-fashioning—a self that lies "hidden within us" as a kind of secreted agency, an inner self—"the person himself" (*anthrōpos*)—that, in its invulnerability, can appear to resemble a mighty citadel (*Meditations* 10.38, 8.48). To this agency we might be tempted to ascribe the power of self-fashioning that Marcus also, at times, acknowledges—the capacity for self-motion and self-alteration, the ability to "arouse itself, and adapt itself, and fashion itself according to its will," and to "make whatever happens to it appear to itself as it wishes to be"—the indices of what he calls an "art of living." (6.8, 4.2, 7.61, 11.29)

But *caveat lector*: self-mastery is not the same thing as self-determination in Marcus' book. For one thing, the soul is never a self-identical object, nor is it the goal of the rational soul to remain self-identical. Quite the contrary. Our natures are not given, they are breathing, changing things, constantly altering in the face of changing realities, constantly taking in and dispersing sensations and perceptions. Such is the composite nature of souls: they are literally "put together" from their environment, and hence literally akin to the natural world. What we are today is not what we were at birth: "for all this was taken in only yesterday or the day before as an influx from foodstuffs or the air breathed in," all of which changes. "Is one afraid of change? Why, what can come about without change?" We are the living proof: "And do you not see that change in yourself is of a similar nature?" (*Meditations* 10.7, 7.18). Change is the law of all that is; it is the characteristic feature of universal nature (as it was for Heraclitus, to whom Roman Stoicism is deeply indebted). And so, when we retreat into ourselves, what we discover there is not the homunculus agent that we putatively are, but rather a connection with everything that "we" are not. We discover a dynamic contingency that is never the same except in some aggregate sense that we will never comprehend but can only dimly glimpse. We stand on a precipice surrounded by "*the abyss of time*" (*Meditations* 4.50, 12.7, 4.3). The best that a rational subject can hope to do is to *yield* to this unalterable set of conditions, to freely become what it is—an emanation of nature—and to accept its own radical contingency and fragility (this is a version of Stoic fatalism, what would later be called *"amor fati"*). Whether peering within itself or within others, whether looking up or down upon all that can be seen, the subject glimpses not so much the universal structures of nature as the absolute deadlock of their conceivability, which is in no way objective or objectifiable in any sense that is meaningful to the human mind. And then she gives way, ceding herself to this quandary of being.

As with Seneca, the ultimate shape that the self assumes comes not from austere measures or regimens or even dialogue, *pace* Foucault and others. Rather, it results from the confrontation with *limits*—its own—in the face of the abyssal character of nature: its endlessness, its sheer meaninglessness (when viewed from the first-personal perspective), and its extremity. For it is only when experiences are had at the limit of what can be experienced, *in extremis*, that the self's true value and estimation can be measured. Radical precariousness and moral urgency come together for a Stoic whenever she thinks such terminal thoughts. For this reason, selves don't ever really "emerge" in antiquity (despite the fact that modern scholars, in search of the ancient self, are bent on pinpointing this moment of emergence): ancient selves are ongoing *emergencies*, ongoing experiments in living on the edge and *in extremis*, the aim of which is to find an ethical relationship not in the first instance to one's self, but rather to the blank contingency and indifference of the world in all its absolute and irrevocable necessity.

Viewed in this light, speculative realism and OOO can be seen to have an identical aim. (In fact, Meillassoux cannot navigate to his final goal without assuming what he calls "the absolute necessity of the contingency of everything"—a fully credentialed Stoic stance.)[49] Even if these most contemporary of ontologies are utterly unconcerned with selves and their formative processes, their principle object, so to speak, is (I would argue) to instill an ethical view of the subject, which limps away from the theory, and the prospect of a "world without thought," with a slower, humbler gait.[50] The ecological variants of the theory are even more obviously committed to such a stance, although the dangers they forecast are of a more imminent sort. On the other hand, this kind of strategic flirtation with the ultimate risk, the radical endangering of the

---

[49] Meillassoux (2008) 54.
[50] I am extrapolating here. But see Meillassoux (2008) 132 n. 15, pointing to a future study of the ethical consequences of his theory, which apparently will build on his 1997 dissertation, *L'inexistence divine*. See Harman (2011a) 187–238 for a relevant excerpt, esp. 187–88: "an imminent ethics is an ethics that *posits this life as the only desirable life*," grounded in a kind of "immortality," which is to say, "the desire that this human life and no other should again and always be lived."

familiar concepts of both self *and* world (beyond their mere empirical perishability),[51] is not unique to the Stoics or to speculative realists. It is the consequence of any attempt to take up a radically third-personal, objective stance, of the sort that is rejected by Diderot but that is more favorably entertained by Thomas Nagel in his book *The View from Nowhere*. To embrace such a stance, from which it can appear not only that you had no reason to exist, but that your "*world* should never have existed" too, is to flirt with absurdity.[52] But not to take this kind of mental step, this view from nowhere, Nagel argues, is to enter into an even greater absurdity: it is to deny ourselves the possibility for an ethical life here in our all-too-human world. But let's procede to our second case study.

Consider Lucretius' account of simulacral films:

> For verily we see many things cast off and give out bodies [i.e., atomic films] in abundance, not only from deep beneath, as we said before, but often too from the surface, such as their own colour. And commonly is this done by awnings, yellow and red and steely-blue, when stretched over great theatres they flap and flutter, spread everywhere on masts and beams. For there they tinge the assembly in the tiers beneath, and all the bravery of the stage and the gay-clad company of the elders, and constrain them to flutter in their colours. And the more closely are the hoardings of the theatre shut in all around, the more does all the scene within laugh, bathed in brightness, as the light of day is straitened.
>
> (*The Nature of Things* 4.72–83; trans. Bailey)

We normally read these simulacral appearances as being destined for the human eye. But they have an actuality of their own, and they are in principle *indifferent* to our view of them and to our existence tout court. Now compare Harman (speaking of a different tent): "Any *appearance* of the tent is only an appearance *for* some other entity.... *The tent itself is an object,* [*a real force,*] *not a phenomenon.*"[53] The play of colors staining the air (and ourselves as its objects) is not *for us*. It subsists in our absence, like the light in the fridge.[54] The laughing show of phenomena can be read as cruel indifference or as a flattering seduction. It is

---

[51] Meillassoux (2008) 62. Knowledge of physics (the heavens, in an empirical sense) is not the object for a Stoic (Seneca, *Letter* 88.14–15, 27–28; trans. Fantham (2010)) any more than it is for an Epicurean (*PHerc.* 831).

[52] Nagel (1986) 212. Closely parallel: Meillassoux (2008) 57: "In order to refute subjective idealism, I must grant that my possible annihilation is thinkable as something that is not just the correlate of my thought of this annihilation. Cf. Meillassoux (2008) 76 and below.

[53] Harman (2005) 17.

[54] Cf. Seneca, *Letter* 54.5 (trans. Fantham (2010)): "wouldn't you say a man was very stupid to think a lantern was worse off when it was put out than before it was lit?"

something of both. Coincidentally (or not), the laughter of the subject-indifferent world of OOO is one of its hallmarks: on this view, too, "sensual objects inevitably become [mere] elements" and relations, "and there is something inherently flat and caricatured about elements, however brilliantly they may sparkle."[55] Their laughter is not for us so much as it is directed *at* us, as we go about groping, senselessly, after the (ever-receding) tangible meaning of objects. To put this in the perspective of ecocriticism and to scale it up to the level of hyperobjects, we can and perhaps should recognize, along with Morton, that

> global warming plays a very mean trick. It reveals that what we took to be a reliable world was actually just a habitual pattern—a collusion between forces such as sunshine and moisture and humans expecting such things at certain regular intervals and giving them names, such as Dog Days. We took weather to be real. But in an age of global warming we see it as an accident, a simulation of something darker, more withdrawn—climate. As Harman argues, *world* is always...a mere caricature of some real object.[56]

And, one should add, of ourselves.

If there were space, I would want to dwell a bit on Empedocles, the fifth-century Greek Presocratic from Acragas (modern-day Sicily) who depicts himself, in his poem on nature, as a fallen angel (a *daimōn*) who has entered into the great cycle of cosmic division and change that runs throughout eternity in tandem with an opposite cycle of aggregation and unification. Identifying himself with the cosmic process, he is finally absorbed into it, its victim and wandering fool, buffeted about with and just like the other *daimones* (the elemental physical constituents of nature, air, earth, water, fire), part human, part thing, undergoing a series of reincarnations for some 30,000 years, some of which included his identity as a boy, a girl, a bush, a bird, and a mute sea fish (fr. 117 DK).[57] In this long view of things, we would have to say that Empedocles' biography no longer traces the life of a subject but that of an object. Is he a hyperobject? Quite possibly he is. The story that he ended his life by hurling himself into the mouth of Etna personalizes this same narrative through-line. Immolating himself in the depths of the volcano, Empedocles does not simply return himself to his elemental nature: he *becomes* Nature. He becomes inhuman again—which he in fact always was. This is an ecological philosophy if ever there was one.

---

[55] Harman (2005) 217.   [56] Morton (2013) 102.
[57] An unflattering list, which ends with fish, creatures that are reputed to be "stupid," condemned to the murky depths, and deprived of light and air (and voice), as in Plato, *Timaeus* 92b.

The volcano of Nature never ceased to erupt, or to petrify the gaze of travelers and poets. One proof that it did not is the *Aetna* poem, composed in Latin a half-millennium after Empedocles died. The poem is not merely a hymn to volcanic Etna. It presents the prospect of a vast, looming Thing, a mass of seething airs, gasses, magma, and liquid. Harboring a crucible of warring forces within (487) and belching forth to the sky where a cloud shrouds its dark underbelly (305–29), Etna is both a recessive object and self-objectifying at once: "Aetna is its own palpable, its own most credible voucher" (177; trans. Ellis). And yet, in its looming presence the volcano is indifferent to everything around it. This is the *contumely* of objects. "If you happen to hold this lava-stone in your hand and try it by its solid part, you would not believe it could burn or disseminate fire; yet the moment you question it with an iron mallet, it returns answer and vents its rage in sparks to the blow" (401–4). Such objectality (indifference, self-absorbed actuality) is the source of Etna's terror, which is a staging place for matter in its most resistant state, that of ruinous ruins. "Often you may look out upon huge gaps in the ground and stretches of land cut off and fallen in ruin or plunged into dense night: it is a wide scene of chaos and debris without end" (137–9). Etna is a uniquely monstrous work of nature and, in its symbolic projection, is tantamount to Nature itself. It contains a fury of potential violence and unspent force that is both inexhaustible and immeasurable. Etna is, for these reasons, a veritable hyperobject: excessive in itself, it resists mythologization and, tendentially, all ascription of meaning. Morton uses the notion of a hyperobject to redescribe our phenomenological experience of nature from an object-oriented perspective that radically undoes first-personal categories of experience. The *Aetna* poet's project has precisely the same goal: he is something of an ecocritic *avant la lettre*, one who is determined to displace the human perspective and to put on show the inner life of things. Nor is he a singularity in the ancient world. There is a veritable subgenre of ancient thought and writing that consists in invitations to observe the life of things from within them and not at a safe distance from without.

Of course, it is a good question to ask how sustainable such perspectives are, but also how coherent and non-self-vitiating they may be. Trying to imagine the world without ourselves imagining it can be a repugnant prospect, logically and psychologically speaking, and it may be politically unviable as well. Jane Bennett's pushback against OOO is worth quoting: "I find myself living in a world populated by materially diverse, lively bodies. In this materialism, things—what is special about them given their sensuous specificity, their particular material configuration, and their distinctive, idiosyncratic history—

matter a lot."[58] Shaviro worries that OOO in some of its variants runs the risk of "isolating [objects] from the world."[59] Harman and Meillassoux would doubtless answer that we need to adjust our definition of the world. No doubt, human-oriented things (as opposed to "objects") do matter, or so we flatter ourselves into believing. But if they do, OOO and speculative realism wager, it is because they originate, somewhere down the line, in an experience of a world that cares little for us and that is unassimilable to our experience of it, however much we may repress the fact.

Object-oriented philosophies existed in antiquity, as did hyperobjects, and they were every bit as potent, and as hypothetical, as current speculative realist and object-oriented philosophies. Unseating the subject, shocking our pet epistemologies and phenomenologies, and inverting our commonplace assumptions, drastic "counter-methods" that lead to both exhilaration and despair or desolation[60]—this was the bread and butter of a great many (not all) views of nature and the universe in Greece and Rome, as I hope my brief forays into a few case studies have served to show. If speculative realism and OOO have any ultimate value, it is not metaphysical or purely philosophical: either their value is ethical or they have no value at all.[61]

But just how hypothetical are thought experiments like these, in fact? Given the impending threats of irreversible climate change and global warming, we may need to start thinking a lot harder about what that unobjectifiable world should mean to us—before we too become a (vanished) antiquity.[62]

WORKS CITED

Bailey, C., trans. (1910) *Lucretius: On the Nature of Things*. Oxford.
Barad, K. (2007) *Meeting the Universe Halfway: Quantum Physics and the Entanglement of Matter and Meaning*. Durham, NC.

---

[58] Bennett (2012) 231. [59] Shaviro (2011) 288. [60] Meillassoux (2008) 116.
[61] This would be one way of mitigating the objections that OOO frivolously personifies and animates objects (see Cole (2015)). On the contrary, it de-centers subjects—an ethical and responsible move. Cf. Williams (1995) 235 addressing, in a prescient way, the problems of ecological catastrophe facing humanity: "Our attitudes to these further kinds of effect are not directed simply to human interests, and in that sense they are not anthropocentric. But they are still our attitudes, expressing our values." This is also the thrust of Bennett (2010). See too now Eagleton (2016), esp. ch. 1. For a possible Adornian line on the problem, see Hammer (2006) 175.
[62] Earlier versions of this essay were presented at Oxford in 2014 and at UCLA and Berkeley in 2015. My thanks to the audiences on each occasion and especially to Brooke Holmes for helpful comments.

Bennett, J. (2010) *Vibrant Matter: A Political Ecology of Things*. Durham, NC.
Bennett, J. (2012) "Systems and Things: A Response to Graham Harman and Timothy Morton," *New Literary History* 43.2: 225-33.
Brassier, R., I. H. Grant, G. Harman, and Q. Meillassoux (2007) "Speculative Realism," *Collapse III*: 306-449.
Brown, B. (2004) "Thing Theory," in B. Brown (ed.), *Things*. Chicago: 1-16.
Bryant, L. R. (2011) *The Democracy of Objects*. Ann Arbor.
Bryant, L. R., N. Srnicek, and G. Harman (eds) (2011) *The Speculative Turn: Continental Materialism and Realism*. Melbourne.
Cole, A. (2013) "The Call of Things: A Critique of Object-Oriented Ontologies," *The Minnesota Review* 80: 106-18.
Cole, A. (2015) "Those Obscure Objects of Desire," *Artforum* (Summer): 319-23.
Davie, J., trans. (2008) *Seneca: Dialogues and Essays*, with an introduction and notes by T. Reinhardt. Oxford.
Diderot, D. (1992) *Political Writings*. Ed. J. H. Mason and R. Wokler. Cambridge.
Eagleton, T. (2016) *Materialism*. New Haven.
Ellis, R. (ed.) (1901) *Aetna: A Critical Recension of the Text*. Oxford.
Fantham, E., trans. (2010) *Seneca: Selected Letters*. Oxford.
Hammer, E. (2006) *Adorno and the Political*. London.
Haraway, D. (2008) *When Species Meet*. Minneapolis.
Hard, R., trans. (2011) *Marcus Aurelius: Meditations, with Selected Correspondence*, With an introduction and notes by C. Gill. Oxford.
Harman, G. (2005) *Guerrilla Metaphysics: Phenomenology and the Carpentry of Things*. Chicago.
Harman, G. (2011a) *Quentin Meillassoux: Philosophy in the Making*. Edinburgh.
Harman, G. (2011b) "On the Undermining of Objects: Grant, Bruno, and Radical Philosophy," in Bryant, Srnicek, and Harman, 21-40.
Harman, G. (2012a) "Concerning Stephen Hawking's Claim that Philosophy Is Dead," *Filozofski vestnik* 33: 11-22.
Harman, G. (2012b) "The Well-Wrought Broken Hammer: Object-Oriented Literary Criticism," *New Literary History* 43.2: 183-203.
Hine, H. M., trans. (2010) *Seneca: Natural Questions*. Chicago.
Hodder, I. (2012) *Entangled: An Archaeology of the Relationships between Humans and Things*. Malden, MA.
Holmes, B. (forthcoming) *The Tissue of the World: Sympathy and the Concept of Nature in Greco-Roman Antiquity*.
Hussey, E. (1999) "Heraclitus," in A. A. Long (ed.), *The Cambridge Companion to Early Greek Philosophy*. Cambridge: 88-112.
Kennedy, D. F. (2002) *Rethinking Reality: Lucretius and the Textualization of Nature*. Ann Arbor.
Kirk, G. S., J. E. Raven, and M. Schofield. (1983) *The Presocratic Philosophers: A Critical History with a Selection of Texts*. 2nd edn. Cambridge.
Knappett, C. (2005) *Thinking through Material Culture: An Interdisciplinary Perspective*. Philadelphia.
Meillassoux, Q. (2008) *After Finitude: An Essay on the Necessity of Contingency*. Trans. R. Brassier. London.

Morton, T. (2013) *Hyperobjects: Philosophy and Ecology after the End of the World*. Minneapolis.
Mueller, M. (2016) *Objects as Actors: Props and the Poetics of Performance in Greek Tragedy*. Chicago.
Mueller, M., and M. Telò (eds) (2018) *The Materialities of Greek Tragedy: Objects and Affect in Aeschylus, Sophocles, and Euripides*. London.
Nagel, T. (1986) *The View from Nowhere*. New York.
Nietzsche, F. W. (1988) *Sämtliche Werke: Kritische Studienausgabe in 15 Einzelbänden*, ed. G. Colli and M. Montinari. 15 vols. 2nd edn. Berlin.
Olsen, B. (2010) *In Defense of Things: Archaeology and the Ontology of Objects*. Lanham, MD.
Porter, J. I. (forthcoming) "Living on the Edge: Self and World *in extremis* in Roman Philosophy," in W. Shearin (ed), *The Oxford Handbook of Roman Philosophy*. Oxford.
Shaviro, S. (2011) "The Actual Volcano: Whitehead, Harman, and the Problem of Relations," in Bryant, Srnicek, and Harman (2011): 279–90.
Smith, A. T. (2015) *Political Machine: Assembling Sovereignty in the Bronze Age Caucasus*. Princeton.
Telò, M. (2016) *Aristophanes and the Cloak of Comedy: Affect, Aesthetics, and the Canon*. Chicago.
The Postclassicisms Collective (forthcoming) *Postclassicisms*. Chicago.
The Petropunk Collective (2013) *Speculative Medievalisms: Discography*. Brooklyn.
Williams, B. (1995) *Making Sense of Humanity and Other Philosophical Papers, 1982–1993*. Cambridge.

11 Nature trouble

Ancient *physis* and queer performativity

Emanuela Bianchi

The question of nature—its value, function, and meaning—has been alive in feminist thought almost from its inception. There exists, of course, a long and well-attested history—perhaps even a prehistory—of associations of women with the domain of the natural, along with a complex history of feminist attempts to negotiate, grapple with, and twist free from their grip. Without offering a comprehensive rehearsal of these histories, I would like to frame the problem as one that emerges with unprecedented philosophical distinctness somewhere in the early 1990s, in a tension whose poles bear the names of Judith Butler and Elizabeth Grosz.[1] Butler, on the one hand, posits the "nature" of gender (that is, sex) as an *effect* of practices, while Grosz draws on an alternate monist ontology to cast the body as natural object as a site of unknowable or unexpected "volatile" activity on the other. In order to interrogate a certain Western inception of this longstanding association of nature and the feminine, I will in this paper return to a phenomenological conception of nature, or *physis*, that first appears in early Greek thinking. In so doing, I will draw on the twin figures of Luce Irigaray and John Sallis for interpretive assistance, as well as the metaphorics of performance and theater found in Butler's thinking, to consider the shape, form, and style of the dynamics of emergence and concealment we might phenomenologically comprehend in relation to Being and beings, and in particular those beings that emerge and withdraw independently of, and alongside, human beings. As phenomenologists in the Heideggerian tradition have emphasized, nature, or *physis*, is understood in these early Greek texts not as a determinate region of Being calling for investigation, not as a hidden essence of things, and certainly not as a hypostatized or totalizable system of parts and wholes (as it will come to be formulated for the Stoics).[2] Certainly, it cannot be addressed as a region of

---

[1] This moment, and its tensions, is beautifully articulated in Pheng Cheah's 1996 review essay discussing Butler (1993) and Grosz (1994).
[2] See Holmes in this volume for an elaboration of the Stoic conception of Nature.

Objecthood against which the human might stand over as Subject, in distinction to Porter's approach (in this volume).[3] Rather, I will show, the complex of natural beings we call *physis* is to be apprehended performatively as a field of dynamic coming to be and passing away, approach and receding, in which the possibility of differentiating essence or truth from dissimulation and display is increasingly compromised, and in which the longstanding Western coupling of "nature" and "the feminine" may be newly discerned as strictly ungroundable.

Butler's famous and arguably almost now hegemonic argument in *Gender Trouble* regards gender as something rooted not in biological sex, but in a sedimentation of practices, gestures, and acts, as something that we *do* rather than something that we *are*.[4] The appearance of this text almost instantly gave rise to feminist worries about the fate of the body, the material substrate, the part of our existence that might be attributed to nature as opposed to culture in this performative scene, and thus to calls for a certain *renaturalization* within feminist discourse.[5] Such calls for a return to nature also required a reconceptualization of nature, which heretofore signified for feminism first and foremost a domain of necessity, of stasis, cyclicity, repetition, and of unfreedom; so conceived, nature is justly a shackle for women, characterizing their bodies, lives, and their labor, from which feminists sought to break free. A reconceptualization of nature or matter as possessing its own sort of motility, vitality, volatility, or vibrancy, then, has been the principal aim of the new materialist and posthuman turn within feminism, whose most pioneering and philosophically penetrating voice up until now has been that of Elizabeth Grosz.

In *Volatile Bodies* and subsequent work, Grosz has drawn upon an alternate, non-dualistic philosophical tradition rooted in the philosophy of Spinoza and which is traced through the thought of Nietzsche, Deleuze, Bergson, Darwin, and Alphonso Lingis. In Grosz's reading of this tradition, political life is primarily constituted by forces, powers, and dynamics that traverse all previously separated spheres of existence:

---

[3] Porter in this volume. Payne's investigation of chorality (in this volume), by contrast, invokes a life of song shared among natural beings and humans as a reparative scene which also seeks to bypass this essentially modern topology of subject and object, though for him (Hellenistic, rather than archaic) poetry as representational form is essentially at odds with the nature it seeks to represent, even if he also offers a vision of an (if momentary) overcoming.

[4] The mainstream acceptance of Butler's thinking in our current moment is evidenced by the June 21, 2016 cover story, "Think Gender Is Performance? You Have Judith Butler to Thank for That" (Fischer (2016)) in The Cut, New York Magazine.

[5] See, for example, Bigwood (1991), published one year after *Gender Trouble*'s appearance.

natural, human, technical, ethical, political. Hasana Sharp has astutely mapped this terrain in *Spinoza and the Politics of Renaturalization*, showing how Grosz's work challenges and turns away from a strictly human politics framed by the Hegelian dialectic of master and slave and the struggle for recognition, which in recent decades has been most trenchantly explored in the work of Judith Butler.[6] As Sharp sees it, the virtue of Grosz's position is that it stresses a politics of empowerment along Spinozist lines, one in which embracing our being as a part of nature counters social designations of unworthiness or abjection by emphasizing our forceful, inherently worthy, energetic becoming, and which sidesteps any requirement that I be *recognized by* an Other in order to accede to legitimate social or indeed personal subjecthood. Grosz's Spinozist-Deleuzian thinking, in which material forces and intensities traverse natural and human worlds, has since been developed by other feminist thinkers such as Rosi Braidotti, Luciana Parisi, Clare Colebrook, and Jami Weinstein, and its echoes may also be found in the vital materialist political thought of Jane Bennett and William Connolly, in the thinking of Négritude from Franz Fanon to Donna Jones, by Zakiyyah Iman Jackson and Diana Leong in recent Black studies, and in the queer of color theoretical work of Jasbir Puar and Mel Chen.[7] At the same time, a quasi-atomist strand of feminist thinking has emerged in the work of Karen Barad, which focuses on the motility and unpredictability or indeterminacy of natural forces at the quantum level, and finds there a resource for thinking through ethical and political relations in and between natural and human worlds. The work of Donna Haraway has in turn inaugurated a new terrain, also traversed by thinkers such as Kathryn Hayles and Patricia Clough, in which the technological, the informational, and the natural ineluctably interpenetrate one another; seeing them as separate spheres of existence has for these thinkers consequently become not just undesirable but perhaps even impossible.[8] This cursory map of new materialist and posthumanist feminist engagements with the natural can only offer a brief glimpse of the paths through which "nature" and its relationship to women or the feminine is being reconceived and reconfigured alongside a newly ecological political sensibility occasioned by global warming, climate change, and the intensification of the interpenetration of the human and the natural

---

[6] Sharp (2011).
[7] See, for example: Braidotti (2013), Colebrook (2009) 77–92, Parisi (2010), Weinstein (2010), Bennett (2010), Connolly (2011), Fanon (1967), Jones (2010), Jackson (2016), Leong (2016), Puar (2007), and Chen (2012).
[8] See, for example, Haraway (1991), Hayles (1999), and Clough (2000).

signified by our newly named if contested entry into the epoch of the Anthropocene. On the one hand, the Spinozist-Deleuzian strain heralded by Grosz relies on a monist ontology in which forces and intensities flow across regions of existence and levels of analysis typically held as distinct, such as the physical and the social; thus *the very same* dynamics (which may, as in the work of Manuel DeLanda,[9] be modeled on nonlinear mathematical equations) are seen to apply in utterly diverse scenarios that have traditionally required different tools for understanding, such as weather patterns, economic booms and busts, flows of information, group power dynamics, food chains, subcellular molecular processes, or even the waves and particles of quantum physics. On the other hand, in the work of Karen Barad, to which I will return toward the end of this paper, it is sometimes unclear whether the forces at work in the entanglements and intra-actions she describes at the level of quantum physics are to be understood as also literally operating at the macro-level, or as a master analogy through which such phenomena (at the levels of the social, cultural, political, technical, human, animal, and vegetable) may be usefully illuminated and understood. While the Groszian philosophical materialism may be more philosophically suggestive and supportable (though perhaps its monism has a flattening effect, especially when contrasted with a phenomenological approach), it will be Barad's version of materialism that I grapple with in this paper. As she develops her physicalist position, Barad embraces too the language of phenomenology and performativity. As the latter comprise the key philosophical apparatus I develop in this paper, it is especially important that these terms be clearly distinguished from what I see as the rather questionable use to which they are put in her philosophical ontology.

If we are to explore the meaning or significance of this move to renaturalization within feminist theory, we must first consider the significance of the notion of a return, a restitution, or perhaps a reconstruction of that from which we have apparently strayed. Does this movement of a return to nature signaled by "renaturalization" in some sense repeat what has always been true of an investigation into nature? As John Sallis puts it, it is "as if in questioning about nature, one could not avoid the circularity of asking about the nature of nature."[10] In this formulation, nature takes on all the abyssal metaphysical weight of essence, principle, or *archē*, that which promises, in its final revelation, to satisfy the hungriest of desires to know. And the figure of woman herself, posed as riddle or mystery, often takes the place of such a lure.[11] Woman as the

---

[9] See e.g. DeLanda (1992).   [10] Sallis (2000).   [11] Hadot (2006).

nontruth of truth, she who must be stripped bare, unveiled, to reveal...? Feminist renaturalizations have thus strenuously sought to avoid charges of essentialism, that is, they have deliberately situated themselves using philosophical resources that are at odds with or have distanced themselves from an essentialist metaphysical tradition rooted in the Platonic *eidos* or *idea* and the Aristotelian *to ti ēn einai*, passed down to us as *essence*: the "what it is to be something". What, then, might a return to Greek antiquity contribute to this terrain?

The Heideggerian tradition in which Sallis writes is certainly concerned with re-opening the philosophical question of nature, and doing so by means of a return to the opening of Western philosophy as such, in Greek antiquity. Especially, such re-opening is anticipated in the philosophical thinking that takes place prior to the sway of Platonic metaphysics, in which, according to Sallis, "philosophy turns away from nature and ventures the *deuteros plous* [the famous "second sailing" of the *Phaedo*] by which it would set out for the intelligible."[12] The earliest thinkers we call philosophers were, after all, designated by later Greeks as the *physikoi*, the ones who investigated nature, or *physis*; this Presocratic thinking about *physis*, from the Greek verb *phyō-phyomai*, to grow, beget, or to be born, will be my concern, and hence we will travel back behind, to the hither side of metaphysics, to Homer, to the Milesians, to Heraclitus, and to Empedocles, to think about first beginnings as such.

Does the move toward first beginnings in some sense repeat and deepen, by pushing further back, the desire for a return to origin as essence? Nature, we might say, still functions here as a lure. Nature-origin-lure. But we are getting ahead of ourselves. For it is precisely the desire for a kind of unveiling or revelation in relation to nature that will be my theme in what follows, along with its ineluctably gendered dimensions. And it is within the terms of a specifically phenomenological approach to nature, developed most fully in relation to Presocratic thinking in the work of John Sallis and Luce Irigaray, that a certain dynamics of revealing and concealment in relation to nature may be discerned. Furthermore, this phenomenology of *physis* will be put into conversation with the Butlerian account of gender performativity. My aims here are multiple. In the first place, the Butlerian turn to a performative account of gender will be resituated and shown to be consistent with a phenomenological ontology in which *physis* is a central term. This approach not only reimagines performativity to be at work in

---

[12] Sallis (2000) 149.

non-human contexts, but it also diverges from the uptake of both the notion of the phenomenon and performativity in the work of Karen Barad, insofar as it emphasizes a phenomenological dynamics of showing, hiding, and responding rather than a dynamics of intra-action and entanglement, derived from quantum physics, upon which her thinking insists. Instead, there will be foregrounded not only the coming to be and passing away of beings, their showing-forth and their withdrawal, but also the simultaneous spacing, clearing, opening, and lighting, not to mention occluding, which necessarily accompanies such showing forth, and constitutes in one sense an elemental surround, but in another the very stage upon which things come into appearance. Here, then, there is a perhaps too-literal thinking of performativity—less as an ontology of acts that congeal into an ontology of substance—but of the dimension of performativity that involves a perceptual, sensory *appearing before and shining forth*, and which is also always a concealment or occlusion. A resuscitation of a dramaturgical dimension of performativity—this time without humans—which returns to the very drag performances and their play of images, of truth and falsity, obfuscation and revelation that are at the carnal, beating heart of the arguments of *Gender Trouble*, will thus be centrally at stake here.

Butler's theory of performativity has been understood by proponents of renaturalization such as Grosz and Sharp (and by others such as Bonnie Honig), as primarily constituted by a humanist dynamics of recognition rooted in the Hegelian dialectic of lordship and bondage.[13] According to this scenario, accession to subjectivity is dependent on recognition by a human other, the Master, the prerequisite of which is a certain legibility and legitimacy whose terms and limits are dictated by the existing hegemonic situation. In this way, some modes of life— heterosexual, cisgendered, white, wealthy, Western—are understood as more worthy of personhood, and the loss of such lives more inherently grievable, than others. In the domain of gender, ways of being gendered are thus only legitimate, worthy of recognition, or even *legible*, if they conform to a preexisting social, cultural, and political hegemony, a presumptive alignment of sex, gender, and sexuality in which biological or "natural" sex is understood as giving rise seamlessly to a corresponding gender expression and sexual orientation. Nature, here, functions as a stable ground or origin that gives rise to varied forms of cultural, social, and sexual expression which may or may not be rewarded for their conformity to the preexisting order. In the face of this, Butler will insist

---

[13] See Grosz (2005), Sharp (2011), and Honig (2013).

that gender does not organically arise out of natural sex, but is rather ontologically constituted and maintained by the iteration and sedimentation of acts in relation to norms (consisting of hegemonically legitimated acts, congealed, sedimented, abstracted, and made "permanent") over time. Gender arises and persists at the surface of the body, and at the level of the social—at once normative, political, and juridical. It is maintained in and through a sociocultural order, a natively conservative heterosexual matrix constituted by regulative limitations on what kinds of bodies, and what coordinated configuration of bodily acts, desires, and sexual proclivities, may appear as legible and legitimate. A key function of this heterosexual matrix is that it also *deploys* nature—naturalized categories of sex, and a naturalized teleology of sex/gender—in order to bolster, legitimize, and eternalize itself. There is a complex movement here, in which life at the level of culture, at the level of meaningful acts, is prioritized over the being of natural life, and sex at the level of nature is thereby reconceived as a function of cultural practices of gender.

Notable here is that the motility, the work—the productive activity that takes place in the construction and perpetuation of the sex-gender system—operates only at the level of the human. If there is a substratum of "matter itself," or "bodies themselves," these only take on social, and thus ontological, significance insofar as they are taken up into a system of legibility: this system and the practices that comprise it may be designated by the human domains of *logos* and of law. Nature then appears *after* the fact, as an effect of human practices, albeit one with an almost limitless power of social legitimation. If anything lies there prior to being taken up into human life, this very "lying there before" only appears itself as a function of human activity. Perhaps we could say, in Heideggerian language, that it lies there as a standing reserve, meaningless in itself, passively waiting to be taken up into a human economy of appearing, meaning, and being. However we think of it, it is clear that, according to this analysis (whose Kantian roots are now evident), it would be incoherent or meaningless to make any claims about how or what it is, or what it does in itself. At stake in Grosz's turn back toward nature, then, is that it returns to nature the power of motility, the power of becoming, the power of appearing and being apprehensible, an apprehendibility in its own right. And it is at this point where the ancient thought of nature as *physis*, as growing, emerging, appearing, and becoming in the non-human, non-technical sense, as essentially *motile and phenomenal*, becomes newly pertinent.

The phenomenological reading of performativity I will develop thus emphasizes a dynamics of performativity *already at work within nature itself.*[14] The force of performativity in this context is such that in emphasizing an interactive field of doing, acting, and perceiving at the expense of preexisting doers, actors, or perceivers ("there is no 'being' behind doing, effecting, becoming; 'the doer' is merely a fiction added to the deed—the deed is everything,"[15] as Butler famously quotes from Nietzsche's *Genealogy of Morals*), it severs the "essential" ties (which are now shown to be hegemonic effects) between the natural or biological, the field of gender expression, and the field of erotic desire, sexual orientation, and sexual expression. There are no fixed destinies of anatomy or of desire except the ones put in place, sedimented and sanctioned by regimes of power, hitherto the hegemonic "heterosexual matrix." In the absence of essential or determinate telic gridlines, there are significations and lines of development at all of these levels (anatomy, gender, desire) that may move and branch in multiple directions, in ways that are not shackled to one another in advance, that is, queerly. Nature, understood both as a dimension of human existence but also as the non-human world, may thus show forth not only in terms of a normative grid or matrix whose terms are always determined and delimited in advance by language, culture, and hegemony, but in and for itself. Contra to any ends-governed version of Darwinism (sociobiological or social Darwinist), nature can be seen to show itself forth, and further, to perform itself to itself, in ways that are insistently wayward, marvelous, excessive, and queer. Nature, *physis*, reconceived as a site of phenomenological performativity may thus be apprehended as always already in a certain excess of itself, always already queer, always already monstrous, and monstrating.

So, let us follow the lure of origin and trace, if not to reconstruct a comprehensive genealogy of *physis* in early Greek thinking, then at least to examine some select *topoi*, with the hope of shedding some light on nature, its mode of appearing, and our thirst for knowledge of nature from which "nature itself" can perhaps never be completely separated. The word *physis* is first recorded in ancient Greece literature in the tenth book of Homer's *Odyssey*, at 10.305. This appearance is a *hapax legomenon*. Although the verb *phyō-phyomai*, to bring forth, to beget, to grow, to be born, occurs relatively frequently, this is the only time it appears in a nominal form in the Homeric corpus. As Gerard Naddaf explains, with recourse to linguist Émile Benveniste, the word formed by adding the *-sis* suffix to *phyō-* is an action noun that denotes "the (completed) realization of a becoming—that

---

[14] By "dynamics" in this context I mean simply to signify the essentially moving and motile quality of phenomena, and less to reference any Aristotelian or post-Aristotelian metaphysics of *dynamis* (potentiality, potency, capacity, power).

[15] Butler (1990) 24.

is to say, the nature [of a thing] as it is realized, with all its properties."[16] However useful (and in the service of Naddaf's more general thesis regarding the meaning of *physis* as an all-encompassing completed process, given from beginning to end), this analysis gives the impression of a quite anachronistic, Aristotelian, teleological overlay. A comparison with similarly formed words, such as *poiēsis* (poetry or technical making), *dosis* (the act of giving or a gift), *phthisis* (decay), shows that a sense of completion is not a necessary aspect of this part of speech, but rather it may refer simply to a process that is ongoing; indeed they are often translated into English as gerunds.[17] And indeed, for present purposes, I would like to de-emphasize a teleological dimension of *physis* even though the paradigm of the animal organism as a developing totality would seem to lend itself supremely to such a conception. To do so, we must turn to the Homeric context.

We find ourselves in the part of the text where Odysseus is relating his adventures with witches, monsters, and the realm of the dead, that is, his encounters with supernatural realms and beings, or as Dennis Schmidt puts it, "with a natural world that is full of strangeness and surprise."[18] Specifically, it is in the episode where Odysseus is seeking to free his comrades who have been captured and turned into pigs by the *pharmakeia*, the sorceress Circe. Hermes appears to Odysseus as a guide, and tells him of a mysterious herb called "Moly": a *pharmakon*—thus both a poison and a cure, indeterminately—that will protect him from Circe's own potions and metamorphic spells. Once it is clear that he is immune to her drugs, Odysseus is to rush upon Circe with his sword in response to her attack with a "long wand," and she will deflect his attack by inviting him to her bedchamber. He is to comply with her request as the path through which he will persuade her to release his crewmen. The pharmacological battle is thus closely allied with and makes way for an erotic struggle, an ever-present field of pleasure and danger for Odysseus. Homer writes,

So saying, Argeiphontes[19] gave me the herb, drawing it from the ground, and showed me its nature (*physis*). At the root it was black, but its flower was like milk. Moly the gods call it, and it is hard for mortal men to dig; but with the gods all things are possible.[20]

---

[16] Naddaf (2005) 12.
[17] See Herbert Weir Smyth, §840 "Names of Actions and Abstract Substantives," in Smyth (1920) 230.
[18] Schmidt (2013) 168.
[19] The epithet means "Argus-slayer." In another battle-scene of eros, charms, and wiles, it was Hermes who liberated Io, the lover of Zeus, from the hundred-eyed giant Argus, who had been ordered by Hera, the jealous wife of Zeus, to watch over her. Hermes charmed the giant with his flute, and while Argus slept Hermes cut off his head and released Io.
[20] Homer, *Odyssey* 10.302–5, trans. A. T. Murray.

The god shows the mortal the plant's *physis*, and what the reader learns is something of its structure, a black root and a flower like milk.[21] The *physis* here does not seem to refer to the magical inner secret of the plant, its pharmacological essence, but rather we are given its outward appearance: a root, black, normally hidden, an underground origin that may not easily succumb to the light of knowledge or to the clear light of day. And a flower, like milk, white, nourishing, natal, maternal, reaching out toward and emerging into the openness of the world. Moly, and its *physis*, is hard for mortal men to dig (the Greek *oryssein*, to dig, does not possess the metaphorical resonance of the English but for us it may be unavoidable). Gods, however, possess the power of unconcealment and may demonstrate (*deiknymi*—to bring to light, to show forth, to point out or explain) *physis* to a mortal.[22] Both Naddaf and Schmidt emphasize the totality of the plant that is thus revealed—as Schmidt puts it, "the movement that makes this plant whole and that brings it to realization."[23] Again, it is less a revelation of a totality, fully present in its completeness, that I wish to stress, although uprooting the plant undeniably reveals its entire outline and structure. Rather, it is an ongoing movement. For the *physis* that is so revealed is one in which revelation itself, *physis* as emerging into openness, is at issue. The outward appearance betrays nothing of an inner "nature." And yet we can observe in the plant's structure a movement that has taken place from a chthonic darkness, a hiddenness of the black root beneath the earth, to a flowering forth into the light, into the open, into appearance: white like milk, maternal and nourishing. Simultaneously vegetal and mammalian, chimerical, monstrous hybrid, this *physis* speaks not only to movements of both emergence and withdrawal, but also to the order of animal and human birthing: the insistent metaphorization of woman as fecund earth in ancient Greece so thoroughly investigated by Page duBois in *Sowing the Body*, as well as to the archaic myth of Demeter and Persephone told in the *Homeric Hymn to Demeter*.[24]

That story also begins with the uprooting of a plant, the wondrous (*thaumaston*) Narcissus "grown as a lure" (*physe dolon*) by Gaia at the behest of Zeus, whose very *physis* might thus be said to constitute a lure. The mirrorings are multiple. Persephone, justly amazed (*thambēsas*),

---

[21] The exact plant that is being referred to is unknown, though has been much speculated upon. Schmidt (2013) cites a number of these investigations, noting that the mystery is hardly surprising since it is a divine name we are given, and not a mortal one (169).

[22] Heubeck's commentary (Heubeck and Hoekstra (1990)), notes that *deiknymi*'s sense of explaining or giving instruction counts as evidence that *physis* may mean "the hidden power within the plant" (60), a reading I counter so as to desubstantialize ancient *physis*.

[23] Schmidt (2013) 169.   [24] duBois (1988).

plucks the flower, but the earth yawns open (Gaia's complicity in rending Demeter from Persephone cannot be overlooked), allowing Hades to abduct her and conceal her beneath. In this, arguably one of patriarchy's supreme founding gestures, the relationship between mother and daughter is interrupted, and Demeter's power to withhold the earth's fruitfulness thereby activated.[25] As Cavarero has deftly shown, the order of generation is here countered by an even greater power than that of death, namely the breathtaking, all-encompassing feminine power of withholding life; a power and a counter-power within *physis* itself.[26] The movement of *physis* transgresses the boundary represented by the surface of the earth. Its nourishing, maternal, animal flowering forth cannot be severed from its vegetal rootedness in the dark earth, a revelation that discloses the unquenchable persistence of concealment, and which in turn grounds the duplicity of the *pharmakon* as cure and poison, as prophylactic and potential danger. As divinely named *pharmakon*, somewhere between animal and plant, the Moly plant is thus distinguished from its environs—the elements of earth, air, fire, and water, and the other plants making up the landscape upon which the scene is set (though the later Empedoclean designation of these "elements" as themselves roots (DK 6) complicates even this separation). Excessive and monstrous, yet capable of protecting Odysseus against monstrous transformation; brought to light and indicated by Hermes, psychopomp and catabatic guide to the underworld; Moly's nature is a double demonstration of monstration, a double dynamic of emergence and hiddenness, in and through itself.

The vegetal provenance of *physis* is echoed in Heidegger's analysis of Aristotle's *Physics* II.i. For Heidegger, the movement of appearing and withdrawal in nature is characterized par excellence by the growth of plants. In *physis*, he writes, "while the blossom 'buds forth' [*phyei*], the leaves that prepared for the blossom now fall off. The fruit comes to light, while the blossom disappears."[27] And "the plant in the form of fruit goes back into its seed, which, according to its essence, is nothing else but a going-forth into the appearance, ὁδὸς φύσεως εἰς φύσιν."[28] This budding, flowering, fruiting, and seeding illustrates the "way by nature into nature" (which, according to Aristotle, is also spoken of as *genesis* or coming to be by nature, as at *Physics* 193b13). It takes place in a constant forward movement that is always also a recession or return, a folding back into itself. It is perhaps easy to read in this cycle of vegetal growth a

---

[25] For a contemporary retrieval of this story for feminist politics see Rawlinson (2016), esp. ch. 4.
[26] Cavarero (1995) 57–90.   [27] Heidegger (1998) 227.
[28] Heidegger (1998) 227.

teleological unfolding of potentiality into actuality that then enters into the reproductive cyclicity of nature, one that emulates the perfect circular motion of the heavens and thus a cosmic order of becoming oriented toward the divine and the good.[29] Heidegger, however, seeks another meaning in *Physics* II.i, which bears continuity with the more archaic Greek sense of *physis*, found in the following passage toward the close of the chapter: "ἡ δέ γε μορφὴ καὶ ἡ φύσις διχῶς λέγεται· καὶ γὰρ ἡ στέρησις εἶδός πώς ἐστιν. Form (*morphē*) and nature (*physis*) are said in two ways, for privation, too, is in a way a form (*eidos*)."[30] *Sterēsis*, privation or absencing, appears alongside presencing and emergence as inherent to, as part of the very movement of *physis*, and thus appears *as such*, as *eidos*, alongside the positive appearance of whatever takes shape in nature. As Heidegger puts it, "The self-placing into the appearance, the μορφή, has a στέρησις-character, and this now means: μορφή is διχῶς, *intrinsically twofold*, the presencing of an absencing."[31] We can see, then, how in Heidegger's reading *physis* designates a realm in which the growing, emerging, and withdrawing motility of nature might be discerned all at once, as well as the later metaphysical overlay, the principle of this nature as a final form, *telos*, or essence.

John Sallis's recent diptych of works on nature, *The Return of Nature* and *The Figure of Nature*, provide a comprehensive post-Heideggerian phenomenological analysis of the early Greek thinking on *physis*, which takes for its bass-note this doubled, motile scene.[32] The Milesian *physikoi* are reputed, through a much contested and distant retrojection by historians of philosophy several centuries later, to have taken *physis* as their subject, turning to elemental principles—water, air, earth, fire, the hot and cold, the wet and dry, as the foundational originary principles—*archai*—of the cosmos. This "*peri physeōs*" tradition, extending onward to the thought of numerous Presocratics including Heraclitus, Empedocles, and Parmenides, is said to have decisively wrenched the discourse on origins from mythology into the sphere of nature, and on this new footing to have founded philosophy as we understand it.[33] While we do

---

[29] For an extended account of the relationship between earthly cycles and heavenly motion as both mimetic and material in Aristotle see my *The Feminine Symptom* (Bianchi (2014)) 157–64.
[30] Aristotle, *Physics* 193b20–1.   [31] Heidegger (1998) 227.
[32] Sallis (2016a) and Sallis (2016b).
[33] See Sallis's careful account of the difficulties with both evidence and interpretation of this tradition in Sallis (2016a) 13–17. Sallis's narration of the passage from myth to philosophical *physis* (3–12) places the Olympian goddess Artemis, the virgin huntress, as the primary representative of the natural, whereas *physis* is arguably represented more vividly in myth in the archaic tradition of fertility goddesses who govern generation, death, and the chthonic proliferation of life, from Inanna and Ishtar in the ancient Near East to

not encounter the word *physis* itself in this tradition until Heraclitus, the early Ionian thinkers Thales, Anaximander, and Anaximenes are said to have looked to elements of the natural world: to water; to the boundless *apeiron* that functions as the source of the opposing natural principles—wet and dry, hot and cold; and to air, respectively, as cosmogonical and cosmological *archai*. This much is familiar from any basic introduction to the Presocratics. And yet Sallis will treat this tradition of early Greek thinking not as a turn to a scientific or "naturalistic" account of cosmic composition or ultimate constituents, nor as a cosmogonic account of origins, and even less as a thinking of natural coming to be on the model of artifactual production or *poiēsis* in which form is imposed upon matter, but as a phenomenological story about *physis* as coming to appearance.[34] The very notion of an "element" is not even fitting in this context, since "element" derives from the more or less direct Latin translation of the Greek *stoicheion*, and its usage in this sense emerges only later; according to Aristotle it initially referred to a constituent from which a thing is composed and which cannot be further divided, such as the letters or sounds from which utterances are made up.[35] Not only does such a compositional or decompositional approach to understanding *physis* as that *from which* things are composed reduce it to something like a metaphysical substance, a thing among things, but as Sallis points out it is already to understand it in the technical-scientific frame of the "mathematical project of modern physics."[36] He reminds us that the Presocratics do not speak of "elements" (*stoicheia*) at all; Empedocles, as we saw, speaks (in DK 6) of the four roots, *rhizomata*. Once again the vegetal analogy—the elements given not as building blocks, but as roots through which passes the manifestation, the flowering forth of things.

In particular, Sallis draws our attention to perhaps the most overlooked of these thinkers, Anaximenes, and his discourse on *aēr*. He reminds us that in the early Greek texts of Homer and Hesiod, *aēr* refers to mist, to cloud, to air that is substantial, damp, dark, thick, and obscuring. This is in contrast to *aithēr*, the bright shining upper air of the highest heavens. Nonetheless, by the sixth century BCE it seems to

---

Gaia, Demeter, and Persephone in Greece. The split in the feminine functions in the Olympian pantheon between Hera as wife and matron, Aphrodite as goddess of sex and love, Athena as goddess of cunning and wisdom, and Artemis as virgin huntress seems to have already apportioned the capricious forces of archaic fecundity according to a patriarchal optic of management and control.

[34] See Sallis (2016b) 30.
[35] Aristotle, *Metaphysics* V.iii. 1014a26–b15. For a fine discussion of the philological evidence and related semantic issues see Crowley (2005) 367–94.
[36] See Sallis (2000) 154.

correspond to the meaning it holds for us—that of the open and transparent medium in which we are immersed, that which we perceive as wind, and that which we breathe and which therefore has a connection to life.[37] A brief reflection on Heidegger's etymology of "phenomenon" in the Introduction to *Being and Time*—as comprised of the middle-voiced construction of the verb *phainō, phainesthai*, to bring into daylight, to place in brightness, gives a hint of why this element *aēr* should be so important for Sallis—"Thus the meaning of the expression 'phenomenon' is *established* as *what shows itself in itself*, what is manifest."[38] For air is at once a "stuff," and thus an entity, a kind of being within the natural world along with earth, fire, and water—perceptible and substantial—*and* that which opens a space, as a material envelope that approximates the immaterial, that allows without resistance for the showing forth of things within it. As Theophrastus' testimonial fragment (DK A5) tells us,

Anaximenes, son of Eurystratus of Miletus, who became a companion of Anaximander, also says, like him, that the underlying nature (*hypokeimenēn physin*) is one and unlimited (*apeiron*), but not undefined as Anaximander said but definite (*hōrismenēn*), for he calls it (*legōn*) *aēr*, and it differs in its substance (*kata tas ousias*) by rarity and density. Being made finer it becomes fire, being made thicker it becomes wind, then cloud, then (when thickened still more) water, then earth, then stones; and the rest come into being from these. He, too, makes motion (*kinēsis*) eternal, and that it is through this that change comes about."[39]

From the outset, we will need to set aside Theophrastus' Aristotelian optic of an "underlying nature," although it is also of course through Aristotle that we understand the Milesian *physikoi* as being concerned primarily with *archē*: first principle, beginning, source, that which rules.[40] Sallis points out that, like Anaximander's *archē*, *aēr* is unlimited, *apeiron*. As one, it has a definition or a *horos* and is identifiable as such in *logos*, but it has no *peras* or limit. As such, if we are to translate *archē* as beginning, "then we could say that it is a beginning that has no beginning, a beginning

---

[37] Sallis (2016a) 20.   [38] Heidegger (2010a) 27, original emphasis.
[39] Kirk, Raven, and Schofield (1983) 145. Using many of the same terms, and more pungent and evocative for my present purposes, though undoubtedly spurious, Fragment B3 reads: "Anaximenes arrived at the conclusion that air is the one, movable, infinite, first principle of all things. For he speaks as follows: 'Air is the nearest to an immaterial thing; since through the outflowing arising therefrom, it is necessary that it should be infinite and abundant, because it is never exhausted.'" The fragment is found in an alchemical text of Olympiodorus (or Pseudo-Olympiodorus), however it is not just context that renders it questionable, but in particular the fragment's anachronistic use of "immaterial" (*asōmatos*). See Renehan (1980) 119–20. I am indebted to Rhodes Pinto, in personal communication, for helpful clarification of these textual and philological issues.
[40] *Archē* is such a key word for Aristotle that it is the first of the thirty entries in his philosophical dictionary, Book Delta of the *Metaphysics* (1012b34–1013a23).

before beginning"[41] (22). This aporia, this duplicity that shows itself at the origin, is further reflected in the necessary division or differentiation that air portends, since air is always there, alongside and in excess of any other being that emerges forth into the open, any manifestation of the other elements. Air *is*, it is a being apparent to our senses, but also a medium *through* which much of what we sense is transmitted—sound, vision, smell—and that *in* which what comes to appearance does so, thus forming the necessary ground to any possible figure, so to speak, but a groundless ground, flowing and excessive. As Luce Irigaray writes in *The Forgetting of Air in Martin Heidegger*, "No other element carries with it, or lets itself be passed through by—light and shadow, voice and silence. No other element is to this extent opening itself—to one who would have not forgotten its nature there is no need for it to open or re-open."[42] Thus, she insists, the terms that then emerge as central for the later Heidegger—clearing, lighting, and opening—require this forgotten medium of air, an element infinite and flowing, for their sustenance. Irigaray shows how air as material envelope, as that which makes possible the region of the open, the clearing, the lighting, is forgotten and left unmourned in Heidegger's phenomenological thinking. This giving of air is moreover also what is given, freely, abundantly, without reserve, as oxygen in the mother's blood. "No gap, breach, spacing, or distancing is possible between the living organism and the blood that has always already nourished it, including with oxygen. Nor is there any more of a gap between it and the ambient air it continuously breathes once born."[43] The mother and air, both giving without reserve as origin and ground of being-there, are forgotten equally in the discourses of philosophy. This intimacy between air/mother and *Dasein*, though in actuality life-giving, then appears according to the terms of Western philosophy and the patriarchal imaginary as—all too ironically—too close for comfort, suffocating, abyssal, terrifying. For Irigaray, this in turn provides the impetus for the phallic standing-out of *Dasein*, its projection into *ek-stasis*. Although he does not cite Irigaray, nor consider the dimension of sexual difference, Sallis might thus be seen as answering Irigaray's call for a philosophical phenomenology of the two.[44]

---

[41] Sallis (2016a) 22.   [42] Irigaray (1999) 8.   [43] Irigaray (1999) 84.

[44] In her key article, "Questioning nature: Irigaray, Heidegger and the potentiality of matter" (Fielding (2003)), Helen Fielding puts Irigaray's critique of Heidegger, equally pertinent to Sallis, thus: "The problem for Irigaray is that even as Heidegger opens up the history of Western philosophy to reveal the forgetting of being, he himself does not recognize the two-fold essence of being as that of sexual difference, despite the fact that sexual difference is phenomenologically and universally evident" (6). While, given the great mass of asexually reproducing "lower" organisms, it is not quite justified to claim universality for sexual difference, it certainly pervades the animal and plant kingdoms in a way that is phenomenologically and ontologically endemic. For views that see the twofoldness of

For Sallis the duplicity of beginnings, of the philosophical desire for origin, is not thematized as riven by sexual difference, nor does he consider the carnal debt to the mother's body as an element and ground of giving. Yet in his phenomenological attention to *aēr* there is an implicit response to Irigaray's critique of philosophy as a "closed universe of thought,"[45] in which the encircling of air—fluid and life-giving—is erased and eclipsed by the Parmenidean circle of being and thought as one, as the One. Irigaray discloses the dimension of desire for the sexually other as intimately linked to the recollection of air as infinitely giving, and infinitely withdrawing, and here, Sallis's attentiveness to its doubled origin might give way to an operation in which sexual difference might, too, begin to appear for the first time.

Listening to Irigaray, we learn that any project of renaturalization within Western philosophical thought, and *a fortiori* a retrieve of ancient *physis*, coming close to the origin, the *archē*, the source, portends great danger; the terror of the maternal abyss, maternal engulfment. The Sallisian embrace of the doubleness that attends every beginning, on the other hand, seems to rest in an attitude of contemplative attunement to the concealments and unconcealments of *physis*. Of Heraclitus' famous "nature loves to hide" (DK 123) he writes:

> Precisely as φύσις lets things come to light so as to reveal themselves in their distinct being, it conceals itself, either withholding itself from the very light that it lets illuminate the expanse of things or hiding itself in the very brilliance of that light, shining with such brilliance that, as it instigates visibility as such, it itself borders on invisibility.[46]

And the Heraclitean emphasis on fire as originary element is, too, interpreted by Sallis as bringing light and visibility rather than destructive force: "it is not primarily its power of conflagration but rather its expansive brilliance that enables fire to say φύσις."[47]

In the remainder of this paper, then, I would like to shift the terms of the scene away from one in which what remains invisible is identified too closely with an unrepayable debt to the maternal-feminine, and the scorching terror of engulfment that then necessarily accompanies such a return to *physis*—or indeed away from a call for a sexual difference whose terms would only count to two. The complex in which air and the maternal are both forgotten envelopes for Being may be, it seems to me, fruitfully dislodged by a consideration of the manner of *physis*'s

---

sexual difference as temporary, unjustified, and on the way to being superseded, see Parisi (2010) and Weinstein (2010).

[45] Irigaray (1999) 96.   [46] Sallis (2016) 32.   [47] Sallis (2016) 38.

emergence—becoming as emerging into the light from the shadows, as indelibly and irreducibly *performative*. The sense of performativity I mean to emphasize here is not primarily that of simply doing or acting, but rather that of doing or acting *before another*. Performativity signifies entry on to a stage in which *physis* gives rise not only to beings *qua* actors, but also to the stage itself as the space cleared for spectacle, the scenery, the lighting, the music, and the action and intrigue that takes place between players: the dramas, whether comedic, tragic, melodramatic, or farcical. Recall here Irigaray's profound reading in *Speculum of the Other Woman* of the allegory of the cave-theater in Plato's *Republic* as maternal womb; the gestational space of semblance out of which birth into the open of the true may be possible.[48] And in concert with this, Irigaray's remarks in "The Power of Discourse" (which, not incidentally, also form the epigraph to Butler's first chapter of *Bodies that Matter*) concerning

the "matter" from which the speaking subject draws nourishment in order to produce itself, to reproduce itself; the *scenography* that makes representation feasible, representation as defined in philosophy, that is, the architectonics of its theatre, its framing in space-time, its geometric organization, its props, its actors, their respective positions, their dialogues, indeed their tragic relations, without overlooking the *mirror*, most often hidden, that allows the logos, the subject, to reduplicate itself, to reflect itself by itself.[49]

Irigaray, here, is offering a critique of the theater of philosophy itself, the theater organized by and for the gaze, the *theōria*, of the subject who finds nothing more than himself and his delusions of domination represented there. And in this patriarchal-paternal imaginary, the maternal womb, as factical, material, literal truth of all our origins, is appropriated and rendered as nothing more than a theater of dissimulation. This mode of the phenomenon as peeled away from the true and concealing it in "mere appearance" or semblance Heidegger calls a *privative* modification.[50] He writes, "This covering up as 'dissimulation' [*Verstellung*] is the most frequent and the most dangerous kind, because here the possibilities of being deceived and misled are especially pernicious."[51] However, it is this very danger of deception that I want to claim is not simply a constant risk, but indeed a constitutive dimension within nature. What illumination, I want to ask, might then be afforded by understanding *physis* itself according to this dramaturgical topography?

---

[48] Irigaray (1985a) 243ff.
[49] Luce Irigaray, "The Power of Discourse and the Subordination of the Feminine," in Irigaray (1985b) 75, original emphasis.
[50] Heidegger (2010a) 27.   [51] Heidegger (2010a) 34.

The Heideggerian tradition has typically approached a phenomenological conception of Being as *physis* in tones of hushed piety. We might recall the approach of night during Heidegger's conversation on a country path, which "brings near the distances of the stars to one another,"[52] or Sallis's citing the *Homeric Hymn to Earth Mother of All* as disclosing the "firmgrounded nourisher of everything."[53] Both Sallis and Irigaray bring to the scene of *physis* an evocative poetizing, a deep reverence expressed in language bordering on the theological. Sallis, for example, asks,

> Who does not have some sense for the sea as its surface sparkles brilliantly under the intense rays of the summer sun; and for the air above (the *aither* as the ancients called it) on days when it superabounds with dazzling, silver light; and for the wind as it is given voice by the swaying pines; and for the dark, rapidly approaching storm clouds and the heavy downpour they will bring; and for the clear night sky of midwinter with its splendent profusion of stars; and for the earth and the forest as once again in early spring they offer their promise of abundance to come?[54]

Who, indeed does not? In a time of ecological devastation, such intense poetic attunements are, in their very refusal of urgency, no doubt intensely urgent and necessary. But I would like to torque this devotional scene by offering a thinking of nature as it is opened up in early Greek thought, precisely in context, as *pharmakon*. We are perhaps all too used to thinking of *technē* as *pharmakon*, but what transpires if we think *physis* in this way? That is to say, a thinking of *physis* as more dangerous, more playful, more performative, more ridiculous, more excessive, more monstrous, than such solemnity would begin to signify.

What this brings to light above all is that nature, too, is surely deceptive, and any "return" to nature must reckon with these inevitable and inescapable dissimulations. Asli Gocer has argued that the *thaumatopoioi* of the cave, literally "wondermakers" but colloquially puppeteers, represent an equivalent of Aristophanic theater, embodying "the burlesque, the vulgar, fantasy and satire."[55] Is the cave then Plato's playground of charlatans, or Irigaray's hidden truth of the maternal body? Aristotle observes at the start of the *Metaphysics* that, "All begin ... by wondering that things should be as they are, e.g. with regard to the wondrous automatons, or the solstices, or the incommensurability of the diagonal of a square."[56] Such apposition posits a strange equivalence between the wonder-causing capacities of a possibly bawdy mechanical

---

[52] Heidegger (2010b) 89. [53] Sallis (2000) 174.
[54] Sallis (2000) 156. [55] Gocer (1999) 121.
[56] Aristotle, *Metaphysics* 983a13–16, trans. H. Tredennick, translation modified.

theatrical performance, a natural phenomenon, and a mathematical puzzle. *Physis* swaggers, embellishes, monstrates, and it, too, is coy and reticent. It shows off, and it hides *as* it shows off. It performs itself to itself, to other aspects of itself, and we, too, observe its many performances. And in part because of its dissimulating tendencies, we in the West have projected upon it a feminine principle, to be sharply distinguished from the direct and fully unconcealed standard of masculine philosophic verifiability and truth.

Inflecting the analysis toward a phenomenological performativity, and away from the classical gendered trope of nature as veiled, here, we are afforded some distance from the deadly beguiling of a feminine lure or seduction. Such seductions may indeed prove fatal to the careless traveler who does not have the proper counterspell, thus providing the ground for millennia of patriarchal misogyny and successive ravagements of the natural world. Instead, we find a nature that manifests itself in the outrageous campery of foliage and plumage, in the exorbitant displays of mating peacock spiders and colobus monkeys, in the spectacularity of the northern lights and massive geological formations of the great continents, and in the earthquakes and tsunamis that ravage the unconscionably inadequate built environments of the global south. The things of nature love to hide and to dissimulate, whether stalking predator or scaredy cat, the stick insect, the famously deceptive orchid, the mysterious underearth mycological networks that resist definite determination, the spores that are said to survive even in the inhospitable conditions of space, and the ghostly traces of subatomic particles such as the Higgs boson. Non-human entities continually play hide and seek, withdraw and manifest, to and with one another, and to and with us, in a dynamic that I suggest must be apprehended less as seriously gendered or obeying any reproductive imperative (despite the Darwinian analyses of sexual selection Grosz's work has helpfully brought to our attention).[57] Rather, they are playfully, dangerously queer.

---

[57] Grosz (2011). Biologists such as Bruce Bagemihl in *Biological Exuberance: Animal Homosexuality and Natural Diversity* (Bagemihl (1999)), and Joan Roughgarden in *Evolution's Rainbow: Diversity, Gender, and Sexuality in Nature and People* (Roughgarden (2004)), have amassed troves of data and examples illustrating the diversity of animal sexual behaviors, and argue that nonreproductive, homosexual, or interspecies sexual displays and behaviors are less the anomalies they have been traditionally assumed to be, standing in need of exceptional explanation, but are overwhelmingly the norm throughout the natural world. I am indebted to a masterful paper by Sarah K. Hansen, "Biology as Refuge: Cis Fragility and the Biopolitics of Gender," presented at the October 2016 meeting of the Society for Phenomenology and Existential Philosophy, Salt Lake City, Utah for alerting me to the breadth of this literature.

Irigaray's epigraph in *Forgetting of Air* is seventeenth-century mystic and poet Angelus Silesius's famous line, "The rose is without 'why'; it flowers because it flowers."[58] Such blooming of this admittedly overdetermined flower, without reference to any given frame or vision, takes us far from the scene of a Butlerian performativity in which recognition within the sedimented terms of a hegemonic matrix is empowered with granting legibility, legitimacy, and ontological status. Irigaray herself comments:

> [Men's] destiny require[s] that they ceaselessly observe that which forms, informs, and surrounds them. That they ceaselessly be in search of reasons, including on the subject of the rose and its secret... As for the rose, it would have no need for this. Since its need is to flower. And its very flowering requires no design [*tracé ouvrant*]—a simple spontaneous blooming/unconcealment. Visible with the unclosing of the rose's gathering [*son receuil*], an exposition with no preliminary objective or lens. With no a priori frame that would produce this flowering as such. With no project that might will it so.[59]

And yet, without wanting to reduce the rose to "reasons," that is, to ontogenic and phylogenetic accounts, to the mechanics of photosynthesis or cell maintenance, or to reproductive and evolutionary imperatives involving insect vectors, horticulture, genetic modification techniques, and so on, the rose would not produce its extravagantly enfolded efflorescences were it not for its being-seen, being-smelled, being-sensed, for its emerging as *physis* onto a scene constituted in the first instance and primarily by *physis*. Even in its unconcerned, vegetal repose, the rose would not be at all without the environment now understood as a stage upon which it blooms: its soil, water, the air and the light from which it feeds, the elements in which it takes root and which, as Empedocles insists, also form its roots, an elemental environment that at once shelters it, and to which it is exposed. And the perceptual apparatuses of the world in which it is immersed, and which it impresses—upon which impressions of it are formed—are no less part of the being of the rose than its own senseless, aimless, flowering. As Michael Marder puts it, "the flower is, at the same time, hypersymbolic and nonsignifying, overloaded with and empty of sense."[60] The rose's lack of a reason, the kind of reason that would satisfy the demands of instrumentality, any relationship to a

---

[58] The verse is also considered by Heidegger in his analysis of Leibniz's principle of sufficient reason in his 1955–6 lecture course, *Der Satz Vom Grund*: the "without why" of the rose discloses the groundlessness of its ground; such "without why" is also the concealed ground of human existence. Heidegger (1991). See also Caputo (1986 [1978]), esp. 60–6, and Miller (2002) 182–3.

[59] Irigaray (1999) 144.

[60] Marder (2014) 201. See also ch. 12, "Irigaray's Water Lily" (213–29).

determinate end, does not however preclude it from referring irreducibly to an outside, to an array of nature's other efflorescences. Such entities are drawn to it, outraged by its abundant imbrications and coloration, lured by the secrets of its disappearing inner petals and the obscene exposure of its bloom, its heady, delicate scent, in incalculable, ephemeral enjoyment. They may be moved to produce and recite poetry sublime and hackneyed in its name, proffer it as a supplement to their own significations of friendship, love, seduction, or mourning, may hybridize and graft it, dye and dethorn it, emblazon it on a standard or tattoo it upon an ankle, and may dig inside to explore its depths and unwittingly pollinate it, or may simply crunch on its blooms as a tasty snack.

A consideration of this vegetal scene permits a sense of *physis* not only as doubled, as both emerging and simultaneously concealing its ground and being, but as multiplied. After all, *physis* constitutes not only both the figure that appears and the ground for the figure's emergence, but also the clearing or opening that constitutes the distance, or interval, between them.[61] *Physis* thus encompasses the being that stands out from its environment, that ek-statically and monstratively emerges, *and* the receding environment from which it emerges and with which it might always remerge, *as well as* the open space as the stage upon which such play of light and shadow may take its place. This excessive outstanding is indeed a form of *ekstasis*, though not the Heideggerian *ekstasis* of a *Dasein* that performs the particular doubling within *logos* that is the questioning of Being. It is, rather, an *ekstasis* that plays with nature's inherent attentiveness to or interest in itself, that draws attention beyond an economic circuitry of gains and losses, that—dare one say—entertains, delights, and seduces.

Alphonso Lingis reports biologist Adolf Portmann's claim that there are "organs to be looked at."[62] Lingis continues: "Before the plumage and display behaviors of the bird-of-paradise, before the coiled horns of the mountain sheep, one has to admit a specific development of the organism to capture another eye."[63] And further: "The symmetry of patterns and the colors have to receive a specific explanation on the level of the phenomenal and not of the operational; there is a *logic of ostentation* over

---

[61] Hill in this volume likewise develops this phenomenological notion of the interval in a feminist frame, but to very different ends, namely in relation to Aristotle's metaphysics of time, rather than in the Heideggerian language of an opening or clearing that is at once a part of *physis* and its condition of possibility.

[62] Portmann (1967) 111, cited in Lingis (1983) 8. I am grateful to Shannon Winnubst, at a presentation of an earlier version of this paper at the 2015 *philoSOPHIA* annual meeting at Emory University, for pointing out the resonance of my analysis with that of Lingis.

[63] Lingis (1983) 8.

and beyond camouflage and semantic functions."[64] While Lingis here risks reinscribing the reign of the visual, and it is the visual that specifically requires the distance that is the clearing as such, these dynamics also apply to all sensory modalities—touch, scent, sonar, sound, taste, as well as sight; nothing here precludes the combinatory, synaesthetic sensorium of the *Gesamtkunstwerk*. However, he is clear that the eye in this context is not the speculative organ of *theōria*, that which seeks to survey, unveil, appropriate, and extract truth. Rather, it is an organ that caresses the surface, whose interest is erotic and excessive, and does not obey in any strict sense a logic of desire indexed to mere lack and satisfaction. Nature's interest in itself, in itself qua the other that it allows to appear before it, is thus riven and traversed by endlessly circulating, aleatory, nonteleological and thus queer eros. As he describes a descent to the luminescent depths of the ocean, Lingis is by no means insensible to the resonances of a return to the maternal origin, and the fears and desires so awakened in this approach. But instead of a monstrous, engulfing feminine, he attends to the (non-petrifying) medusas, nudibranches, anemones, octopuses, the proliferation of wonders in the deep that lead to a sensation of one's own body as an assemblage of monstrous organs, whose extraordinary and paradoxical visual diversity in the murky depths cannot be accounted for by any survivalist evolutionary schema.

Sallis himself is distinctively attuned throughout his work to the appearance of the monstrous in Plato, especially insofar as that it is *thaumazein*, wondering, encountering what is wondrous or monstrous, that sets off the philosophical impulse as such.[65] Furthermore, this monstrous excess is an excess of nature, of nature as figure, of nature as encountered by the philosopher: "Monstrosity as such—as in monstrous wonder—takes place as an exceeding of nature within—or from within—nature."[66] Indeed truth itself for Sallis is both monstrous and deformed.[67] While Sallis then locates such deformation in the philosophical *logos*, it would seem that this propensity for monstrosity operates always already within nature, as nature itself monstrates its wonders, in the depths, far from the gaze and projects of philosophers. If nature constitutes a stage for itself, is constituted by continual acts of self-staging, can it be justified to bring to bear upon it the entire technical weight and apparatus of the theater? This is, after all, the substance of Irigaray's critique of Plato, in which the maternal body is replaced with the scenography of the cave, and the stage thus set for a narrative of

---

[64] Lingis (1983) 9. My emphasis.
[65] See Sallis's discussion of Plato, *Theaetetus* 155d at Sallis (2016a) 101–3.
[66] Sallis (2016a) 136.   [67] Sallis (1993) 39.

emergence from semblance to truth. And yet nature is surely engaged in a continual dynamics of performance. Bringing to bear the material apparatus of the theater upon the natural world—proscenium, skene, machina, wings, cyclorama, stage, orchestra, spotlights, gels, gobos, upon its movements of shadow, lighting, clearing, showing, make-believe, concealment, inception, dramatic action, and conclusion—would seem to offer an unparalleled kind of illumination of its activities. Early twentieth-century phenomenological conceptions of animal life, such as Jacob von Uexküll's description of the lifeworld of the tick, begin to open up this multiple, dizzying world of natural encounters involving organism and milieu that necessarily encompass a performative element, although Uexküll in particular folds his observations back all too neatly into a Kantian schema of transcendental subjective philosophy.[68] Roger Caillois's ruminations upon the mimicry of insects—springing from his observation that deceptive adaptations fall far short of conferring an evolutionary advantage as a defense strategy—come close to articulating this sense of excessive, ludic performativity in nature. Instead he concludes that, far from representing an energetic proliferation, such mimetic deceptions display a loss of individuation insofar as the creature merges and blends with its environment.[69] He thus finds them to represent a kind of letting go, an exhaustion or "psychasthenia"—using a term from Pierre Janet's studies in schizophrenia—a tendency we might gloss (no doubt too quickly) as the operation of a death drive in nature. Contrast this with the most famous of deceptive plants, the orchid, whose vast global diversity and exuberant proliferation would seem to illustrate quite the opposite—indeed the orchid would seem to be the very paradigm of the "abominable mystery" of the flowering plant famously remarked upon by Darwin in a letter to Sir Joseph Hooker in 1879.[70]

Lingis, evoking Nietzsche, describes the theatrical pleasures of disguise, masquerade, and unmasking, and analyzes tragedy not simply in terms of a confluence of Apollonian and Dionysian elements, but as a technology in which the transience of form is rendered visible and ecstatic.[71] In this queer performativity as theatricality of nature, the

---

[68] von Uexküll (2010 [1934]).
[69] Caillois (1984). First published in the surrealist magazine *Minotaure* in 1935, this longer version appeared in Caillois's monograph *Le mythe et l'homme* (Paris, 1938). I am grateful to Carla Freccero, in a lecture entitled "Queer/Animal/Theory: Psychoanalysis and Subjectivity," given to the Department of Performance Studies, New York University, November 2016, for brilliantly laying out this early twentieth-century theoretical terrain and thus demonstrating its relevance for my project.
[70] I thank Brooke Holmes for reminding me of Darwin's "abominable mystery."
[71] See Lingis (1983) 84–5.

comings to be and passings away of nature are precisely mimicked by the very structure of the theater's *mise en scène*, and the infrastructure of theater comes to metaphorize nature, in such a way that the true and the false, and *physis* and *technē* for that matter, can no longer be properly distinguished. *Mise en scène* as *mise en abyme*...deadly serious and yet unutterably frivolous, *physis* yields the tragedy of the last laugh, and yet another....

In a recent essay, Karen Barad has explored what she calls the "queer performativity" of nature, and within her agential realist approach more generally the concepts of phenomenon and performativity have central importance.[72] She is explicit, however, that her concept of phenomenon is not that of the phenomenologists. Rather, she is concerned with how entities precipitate out of phenomena, which seem to be for her matrices of entangled and intra-acting agencies in which practices of human knowing, observing, and theorizing as well as material agencies act (this is her performativity), and thus have a constitutive role in producing the objects they observe as well as the knowledge practices that observe them. Phenomena for Barad are "ontologically primitive relations—relations without pre-existing relata."[73] In this onto-epistemic scenario the phenomenon of observer-dependence in quantum physics is taken as central. And while for her the non-human and material world *acts*, she is less concerned with including non-human nature within performativity's range of applicability than with expanding the strangeness of quantum physics at the atomic level to larger scale phenomena. On her account, queer performativity is constituted by observations of natural phenomena that appear to disobey a classical ontological conception of cause and effect, and she includes in her analysis lightning, stingray neurons, a fish-killing micro-organism, human coincidence, and atoms, surely all strange, wondrous, classical-causation-confounding phenomena. The "queer performativity" she identifies is thus less related to a dynamics of display and concealment within and among the entities of nature as I understand it here, than constituted by empirical results and theoretical speculations that demonstrate a kind of uncanny flouting of laws of nature understood at the macro level, as they have emerged in the primarily Newtonian scientific paradigm of modernity. Her reliance on one model within contemporary physics (and there are of course competing ones) thus falls prey to what Sallis calls "compositionism"—a reductive ontological approach that breaks nature down into proposed parts and seeks to show how those parts come to constitute what is

---

[72] Barad (2012) and Barad (2007).   [73] Barad (2007) 139.

observed. This is quite at odds with a phenomenology of what appears, or what "comes into manifestation." Despite her claim that she is providing an empirical support for Derridean *différance*, her quantum physics vocabulary of entanglement, intra-action, differentiation, and enfolded materialization aspires to a kind of orthodox scientific correctness in which the goal appears to differ not at all from the traditional one of science, which I have characterized as the lure of nature, that of uncovering nature's secrets once and for all. Indeed, her theoretical exposition conforms to the formal requirements of the "view from nowhere," which the content would seem to push against, or more strictly render impossible. Here, the phenomenological dimension is entirely elided, a dimension that necessarily exceeds the metaphysics of presence underpinning scientific inquiry insofar as within it absence and presence are constantly implicated in one another. Performativity here loses its dramaturgical resonances, but is understood merely as the sedimentation of iterative practices, acts, or activities that emerge at the conjuncture of the human and non-human.

By contrast, in the phenomenological account of nature's queer performativity I am developing here, the humanist focus of Butler's performativity, and the scientific-epistemic focus of Barad's, which in both cases never required a conscious, volitional subject capable of recognition for its operation, evaporates. Nature's queer performativity thus understood in relation to ancient *physis* describes how entities expose themselves to and conceal themselves and their grounds from one another in ways that are hubristic, excessive, sublime, monstrous, mysterious, seductive, dangerous, wondrous, and pleasurable. Intra-action or entanglement here is not simply causally constitutive or sensory, but dramaturgic: nature's drama unfolding on nature's stage. Violent and vulnerable, playful and serious, truthful and deceptive, comedic and tragic, nature's exorbitant appearing and concealing moves away too from a Groszian-Spinozist renaturalization of politics as an increase of power and pleasure, as it attends to and values not simply the expansive vector, but also the contractive, the hidden. It attends to the kind of grounds that recede, hitherto unnoticed and unmourned: air, maternal body, the roots, the conditions of openness that withdraw into obscurity so that the entities they nourish might live. An Irigarayan understanding of sexual difference that demands acknowledging the mother not simply as locus of endless, unpayable debt or abyssal terror, but as a sexuate, sexually other being is indispensable here, and yet nature's queerness also torques the seriousness of gender, making of it something elusive, mobile, excessively demonstrative, as so powerfully theorized in *Gender Trouble*'s consideration of drag. Gender, sexual difference, sexuality is, like *physis*, a site of both utmost gravity and utmost levity. What, then, is the task of humans in relation to such a nature? As Homer tells us of the Moly plant's nature, it is hard for mortals to dig. It is not for us to lay bare, nor master, but neither to pay only reverent obeisance. It is to be knowingly beguiled and fascinated by its lures and powers, to read its pharmacological signs with care and even with guile, to respond sensitively, with attunement, wonder, terror, horror, awe, hilarity, credulity, suspicion, flexibility, and play: endless incredulousness and endless responsibility.[74]

WORKS CITED

Aristotle. (1933) *Metaphysics, Vol. I.* Trans. H. Tredennick. Cambridge, MA.
Bagemihl, B. (1999) *Biological Exuberance: Animal Homosexuality and Natural Diversity.* New York.
Barad, K. (2007) *Meeting the Universe Halfway: Quantum Physics and the Entanglement of Matter and Meaning.* Durham, NC.
Barad, K. (2012) "Nature's Queer Performativity," *Kvinder, Køn og forskning/ Women, Gender and Research* 1–2: 25–53.
Bennett, J. (2010) *Vibrant Matter: A Political Ecology of Things.* Durham, NC.
Bianchi, E. (2014) *The Feminine Symptom: Aleatory Matter in the Aristotelian Cosmos.* New York.
Bigwood, C. (1991) "Renaturalizing the Body (with the Help of Merleau-Ponty)," *Hypatia* 6: 54–73.
Braidotti, R. (2013) *The Posthuman.* Cambridge.
Butler, J. (1990) *Gender Trouble: Feminism and the Subversion of Identity.* New York.
Butler, J. (1993) *Bodies That Matter: On the Discursive Limits of "Sex."* New York.
Caillois, R. (1984) "Mimicry and Legendary Psychasthenia." Trans. J. Shepley. *October* 31: 16–32.
Caputo, J. D. (1986 [1978]) *The Mystical Element in Heidegger's Thought.* New York.
Cavarero, A. (1995) *In Spite of Plato: A Feminist Rewriting of Ancient Philosophy.* Trans. S. Anderlini-D'Onofrio and Á. O'Healy. New York.
Cheah, P. (1996) "Mattering: *Bodies That Matter: On the Discursive Limits of 'Sex'* by Judith Butler; *Volatile Bodies: Toward a Corporeal Feminism* by Elizabeth Grosz," *Diacritics* 26: 108–39.
Chen, M. (2012) *Animacies: Biopolitics, Racial Mattering, and Queer Affect.* Durham, NC.
Clough, P. T. (2000) *Autoaffection: Unconscious Thought in the Age of Technology.* Minneapolis.

---

[74] It will not have escaped the attentive reader that the natural world is acting in ways that are far from amusing at the present time, a situation that demands urgent redress. Growth (*physis*) as natural phenomenon, untempered by withdrawal, is patently misapplied when reformulated as an imperative within the human sphere of economics.

Colebrook, C. (2009) "Queer Vitalism," *New Formations* 68: 77–92.
Connolly, W. (2011) *A World of Becoming*. Durham, NC.
Crowley, T. J. (2005) "On the Use of *Stoicheion* in the Sense of 'Element,'" *Oxford Studies in Ancient Philosophy* 29: 367–94.
DeLanda, M. (1992) "Nonorganic Life," in J. Crary and S. Kwinter (eds), *Incorporations*. New York: 129–67.
duBois, P. (1988) *Sowing the Body: Psychoanalysis and Ancient Representations of Women*. Chicago.
Fanon, F. (1967) *Black Skin, White Masks*. Trans. C. L. Markmann. New York.
Fielding, H. (2003) "Irigaray, Heidegger and the Potentiality of Matter," *Continental Philosophy Review* 36: 1–26.
Fischer, M. (2016) "Think Gender Is Performance? You Have Judith Butler to Thank for That," *New York Magazine*, June 13, viewed June 30, 2016, <http://nymag.com/thecut/2016/06/judith-butler-c-v-r.html>.
Gocer, A. (1999) "The Puppet Theater in Plato's Parable of the Cave," *The Classical Journal* 95: 119–29.
Grosz, E. (1994) *Volatile Bodies*. Bloomington, IN.
Grosz, E. (2004) *The Nick of Time*. Durham, NC.
Grosz, E. (2005) *Time Travels*. Durham, NC.
Grosz, E. (2011) *Becoming Undone: Darwinian Reflections on Life, Politics, and Art*. Durham, NC.
Hadot, P. (2006) *The Veil of Isis*. Trans. M. Chase. Cambridge, MA.
Haraway, D. (1991) *Simians, Cyborgs, and Women: The Reinvention of Nature*. New York.
Hayles, N. K. (1999) *How We Became Posthuman: Virtual Bodies in Cybernetics, Literature, and Informatics*. Chicago.
Heidegger, M. (1991) *The Principle of Reason*. Trans. R. Lilly. Bloomington, IN.
Heidegger, M. (1998) "On the Essence and Concept of Φύσις in Aristotle's *Physics* B, 1," trans. T. Sheehan, in Q. McNeill (ed.), *Pathmarks*. Cambridge: 183–230.
Heidegger, M. (2010a) *Being and Time*. Trans. J. Stambaugh, ed. D. Schmidt. Albany.
Heidegger, M. (2010b) *Country Path Conversations*. Trans. B. W. Davis. Bloomington, IN.
Heubeck, A., and A. Hoekstra (1990) *A Commentary on Homer's Odyssey, Vol. II*. New York.
Homer (1919) *The Odyssey*. Trans. A. T. Murray. Cambridge, MA.
Honig, B. (2013) *Antigone, Interrupted*. Cambridge.
Irigaray, L. (1985a) *Speculum of the Other Woman*. Trans. G. C. Gill. Ithaca, NY.
Irigaray, L. (1985b) *This Sex Which Is Not One*. Trans. C. Porter. Ithaca, NY.
Irigaray, L. (1999) *The Forgetting of Air in Martin Heidegger*. Trans. M. B. Mader. London.
Jackson, Z. I. (2016) "Sense of Things," *Catalyst: Feminism, Theory, Technoscience* 2.2: 1–48. <http://catalystjournal.org/ojs/index.php/catalyst/article/view/74/212>. Accessed May 21, 2018.
Jones, D. V. (2010) *The Racial Discourses of Life Philosophy: Negritude, Vitalism, and Modernity*. New York.

Kirk, G. S., J. E. Raven, and M. Schofield (1983) *The Presocratic Philosophers*. Cambridge.

Leong, D. (2016) "The Mattering of Black Lives: Octavia Butler's Hyperempathy and the Promise of the New Materialisms," *Catalyst: Feminism, Theory, Technoscience* 2.2: 1-35. <http://catalystjournal.org/ojs/index.php/catalyst/article/view/100/203>. Accessed May 21, 2018.

Lingis, A. (1983) *Excesses*. Albany, NY.

Marder, M. (2014) *The Philosopher's Plant: An Intellectual Herbarium*. New York.

Miller, E. P. (2002) *The Vegetative Soul: From Philosophy of Nature to Subjectivity in the Feminine*. Albany, NY.

Naddaf, G. (2005) *The Greek Concept of Nature*. Albany, NY.

Parisi, L. (2010) "Event and Evolution," *The Southern Journal of Philosophy* 48, Supplement s1 29-46: 147-64.

Portmann, A. (1967) *Animal Forms and Patterns*. New York.

Puar, J. (2007) *Terrorist Assemblages: Homonationalism in Queer Times*. Durham, NC.

Rawlinson, M. (2016) *Just Life: Bioethics and the Future of Sexual Difference*. New York.

Renehan, R. (1980) "On the Greek Origins of the Concepts Incorporeality and Immateriality," *Greek, Roman and Byzantine Studies* 21:105-38.

Roughgarden, J. (2004) *Evolution's Rainbow: Diversity, Gender, and Sexuality in Nature and People*. Berkeley.

Sallis, J. (1993) "Deformatives: Essentially Other than Truth," in J. Sallis (ed.), *Reading Heidegger: Commemorations*. Bloomington, IN: 29-46.

Sallis, J. (2000) *Force of Imagination*. Bloomington, IN.

Sallis, J. (2016a) *The Figure of Nature: On Greek Origins*. Bloomington, IN.

Sallis, J. (2016b) *The Return of Nature: Coming as if from Nowhere*. Bloomington, IN.

Schmidt, D. J. (2013) "From the Moly Plant to the Gardens of Adonis," *Epoché* 17: 167-77.

Sharp, H. (2011) *Spinoza and the Politics of Renaturalization*. Chicago.

Smyth, H. W. (1920) *A Greek Grammar for Colleges*. New York.

von Uexküll, J. (2010 [1934]) *A Foray into the Worlds of Animals and Humans with a Theory of Meaning*. Trans. J. D. O'Neill. Minneapolis.

Weinstein, J. (2010) "A Requiem to Sexual Difference: A Response to Luciana Parisi's 'Event and Evolution,'" *Southern Journal of Philosophy* 48, Supplement s1: 165-87.

On Stoic sympathy

Cosmobiology and the life of nature

Brooke Holmes

The concept of sympathy is familiar to us as a form of affective intersubjectivity: I feel for you. By contrast, the ancient Greco-Roman concept of sympathy, which thrives well into the eighteenth century, is not primarily human nor is it imagined from a predominantly first-personal perspective.[1] In the wake of its emergence in extant Greek texts in the fourth century BCE, sympathy comes to describe a mode of relationality distributed throughout the world, from worms and fungi all the way up to celestial bodies, as well as within human beings (between bodies and souls and between the different organs and other parts of the body).

One of the most remarkable things about ancient sympathy is its seemingly sudden appearance across a range of domains engaged in making sense of the natural world in the late classical and early Hellenistic period—from philosophical psychology to natural history, learned magic to medicine, cosmology to astrology. The rapid efflorescence of sympathy in this period signals a multi-focal and multi-faceted engagement with the question of how non-human natures, including the parts of human bodies, relate to one another in a way that is neither anthropomorphic (as in Greek cult and myth) nor reductively materialist but, rather, sustained by the explanatory force of nature itself. It indexes, too, a deep engagement with the question of where humans are or should be situated within this tissue of relations.[2] These are not easy questions, as their widespread resurgence in a range of discourses and debates in the early twenty-first century makes clear.

I am very grateful to my co-organizers of the conference "Posthuman Antiquities," Sara Brill and Emma Bianchi, and the other participants and audience members for their feedback on this paper. I also want to thank audiences at the University of Chicago, the University of Leiden, the University of Pennsylvania, the University of California, Berkeley, and University College London for their feedback. Many thanks as well to Mark Payne, Gabriel Lear, Jonathan Lear, Shaul Tor, Jim Porter, André Laks, Susan Bielstein, and the anonymous readers for the Press.

[1] See Hanley (2015) on this shift in the eighteenth century.
[2] See further Holmes, Forthcoming.

Indeed, one of the reasons why sympathy is so fascinating is because of the way in which it helps makes possible, through its emphasis on the relation, the emergence of a concept of Nature, a concept that is addressed to the totality of beings and their relations in the world and therefore distinguished from the concept of (little-*n*) nature, that is, the nature of an x—a platypus, an amethyst, a human being—as it is articulated, above all, in Aristotle, but also in the early medical writers.[3] At the same time, sympathy exposes tensions within what I call *organismic* thinking and, more specifically, in the theorization of the relationship of mind and matter and the relationship of parts and wholes on a cosmic scale. In this chapter, I focus on these tensions as they are disclosed in the expansive version of cosmic sympathy that can be elicited from the lacunose remains of the Stoics. The Stoics are the most committed cosmobiologists in antiquity. Their theorization of the cosmic organism enacts a scenario in which the idea of Nature as a totalized whole is taken to its absolute limit, offering fertile ground to understand the powerful attraction of Nature as a totalized whole or a superorganism, organized by a single governing force of life.[4] At the same time, Stoic sympathy often seems to be something that escapes the web of causes, hovering above it all as a kind of film of becoming.

In Stoic sympathy, we find a pious commitment to the unity, completeness, and perfection of the world together with a tarrying with its parts and its particulars. Whether observing symbiotic plants or tidal patterns, magnetic attraction or the lunar cycles of shellfish, they do not simply see two bodies experiencing *pathē*, affections, together. The Stoics see a principle of connectivity as a feature of the world—indeed, its defining feature, symptomatic of the immanence of god (also called Reason, Fate, Providence, and Nature). At the same time, sympathy leads the other direction, away from totalizing concepts of wholeness towards the world's diversity and singularities: the waxing and waning of a mouse's liver, the bloom of pennyroyal. With sympathy, we move across a plane of beings all participating in the incalculably complex life of the cosmos, but we also meet the master order imposed on the many different parts. The cosmos is at once micro and macro, one and many. We scale up and down in the same breath.

---

[3] On a reading of nature in early Greek philosophy that doesn't fit easily into either of these categories, see Bianchi in this volume. Brill in this volume points to the ways in which Aristotle does explore the interconnectedness of natures despite his resistance to cosmic teleology and an immanent transindividual Nature.

[4] On Stoic "cosmobiology," Hahm (1977) 136–84 remains foundational. On Earth as superorganism, see Latour (2017) 94–101.

The breath, pneuma, is what lies behind or beneath or, perhaps, alongside Stoic sympathy, the two entwined as cause and effect. The Stoics have a unique, arguably lunatic philosophy of cause and effect that insists on a radical ontological division of the former from the latter. They are thoroughgoing corporealists, subscribing to a continuum theory of matter and holding that everything that exists—including the soul—is a body (*sōma*). A body is that which acts and/or is acted upon. Therefore, only bodies can be causes, and only bodies undergo affections. But effects are themselves classified by the Stoics as incorporeal. For effects belong to one of the four categories of incorporeals, namely, *lekta*, "sayables" (the other three categories of incorporeals are place, time, and void), which do not exist but, rather, the Stoics say, *subsist*.[5] In a classic example reported by Sextus Empiricus, if a scalpel cuts flesh, two bodies have come into contact, one acting on the other, but the effect, "being cut," floats as an incorporeal.[6] It cannot itself cause anything but neither is it, technically speaking, caused. Rather, the predicate "being cut" expresses something that has happened to a body without that body ceasing to be what it is. It captures not a quality or a property—these are also bodies, according to the Stoics—but an event, ghostly, and yet real in its way, "a thin film at the limit of things and words" or "the faint incorporeal mist which escapes from bodies," "extra-being," as Gilles Deleuze writes in the *Logic of Sense*.[7]

The Stoics in fact occupy a privileged space in the *Logic of Sense*, credited by Deleuze with the first "reversal" of Platonism.[8] Their claim to the title lies in the way they embrace what Plato in the *Philebus* calls the "unlimited"—the flow of becoming, the going to-and-fro of things that eludes the disciplining power of the Idea—and raise it to the surface as at once ethereal and manifest, what Deleuze calls a "becoming-mad" of the

---

[5] Technically speaking, a predicate (e.g. "is cut") is classed as an "incomplete" sayable; it becomes complete when it acquires a subject or substantival form (e.g. "the flesh is cut"): see Diogenes Laertius, *Lives of the Philosophers* 7.63.

[6] Sextus Empiricus, *Against the Professors* 9.211.

[7] Deleuze (1990) 10, 21, 31. Note that for the Stoics, qualities are also causes of the steady state of the unified body. The Stoics call these causes "containing" causes, and I discuss them further below, p. 267.

[8] Plato is in fact the first to reverse his own Platonism, in the *Sophist*, in the reading that appears as the first part of "The Simulacrum and Ancient Philosophy" in the appendix to the *Logic of Sense* ((1990) 253–66), but the problem is that Plato represses that which escapes the Idea (i.e. the simulacrum), whereas in the Stoics, "everything...returns to the surface.... What was eluding the Idea climbed up to the surface, that is, the incorporeal limit, and represents now all possible *ideality*, the latter being stripped of its causal and spiritual efficacy. The Stoics discovered surface effects" ((1990) 7, emphasis original). In turning to the Stoics, Deleuze shifts attention away from the Epicureans, despite an earlier interest in a reversal of Platonism in Lucretius: see Holmes (2012) 339–40 n. 66.

world. Effects become manifest in language, as what is literally "sayable." It is in this way, Deleuze points out, that they must be differentiated from qualities: they are not physical attributes, but logical ones. It is important here that the idea of the sayable, with its sense of possibility, signals a gap between the subsistence of the event and the event's expression in words or thought, because it emphasizes that the event is independent of actual thought and speech. At the same time, spoken language is a body and, as such, capable of causing changes in other bodies: philosophy is therapy in Stoicism as in the other ancient schools. The body of language cups the incorporeal event, the being-cut of flesh. For Deleuze, this cupping of the event *is* sense, the non-existing bond between things and propositions that in Stoicism makes possible the understanding of the world in its total unity that is the hallmark of the sage.[9]

Elizabeth Grosz has recently returned to the Stoics in her Deleuze-inspired inquiry into "the incorporeal," the term that she adopts from the Stoics to name a tradition of "extramaterialism" that, she argues, extends from the Stoics through Spinoza and Nietzsche to Deleuze, Gilbert Simondon, and Raymond Ruyer.[10] In turning to the incorporeal, Grosz aims to demonstrate how any materialism, including different forms of new materialism, is indebted to ideality and form.[11] The project has Aristotelian roots, insofar as Aristotle was working against Platonic idealism to develop his concept of immanent form. It is not a surprise that Aristotle has been an ally of Graham Harman, for example, in his own war against reductive materialism under the aegis of object-oriented ontology.[12] But Grosz bypasses Aristotle, no doubt in part because Aristotelian hylomorphism skews so heavily towards form and consigns matter to passive femininity in the later tradition, but primarily

---

[9] It is through sense that I take Deleuze to be addressing the problem of how incorporeals are thought and spoken by us, given that they cannot, technically, act in the world. Sextus Empiricus reports that the Stoics thought that the mind (*hēgemonikon*, the "commanding faculty") was impressed not by incorporeals but *in relation to* them (*Against the Professors* 8.409). Long and Sedley (1987) 1:241 see this as "too mysterious" and suggest instead incorporals are perceived through "transition," a form of abstraction, as at Diogenes Laertius, *Lives of the Philosophers* 7.53. In closing the circuit between denotation, manifestation, and signification, Deleuzian sense is a different solution to the problem of moving between the corporeal and the incorporeal, though not without mystery.

[10] Grosz (2017) 5. Grosz's project recalls Nagel (2012) on the other side of the continental/analytic divide.

[11] "Today just about everyone is a materialist" ((2017) 16). In this camp of reductive materialists, Grosz groups historial materialism, new feminist materialisms, and object-oriented materialisms together with the bulk of the physical sciences, though in so doing, she downplays the vitalist strain in new materialism, associated most strongly with the work of Jane Bennett.

[12] e.g. Harman (2011). On OOO and Greco-Roman antiquity, see Porter in this volume.

because of Deleuze's privileging of the Stoics. Hence it is the Stoics who christen her genealogy of a third way between materialism and idealism—namely, the incorporeal.

I share Grosz's—and Deleuze's—interests in the seam between matter and mind, and I am strongly committed to the position that the twenty-first-century renaissance of a materialist imaginary needs to surface ancient resources to grapple anew with the complex ways in which matter takes shape; the ways in which mindful bodies orient towards ends; the ethical labor of living with and through bodies; and the tensions between individual organisms and the collectives and systems within which they flourish and suffer. In its emergence as a locus of organismic thinking at both a micro- and a macro-level, sympathy thus repays attention in the context of contemporary debates about materialism and the ethical, political, and aesthetic implications of relations between the non-human and the human. Moreover, sympathy is crucial to Stoicism, although it is virtually always taken for granted by commentators, rather than interrogated, perhaps due to its longtime status as too mystical or magical for serious philosophical consideration.[13]

Let me specify more precisely two major reasons for the importance of sympathy to contemporary debates about materialism and the non-human, the ontology of life, and the philosophical stakes of Nature. First, the Stoics, pursuing an inquiry begun by the classical medical writers and Aristotle into the immanence of nature in bodies, are pushing beyond the parameters of *a* nature to understand natures as embedded in a larger network of bodies governed by Nature. The onto-ethics of the Stoics have to be understood in light of this vast non-human web, which Grosz largely ignores. The web of natures elevates the relation between natures to a place of privilege in the Stoic system while seeming to offer, too, a kind of flat ontology. Yet, in pushing cosmobiology to its limits, the Stoics end up offering us the earliest version of a cosmic

---

[13] Grosz (2017) 28–9 mentions sympathy briefly immediately after introducing incorporeals and before a discussion of the mixture of bodies, but it isn't clear what role she thinks it plays. Bobzien 1998, the definitive work on Stoic fate and causal determinism, makes only passing reference to sympathy (e.g. 13, 41, 296). Long and Sedley (1987) 1:287 write only that the Stoics "recognized that the coherence of the world-order is a fact requiring explanation" and do not single sympathy out as a core Stoic concept. Besnier (1996) 143 describes sympathy as "connaissance qui n'est pas savante, qui résulte d'une expérience sur laquelle tout le monde peut avoir réfléchi." Even Brouwer (2015), the chapter devoted to Stoic sympathy in the recent Oxford Philosophical Concepts volume on sympathy, does little to explain why sympathy mattered so much to the Stoics. On its status as a magical concept, see Lehoux (2012) 133–54. Cf. Laurand (2005) 525, rightly emphasizing how seductive the apparent intuitiveness of sympathy was (and in some ways, still is).

superorganism in all its danger and seduction, demonstrating how totality always lurks within a concept of big-N Nature.[14]

The Stoics are also radical human exceptionalists, precisely because they elevate mind over matter. The tension between an expansive community of mostly non-humans and the exceptionalism of the human, which mirrors the tension between blind (but *natural*) embodiment and sagehood, is the second reason why sympathy is so important. For in the folds of sympathy the relations between matter and mind, corporeality and incorporeality, are shown to be more fractious and complex than Grosz allows in her largely descriptive account of Stoicism, calling into question her use of the Stoics to ground the happily hyphenated material-ideal that she claims as the catalyst for "a *new* new materialism."[15] In sympathy, we encounter the openness of bodies to becoming *and* the rigorous disciplining of every body by the totalizing truth of Stoic Fate. In sympathy, we encounter surface effects and causal depths.

In what follows, I first unpack what the Stoics think they are seeing and showing when they speak of sympathy before tracing the two sides of sympathy and, with it, the complex terrain of Stoic materio-idealism, in the spirit of a project that finds resources for a newer materialism in materialism's ancient puzzles.

12.1. The web of natures

Before going further, a caveat is necessary. We have virtually nothing from the major Stoic thinkers writing in Greek with the result that we have to rely largely on their later, especially Roman, adherents, doxographers, and critics, all of whom had their own agendas. The status of the evidence makes it difficult to reconstruct a diachronic development for sympathy within Stoicism, or even to establish it as the doctrine of any one thinker, although there are strong indications that it owes much to Chrysippus. What is clear from extant sources is that the Stoics were keen to see and, more important, to *show* sympathy in the world as manifest proof of their cosmological and theological claims. Indeed, the Stoics seem to have been instrumental in making sympathy at the cosmic level visible even to those who rejected their explanations of it.

---

[14] The concept of the superorganism has appeared as something that must be resisted in Haraway (2016); Latour (2017).
[15] Grosz (2017) 14 (emphasis original).

One of the best places to start observing the Stoics' deictic invocations of sympathy is Cicero's *On the Nature of the Gods*. Early on in a series of arguments for the existence of god, Balbus, the dialogue's mouthpiece of Stoicism, invokes sympathy as an especially decisive proof for a divine presence in the world:

> Now again who would not be compelled to assent to the things I have said by such a sympathetic, continuous affinity of things, joined together in its breathing (*vero tanta rerum consentiens conspirans continuata cognatio*)? Would it be possible for the earth to bloom at a single time and then, in turn, turn bare and stark, or for the sun's approaches and retreats at the summer and winter solstices to be known by the spontaneous transformation of so many things, or for the sea tides and the narrow straits to ebb and flow with the rising and setting of the moon, or for different courses of the stars to be maintained by a single revolution of the whole sky? These things could not happen in this way with all the parts of the world harmonizing together if they were not held together by a single divine all-pervading breath (*uno divino et continuato spiritu*).[16]

What the careful observer will realize, Balbus argues, is that the coordinated transformations of the many disparate parts of the cosmos require something binding them all together. He insists without further argument that the unifying force must be a "single divine all-pervading breath." In another *locus classicus* for Stoic sympathy, Sextus Empiricus relays a similar series of examples—the coordination between the phases of the moon and the waxing and waning of animals on land and sea, the tides, and the large-scale effects of climactic change—in order to establish the more modest claim that the cosmos is unified: "and from these facts, it is obvious that the cosmos is a unified body."[17]

In these examples, sympathy is treated as a phenomenon given to us unproblematically through observation. The conspicuous fact of cosmic sympathy compels us in turn, the Stoics insist, to accept the reality of less obvious things, such as the unity of the body of the cosmos and the absence of interstitial void; a breath pervading all things; and, finally, the existence and nature of god. The decision to begin with the visible world accords with the Stoics' thoroughgoing empiricism: all concepts have their origins in sense-perceptions. In mature human beings (over the age of 14), these perceptions correspond to (incorporeal) propositions, to which a person chooses to assent, thereby accepting the proposition as a

---

[16] Cicero, *On the Nature of the Gods* 2.19. Cf. 2.119 on the union of things and the sympathetic synthesis of nature (*copulatio rerum et quasi consentiens ad mundi incolumitatem coagmentatio naturae*).

[17] Sextus Empiricus, *Against the Professors* 9.79.

true statement about the world.[18] Some propositions can be classed as "indicative signs" (*sēmeia endeiktika*) that function as springboards enabling reason to move inferentially from sense-perceptions to non-evident truths, most notably about the nature of god.[19]

Balbus and Sextus suggest that sympathy was deployed by the Stoics as just such a springboard. But what is it, exactly, that we assent to when we take sympathy as a fact about the world? It is neither the presence of a crescent moon, nor a green tree. Rather, we must first grasp that a body is undergoing an affection: the moon waning, the tree greening. We must then grasp that the change in one body is occurring together with another body's transformation (e.g. with celestial movements). Neither the coordination between bodies nor even the change of one of them is a simple thing to perceive. Rather, each case involves a process that the Stoics perhaps called "remembering together" (*symmnēmoneusis*), that is, "holding two things in mind in order to construct some single thing from them."[20] It requires recognizing the ways in which bodies are related to themselves in time and to one another—in other words, the labor of making sense.[21] At the same time, the conceptual labor required to sense sympathy is strategically obscured by the Stoics' invocation of a world coordinated in its becomings as uncontroversially manifest.

We should nevertheless pause before giving cosmic sympathy too easy a foothold in the phenomenal landscape and ask instead how the Stoics managed to establish cosmic sympathy as blindingly obvious to those around them, including their most strident opponents. The Stoics were not, of course, the first to observe seasonal change, nor were they the first to put the waxing and waning of terrestrial life in communication with

---

[18] The stage of assent is crucial to Stoic moral psychology, but we should imagine it as sub-phenomenal and therefore automatic in most cases, as Brennan (2006) 262 argues.

[19] The existence of god/providence is the main object requiring demonstration at Diogenes Laertius, *Lives of the Philosophers* 7.52.

[20] Barnes (1988) 254. The term is in Sextus, who points out that "co-remembering" is needed to perceive any change and in complex concept formation (*Outlines of Pyrrhonism* 3.108; *Against the Professors* 1.129). Barnes (1988) 250–9 discusses co-remembering in the case of the perception of the relation of part to whole.

[21] The ways in which bodies are "relatively disposed" to another is the fourth genus (of four genera) in Stoic ontology, covering cases of extrinsic relation—say, being Dion's neighbor or being father and son. In the cases of sympathy above, the emphasis is on observing how two bodies change at the same time, with the inference that they must be responding to a single cause. In this way, the observation of sympathy participates in recognizing that every body in the cosmos is relatively disposed to the cosmos as a whole—hence the need for the fourth genus. But other cases of sympathy (e.g. the influence of the moon on the tides) emphasize that one body is relatively disposed to another as cause. I discuss these two forms of sympathy below, pp. 263–65.

the sun and the moon. Lunar cycles, to take just one example, had long been seen as having a wide range of effects on life on earth.[22] Cicero gives a hint of Stoic practice in his *On Divination*, where we find a particularly impressive catalog of sympathies that bears more than a passing resemblance to what Ian Bogost has called "Latour litanies," the lists favored by Latour and object-oriented ontologists as a way of flattening entrenched metaphysical scales of Being.[23] Cicero says that the Stoics have "collected much evidence" to prove that even things far removed from one another have a natural kinship (*cognatio naturalis*).[24] He goes on to enumerate the waxing of the "little livers of mice" in winter, the blooming of pennyroyal, and the bursting of its seed pods on the day of the winter solstice, the sympathetic sounding of the strings of the lyre, and the waxing and waning of shellfish with the phases of the moon, before wandering into ellipsis: "Why should I mention the seas and straits with their tides, whose ebb and flow are governed by the motion of the moon?"

Whereas the Latour litanies resist totalization, the Stoic list is designed to point to a principle of order behind the apparent heap of relationships it names. In his commentary, A. S. Pease exhaustively catalogs other ancient Greek and Roman references to the "facts" listed by Cicero.[25] Interestingly, in the majority of those references, we find no mention of sympathy or its Latin cognates, though the other sources confirm that these claims (e.g. that the livers of mice grow in winter) were in wide circulation. It seems likely, then, that the Stoics mined the annals of natural history and a stock of shared popular beliefs for facts to be amassed as evidence of sympathy on a cosmic scale. I am not arguing here that the Stoics singlehandedly created sympathy. There are different threads of evidence that imply a push from a range of quarters to see the world in terms of sympathy in the early Hellenistic period. But Cicero does imply that the Stoics played an important role in making sympathy visible insofar as they stockpiled existing observations into a common repository of facts all attesting to the existence of a single phenomenon—that

---

[22] For archaic and classical beliefs about the moon, see Préaux (1973). Arguments for the lunar influence on the tides appear to have owed much to the first-century BCE Stoic Posidonius, who was probably responsible for making the tides star examples of sympathy: see Frr. 138, 217–20 (Edelstein-Kidd), with Kidd (1988) 524.

[23] Bogost (2012) 38. Many thanks to Emma Bianchi for drawing my attention to the parallel.

[24] Cicero, *On Divination* 2.33. On the Stoics as collectors and list-makers, see Pease (1920–3) 402, *ad* 5. See Weidlich (1894) 8–11 and Lehoux (2012) 140 more generally on the lists used to establish sympathy.

[25] Pease (1920–3) 402–12.

is, sympathy. The argument from induction helped establish sympathy as the home for a range of observations about the non-human world that used to be explained, when they were explained at all, in local and disconnected ways.

In this project of showing sympathy the Stoics seem to have been remarkably successful. Cicero says, in *On Divination*, that in the face of such an accumulation of evidence, one has to concede the existence of "natural kinship," and in *On the Nature of the Gods*, Balbus' Academic critic, Cotta, also accepts that sympathy exists. But Cotta rejects the explanation offered by the Stoics—one immanent divine breath—and instead chalks sympathy up to "forces of nature" (*naturae viribus*, 3.28). A similar response is found in other anti-Stoic authors. The first-century BCE Platonizing Jewish philosopher Philo of Alexandria, responding to a more strictly astrological concept of sympathy associated with the Chaldeans (a term used in Greek and Roman texts of Babylonian scholars of astrology), explains sympathy in terms of "indissoluble chains" used by a (transcendent) demiurgic god to hold the cosmos together. The second-century CE Peripatetic Alexander of Aphrodisias, responding directly to the Stoics, accounts for sympathy by pointing to the aether surrounding the sublunary world, whose continuous motion causes bodies to be exchanged with regulated order, as well as to what he calls the "commonality of matter."[26]

Stoic critics thus disagreed vigorously about the causes of sympathy. They disagreed, too, about its scope. For the Stoics, sympathy extends beyond lunar or seasonal changes to the relationship of every single event to a unified Fate. Here, Cicero, like many others in antiquity, resisted, refusing to see a connection between, say, the liver of a sacrificial animal and a lucky windfall.[27] Nevertheless, the fact that "natural" sympathy becomes widely accepted as a manifest feature of the cosmos was very likely a victory of the Stoic catalogs. That is, with sympathy, the Stoics help to establish a vast web of interconnected natures as a shared reality with ricocheting implications for future philosophies of Nature. But the Stoics thought that making sense of such a web required surfacing much more, of course. I turn now to take a closer look at their claims about the cause of sympathy, before returning to the scope of cosmic sympathy and the concept's animating tensions.

---

[26] Philo, *On the Migration of Abraham* 178–81; Alexander of Aphrodisias, *On Mixture* 223.10–14 (Bruns); 223.32–4 (Bruns), on "the commonality of matter" (διά τε τὴν τῆς ὕλης κοινωνίαν).

[27] Cicero, *On Divination* 2.33. For similar complaints about the explanatory limits of sympathy, see Cicero, *On Fate* 7–8; Aulus Gellius, *Attic Nights* 14.1.4–5 (technically also about Chaldean astrology, but the argument is the same); Plotinus, *Ennead* 3.1.

12.2. The breath of sympathy

In the invocation of sympathy in *On the Nature of the Gods*, Balbus triumphantly wields cosmic sympathy at the climax of a series of arguments for the existence of god, as if its evidentiary value were indisputable (and, as we have just seen, his critic Cotta accepts sympathy as a fact). The persuasive force of his claim relies on transferring the facticity of sympathy enthusiastically observed at scattered sites in the world to a single unseen thing that holds together all these simultaneously changing but distant bodies (stars and flowers and the sun and tides and so on)—namely, a divine breath. He accomplishes this task rhetorically with his insistent language of many and One (*so many* things transformed, *different* courses of the stars; at *one* time, by a *single* revolution of the sky), with which he prepares the listener for a final inductive leap from all these examples to the crucial pairing of *all* the parts of the world with a *single* breath.[28] But despite Balbus' treatment of sympathy as a deictic sign pointing to the presence of the single immanent breath of god, he offers little to convince us that the unifying cause of sympathy must be a breath or divine at all, though of course these were the features of Stoic sympathy that were most controversial.

Sextus tarries a bit longer with the argument from sympathy, spelling out steps that are glossed over in Balbus' account, and he invokes sympathy on behalf of a more limited claim—namely, that the cosmos is a unified body.[29] The argument repays closer attention. The expression "unified body" (*hēnōmenon ti sōma*) is a technical term in Stoic physics, one of three types of bodies, as Sextus describes here.[30] The simplest of these are flocks, choruses, and armies—in other words, loose groupings composed of separate elements (*diestōta*). The next category includes bodies whose elements are joined together (*synaptomena*), like ships or cables. In both these types of bodies, the parts can survive the destruction of the whole. For example, even if an entire army, save one soldier, dies,

---

[28] That is, *uno tempore* and *una totius caeli conversione*, contrasted with *tot rebus* and *cursus astrorum dispares*, leading up to *omnibus inter se concinentibus mundi* taken with *uno divino et continuato spiritu* (2.19). Induction was an important tool in the Stoic understanding of a science (*technē/ars*). That the unifying force is all-pervasive is underscored by the repetition of the crucial adjective *continuatus* (Greek: *synechēs*) at the start and the end of the passage.

[29] See also Epictetus, *Discourses* 1.14.1–2, where sympathy between terrestrial things and the heavens more loosely attests to cosmic unity. Elsewhere sympathy is used to demonstrate the absence of (intracosmic) void: see Cleomedes, *On the Heavens* 1.1.13 (Todd); Galen, *On the Natural Faculties* 1.13 (2.39 Kühn); Diogenes Laertius, *Lives of the Philosophers* 7.140.

[30] Sextus Empiricus, *Against the Professors* 9.78; see also 1.102.

the lone survivor does not suffer anything "by transmission" (*kata diadosin*).[31] By contrast, in unified bodies, there exists "a certain sympathy": "if a finger is cut, the whole body shares in the pain."[32] The claim that the suffering of one part of a (human) body affects the whole is already found in the late fifth-century or early fourth-century BCE medical text *On Places in a Human Being*, and it appears as well in Plato's *Republic*, suggesting that the embodied person had become a paradigmatic case of a unified whole in the late fifth or early fourth century BCE.[33] But if it is a stock example, it all the more useful for inviting the listener to assess empirically the truth of the claim that sympathy occurs only in unified bodies not simply from the observation of other bodies (stars, starfish) but from the experience of her own corporeal unity. Insofar as sympathy occurs *only* in unified bodies, as the Stoic division of bodies assumes, it functions in the argument that Sextus reports as an indexical sign. That the cosmos exhibits sympathies therefore confirms that it is a unified body.

Nevertheless, these arguments take us only so far. We want to know what makes a body unified, and why the cosmos is divine. Sextus does not explain here what accounts for a body's unity. Instead he launches into a discussion of the ascending types of unified bodies, by which ladder he will eventually get to the divinity of the cosmos. Before returning to the place of sympathy in this context, however, I want first to look closer at the role of breath—that is, pneuma—in securing the unity of a unified body. A single, all-pervading breath was the cause of sympathy invoked by Balbus, and we find the same claim ascribed to Chrysippus by Alexander of Aphrodisias: "he posits, first, that the whole of substance is unified, a pneuma pervading all of it, by which the whole is held together and holds fast and is sympathetic with itself."[34]

---

[31] Sextus Empiricus, *Against the Professors* 9.80. On the army as an example used to prove "the innocence of composition" (for the Stoics it is a "denumerable entity" [*arithmōi leptos*]), see Plato, *Theaetetus* 204b10–e10 with Harte (2002) 41–7, esp. 45.

[32] Sextus Empiricus, *Against the Professors* 9.80. See also Alexander, *Mantissa* 3 (117.9–23 Bruns).

[33] [Hippocrates], *On Places in a Human Being* 1 (Littré 6.278); Plato, *Republic* 5, 462c–d (thanks to André Laks for pointing out this passage). A couple passages from Aristotle's *Parts of Animals* are relevant here. At 653b5–8, the heart (as *archē*) is *sympathestaton*, being affected by the changes of everything around it; at 690b4, Aristotle says that if the foot were not divided at the tip, then the whole foot would be sympathetic with the suffering of a part (ἅπαν γὰρ ἂν συμπαθὲς ἦν ἑνὸς μορίου πονήσαντος). But cf. *On Sleep and Wakefulness* 455a34, where the common sense does not "sympathize" (*sympaschein*) with the individual senses. The Stoics often drew examples of sign-relations from medicine (e.g. if sweat flows from a surface, then there are imperceptible pores), though they did not see them as universally true: see Bobzien (1998) 162–3, 174.

[34] Alexander of Aphrodisias, *On Mixture* 216.14–17 (Bruns): ἡνῶσθαι μὲν ὑποτίθεται τὴν σύμπασαν οὐσίαν, πνεύματός τινος διὰ πάσης αὐτῆς διήκοντος, ὑφ' οὗ συνέχεταί τε καὶ συμμένει καὶ συμπαθές ἐστιν αὑτῷ τὸ πᾶν (the μέν clause is followed by a δέ clause

In this context, sympathy is but one consequence of the unity secured by pneuma, in addition to the whole of Being being cohesive and stable. So what is pneuma, and why is it capable of endowing bodies with unity?

The majority of our sources treat pneuma in the Stoic system as a compound of (cold) air and (hot) fire, the two "active" elements in Stoic physics (against the two "passive" elements, water and earth).[35] In this way, pneuma is identified with the active principle (*archē*) itself, and so with the governing force of the cosmos, called god, reason, fate, providence, and nature (for the Stoics, all these names point to different aspects of what is essentially the same thing). It is opposed to the passive principle, equated with unqualified substance (*ousia*) or matter (*hylē*). Both these principles were almost certainly classified as bodies, consistent with the Stoics' corporealism.[36] It is by means of pneuma that god (reason, mind, etc.) becomes immanent in the whole of the cosmos, imbuing every last bit of matter so that it participates in cosmic unity while retaining its own special properties in the same way that a soul permeates and organizes a body.[37] The cosmic significance of pneuma is almost certainly due to Chrysippus. For Zeno, the founder of the school, what he called "creative" or "craftsmanlike" (*technikon*) fire was master, analogous to the vital heat in the organism and equated with a form-giving seed (*spermatikos logos*).[38] Chrysippus retains creative fire, but invests pneuma with the capacity to carry out the embryological potential of the cosmogonic moment into the life of the cosmos. It is with

---

introducing the presence of different mixtures within the unified cosmic-body); cf. *On Mixture* 223.6–9 (Bruns). Note that to the extent that Alexander is using τὸ πᾶν to gloss τὴν σύμπασαν οὐσίαν, he cannot be using the term with its proper Stoic meaning. For the Stoics, τὸ πᾶν includes the cosmos and void and therefore cannot be unified. It is the cosmos that is a "whole." On the difference, see Sextus Empiricus, *Against the Professors* 9.332. Alexander's lack of precision is understandable if we remember that the Peripatetics denied void and therefore predicated wholeness and totality of bodies alone.

[35] e.g. Alexander of Aphrodisias, *On Mixture* 224.14–17 (Bruns), 225.6–8 (Bruns). Alexander goes on to criticize the classification of pneuma as a compound element (225.8–10 [Bruns]), a criticism echoed by other ancient commentators. For a modern response, see Gourinat (2009) 62–6.

[36] If the definition of a body is to act and be acted upon, it seems impossible to isolate the principles as independent bodies. Some modern commentators have thus argued the principles are incorporeals that conceptually isolate aspects of a single substance. Long and Sedley (1987) 2:274 defend the corporeality of the principles: nothing bars us from imagining that the definition of body includes bodies that exhibit only one of the two features, capable of acting (active principle) and capable of being acted on (passive principle).

[37] Chrysippus developed the theory of "total blending" to account for this special relationship: see Todd (1976) 29–73, esp. 71–2; Nolan (2006) 169–77.

[38] See Diogenes Laertius, *Lives of the Philosophers* 7.135–6 and Cicero, *On the Nature of the Gods* 2.23–31. On the limitations of fire as a principle of immanence, see Todd (1978).

pneuma that the idea of a unified cosmos totally imbued with god reached its full realization in Stoicism.

What enables pneuma to grant unity to a body—whether the cosmos as a whole or a unified body within it—is its *tonos*, "tension." It is tempting to think of *tonos* as a kind of cosmic glue, and in some sense it is, holding bodies together and keeping them in place.[39] But if pneumatic tension makes bodies and the whole of substance hang together, it does much more than this. Our sources speak not only of tension but also of tensional motion (*tonikē kinēsis*) and pneumatic motion (*pneumatikē kinēsis*), as well as pneumatic "currents" and a breath that is ever running a double course.[40] By developing the concept of tensional motion, the Stoics elaborate cohesion as a force: "the geometrical continuum of Aristotle is in this way transformed into a dynamic one."[41]

The tension of a unified body is usually described as a *simultaneous* movement of contraction and expansion.[42] In contracting, pneuma imparts the tensile strength that enables a body to resist dissolution, providing an internal bond that is not unbreakable but "hard to dissolve."[43] Simplicius describes parts "grown together" (*symphyēs*) towards one another, language that suggests a kind of organic whole, not an aggregate.[44] By expanding, pneumatic currents, themselves categorized as bodies, imbue unified bodies with qualities, shaping their matter with definite form: the sheen of silver, the hardness of iron. Indeed, only unified bodies possess qualities by virtue of being governed by a

---

[39] Alexander of Aphrodisias reports that Chrysippus has pneuma giving the cosmos both cohesion and stability (in addition to sympathy). Both questions may be addressed to the position of the cosmos in the surrounding void, which was seen as having the potential to displace the cosmos and scatter its parts. Zeno was already aware of the problem and seems to have addressed it by positing a centripetal force pulling the elements of the cosmos towards its center and stabilizing it within the void: see Stobaeus 1.19.4, with Hahm (1977) 110–22. Chrysippus kept the theory of elemental motion but added the containing force of pneuma: see Plutarch, *Moralia* 1054F–1055C, with Hahm (1977) 168 and n. 80. Chrysippus may have answered the problem of the immobility of the cosmos independently, by following Aristotle in arguing that no direction is possible in the void, as Hahm (1977) 122–3 argues, but the concept of stability probably retained a wider reference to the cohesive integrity of the cosmos within the void. For example, at *On the Nature of the Gods* 2.115, after discussing the movement of parts towards the center of the cosmos, Balbus adds an argument about the cohesive role played by the divine stuff pervading the world.

[40] Sambursky (1959) 21–48.   [41] Sambursky (1959) 4.

[42] Nemesius, *On the Nature of a Human Being* 164: contraction is from cold air, expansion from hot fire. At 70–1, the *tonikē kinēsis* "moves simultaneously inward and outward, the outward movement producing quantities and qualities and the inward one unity and substance" (trans. Long and Sedley).

[43] Philo, *On the Incorruptibility of the World* 24.

[44] Simplicius, *On the Categories of Aristotle* 214.36–7. Simplicius is probably not marking a subcategory of organic bodies among unified bodies, as Long (1982) 37–8 suggests. Cf. Plutarch, *Moralia* 1055B.

single pneumatic "something" or a single *hexis*, sometimes translated as "tenor."[45] As we saw above, a chorus or a flock does not satisfy this criterion; a stone does. In a unified body, every part is bound up with every other part and the whole. As Cato describes Stoic philosophy itself in Cicero's *On Ends*, the entire system is so tightly interconnected that if you alter a single letter, you disrupt the whole.[46] In short, it is clear that pneuma creates wholes that are greater than the sum of their parts, wholes that triumph as unities despite their many parts.

The negotiation between plurality and unity is arguably best captured by the third consequence of pneumatic tension mentioned by Chrysippus—namely, the whole of substance is "sympathetic with itself." But sympathy also focuses attention on the very conditions by which a unity is also a plurality. What creates the gap that a reflexive construction like "sympathetic with itself" is required to close? For the Stoics, parts are not the *same* as wholes, but nor are they *other* than the whole.[47] In the case of sympathy, a whole contains many parts and so it undergoes many affections, *pathē*, but these affections are nevertheless coordinated. More specifically, as the reflexive construction asks us to recognize, coordination is governed by the structure of the whole such that all of the affections *belong* to the whole, in two ways. On the one hand, the affection of any part is necessarily also an affection of the whole to the extent that the part is not *other than* the whole. On the other hand, the very doubling of the reflexive underscores the multiplicity of the whole. Each part suffers an affection proper to it and the whole suffers *with* it to the extent that the part is not *the same as* the whole.

Thus sympathy most vividly triggers the double vision needed to grasp the unified body as parts *and* a whole, as we have already seen in the lists cited by Cicero and Sextus, lists that survey the plenitude of the cosmos—tides and stars and blossoming trees—while at the same time gathering these many parts into a whole unified by a single breath. In the arguments from sympathy, we see not just oneness but something like *the making of oneness out of multiplicity*, the creation of bonds

---

[45] Simplicius, *On the Categories of Aristotle* 214.29 speaks of *pneumatikon ti hen*. On qualities, see Plutarch, *Moralia* 1053F–1054B. The qualified body is the second of the Stoic genera, encompassing common qualities (e.g. "man") and particular ones (e.g. "Socrates") as well as essential and contingent qualities. Only unified bodies possess qualities: Simplicius, *On the Categories of Aristotle* 214.24–37 (where non-unified bodies, such as choruses, can nevertheless *be qualified*—they cooperate towards a common end).

[46] Cicero, *On Ends* 3.74.

[47] Sextus Empiricus, *Against the Professors* 9.336: "But the Stoics assert that the part is neither other than the whole nor the same; for the hand is neither the same as the man (for it is not a man) nor other than the man (for it is included in the conception of man as man)." See further Barnes (1988) 260–8.

between the parts so that, as the Stoicizing poet Manilius writes, "each may furnish and receive another's strength and the whole may stand fast in kinship *despite its variety of forms (per varias figuras)*."[48]

The sympathy of the cosmos is especially dramatic, Manilius emphasizes, because its parts are so many and so variegated. In fact, variations in the pneumatic tension (more specifically, the ratio of passive to active elements) of different bodies gives rise to an ascending scale of bodies within the class of unified bodies. The term *hexis*, which I have been using of structure in general, also names, more narrowly, the structure of the simplest unified bodies, inanimate objects such as wood and rocks, which are said to be held together by *hexis* alone. The next rung up the scale is occupied by plants, whose organization, realized over time as growth and development, is called "nature" (*physis*); after plants are animals and children, structured by soul (*psychē*), which is responsible for perception and locomotion.[49] In a mature human being, the soul acquires the capacity for reason through a further modification of pneumatic tension. Finally, in gods and sages, pneumatic tension generates a state of virtue. Much as in Aristotle's better known *scala naturae*, each new level in the Stoic system encompasses the lower level(s). The result of this nesting is that complexity describes not only the higher-level faculties possessed by bodies at the top of the scale (perception and impulse in animals, for example, or reason in people) but also the integration of increasingly heterogeneous parts into a unified whole.[50] The cosmos, at the top of the scale, thus comprises different parts belonging to the lower levels. Mind is everywhere, but it is not equally distributed, changing as it passes through different kinds of unified bodies (worms and stars, oysters and toddlers). And yet, as the pneuma of the cosmic animal, Mind recuperates these diverse bodies into a single whole.

One of our best sources for the scale of unified bodies is Sextus, who, right after invoking the argument from sympathy to prove the unity of the cosmos, climbs it in order to move from the lowest-level cohesion of stones to the divinity of the cosmos.[51] Sextus has to climb upwards one step at a time because sympathy on its own, despite Balbus' efforts, cannot prove that the cosmos is divine. The argument from sympathy, rather, proves only that a body is unified, held together at the most minimal level by (a single) pneumatic tension. Neither reason nor

---

[48] Manilius, *Astronomica* 1.253–4. See also the list of sympathies at 2.60–135.
[49] As Meyer (2009) 74 emphasizes, nature and soul are "seminal" (*spermatikoi*) causes "so called because their effects typically unfold in an orderly sequence of events." There is one cause, namely, the nature or the soul that persists through the sequence.
[50] On this nesting, see Long (1982) and Inwood (1985) 24–7.
[51] Sextus Empiricus, *Against the Professors* 9.81–5.

perception nor even life or a nature—let alone divinity—is a necessary property of a unified body. It is only with further refinement, when the passive, more material, elements have been offset by the active, more mindful elements, that pneumatic tension imparts qualities more complex than unity and coherence: life, perception, reason, wisdom, divinity. To put it another way, cohesion is both necessary and sufficient for sympathy: sympathy is exhibited as much by lifeless bodies as by living ones, by stones as much as by sages. The argument from sympathy is in fact surprisingly limited in how much it can prove about the cosmos.

Then again, the Stoics usually do not try to claim otherwise. They lean on other arguments to support their claims that the cosmos is alive, sentient, rational, and divine. These include a battery of syllogisms credited to Zeno that turn on the argument that the cosmos cannot lack anything—or, more specifically, anything uncategorically good— possessed by one of its parts.[52] One of Zeno's favorites, we are told by Cicero, goes something like this. If flutes that played tunes grew on an olive tree, you would hardly question that the olive tree had some knowledge of the art of flute-playing. Why, then, would anyone question that the world is animate and wise when it produces offspring like us who are animate and (potentially) wise?[53] Whatever the flaws of these arguments, we cannot blame the Stoics for not backing up the claim that the cosmos is an animal endowed with reason and, moreover, a god. It is simply that these arguments do not really have to do with sympathy.

Yet the arguments from sympathy often betray greater ambition. Recall that for Balbus, the spectacle of cosmic sympathy requires an all-pervading, divine breath. If Balbus does not prove the divinity of this breath, or even explain why we need to attribute sympathy to breath at all, he arguably aims for a sense of wonder with his Latourian litany of sympathies. Much as Lucretius writes *On the Nature of Things* to help Memmius see the world in terms of *atomization*, the Stoics, in waxing poetic about sympathy, exhort their readers to understand the cosmos in terms of *connectivity* and *complexity*, unity in the midst of seemingly infinite variability.

The place of wonder in the passage assigned to Balbus suggests that we have to see the work performed by sympathy in Stoic arguments as exceeding the parameters of technical argumentation in any one context. That is not to say that it was not a bold move to make the claim that

---

[52] On the argument about parts and wholes, see Cicero, *On the Nature of the Gods* 2.30; Sextus Empiricus, *Against the Professors* 9.108–10, with discussion at Schofield (1983) 43; see also Powers (2012) 266–8.
[53] Cicero, *On the Nature of the Gods* 2.22.

sympathy is meant to demonstrate, that is, that the cosmos is a unified body. It surely was, and the claim plays a critical role in Stoic cosmology and physics. Nevertheless, I want to defend the stronger position that sympathy matters so much to the Stoics because of the ways in which it fleshes out and sustains the difficult but compelling idea that the cosmos is alive, and therefore is as complex as any plant or animal. More specifically, the life of the cosmos is not just a *form* of life, enacted for the most part by different animals in a species according to nature. It is, rather, the very specific realization of *a* life, unfolding in time according to a seed-like *logos*.[54] Despite the fact that sympathy fails to securely index life, sentience, intelligence, or *a* life, I argue that because of the way it negotiates the relationship between parts and wholes at a microcosmic and a macrocosmic level, it enables thinking about organisms as complex wholes embedded in time—at once natural and historical—in a way that is formative for the elaboration of cosmobiology in all its tensions.

12.3. The two sides of sympathy

The belief that the cosmos is an (intelligent, divine) animal has important antecedents. Despite some evidence of the idea in the Presocratics, the watershed moment undoubtedly comes with Plato's *Timaeus*, where the cosmos is expressly envisioned as an animal—alive, sentient, intelligent.[55] The influence of that dialogue on the Stoics is widely accepted.[56] Yet biology only goes so deep in the *Timaeus*. The cosmos has structure—indeed structure, in the *Timaeus*, "goes all the way down"— but structure is understood in terms of geometry and the microscopic triangles that occupy the most basic ontological stratum.[57] For the elaboration of biological models of parts and wholes the Stoics could have looked to Aristotle. Aristotle's biology, however, is worked out at the level of individual organisms. He rejects Plato's World Soul, as well as the Demiurge, and the nature immanent in individual beings is not cosmic. Theophrastus may have played a crucial role in developing the idea of biological life on a cosmic scale. His *Metaphysics* is tantalizing

---

[54] Diogenes Laertius, *Lives of the Philosophers* 7.137-8: the cosmos is god as "peculiarly (*idiōs*) qualified."
[55] See Laks (Forthcoming), arguing caution about the evidence for this belief in the Presocratics.
[56] See Reydams-Schils (1999), esp. 42–60, Sedley (2002), Powers (2013).
[57] Harte (2002) 226, 241, 246-7. It is telling that in Harte's analysis mereology is never biological for Plato.

here, and especially a passage where he describes the cosmos as "symphonious with itself" (*symphōnon heautōi*), though like Aristotle he rejects large-scale teleology.[58] But it is undoubtedly in the Stoics that cosmobiology comes to full fruition alongside sympathy.

It is true, as we have just seen, that at a minimum sympathy points to the unity of a body, but not more—not life, sentience, or intelligence. In canonical examples, however, sympathy behaves like the mark of a sentient body. The idea that a unified (animal) whole will experience the pain of its parts was already found, as we saw earlier, in the Hippocratic Corpus and in Plato, and of course it is precisely the experience of the cut finger that is invoked when Sextus establishes sympathy as a property of unified bodies. That we have first-personal experience capable of verifying this claim secures its validity as a premise that can then allow us to identify unity in other bodies whose sympathies we witness from the outside—sympathies that may not even be perceived by the body itself, if it is insensate—including in the most macro of bodies, that of the cosmos itself. The first-personal experience of sympathy is also used to secure one of the premises of another cardinal Stoic claim, that the soul is corporeal. As the argument is reported to us by Nemesius, the Stoics first claim that no incorporeal suffers together with a body, and no body with an incorporeal before observing that "the soul suffers together with the body when it is sick and being cut, and the body with the soul; thus when the soul feels shame and fear the body turns red and pale respectively."[59] The experience of inhabiting a psychosomatic compound is thus marshalled to prove that the soul is a body. Here, as with the case of the cut finger, we live the truth that our parts are neither entirely the same as the "I" nor are they entirely other to the "I." That sympathy is a phenomenon first secured through first-personal experience is one reason why, when sympathy travels from the microcosm to the macrocosm, it trails a knot of ideas about life.

Recall, too, that the stock examples of cosmic sympathy we have seen are drawn primarily from the natural world. It is true that the Stoics go further, as we saw above, in extending sympathy into the order of events, which is why they embraced divination. But it is worth reiterating that, while their many critics resisted the total expansion of sympathy to the

---

[58] See Theophrastus, *Metaphysics* 8a3–7 where the whole cosmos (*ho holos ouranos*; I read this as denoting the cosmos and not only the heavens) is symphonious with itself and perfect like a city, animal, or other composite entity, with van Raalte (1988).

[59] Nemesius, *On the Nature of a Human Being* 2 (21.6–9 Morani). See also Alexander of Aphrodisias, *Mantissa* 117.15–16, opposing the Peripatetic interpretation of these examples, which Aristotle had already hesitated to explain in terms of sympathy: see Holmes (2013) 156–9.

point of Fate, they seem to have broadly accepted a concept of "natural" sympathy at least in part as a result of the Stoics' efforts at compiling lists of non-human, largely organic sympathies. Insofar as sympathy expressed the workings of Nature, it would have been understood by the Stoics as expressing the form of cohesion distinctive of plant and animal life.[60] Thus, as Balbus says later in the *On the Nature of the Gods*, when the Stoics speak of *natura* as the sustaining and governing principle of the world, "we do not mean that the world is like a clod of earth or lump of stone or something else of that sort, which possesses no natural principle of cohesion, but like a tree or an animal, displaying no haphazard structure, but order and a certain semblance of design."[61] The notion of order is not exhausted by sympathy. Nevertheless, sympathy plays a critical role in demonstrating its presence in the cosmos qua *natural* body, a body with a life unfolding in time.

For the Stoics, then, sympathy functions as a concept deeply bound up with organic life, and indeed, with our own experience of being a unified collective of parts undergoing constant change. Perhaps there is nothing surprising about this. What else would you expect from a school of radical cosmobiologists? And as I have emphasized, Stoic sympathy is often treated as unsurprising or at least as an unproblematic concept in the Stoic arsenal. But I prefer to see the organicism trailed by sympathy as an invitation to think about sympathy as a concept that exaggerates the double nature of Stoic unities as parts *and* wholes, body *and* mind, matter *and* god, while at the same time carving out a conceptual space to hold these aspects of life together in dynamic tension.

More specifically, the two sides of sympathy speak to the double perspective of living beings embedded in cosmic life, signaling, on the one hand, their openness to being acted on by the world beyond them and to change; and, on the other hand, the inborn cohesion of their natures and the apparent mindfulness of their lives. From within the increasingly rational perspective of the ethical agent, sympathy is again double, resignifying her openness to the world beyond her as a critical aspect of her participation in *its* unity and *its* life, and so becoming part

---

[60] The Stoics held that all bodies cohering with nature (plants) or soul (animals) are distinguished by having a "ruling part" (*hēgemonikon*): see Powers (2012) 253–62 and above, n. 48, on the importance of "seminal" causes in plants and animals.

[61] Cicero, *On the Nature of the Gods* 2.82. I follow Pease and the MSS in reading *nulla cohaerendi natura* ("no natural principle of cohesion"). In the Loeb Rackham prints *sola cohaerendi natura* ("only the natural principle of cohesion"). As Pease (1979) 2:754 notes, the sense of *natura* is obviously different here than the *natura* under discussion, but this alone does not justify rejecting the manuscript reading. For Nature as the name of the *hexis* of the cosmos, see Diogenes Laertius, *Lives of the Philosophers* 7.148. On Nature as the active principle of the cosmos, see below, pp. 263–64.

of her increasingly stable grasp of cosmic truth. For Stoic ethics aims to transform the experience of what we might call radical vulnerability into an understanding of one's own place in cosmic sympathy, understood in its finest intricacy as fate. The importance of "cosmological ethics" to Stoicism is obvious, though what it entails for human action is stubbornly opaque.[62] Suffice to say here that in yielding access to the unity of cosmic truth through the scattered parts of the world in their translocal entanglements, sympathy was always about yoking the smallest of events to a logic of sense aspiring to encompass the whole of the world not with the form or the concept or the proposition or a set of rules but *with the net itself*.

Let us begin, then, with the notion of openness by considering what sympathy is not—namely, the kind of participation we see in the *Timaeus* or in other Platonic dialogues. In these contexts, unity on a grand scale is often cast in terms of *symphōnia* or *harmonia*, words that probably had associations with Pythagoreanism. When classical writers talk about *symphōnia*, they imply that two or more things are in agreement with one another in a way that is like the concord produced by a harmony of two or more musical notes. Plato, for example, talks about the *symphōnia* of the parts of the soul, which can be brought about by certain kinds of music or star-gazing.[63] If music or astronomy is efficacious it is because the soul has a share in a mathematicized reality. For Plato as well as for the Pythagoreans, the more ideal the object, the less entangled in matter, and so the purer its harmonies: participation is located at what we might call the highest common denominator.

By contrast, the common property of bodies that are connected through sympathy is their ability to be affected by other bodies, to undergo *pathē*. The fact that affectability is in play here is not surprising, given the Stoic definition of body as that which affects and/or is affected. But it is worth emphasizing that by shifting the terms of cosmic participation to bodies, the Stoics level the ontological playing field: all bodies, no matter how small or seemingly inconsequential, are entangled in the life of the cosmos and worthy of the breath of god. In the domain of cosmic sympathy, we find an attention not only to the stars and seasons but to the smallest things—little mouse livers, seed pods—lacking in the

---

[62] Most modern commentators accept the significance of "cosmological ethics" to Stoic ethics but no one agrees what the alignment of one's own life with the life of the cosmos looks like (probably also in antiquity, which is why the lives of animals and children played such an important role in the Stoic theory of *oikeiōsis*: see Brunschwig (1986); Holmes (2014)). For recent discussion of cosmological ethics, see Boeri (2009).

[63] Plato, *Laws* 7.817e–822c; Sextus Empiricus, *Against the Professors* 7.94 on the *symphōniae* of the Pythagorean cosmos.

metaphysics of Plato and even Aristotle. It is this flattening of the world to the level of invertebrates that Favorinus complains about in a critique of the astrological sympathy associated with the Chaldeans, where he laments a fate that would bind the lives of men to those of flies, worms, sea urchins, frogs, and gnats.[64] What marks a worldview oriented around cosmic sympathy is a commitment to the shared capacity of bodies to be acted upon as a criterion for inclusion within the life of the whole.

The sympathetic incorporation of the smallest beings into the cosmic whole mirrors analogically the animal's structure at the micro-level, where even a cut to the finger causes the whole to suffer, due to the total blending of soul and body. At the same time, it is precisely in this paradigmatic example of unity that sympathy speaks not only to the interaction of bodies but also to the magnification of vulnerability *within* a unified body. For if each part acts as a portal to the whole (cosmos), the affection of any one part puts the whole (organism) at risk. And, for the Stoics, the risk of being cut or rocked by what lies beyond the body always seems high. Think of the examples of psychosomatic sympathy from Nemesius, where the body turns red or pale when the soul experiences shame or fear, and the soul, in turn, suffers when the body is sick or cut. Or think of the paradigmatic case of cause and effect, the flesh yielding to the scalpel. Bodies are open to the world. And in the sympathetic body, affections travel from one part to another, implicating the whole in a torrent of successive becomings.

The storm of becoming defines what it means to be a whole made up of parts, each communicating with that whole. It defines, too, what it means to be part of a larger whole, responsive to the becomings of other bodies and capable of becoming a cause to another body, in turn, within the vast tissue of cosmic sympathies.[65] The radical openness to the world exhibited by unified bodies, that is, their vulnerability to scalpels and sickness, is simply the obverse, shadowed side of total connectivity among the (unified) parts of the cosmos. Yet many of the paradigmatic images of cosmic sympathy—flowering trees, tidal flows—do not suggest a world in pain at all. They express, rather, a world that is dynamic and alive, a world permeated by a quivering and vital sensibility. These two ideas, vulnerability and vitality, are, of course, not unrelated. In sympathy, the Stoics see the vulnerability of the interconnected body as a risky openness to the world that is magnified by the communicability

---

[64] Aulus Gellius, *Attic Nights* 14.1.31.
[65] Meyer (2009) 73–8 usefully distinguishes this kind of "chain" from a modern notion of cause and effect, which trades in events (which are incorporeals, for the Stoics, and so incapable of being causes).

of affection within a cohesive body. But they also see sympathy as a body's pulsing connection to the rhythms of other bodies due to a common receptivity to a vital force that is at once immanent within the very matter out of which a body is made *and* extends beyond the boundaries of any one unified body. On both counts, sympathy exaggerates the passive principle as the openness to being affected. The risk of being open simply *is* the condition of dynamic becoming in an entangled cosmos.

The concept of sympathy thus powerfully expands the boundaries of a living being after Aristotle, emphasizing the way in which each living being must be understood in terms of its relations—that is, through its enmeshment with other lives. The idea that a living being can pursue its own end only through its inborn orientation towards other beings is most clearly expressed in the Stoic theory of *oikeiōsis*, which posits that Nature has fashioned each animal in such a way that it knows how to pursue benefit and avoid harm in the interest of caring for its own life.[66] But the way that sympathies are mobilized within the theory of *oikeiōsis* as expressions of the larger web in which an animal finds itself is itself just one example of how sympathy surfaces a cosmic web. Sympathy could be adduced to prove the claim that the whole of the cosmos is governed by a single Nature, as in the opening of Cleomedes' treatise *On the Heavens*. Cleomedes wants to prove that the cosmos is limited, a claim that he supports by the evidence that it is administered throughout by Nature.[67] The total control of Nature is attested, he argues, by the order exhibited by the cosmos (the ordering of its parts, the orderly succession of time) and also by its sympathies, together with the fact that everything in the cosmos *is created in relation to something else* and renders services to other beings (especially humans, who sit at the top of the food chain).

The sophistication of symbiosis among living beings is no doubt what Balbus, too, was getting at in his invocation of sympathy in *On the Nature of the Gods*. If we focus on this vital side of the sympathetic cosmos, we will see how sympathy is so crucial to cosmobiology because it functions as the tissue joining living beings in the cosmos. It is one thing for a part to communicate pain to the whole. It is another for parts to thrive through their cooperation with one another in pursuit of the flourishing of the whole over time. It is another thing still for the

---

[66] The locus classicus on *oikeiōsis* is Diogenes Laertius 7.85.
[67] "For it is impossible for Nature to belong to anything unlimited, since Nature must control what it belongs to" (Cleomedes, *On the Heavens* 1.3). See also ps.-Plutarch, *On Fate* 574D, where again Nature is credited with the order of the whole.

flourishing of one life to be dependent on its interactions with other lives. The very imbrication of the boundaries of one life in others seems to have been part of what encouraged the Stoics, and others, to move towards conceptualizing a global concept of Nature to function as the only true whole whose mind governs the ordering of the partial wholes that constitute its own parts. We have thus traversed the semantic spectrum of sympathy to the other side, away from openness and affectability to the immanent, total order that goes by the names of god and Nature, a trans-individual principle stitching together all the aspects of the cosmos, non-human and human alike, trivial and great, into a single, coordinated community and thereby capturing at the most macro scale the cohesion that is a feature of every unified body.

But it is here, too, that we hit the limits of the guiding analogy of cosmobiology. For unlike the unified bodies it contains, the cosmos is complete (*teleios*); "it alone is said to be self-sufficient because it alone contains in itself everything that it needs."[68] What happens to the cosmos does not open it to bodies outside itself because there *are* no bodies that lie outside of it to affect it—only void (from which it is protected by pneumatic tension). Beyond the analogy between the body with the cut finger and the cosmos lies a powerful disanalogy: there is nothing outside the cosmos that can cut it, nothing that could *do* anything to it. But what kind of an animal is this, then?[69] Plato's world animal in the *Timaeus*, which eats its own waste in a cycle of perfectly balanced input and output, performs the difficulty of an organism that must make a life, understood as the most minimal state of self-differentiation in time, by cannibalizing itself under cover of waste production (33c8–d3). Kristevan abjection here acts as the extreme expression of the organism's internal heterogeneity—and its salvation.

The Stoics, too, had to grapple with the question of what it means for the cosmic animal to be alive without a world to live in, without a proper environment or other bodies to sympathize with. For the Stoic cosmos does have a life, which, as we have seen, they imagine unfolding from something like a biological seed. Zeus grows—and goes on growing until everything has been consumed by his growth.[70] But again the question arises, from where does the cosmos draw the nourishment it needs to grow? One answer we find takes us back to the parts: "it gets from itself

---

[68] Plutarch, *Moralia* 1052D, 1054E–F.
[69] The critique of Sextus Empiricus (*Against the Professors* 9.138) is instructive here: if god is an animal, he has sensation, and experiences negative sensations, is vexed, changed for the worst, and so perishes.
[70] Plutarch, *Moralia* 1052C.

its nourishment and growth by the interchange of its different parts into one another."[71] The becomings inside the cosmos therefore fuel its own becoming, acting as the motor of self-differentiation within, rather than acting on the cosmos from outside.

The transformations described here almost certainly refer to the mechanisms in Stoic physics whereby the master element, fire, morphs into the other three elements (air, water, earth) and, in so doing, enables the emergence of difference and parthood after the cosmogonic moment. It is just the possibility of variable elemental ratios (and especially the ratio of the active elements, air and fire, to the passive ones, earth and water) that accounts for tensional variability within the pneuma and, so, the diversity of the world. In this state, sympathy becomes all important as that which reasserts unity in the face of a wild heterogeneity of unified bodies and their manifold becomings. For as in the (non-cosmic) animal, cosmic sympathy indexes the cohesive power that maintains identity even as the world animal is undergoing constant corporeal change within. What drives that change is not an encounter with the outside world but time itself.[72] Perhaps we could say that the cosmic animal eats its future. If sympathy is so crucial to the Stoics, it is because through sympathy, we sense the very life of the cosmos unfolding in time.

It should not come as a surprise, then, that sympathy holds within itself the deepest tensions within cosmobiology, tensions within the concepts of (*a*) life and (*a*) nature. Think back again to the question I posed at the outset—namely, what does sympathy show? The question is harder to answer than it may appear. On the one hand, the canonical examples of sympathy suggest bodies acting on one another at a distance, such as the moon acting on the tides. In a case of this kind, the situation involves not the finger communicating with the whole but the finger communicating with another part of the organism. On the other hand, sympathy in other contexts implies various bodies all reacting to a single unifying active principle. These options (part-to-part; part-to-whole) are not mutually exclusive alternatives. Nevertheless, they do offer different perspectives. In the first instance of part-to-part sympathy, pneuma is a medium for the communication of one body's causal power to another; in the second, all sympathies are referred to a larger principle of order.[73]

---

[71] Plutarch, *Moralia* 1052D. Plutarch complains Chrysippus contradicts himself in claiming that god both grows and does not take nourishment.
[72] On time as difference, see Hill in this volume.
[73] It is this compatibility—and with it, the different implications of the two perspectives—that is lost in the conflicting interpretations of cosmic sympathy in Laurand (2005) and Meyer (2009). Laurand (2005) 530 argues that even in cases where it looks like one entity is affecting another, what matters is the overarching single cause ("*tient*

Each perspective holds different implications that are worth unpacking because in so doing, we can see how sympathy holds together different ways of conceptualizing the cosmic whole.

It is easiest to imagine sympathy as the action of one body on another (that is, part-to-part sympathy) under the guise of Nature because such interaction accords well with the way that parts cooperate with one another in an organism. Moreover, part-to-part interaction at the cosmic level—such as the sun or other celestial bodies affecting terrestrial natures—frequently expresses cyclical or otherwise regular patterns that are read as the work of Nature.

Now insofar as parts work together for the best vis-à-vis the life of the whole, Nature starts to shade into Providence. The turn to Providence shifts attention from the ways in which parts act on parts to the immanent, transindividual principle of order that ensures these actions accord with a larger plan for the flourishing of a nature, whether that nature is species-nature or cosmic nature. It is worth noting that even if we are now at the level of part-to-whole, the "plan" of the whole (Nature, Providence) can be understood as what happens most of the time but not *necessarily* what happens. That is, with Providence, the Stoics continue to emphasize Nature in its regularities, whether these are manifest in the behaviors of rabbits or mice or in the coordinated blooming of a garden with the coming of spring. They do so because they read the everyday successes of being alive as evidence that the cosmos has been organized in the best possible way. In this way, part-to-part sympathy retains significance as the predictable expression of a nature or Nature as a whole.

By contrast, the order of cosmic sympathy goes beyond these regularities to encompass the whole of what the Stoics called the web (*symplokē*) of causes, by which they meant every single cause that has ever and will ever exist. In this guise, sympathy becomes allied with Fate. For, the Stoics argued, the entire cosmos was structured at the moment of creation so that certain causes precede others even at vast removes of space. The life of the cosmos in each and every one of its particulars is programmed at the moment god generates it out of fire, and it is played out in time without a single error. Fate is thus sympathy at its most closed and even claustrophobic, signaling the incorporation of every last particular into the predetermined unfolding of cosmic life across a

---

moins dans les interactions entre les êtres du monde que dans l'action de l'air sur ces êtres ainsi co-affectés," emphasis original). Meyer (2009) 82–4 disagrees and tries to show that every instance of sympathy involves the action of one (non-cosmic) body on another. But as Bobzien (1998) 144–79 shows, this cannot be true at least of astrological sympathy.

network of causes—every lucky discovery, every cut finger, every muddy foot.[74] What may look like a disaster from the perspective of an individual life is redeemed at the level of the life of the cosmos. Fate gathers up all the apparent disruptions of natural regularities and recodes them as fated events within the singular life of Nature. More important still, Fate obliterates the difference between the generic cyclicities of non-human life and the particularities thought to be constitutive of a specific human life, referring every single event in every single life, human or non-human, to the life of the cosmos. The possibility of some form of part-to-part sympathy remains. After all, divination relies on the fact that some causes were fated to precede others regularly and so can be invested with predictive value; it is like medicine insofar as it is an inductive science. But because these causes seem to be signs of future events, rather than direct causes of them, we end up with a situation where human lives are directly implicated in the life of the cosmos qua Fate, as opposed to a situation where humans are situated within natural cycles of parts acting on parts: theology overtakes physics.[75] But all along we are under the aegis of sympathy.

Many in antiquity resisted the extension of sympathy beyond Nature to Fate. Just as we saw earlier with Cicero, it is one thing to accept there is some *cognatio*, "connection" or "kinship," in the nature of things, another to assume that each and every event is fated. The worry was a serious one—namely, that Fate threatened to erase all the grounds for taking responsibility for our actions and, so, the very basis of ethics—and it remains an abiding concern for modern interpreters of Stoicism. What life is left to each of us to live as her own if, it turns out, we are just parts of cosmic life? Part of the objection is that in essentially conflating Fate with Nature, the Stoics reduce us to animals, or babies, or madmen, moving through our environments according to "blind impulses" alone, as Plotinus writes.[76] If the Stoics were right, we would be nothing more than the mindless parts of the cosmic animal. Put another way, in conflating Nature with Fate, the Stoics shift from imagining that the cosmic animal simply exhibits a *form* of life, perceptible in its regularities, to imagining that the cosmic animal is living out *a* life, in which every

---

[74] Chrysippus is famously credited with saying that if the foot had intelligence and knew it was fated to get muddy, it would gladly get muddy, just as I would gladly be sick if I knew it was fated (Epictetus, *Discourses* 2.6.10).

[75] Though humans may *also* be situated within natural sympathies. The ancient belief in environmental determinism was often given as an example (e.g. Cicero, *On Fate* 7–8) but crucially it is a case that Stoic critics of Fate were willing to accept, precisely because it seems to speak to Nature, not Fate.

[76] Plotinus, *Ennead* 3.1.7.

particularity is fixed for eternity. It is the fixity of these particulars that seems to crowd out the possibility of truly human lives unfolding within the belly of the cosmic beast.

On the one hand, the Stoic response would simply be, "yes!". I am a part of a whole governed by Nature, writes Marcus Aurelius, one of the most enthusiastic adherents of cosmological ethics.[77] On the other hand, the Stoic most closely associated with what becomes the canonical line on Fate, Chrysippus, clearly worked hard to protect the domain referred to in ancient Greek philosophy as what is "up to us." In a famous analogy, he argues that a cylinder rolling along rolls not only because it was pushed by someone's hand but also because of its own nature, which becomes the "sustaining cause" of its movement.[78] The example draws a crucial line between an external cause (the hand) and an internal one (the shape of the cylinder), and, in allowing the latter causal power, tries to salvage the case for responsibility. In human beings, the difference between a stimulus and an action is further protected by the mechanism of assent, whereby the rational human being accepts the truth value of a proposition generated by a sense-perception. The critical stage of assent explains the status of *pathē*, emotions, which the Stoics understood as beliefs and, more specifically, as false beliefs about what is valuable that, as bodies, cause people to act in largely regrettable ways (pursuing wealth, for example, or fame). The sage, by contrast, has no emotions: the ethical ideal in Stoicism is *apatheia*. The ideal can only be achieved by "living in agreement with Nature," which the Stoics glossed as "living in accordance with virtue."[79] One way of understanding such a state is as the expression in humans of the state that all animals exist in. What makes it properly human is that it is achieved through reason. It is the affirmation in the terms of one's own nature, in the terms of what is "up to us," of the Nature of the cosmos, that is, cosmic life.

Still, insofar as we are bodies—and our souls, beliefs, impulses, vices, and virtue are bodies—we remain within Fate, within the universal nexus of causes expressed by sympathy. This nexus, as we saw earlier, is eternal. It is in place at the moment the cosmos is born. It is the *spermatikos logos*, the mind of god coiled inside the seed at the start of the world. The life of the cosmos is the unfolding of this *logos* in time, as the future becomes the past, god consuming the not-yet-realized world. From this

---

[77] Marcus Aurelius, *Letters* 10.6.1.   [78] Cicero, *On Fate* 39–43.
[79] Diogenes Laertius, *Lives of the Philosophers* 7.86–9, where "living in agreement with nature" and "living in accordance with virtue" are already ascribed to Zeno. Chrysippus is said to have written that "living in accordance with virtue" is the same as "living in accordance with experience of what happens by nature," because "*our natures are parts of the nature of the whole*" (trans. Long and Sedley).

perspective, the mastery of mind over matter in Stoicism is absolute; sympathy aligns with and sometimes seems to be another name for fate, the recuperation of every last part into the whole. There is no errant matter, as in Aristotle, nothing that escapes the universal nexus of causes, no true symptoms.[80] The sage may not grasp every last body in this nexus—such complexity exceeds our comprehension—but she knows that Fate is watertight.

What is not within the web of causes, as Deleuze stressed, is the event, the becoming of bodies. Effects are incorporeals, ghosts and mists hovering at the edge of bodies. They do not exist but subsist in a present that floats free from past and future. Can the same be said of sympathy?

Our sources speak of a unified body as being "sympathetic" with itself. It is best to understand "being sympathetic" here as an incorporeal predicate resulting from the cause of the sustaining breath (tenor). It is worth reiterating that Stoic causes encompass not only antecedent causes (the scalpel cutting the flesh) but also the underlying nature of any body (the way that flesh responds to the blade). The tree "greens" not only with the coming of spring, but at each and every moment it is green. The very possibility of a body having qualities is due to it being unified by a single tenor. From this angle, sympathy is the way in which "green" for example, belongs to the whole body, despite being a part. The tree is green because it is a unified body that is at each moment "being sympathetic with itself," part communicating with whole, internal heterogeneity cohering into unity. Remember that the Stoic speak of cohesion as dynamic, as Sambursky emphasized. Thus, sympathy is the distributed but nevertheless simultaneous effect of a tenor throughout a unified body. It expresses what it is to be a certain kind of qualified body at any moment in time (a green tree) *and* as the result of each contact with an external cause (a tree that turns green with the change of seasons) over the course of a life. The becoming marked by sympathy is always, to adopt Donna Haraway's formulation, a "becoming with."[81]

We may therefore understand sympathy not as a cause but as the event par excellence. Through a series of events, a non-cosmic body remains one in time and over time, through the things that happen to it and through its seeming to stand in place. We can call this series of events a life. In the same way, because it is sympathetic with itself, the cosmos holds itself together in the way we imagine bodies hang together over time but also, more profoundly, it becomes itself; it lives *its* life. The

---

[80] On errant matter and the symptom in Aristotle, see Bianchi (2014). On the concept of the symptom in antiquity, see also Holmes (2010).
[81] Haraway (2007) 244, amending Deleuze and Guattari on "becoming."

plotting of materialism and idealism is indeed scrambled here. On the one hand, in the eternal nexus of causes symptomatized by sympathy, mind has disciplined matter completely. We are here in the realm of the superorganism or a totalized Nature that has been evacuated of contingency. On the other hand, sympathy can be understood as the life of the cosmos in the present-tense of being lived or, in other words, the incorporeal becoming of god, the mist through which the future releases its strange kernel of difference—its possibility of feeding god—and hardens into the past. In its incorporeality, this becoming is what can only be thought by the mind. Insofar as it is thought, it remains inactive and incapable of participating in the nexus of bodies however much it subsists as the relation between them. Sympathy would be nothing more, nothing less than all surface effect in its efflorescence.

WORKS CITED

Barnes, J. (1988) "Bits and Pieces," in J. Barnes and M. Mignucci (eds), *Matter and Metaphysics: Fourth Symposium Hellenisticum*. Naples: 223–94.

Besnier, G. (1996) "La nature dans le livre II du *De Natura Deorum* de Ciceron," in C. Lévy (ed.), *Le concept de nature à Rome: la physique; actes du séminaire de philosophie romaine de l'Université de Paris XII–Val de Marne (1992–1993)*. Paris: 127–75.

Bianchi, E. (2014) *The Feminine Symptom: Aleatory Matter in the Aristotelian Cosmos*. New York.

Bobzien, S. (1998) *Determination and Freedom in Stoic Philosophy*. Oxford.

Boeri, M. D. (2009) "Does Cosmic Nature Matter? Some Remarks on the Cosmological Aspects of Stoic Ethics," in R. Salles (ed.), *God and Cosmos in Stoicism*. Oxford: 173–200.

Bogost, I. (2012) *Alien Phenomenology, or What It's Like to Be a Thing*. Minneapolis.

Brennan, T. (2006) "Stoic Moral Psychology," in B. Inwood (ed.), *The Cambridge Companion to the Stoics*. Cambridge: 257–94.

Brouwer, R. (2015) "Stoic Sympathy," in E. Schliesser (ed.), *Sympathy*. Oxford: 15–35.

Bruns, I. ed. (1887) *Supplementum Aristotelicum* 2.1. Berlin.

Bruns, I. ed. (1892) *Supplementum Aristotelicum* 2.2. Berlin.

Brunschwig, J. (1986) "The Cradle Argument in Epicureanism and Stoicism," in M. Schofield and G. Striker (eds), *The Norms of Nature: Studies in Hellenistic Ethics*. Cambridge: 113–44.

Deleuze, G. (1990) *The Logic of Sense*. Trans. M. Lester. New York.

Edelstein, L., and I. G. Kidd (1989) *Posidonius, Volume 1: The Fragments*. 2nd edn. Cambridge.

Gourinat, J. (2009) "The Stoics on Matter and Prime Matter," in R. Salles (ed.), *God and Cosmos in Stoicism*. Oxford: 46–70.

Grosz, E. (2017) *The Incorporeal: Ontology, Ethics, and the Limits of Materialism.* New York.
Hahm, D. E. (1977) *The Origins of Stoic Cosmology.* Columbus.
Hanley, R. P. (2015) "The Eighteenth-Century Context of Sympathy from Spinoza to Kant," in E. Schliesser (ed.), *Sympathy.* Oxford: 171–98.
Haraway, D. (2007) *When Species Meet.* Minneapolis.
Haraway, D. (2016) *Staying with the Trouble: Making Kin in the Chthulucene.* Durham.
Harman, G. (2011) *The Quadruple Object.* Winchester, UK.
Harte, V. (2002) *Plato on Parts and Wholes: The Metaphysics of Structure.* Oxford.
Holmes, B. (2010) *The Symptom and the Subject: The Emergence of the Physical Body in Ancient Greece.* Princeton.
Holmes, B. (2012) "Deleuze, Lucretius, and the Simulacrum of Naturalism," in B. Holmes and W. H. Shearin (eds), *Dynamic Reading: Studies in the Reception of Epicureanism.* New York: 316–42.
Holmes, B. (2013) "Disturbing Connections: Sympathetic Affections, Mental Disorder, and Galen's Elusive Soul," in W. V. Harris (ed.), *Mental Disorders in Classical Antiquity.* Leiden: 147–76.
Holmes, B. (2014) "Greco-Roman Ethics and the Naturalistic Fantasy," *Isis* 105: 569–78.
Holmes, B. (Forthcoming) *The Tissue of the World: Sympathy and the Concept of Nature in Greco-Roman Antiquity.* Chicago.
Inwood, B. (1985) *Ethics and Human Action in Early Stoicism.* Oxford.
Kidd, I. G. (1988) *Posidonius, Volume 2: Commentary, Part 1.* Cambridge.
Kidd, I. G. (1999) *Posidonius, Volume 3: The Translation of the Fragments.* Cambridge.
Laks, A. (Forthcoming) "How Preplatonic Worlds Became Ensouled."
Latour, B. (2017) *Facing Gaia: Eight Lectures on the New Climatic Regime*, trans. C. Porter. Cambridge.
Laurand, V. (2005) "La sympathie universelle: union et separation," *Revue de Métaphysique et de Morale* 4: 517–35.
Lehoux, D. (2012) *What Did the Romans Know? An Inquiry into Science and Worldmaking.* Chicago.
Long, A. A. (1982) "Soul and Body in Stoicism," *Phronesis* 27:34–57.
Long, A. A., and D. N. Sedley (1987) *The Hellenistic Philosophers.* 2 vols. Cambridge.
Meyer, S. S. (2009) "Chain of Causes: What is Stoic Fate?" in R. Salles (ed.), *God and Cosmos in Stoicism.* Oxford: 118–34.
Nagel, T. (2012) *Mind and Cosmos: Why the Materialist Neo-Darwinian Conception of Nature Is Almost Certainly False.* New York.
Nolan, D. (2006) "Stoic Gunk," *Phronesis* 51:162–83.
Pease, A. S. (1920–3) *M. Tulli Ciceronis* De Divinatione, repr., 2 vols. Darmstadt.
Pease, A. S. (1979) *M. Tulli Ciceronis* De Natura Deorum, repr., 2 vols. New York.
Powers, N. (2012) "The Stoic Argument for the Rationality of the Cosmos," *Oxford Studies in Ancient Philosophy* 43: 245–70.

Powers, N. (2013) "Plato's Demiurge as Precursor to the Stoic Providential God," *Classical Quarterly* 63: 713–22.
Préaux, C. (1973) *La lune dans la pensée grecque.* Brussels.
Reydams-Schils, G. (1999) *Demiurge and Providence: Stoic and Platonist Readings of Plato's* Timaeus. Brepols.
Sambursky, S. (1959) *The Physics of the Stoics.* London.
Schofield, M. (1983) "The Syllogisms of Zeno of Citium," *Phronesis* 28: 31–58.
Sedley, D. N. (2002) "The Origins of Stoic God," in D. Frede and A. Laks (eds), *Traditions of Theology: Studies in Hellenistic Theology, Its Background and Aftermath.* Leiden: 41–83.
Todd, R. B. (1976) *Alexander of Aphrodisias on Stoic Physics: A Study of the* De mixtione *with Preliminary Essays, Text, Translation and Commentary.* Leiden.
Todd, R. B. (1978) "Monism and Immanence: The Foundations of Stoic Physics," in J. Rist (ed.), *The Stoics.* Berkeley: 137–60.
van Raalte, M. (1988) "The Idea of the Cosmos as an Organic Whole in Theophrastus' *Metaphysics*," in W. Fortenbaugh and R. Sharples (eds), *Theophrastean Studies on Natural Science, Physics, and Metaphysics, Ethics, Religion and Rhetoric.* New Brunswick: 189–215.
Weidlich, T. (1894) *Die sympathie in der antiken litteratur.* Stuttgart.

13 Immanent maternal

Figures of time in Aristotle, Bergson, and Irigaray

Rebecca Hill

This chapter affirms a thinking of time as difference.[1] It does not claim to figure time as such, because whatever time is, time remains essentially in excess of figuration. Instead this chapter elaborates instances of the effort to think time as difference in Aristotle, Henri Bergson, and Luce Irigaray. I suggest that each of these philosophers affirms the fundamentally elusive nature of time while also articulating valuable ideas for thinking time as difference. Given that time remains beyond presentation, these ideas remain necessarily figural.

The selection of Aristotle in the effort to think time as difference might surprise some readers, since the time chapters in *Physics* IV explicitly frame the problem of time in subordination to the measurement of motion. I do not dispute this reading of Aristotle; the dominant concept of time (*chronos*) in his corpus is a figuration of time as the measurement of motion. Nonetheless, in excess of this construal, there is a thinking of time in the last few chapters of *Physics* IV that cannot be understood in terms of motion or constrained to any kind of figure. This other thinking of time offers a glimpse of immanent time. It is not developed

---

[1] An earlier version of this chapter was composed on the country of the Kulin Nations (Melbourne) and in New York in 2014. The final version of the text was redrafted on the country of the Kulin Nations in 2016. I acknowledge the unceded Sovereignty of First Nations people in what is called "Australia" and pay my respects to the First Nations people throughout the world. This chapter extends the argument of my book *The Interval: Relation and Becoming in Irigaray, Aristotle and Bergson* (2012). Where my book focuses on Aristotle's concepts of *physis* and *topos* and Irigaray's radicalization of the excesses of these Aristotelian concepts in her elaboration of the interval of sexual difference, the present chapter focuses on Aristotle's account of time in chapters 10–14 of *Physics* IV, texts that *The Interval* does not read explicitly. In this chapter, I am particularly interested in one of Aristotle's figurations of time as "always other and other" (*aei allo kai allo*). I argue that this figuration is a thinking of time as difference that is close to Bergson's concept of the virtual "whole," to Irigaray's figuration of the interval, and to her affirmation figuration of woman as becoming in *Speculum of the Other Woman*. My book does not address the figure of time as "always other and other" in Aristotle and it does not ponder the status of Irigaray's figuration of woman as becoming as a figure of time.

systematically in Aristotle's thought and it sits in tension with the dominant conception of time as the measure of motion bequeathed by his metaphysics.[2] This other time, always other and other (*aei allo kai allo*), is the groundless ground of the concept of time as the measurement of motion. I argue that this is a time of difference, which is a source of inspiration for Bergson's postulation of duration and is resonant with Irigaray's thinking on the interval of sexual difference and with her strange impersonal formulation of woman as becoming in the early essay "Volume without Contours."[3]

13.1. Time and motion for Aristotle (*Physics* IV)

Aristotle notes that time (*chronos*) is often thought to be motion (*kinēsis*) because motion and time are apprehended together.[4] While time is apprehended with motion, time and motion cannot be identical. There are many motions in the *kosmos* and each motion is specific to that thing which is changing, while "time is equally everywhere and with everything" (*chronos homoios kai pantachou kai para pasin*). Aristotle claims that it is through time that we measure motion; for instance, a fast change or a slow change is defined by time (218b9–20).

Aristotle elaborates on the implication of time and motion with a formulation of the "now" (*nyn*) as what is in between "the before and the after" (*to proteron kai hysteron*) (219a30). In a passage that Jacques Derrida describes as proto-phenomenological, Aristotle points out that our awareness of movement involves a marking off of "the before and the after" in motion.[5] As we mark off the "before and the after" of a motion,

---

[2] In the notes to the Clarendon Press translation, Edward Hussey suggests at least four senses of *chronos* at work in chapters 10–14 of Book IV, which Aristotle does not take the trouble to distinguish. Hussey writes:

First, a time as the "number" of change is just a quantity belonging to a change, or that quantity expressed as a number. Secondly, a time as a temporally extended interval abstracted from changes is something having not merely a time-quantity but also a *date*. Thirdly, there may be an intermediate sense of "dateless interval," something having, but not being, a time-quantity. Fourthly, there is a sense of "time" in which it denotes the sum of all temporal intervals, and (allied to that) looser ways of speaking in which time may be spoken as a force or an agent and so on" (145).

All translations from Aristotle, unless otherwise noted, are from Hussey (1983).

[3] Irigaray (1991) 53–67.

[4] The basic concepts of time are derived from a series of analogical relations of dependence that Aristotle maintains between magnitude (*megethos*) and place (*topos*), motion (*kinēsis*) and time (*chronos*).

[5] Derrida (1982) 48–9.

we also mark off "the before and the after" in time. Aristotle says that if we are not aware of motion, we are not aware of time. And yet we also know the passage of "the before and the after" of time in the dark, when we are unaffected by any bodily movement whatsoever. He does not develop the implications of his description of the awareness of the passing from the before and to the after in the *psychē* occurring without an experience of embodied motion.[6] This is an instance in *Physics* IV in which time escapes from its subordination to motion.

Let us examine how Aristotle deploys the "before and the after" (*to proteron kai hysteron*) in relation to the now (*nyn*) in more detail. For Aristotle:

> We say that time has passed when we get a perception of the before and after in motion. We mark off motion by taking... [the before and the after] to be different things, and some other thing [in] between them; for whenever we conceive of the limits as other than the middle, and the soul says that the nows are two, one before and one after,... this it is that we say time is.[7]

The movement from the now that is "before" to the now that is "after" is a movement from one limit to another limit. Aristotle also says that there is something in between the now-limit, which is before, and the now-limit, which is after. (That something, which resides in between the two limits, is what Henri Bergson draws from to posit the very becoming and mobility of duration's progress as continuous and heterogeneous change.)[8] But Aristotle's focus is on the difference noticed by the soul between the now that comes before and the now that comes after.

Aristotle declares that time is the counting of a sequence of nows by which we measure *kinēsis*. Time is defined as "a number of motion in respect of before and after."[9] On this definition, time is that aspect of motion that can be counted.

For Aristotle, time is not number in the sense of being that by which we count, time is that which number counts. He gives an analogy; we can count a hundred horses or we can count a hundred men, while we get the same number, the beings that are counted (the horses and the men) are

---

[6] This Aristotelian formulation is emphasized by Jacques Derrida in "*Ousia* and *Grammē*." Aristotle: "*hama gar kinēseōs aisthanometha kai chronou.*" (219a4–5) "Together when we are aware of *kinēsis*, we are aware of *chronos.*" For Derrida this formulation is what prepares for Immanuel Kant's association of time with the form of inner sense and the condition of all outer appearances, of time no longer dominated by thought of presence. In the dark and unaffected by any body: "*kai gar ean hēi skotos kai mēden dia tou sōmatos paschōmen kinēsis de tis en tēi psychēi enēi, euthys hama dokei tis gegonenai kai chronos*" (*Physics* IV 219a5–9, in Derrida (1982) 48–9).
[7] Aristotle, *Physics* IV 219a23–9, translation modified.
[8] Bergson (1983) 1–4.   [9] Aristotle, *Physics* IV 219b1–2, translation modified.

not numbers (220b10–15). Here, time is analogous to the horses or to the men rather than to the numbers, which are added up to produce a sum.

The definition of *chronos* "as a number of motion in respect of before and after" is frustrating. Whether "the before and the after" is figured as the different nows or as different limits or as different numbers, the whatever-it-is-ness that is in between, what Bergson calls the very interval of time, remains elusive.[10]

Following Martin Heidegger in "*Ousia* and *Grammē*," Derrida argues that the Aristotelian conceptualization of time is constrained by trying to think time in terms of its being and that being is "already silently predetermined in its relation to time" as presence.[11] Focusing on the figure of the now, Derrida writes:

> The now is given simultaneously as that which is no longer and as that which is not yet. It is what it is not, and is not what it is ... [Derrida then quotes Aristotle from the opening of his chapters on *chronos*] "In one sense it [the now] has been and is *no longer*, and in another sense, it will be and is *not yet*." (217b) Thereby time is *composed* of nonbeings. Now, that which bears within it a certain *no-thing*, that which accommodates non-beingness, cannot participate in presence, in substance, in *beingness* itself (*ousia*).[12]

While Aristotle's definition of time is constrained by thinking in terms of presence, Derrida praises Aristotle's proto-phenomenological description of telling time in the dark unaffected by any moving body as a glimpse of a thinking of time that cannot simply be present.

13.2. Aristotle's figures of time

Let us consider another passage from *Physics* IV. In this passage, Aristotle speaks of the difference and the sameness (*autos*) of time. Once again, Aristotle presents time in subordination to motion and he makes use of the "now" to figure time.

> *Kai hōsper hē kinēsis aei allē kai allē, kai ho chronos. Ho d' hama pas chronos ho autos to gar nyn to auto ho pot' ēn, to d' einai autōi heteron to de nyn ton chronon metrei hēi proteron kai hysteron.*

As motion is always other and other, so is time, though at once time as a whole is the same. For the now is the same, whenever it is, but its being is different. It is the now that measures time as before and after.[13]

---

[10] Bergson (1992) 12.   [11] Derrida (1982) 47.   [12] Derrida (1982) 39–40.
[13] Aristotle, *Physics* IV 219b9–13. This is a translation Kristin Sampson generously wrote for me after several discussions about this passage in Aristotle's Greek and its frustratingly

On the one hand, the elements of time, which Aristotle calls "the nows," are always differing, they are always other and other (*aei allē kai allē*). On the other hand, time considered as a whole is identical (*to auto*), otherwise it could not be time as such.

Where Edward Hussey translates "*hama pas chronos ho autos*" as "the whole of time in sum as the same", Phillip Wicksteed and F. M. Cornford render "*hama pas chronos ho autos*" as a moment that "is the same everywhere." On Cornford and Wicksteed's translation, time exists in the moment of the now as self-identical, as being-present. Derrida points out that by being present, the now cannot be temporal, for temporalization is what evades presence:

> ...the now, which itself is affected—as if it were not already temporal—by a time which negates it in determining it as a past now or a future now. The *nyn*, the element of time, in this sense is not in itself temporal. It is temporal only in becoming temporal, that is, in ceasing to be, in passing over to nothing-ness in the form of a being-past or being-future.[14]

The difference in being between the nows is construed in Wicksteed and Cornford's translation of Aristotle in terms of a comparison between different present beings (the nows situated at different points in the movement of time from a past now to a future now). Difference is thought on the basis of a more primordial identity between the nows. The temporalizing work of difference, the dynamic progress of difference, that which makes possible the identity of these now-moments, is outside of the focus of Aristotle's formulation.

In the logic of Derrida's argument, Hussey's translation of "*hama pas chronos ho autos*" as the "the whole of time in sum" does not change the status of difference or the status of the thinking of time. For, the "whole of time in sum" is determined as being-present.[15] And yet, as Derrida

---

divergent rendering in the English translations by Edward Hussey for the Clarendon Press and F. M. Cornford and Phillip Wicksteed for the Harvard University Press.

Just as change is always other and other, so the time is too, though the whole time in sum is itself the same. For the now is the same X, whatever X it may be which makes it what it is; but its being is not the same. It is the now which measures time, considered as before and after. (Edward Hussey)

And as motion is a continuous flux, so is time; but at any given moment time is the same everywhere, for the "now" itself is identical in its essence, but the relations into which it enter differ in different connexions, and it is the "now" that marks off time as before and after. (Phillip Wicksteed and F. M. Cornford)

[14] Derrida (1982) 40.
[15] Derrida (1982) 46. Derrida draws attention to the crucial status of the word "*hama*" in Aristotle's Greek. Sometimes *hama* is translated as "simultaneously," sometimes it is translated as "at the same time," sometimes it is rendered as "coincide" and sometimes it is presented as "together." "Same" is an English word derived from the Greek *hama*

notes, Aristotle recognizes that the now and time are not identical.[16] The following passage brings out this point forcefully. Aristotle writes:

Considered as a limit, the now is not time but is accidentally (*symbebēken*) so, while, considered as counting, it is a number. (For limits are those of that alone of which they are limits, but the number of these horses, the ten, is elsewhere too).[17]

Aristotle makes use of other figures for time—the point and the line and the convex and concave in the figuring of a circle—my contention is that Aristotle *acknowledges* that these figures are not able to present time in a definition. We can read Aristotle's discourse as one that admits that these figurations are ways in which time appears to us while time "itself" remains fundamentally different from any of these structurations.

I want to emphasize another phrase in a passage of *Physics* IV that was analyzed earlier that is crucial for discerning a thinking of time in excess of presence in Aristotle. In a line that is reminiscent of Heraclitian flux, Aristotle says that *kinēsis* and *chronos* are "always other and other" (*aei allo kai allo*).[18] Time and motion *always differ*.[19] If difference is conceived here in terms of the difference between present moments such as a figuration of nows that are compared to one another, we remain

---

(Derrida [1982] 56). See also the entry on *hama*, which is translated in Liddell and Scott as "at the same time" (Liddell and Scott [1996] 71). Derrida argues for a reading of *hama* in Aristotle's time chapters in *Physics* IV as the temporal-intemporal pivot which makes it impossible for time to have an essence (*ousia*). Derrida's reading of *hama* as difference is very close to Heidegger's argument in *Identity and Difference* (1969):

"If time... appears not to take part in pure *ousia* as such, it is that it is made of nows (time's parts), and that several nows cannot: (1) either follow each other by immediately destroying one another, for in this case there would be no time; (2) or follow each by destroying each other in a not immediately consecutive way, for in this case the intervallic nows would be simultaneous, and again there would be no time; (3) or remain (in) the same now, for in this case things that occur at intervals of ten thousand years would be *together, at the same time*, which is absurd. It is this absurdity, denounced in the self-evidence of the "at the same time", that constitutes the aporia [of the non-being of time's being] as aporia" (Derrida [1982] 56).

For Derrida, *hama* generates the very difference between space and time and is the locus of its collapse.

[16] Derrida (1982) 47.   [17] Aristotle, *Physics* IV 220a24.

[18] Aristotle, *Physics* IV 219b10. As Mark Payne suggested to me when I presented an earlier version of this chapter at the *Posthuman Antiquities* conference at New York University in 2014, Aristotle's phrase "*aei allo kai allo*" is practically a quotation of Heraclitus. In Fragment 12, Heraclitus says "As they step into the same rivers, different and [still] different waters flow upon them (*potamoisi toisin autoisin embainousin hetera kai hetera hydata epirhei*)" (Heraclitus [1987] 16–17). It is noteworthy that Aristotle's text inscribes time and motion as *allo kai allo* where Heraclitus' Fragment 12 presents the rivers as *hetera kai hetera*. If we read Aristotle as citing Heraclitus, Aristotle, in this instance at least, understands *allo* and *hetera* interchangeably.

[19] My shift to the words "differ," "difference," and "differentiation" in this paragraph is done in fidelity to a modern sense of difference as the groundless ground of thought and life.

in the contradictory metaphysics of presence that Derrida diagnoses so acutely. But what if the differentiations of time and motion are not thought as the measurements of a succession of moments? *Chronos* and *kinēsis* can be read as figures of presence dependent upon the "always other and other" in order to be as such. In this sense, Aristotle affirms an order of time as difference that cannot be contained by the thought of presence. The "always other and other" is the groundless ground that gives *kinēsis* and *chronos* as it contaminates that which it gives, in its very otherness.[20]

13.3. Bergson's postulation of duration

Bergson's postulation of duration as heterogeneous *and* continuous change, without any affiliation to number, is a rewriting of Aristotle's claim that time and movement are grounded by the "always other and other."[21] Duration is difficult to conceptualize because the dominant form of thought to evolve in human beings emerged to fulfill the fundamental law of life, the law that confronts all living beings: to fulfill their bodily needs and to act in order to survive in the world.[22] Bergson argues that homogeneous space is the medium of practical human knowledge (what he calls the intellect), and the intellect is indispensable to the demands of practical life and to science. It is particularly useful for comprehending matter. Homogeneous space functions as an immobile medium in which matter can be readily measured, juxtaposed, and divided.[23] The problem is that homogeneous space has become such a habitual form of human knowledge that the metaphysical tradition has not recognized the way in which it is used to translate real time into spatial symbols that are predicated on the exclusion of the change specific to duration. The representation of time in terms of number, points and lines, nows, and convex and concave aspects of a circle is

---

[20] This claim is influenced by Pheng Cheah and Suzanne Guerlac's succinct formulation of Derrida's thinking on the figures of the aporia of time:

"Simply put, Derrida's argument is that under conditions of radical finitude, time can only be thought as coming from an absolute other beyond presence. But because the relation to alterity also constitutes the order of presence and experience in general—since presence or experience presupposes persistence in time—any presence is subject to a strict law of contamination by an other that destabilizes, disrupts, and make presence impossible even as it maintains, renews, and makes presence possible by giving it a to-come."   (Cheah and Guerlac [2009] 13)

[21] Bergson (1913) 105.   [22] Bergson (1981) 173.
[23] Bergson (1992) 133.

accidental for Aristotle (220a24); in Bergson's terms, these representations are not accidents. They are the intellectual procedures that human beings evolved in order to fulfill their bodily needs.

To get an intuition of duration, Bergson says that all forms of spatial symbolism must be put out of play.[24] When he says that duration is heterogeneous, the word "heterogeneous" should not be read in spatial terms. It refers to the qualitative alteration of duration in relation to itself. The heterogeneity of duration designates an evolving whole, whose aspects do not externalize themselves. Duration is purely qualitative.[25]

Bergson figures duration as the hyphen or connecting link that brings the past into the future; it is the threshold of emergence that brings into being what did not exist.[26] In his first major work, *Time and Free Will*, the self is defined as duration and is celebrated as the very condition of qualitative difference, the threshold of invention that introduces free acts into the world. In *Creative Evolution* Bergson extends duration beyond human consciousness to all that lives. Life "corresponds to an inner work of ripening or creating."[27] Isolated systems are readily measureable in scientific experiments and this could be read to suggest that the past, present, and future of matter could be given instantaneously.[28] Bergson emphasizes, however, that insofar as matter is bound up in the duration of the whole universe, it also endures. For example, if sugar is mixed in a glass of water, the observer cannot speed up or draw out the process of the sugar melting. The observer's impatience is not something thought, such as the measurable time of the physicist; it is lived time. Waiting for the sugar to melt is not relative because the parts of time cannot be unfurled at will. It is absolute. The whole universe has a particular, irreducible rhythm of duration that is something *like* a consciousness.[29]

Bergson repudiates the instantaneous present as a feature of real time. The instant is an intellectual projection into the lived time of an organism acting and reacting in its environment.[30] He does affirm a concept of the lived present, as that which is actually perceived and felt by a living being. The lived present is that which interests the creature, that which calls her to action, through her perceptions and sensations. From the

---

[24] Bergson (1913) 180.
[25] Bergson (1913) 104. Bergson constantly deploys spatial and sensible imagery to present duration because language is entwined in space and sensibility. Bergson claims it is possible to suggest the intuition of duration through images but the intuitive philosopher must do the work of transcending these spatial and sensible forms to conceive duration in their own thought. I have argued elsewhere that Bergson's desire to transcend space and sensibility and attain pure intuition is logocentric in Derrida's sense. See Hill (2012) 107–11.
[26] Bergson (1983) 22.   [27] Bergson (1983) 11.   [28] Bergson (1983) 9.
[29] Bergson (1983) 10.   [30] Bergson (1981) 137.

abstract point of view of an instant, this lived present is made up of the immediate past and the impending future of the organism's imminent actions and reactions. For instance, imagine the lived present of a lizard on a rock; the lizard catches sight of a passing insect, leaps in the air, opens her mouth and shoots her tongue out and catches the passing creature. Then she curls her tongue back into her mouth and swallows the insect. This ensemble of actions occurs over a certain span of her duration, which could be abstracted into the terms of intellectual time that is measured by homogeneous segments such as seconds. In contrast, in the animal's lived present, this span of time is undivided.[31]

Bergson attributes distinct durational rhythms to living beings and to inanimate matter. For instance, the lizard is characterized by a durational rhythm, the insect is characterized by different rhythm of time and the rock is constituted by another durational rhythm. Bergson is more Aristotelian than this figuration of multiple durations would suggest. In *Duration and Simultaneity*, he says we should not speak of individuated durations; there is only one duration, which articulates a manifold of different durational rhythms—the lizard's rhythm, the rock's rhythm, the rhythm of the insect are all implicated together in the duration of the Whole.[32]

13.4. The virtual Whole

In Bergson, the enduring Whole should not be read as the living present or the actuality of the universe; the Whole is virtual. The living present denotes the activity and reactivity of an organism or a group of organisms. In other words, the present is a joint system of sensations and movements. In contrast, the virtual Whole is absolutely unextended; it is a becoming preserved automatically and in itself. Bergson therefore distinguishes the virtual whole (which he also calls the past) from the extensive living present by a difference in nature.[33]

Let us go into the difference between the actual and virtual in more detail. In the context of human being, Bergson contends that the history of a man's life is preserved, in its entirety, in the past itself.[34] Unlike the actuality of the lived present, the past concerns no part of a man's body. It is not stored in his brain; it does not occupy any space whatsoever. The past is unextended, and, because it is not useful for action, it is virtual.[35]

---

[31] Bergson (1981) 139.
[32] For a succinct account of the interimplication of rhythms in a single duration in Bergson's *Duration and Simultaneity*, see Deleuze (1991) 80.
[33] Bergson (1981) 140.   [34] Bergson (1983) 5.   [35] Bergson (1981) 140.

In this sense the virtual and the actual denote two radically different aspects of life. Moreover, these two orders—the virtual and the actual—coexist. The present does not fade into something constituted as the past once it has ceased to act. If it did, present and past could only be distinguished by a difference in degree.[36] Present and past are two separate elements that are constituted "simultaneously."[37] For Bergson, the past "duplicates" the present at every "moment," to arise with it, to be articulated at the "same time" and to survive it because it is of a different nature.[38] Gilles Deleuze astutely describes this as the most profound paradox of the past and the present.[39]

The paradoxical co-existence of present and past constitutes a split at the heart of Being. In the psychic life of human beings,

> every moment of our life presents two aspects, it is actual and virtual, perception [the living present] on the one side and memory [the past] on the other. Each moment of life is split up (*se scinde*) as and when it is posited. Or rather, it consists in this very splitting (scission).[40]

In *Matter and Memory*, Bergson says that the duplication of the present by the past occurs at the psychological level of a human being's becoming and also, probably in the lives of animals.[41] In *Creative Evolution* all of life is characterized by this scission. Though Bergson does not spell it out, this must also be the case for the bodies made up of (so-called) inert matter because it is the virtuality inherent in matter that allows matter to form a bridge between two of its moments and to repeat its configuration of particles in order to make itself.[42]

Rigorously speaking, the constitution of past and present do not "duplicate" each other, nor are they constituted "simultaneously"; for these phrases are too presentist, too extensive, and what is made in the scission as the living present and as the past respectively are modes of existence that are different in nature.[43]

To posit a scission in duration is to effect a profound displacement of presentist descriptions of Being. It reveals the plane of the living present as merely an aspect of a living being's experience. In the sphere of action, an animal has everything to gain by privileging the actuality of her becoming at the expense of the past.[44] But a philosophy of time cannot

---

[36] Bergson (1981) 135–57. [37] Bergson (1920) 160.
[38] Bergson (1920) 164. [39] Deleuze (1991) 58.
[40] Bergson (1920) 165; Bergson (1959) 917.
[41] Bergson (1981) 82; Bergson (1959) 228.
[42] Bergson (1920) 201. I have problematized Bergson's treatment of "inert" materiality as entangled in the phallocentric idea of feminine passivity in "Beyond Man: Life and Matter in Bergson," chapter 5 of *The Interval* (Hill (2012)).
[43] Bergson (1981) 82. [44] Bergson (1981) 144–5.

afford to ignore the virtual. The virtual past is immensely wider than the actuality of the lived present. The lived present *is* only insofar as it acts. Once a human being has accomplished a particular action, the perceptions that prepared the act and the motor movements that affected it expire. In contrast, the virtual Whole is independent of action. It survives in its entirety, automatically.[45]

For Bergson, the virtual Whole is the ground of invention on which an organism draws to actualize new movements in her or his living present.[46] Beyond the functional significance of the virtual as ground for the invention of acts in an organism's living present, the virtual Whole is the plane of Being in which duration is always becoming other and other. The duration of the whole in Bergson can be conceived as all the rhythms of duration of all living beings (to speak in overly individuated terms). This duration cannot be known in an instant, even by a superhuman intelligence, for there is an extraordinary multiplicity of fluxes making up this becoming, prolonging themselves indefinitely from the time of the emergence of life into the evolving becoming of the new which continues to grow without ceasing. The virtual Whole is never given as such.

13.5. Irigaray's elaboration of the time of the interval

In the introduction to *An Ethics of Sexual Difference*, Irigaray argues that the articulation of sexual difference must involve a rethinking of space and time.[47] Aristotle is an important touchstone in this effort. One of the longest chapters in her book is devoted to a close deconstructive reading of his theory of place (*topos*) in *Physics* IV 1–5. While the chapters focused on time in *Physics* IV are not explicitly addressed, I think that Aristotle's conceptualization of *chronos* and *kinēsis* and his fleeting affirmation of the time of difference are legible in the argument of *An Ethics of Sexual Difference*. This is striking in Irigaray's account of the interval, which is remarkably close to Aristotle's construal of the time of difference and to Bergson's postulation of duration.

---

[45] Bergson (1983) 5.
[46] See chapters 2 and 3 of *Matter and Memory* (Bergson (1981)) for an account of this process in human beings.
[47] Irigaray (1991) 166.

The interval is never defined in Irigaray's corpus; she says that the interval needs to be conceived as the very attractions, tensions, and acts between form and matter and also as the remainder that subsists after each *oeuvre* and *between* what is already identified and what remains to identified.[48] In this sense the interval cannot be defined. The interval is not present but is the condition for presence. Irigaray's descriptions of the interval are framed in terms of the question of her project, the question of sexual difference, but that does not mean that the interval only applies to sexual difference. As I read her, the interval permeates all things as the very giving of space and time.[49]

In the context of elaborating nonhierarchical sexual difference, the interval is the emergence, here and now, of the relationship between the sexes. For instance, in terms of human being, the interval designates the unassimilable difference between woman and man that prevents one sex from ever being substitutable with the other sex.[50] The "here and now" does not designate an instant abstracted from the flow of lived time. It is a flowing and evolving present. To affirm the interval as "here and now" is to say that the present is never given as such but is always (in) the process of actualization. The interval is also the haunting of the present by the past. By the past, I mean everything that has happened in the respective experience of a woman and the experience of a man. The past in the interval of woman and man's specific encounter is also the whole of the past of the universe. Another way of describing the concept of past time is to describe it in Bergsonian terms as virtual time. For example, the invasion of Sydney Cove by the British Empire in 1788 is the virtual past of an actualized event that haunts the evolving of the present flow of the actualization of the relationship between woman and man.

The interval is more than the movement of the living present and the movement of the past of actualized time. The interval is traced with other potential mutations, with other possible actualizations of different relationships. These potentialities are not life-assured, future becomings that are given in advance, programmable, and foreseeable. They are potentials, which might be invented, actualized in the becoming of the present and virtualized in the becoming of the past. "The interval always remains in play."[51] It is necessarily open to an unforeseeable future.

Irigaray has been writing on sexual difference since the 1970s and unsurprisingly, the emphasis of her formulation of sexual difference has

---

[48] Irigaray (1991) 167–8.
[49] This Irigarayan concept is a central concern of my book, *The Interval* (Hill (2012)).
[50] Irigaray (1993) 112.   [51] Irigaray (1993) 49, translation modified.

shifted over the ensuing decades. In the text published in French in 1984 that we have been discussing, Irigaray concentrates on figuring the interval as a generative threshold for the non-hierarchical relationship between woman and man. But the interval is not human; it is the threshold (of) difference, becoming in the broadest sense. The interval does not figure explicitly in her groundbreaking work from 1974, *Speculum of the Other Woman*. And yet, there is a figuring of the time of difference at work in her formulation of woman as becoming. On the one hand, "woman" (*la femme*) has an undeniably anthropocentric sense. On the other hand, I argue that in positing woman as becoming Irigaray avows an impersonal concept of the time of difference.

13.6. Woman as becoming

According to the terms of Irigaray's critical description of philosophy, Western metaphysics is founded on the elision of the maternal and the valorization of conceptual architecture that is isomorphically congruent with the phallocentric idea of man.[52] For instance, in "How to Conceive of a Girl?" in *Speculum of the Other Woman*, Irigaray suggests that the mother is the effaced ground on which Aristotle's unmoved mover is erected.[53] The source of movement and order in the *kosmos*, the unmoved mover, is figured as masculine—as a beautiful boy as Emanuela Bianchi argues in her brilliant queer reading of Aristotle's cosmology.[54] For Irigaray, the maleness of the unmoved mover is a phallomorphic projection on the cosmic scale. Obliquely, the supreme "self-principle" conceals man's debt to *the* mother.[55]

Irigaray's evidence for the suppression of the maternal in Aristotle is based on a close reading of the *Physics* and his theories of sexual reproduction in the *Generation of Animals*. She finds that woman, the female sex, and matter, which Aristotle figures as feminine in his thought, have a contradictory status. Woman is both privation (*sterēsis*) and potentiality (*dynamis*) and she is equally *neither one nor the other*.[56] These derogated and ambiguous figurations of woman are traces of the

---

[52] The idea of the maternal as the repressed ground for the postulations of metaphysics is central to Irigaray's critical engagement with the tradition of Western philosophy as such. I discuss this in more detail in *The Interval*. Also see Bianchi in "Nature Trouble" in this volume.
[53] Irigaray (1985) 161–2.   [54] Bianchi (2014).
[55] Irigaray (1985) 161–2.   [56] Irigaray (1985) 165.

omnipotent power of the mother as the groundless ground of Aristotle's metaphysics, which cannot be resolved to be or not to be.[57]

It is not only as the repressed ground of the pure actuality of the unmoved mover that Irigaray discerns the maternal. There is a sense in which the maternal is all of time-space from which "we" never separate. This is a concept of maternal as absolutely impersonal, as what she calls woman (*la femme*). We cannot even speak of the "we," of the "I" in this conception of woman. The hints of the idea of woman are presented in another essay from *Speculum*: "Volumes without Contours." Her description is resonant with Aristotle's construal of time as always and other:

> Woman is neither open nor closed. She is indefinite, in-finite, the form is not accomplished in herself. She is not infinite but neither is she a unit(y): letter, number, figure, number in a series, proper noun, unique object (in a) sensible world, simple ideality in an intelligible whole, entity of a foundation etc.... This incompleteness of her form, of her morphology, permits her (at each instant) to become something else.[58]

Where Irigaray figures woman's incompletion in terms of the progress of instants, I suggest woman should not be spoken of in terms of becoming at each instant, for there is no instantiation of becoming, but only a virtual progress that takes place between moments.[59]

Irigaray would not agree with what I have suggested here if woman is read as the ground distinct from the figures that emerge in the living present. In her diagnosis of sexed hierarchy that I discussed above, she protests against the appropriation of woman in the phallocentric constitution of metaphysics—for instance, in the dominant formations of Aristotle's project, which presents a phallomorphic conceptual architecture. Here, the maternal does not appear as such but lurks implicitly as metaphysics' repressed ground.[60] But if we take up Irigaray's affirmative figuration of woman as becoming we can dissolve masculine appropriation—no more self and disavowed other, no castration, no more ground and figure, but only virtual rhythms, always other and other.

---

[57] Aristotle's misogynist figurations of materiality are notorious. Irigaray's subversion of Aristotle's contradictory figuration of "woman-matter" is much more than a critique, as it becomes the basis for Irigaray to dismantle the strictures of his metaphysics. I address her argument at greater length in Chapter One of *The Interval* (Hill (2012)). Bianchi also moves beyond diagnosing the Stagirite's misogyny to articulate a rigorous and original argument for re-thinking Aristotelian matter as feminine symptom and the very force of aleatory becoming in radical excess of teleology (Bianchi (2014)).

[58] Irigaray (1991) 55 and Irigaray (1974) 284, translation modified.

[59] My argument that woman's incompletion should be conceived in terms of a virtual progress that takes between moments is influenced by Deleuze's thought on becoming. For instance, see Deleuze (2005) 29.

[60] Irigaray (1991) 169.

What is the value of Irigaray's designation of woman as becoming in "Volumes without Contours"?[61] It is the strategic gesture of a combatant drawing on metaphysicians who posit cosmologies that should exceed human being that nonetheless draw on hierarchically sexed images—I am thinking of Aristotle's image of the unmoved mover as a beautiful boy and Bergson's figuration of the creativity of duration and evolution with images of paternity and the explosive action of sperm.[62] Becoming is not reducible to the figure of woman or to Aristotle's formulation of the time of difference as always and other; time is beyond any figuration.

WORKS CITED

Bergson, H. (1913) *Time and Free Will: An Essay on the Immediate Data of Consciousness.* Trans. F. L. Pogson. London.
Bergson, H. (1920) *Mind Energy.* Trans. H. Wildon Carr. New York.
Bergson, H. (1959) *Oeuvres.* Paris.
Bergson, H. (1981) *Matter and Memory.* Trans. N. M. Paul and W. S. Palmer. New York.
Bergson, H. (1983) *Creative Evolution.* Trans. Arthur Mitchell. Lanham, MD.
Bergson, H. (1992) *The Creative Mind: An Introduction to Metaphysics.* Trans. M. L. Andison. New York.
Bianchi, E. (2014) *The Feminine Symptom: Aleatory Matter in the Aristotelian Cosmos.* New York.
Cheah, P., and S. Guerlac (2009) "Introduction: Derrida and the Time of the Political," in P. Cheah and S. Guerlac (eds), *Derrida and the Time of the Political.* Durham, NC.
Deleuze, G. (1991) *Bergsonism.* Trans. H. Tomlinson and B. Habberjam. New York.
Deleuze, G. (2005) *Pure Immanence: A Life.* Trans. A. Boyman. New York.
Derrida, J. (1982) *Margins of Philosophy.* Trans. A. Bass. Chicago.
Heidegger, M. (1969) *Identity and Difference.* Trans. J. Stambaugh. New York.
Heraclitus (1987) *Fragments: A Text and Translation with a Commentary by T. M. Robinson.* Toronto.
Hill, R. (2012) *The Interval: Relation and Becoming in Irigaray, Aristotle and Bergson.* New York.
Hussey, E. (trans.) (1983) *Aristotle's Physics: Books III and IV.* Oxford.
Irigaray, L. (1974) *Speculum de l'autre femme.* Paris.
Irigaray, L. (1985) *Speculum of the Other Woman.* Trans. G. C. Gill. Ithaca, NY.
Irigaray, L. (1991) *The Irigaray Reader.* Ed. M. Whitford. Oxford.

---

[61] My reading of Irigaray's woman as becoming in the affirmative sense is a figuration of time as difference and can be read as a figuration of nature as difference in the sense proposed by Bianchi in her chapter "Nature Trouble" in this volume.
[62] Bianchi (2014) 140–82, Bergson (1913) 173, and Bergson (1983) 92.

Irigaray, L. (1993) *An Ethics of Sexual Difference*. Trans. C. Burke and G. C. Gill. Ithaca, NY.
Liddell, H. G., and R. Scott. (1996) *A Greek-English Lexicon*. 8th edn. Oxford.
Wicksteed, P. H., and F. M. Cornford (trans.) (1937) *The Physics*. 2 vols. Loeb Classical Library. Cambridge, MA.

14 In light of *eros*

Claudia Baracchi

14.1. Foreword, on Aristotle

Aristotle underlines in many ways the finitude of knowledge (*epistēmē*). He is one of the most indefatigable analysts of reason and of the variegated possibilities of formalization; yet he also consistently casts light on the non-logical foundation of *logos* and logic. The sciences rest on non-scientific foundations, that is, on an abyss: this sobering reminder alone would warrant a rigorous reorientation in Aristotelian studies. Aristotle variously names that which exceeds discursive/scientific knowledge. One of these names is *eros*.

In the treatises gathered under the title of *Metaphysics* Aristotle raises the question regarding "the first causes and principles"[1] of all that is—the causes and principles of being. Book Alpha opens with a customary gesture: the philosopher turns to his predecessors, consciously receiving a certain legacy and undertaking to send it forth critically reconfigured. Of crucial importance at this stage is the analysis and articulation of causality, particularly given the perceived inadequacy of accounts focusing on material principles alone. Hence,

> when someone said that intelligence [*nous*] is in nature, just as in animals, and that it is the cause of every order and arrangement, he appeared like someone sober in contrast to the erratic statements of his predecessors. We know that Anaxagoras explicitly spoke in this way, but Hermotimus of Clazomenae is credited with having done so earlier. Thus, those who held this belief posited, as principles of beings, simultaneously the cause of the beautiful and the cause by which motion inheres in beings.[2]

We should not fail to note a couple of issues here. The investigation of first principles is unveiled in its pre-philosophical inception: in broaching such a primordial question the philosophical discourse acknowledges its own mysterious provenance. The fabulous figure of Hermotimus of Clazomenae mentioned as a precursor of Anaxagoras, the inscription of *nous* in nature (indeed, in living beings broadly understood), and

---

[1] *Metaphysics* 981b28–9.
[2] *Metaphysics* 984b15–22. Here and throughout the translations from the Greek are mine.

therefore the delineation of an inquiry not organized around the centrality of the *anthrōpos*, are indications of alterity—of an outside utterly vital to the unfolding of the philosophical discourse.

While Aristotle typically does not hesitate to expose the inadequacies of the forefathers, he seems to vacillate quite conspicuously when considering two figures: Hesiod the archaic poet and Parmenides the Presocratic philosopher. Regarding them and the name that both of them attribute to the first and ultimate principle of all beings, Aristotle suspends the final word:

> One could make the hypothesis that Hesiod was the first one who undertook to seek such a cause, or anyway someone else who posited *eros* or desire as the principle in beings, as Parmenides does also; for the latter, in describing the generation of all, says:
>
> > she conceived [*mētisato*] *eros* first of all the gods.
>
> And Hesiod says:
>
> > first of all chaos came to be, then
> > broad-chested earth...
> > and *eros* supreme [*metaprepei*] among all immortals.
>
> And this suggests that there must be some cause belonging in beings that moves them and holds them together. As for the preeminence to attribute to these thinkers for such opinions, let us postpone judgment.[3]

According to Hesiod's and Parmenides' hypothesis, love (*eros*) would be the principle "of beings"[4] or "in beings,"[5] that is, "the cause of that which is beautiful" and that thanks to which "motion belongs to beings."[6] This hypothesis is never properly rejected. Aristotle pauses before it and apparently never returns to it for an assessment.

Yet, this primordial intuition will find an echo, even an amplification, in Book Lambda. In this treatise the principle "of beings" and "in beings" is identified with *nous*—the intelligence that, unlike *logos*, presents itself as immediate, non-mediated, non-discursive. Indeed, *nous* names the intellect in its numinous, intuitive dimension. At the heart of all beings, it is said to be the source of their movement, the cipher of their becoming and of their unitary articulation—that which, unmoved, moves everything.

Understanding the mover of all as itself unmoved intimates that it moves otherwise than mechanically, otherwise than a body in movement impacting another body and imparting its own motion to it. *Nous* moves as "that which is desired" (*orekton*)[7] and as the "beloved" (*eromenon*).[8]

---

[3] *Metaphysics* 984b23–32. [4] *Metaphysics* 984b21.
[5] *Metaphysics* 984b24. [6] *Metaphysics* 984b21–2.
[7] *Metaphysics* 1072a26. [8] *Metaphysics* 1072b3.

Moreover, *nous* is illuminated in terms of beauty, that is, of phenomenality, for "what is desired is what appears beautiful [*to phainomenon kalon*],"⁹ what expands in a radiant splendor. It is because of such an appearing that we desire, that we are enraptured, caught in the insuppressible movement of attraction: "we desire because it seems, rather than it seems because we desire."¹⁰ Thus, the principle outlined in treatise Alpha as "the cause of the beautiful,"¹¹ is exposed in treatise Lambda as itself beautiful. However irreducible the cause may be to that which is caused, still, it may prove impossible for us properly to formulate such an irreducibility and tell the cause simply apart from its fruits. For it is only through its fruitfulness that it shows itself at all.

In the lack of an explicit evaluation of the verse by Hesiod echoed by Parmenides, the return to the language of *eros* in conjunction with *nous* seems a confirmation of their hypothesis. Or at least we must hear the consonance between this moment in *Metaphysics* Lambda and the poetic intimation (an intimation older than philosophy itself) recalled in Alpha: everything (the celestial spheres as well as the sublunar world, which is the region of human dwelling) moves *for love* and *out of love*, stretching out in a desiring thrust. Such a movement tending to the beloved is inscribed within the physical and phenomenal domain, of which beauty is the radiant intensification. This aspect of Aristotle has become almost completely inaudible in our culture (whatever "our" may mean here).¹² And yet, Dante, who receives Aristotle through the decisive reading of the Islamic commentators (particularly Averroes), concludes the Paradiso evoking in his own way, but with utmost precision, the Aristotelian unmoved mover of every thing: "*amor che move il sole e l'altre stelle.*"¹³

We should note, moreover, Aristotle's adherence to the Platonic teachings, which involve analogous problems relative to the inscription of first principles, even of the good, in the domain of beauty, and hence in the incessant motility of sensibility and desire.¹⁴ As a matter of fact, in

---

⁹ *Metaphysics* 1072a28.
¹⁰ *Metaphysics* 1072a29.   ¹¹ *Metaphysics* 984b21–2.
¹² For altogether essential reasons, the analysis of which lies beyond the scope of the present essay, it might be a desirable sign of sobriety to refrain from sweeping claims regarding the "Western tradition," as if it were one and simple—the univocal ground of identification, propriety, possession, and self-possession.
¹³ *Divina Comedia*, Paradiso XXXIII, 145.
¹⁴ Despite the emphasis on the hyperbolic character of the good with respect to the domains both of seeming and of being, the discourse of the *Republic* never manages safely to emancipate itself from the language of images, of beings appearing in their multiplicity. In the *Philebus*, the imaginal character of the discourse of philosophy is revealed as insurmountable (64e). This may not necessarily mean that the good simply resolves itself into the beautiful (as H. G. Gadamer has argued in Gadamer (1978)). However, it minimally entails

the passage from *Metaphysics* Alpha considered above, Aristotle is closely following (literally quoting) the *Symposium*, where Plato adds Acusilaos to Hesiod and Parmenides, and radicalizes the primordiality of Eros, acknowledged "among the oldest" or as "the oldest."[15] Eros is not mentioned in the Homeric cycles and Hesiod's *Theogony* is the earliest text reaching us in written form to celebrate the god in its cosmogonic function.[16] Situated among the primeval powers of Chaos (the open), Gaia (the earth), and Tartaros (fearsome darkness), Eros differentiates itself by inaugurating light, for it is "the most beautiful." Interestingly enough, Aristotle cites the Hesiodic verse[17] in a variant that, precisely in dropping the superlative *kallistos* ("most beautiful"), elucidates what is at stake in utmost beauty. According to this alternative version, Eros is supremely beautiful in the sense that it "distinguishes itself" (*metaprepei*) from the other immortals, outdoing them and shining forth in a dazzling glow—the same glow associated with heroic fame. The distinctive trait of *eros* is luminosity, that especially bright mode of appearance that is outstanding beauty. As we saw, Aristotle himself attributes a crucial importance to this trait in developing the unmoving mover as *eromenos*, the beloved.

In its defining, radiating beauty, Eros is a figure of primordial manifestation, of the resplendent appearance of all things and of the cosmos as such—the place of the expansive disclosure of light, *phōs*, wherein all things come to shine (*phainomena*). The cosmogonic character of Eros merges with the divinity ubiquitous in the Orphic fragments: Phanes, the first born, *protogonos*, winged deity rising from the nocturnal abyss, as ancient as *physis* itself. Far from a pretext, the mention of these intertwined, indefinitely remote traditions is necessitated by the register of Aristotle's reference to Eros. For, while Hesiod touches as well on the altogether human experience of *eros* (we shall come to this shortly),[18] Aristotle skips those lines in order to maintain the parallelism between the poet and Parmenides, setting into relief only the more encompassing sense of *eros* as a creative and unitive force, able to form, (re)compose, and harmonize through attraction, and hence to heal. In this sense *eros* is literally a principle "of" things and "in" things—essential to the

---

that, "for us," the good remains elusive, a fugitive that cannot be properly said but only evoked through the perceivable gesture of the beautiful, that is, the perspicuity of phenomena endowed with measure and balance. On the good as the site where aesthetic, ethico-political, and mathematical questions converge, see Baracchi (2004).

[15] *Symposium* 178b–c. [16] *Theogony* 116–22.
[17] *Theogony* 120. [18] *Theogony* 121–2.

constitution of things and, at the same time, sustaining their cohesion and continuity. It is that which grants, maintains, and cures.

Eros is the hatched egg: the shell broken into the two halves (the ark of the earth, the arc of the sky) and the all (the cosmos) that emerges from this rupture and begins to unfold. A passage from Aristophanes' *Birds* evokes the theme of primeval divinity Eros/Phanes,[19] and is one of the earliest written sources of what goes under the name of Orphism:

> First of all Chaos, Night, black Erebos and vast Tartaros came to be; the earth, air, and sky were not. At first black-winged Night laid an egg without semen in the infinite depth of Erebos, from which, in the turning of time, surfaced lovely Eros unfolding golden wings gleaming, swiftly whirling. In vast Tartaros it joined nocturnal Chaos, itself winged, and our race came to be, the first to emerge to the light. At first there was no immortal race, until Eros mixed together all [the components]: from the mixture of each with the other came to be the sky, ocean, earth, and the indestructible race of all the blessed gods.

14.2. *Symposium*: the life of the cosmos

Thus, love holds together the differing, protects the cohesion of all that is composite, animates the articulate organism. It is a principle of composition and friendship—think of the laws of gravitation, regulating the attraction among celestial bodies, in the choreographies and circuits they draw; think of harmony as the work of joining and junctures, whether in sounds, landscapes, or living bodies. It indicates the accord, the benevolent bond with the all, conjoining every being with every other, and preserving each one in its own unique integrity.

But if *eros* operates as a cosmic force gathering, providing sustenance, and balancing the flow of the all, it cannot not include its counterpart: that which moves in the mode of countermovement, which proves intractable and recalcitrant, resistant and even destructive in the face of the unifying and creative thrust. Eros is the name of an inherently agitated, self-differing unity.

It is in this way that *eros* is presented by Eryximachus, the physician in Plato's *Symposium*. *Eros* comes to the fore, on the one hand, as a principle of healing, working so as to recompose fractures and close wounds: law of sympathy, consonance, harmony even in the sonorous, vibratory sense—the unfolding of nature as a musical score. On the other

---

[19] *Birds* 693–702.

hand, *eros* is devastating fury and cacophony. In its dual function, *eros* informs the entire cosmos: it resides in "the souls of human beings," but also "in the bodies of all the other animals, in the plants that grow on the earth" and "in all there is."[20] Thus, one ascribes to the power (the *dynamis*) of Eros both the "wise mixing" that articulates the rhythm of the seasons, granting the composition of the all, and the violence that characterizes disasters and upheavals perdiodically disrupting the natural environment:[21]

When...the hot and the cold, the dry and the wet, happen to arise in a proportionate manner by means of the proper love, they realize a harmonious and intelligent mixture and bring about a good, healthy season for human beings as well as the other animals and plants, and cause no harm. However, when the hubristic love is more in control of the seasons, it causes a lot of injury and destruction. Plagues tend to develop in such a situation, and many other abnormal diseases among animals and plants, including frost, hail, and blights, which develop from the greed and disorderliness of the activities of this sort of Eros in the movements of the stars and seasons of the year.[22]

In this oscillation, the serene countenance of *eros* only marginally prevails over the unruly aspect, intermittently "bringing happiness" and the inclination to gather in friendship with other human beings and, beyond the human, with the gods.[23] Note then: the unity results from a struggle—a balanced one, whose outcome tends to be uncertain. The powers that loosen, disarticulate, disintegrate are forced into some relation with the rest: that which does not want to mix is somehow brought into the mixture. "Force does not touch love," says Agathon.[24] Nor does love utilize force, manipulation, or brutality. This means that love acts only by giving rise to consensus; it moves (another) to the extent that it is recognized and that one gives assent to it. Yet, as we noted, not everything submits to love, not everything responds to love's demands. But, if love is to be the all-encompassing gesture, it must embrace also that which repels it. (This is probably why in Plato's *Timaeus* the demiurge is said to employ a kind of *bia*, force or violence, in carrying out the mixing constitutive of cosmic aliveness.)[25]

---

[20] *Symposium* 186a; also 186b–d, 187b–c.
[21] The god with wings of gold is the same one portrayed as the monstrous combination of many different beasts, many-headed, crying out with their many thunderous voices. Proclus (in Plato, *Timaeus* 30c–d) attributes this characterization of Phanes to Orpheus (Kern fr. 79).
[22] *Symposium* 188a–b.   [23] *Symposium* 188d.   [24] *Symposium* 196b–c.
[25] *Timaeus* 35a.

14.3. *Symposium*: human *pathos*

But Hesiod speaks of the human experience of *eros* as well. He rhapsodizes (literally sews together) *two* lines of development of the figure of Eros: in the *Theogony*, after the verse on Eros the primordial god, he recalls *eros* as the *pathos* undergone by the human and the divine races alike. In these two lines, Eros, "fairest" among the immortals, is portrayed as the dismembering, overwhelming one, "who melts the limbs [*lysimelēs*], and overcomes [*damnatai*] the mind [*noon*] and wise counsel [*epiphrona boulēn*] in the chest [*en stēthessi*] of all gods and human beings."[26] Eros is *lysimelēs*, undoes the limbs, as Sappho also will say,[27] and sweeps away whatever order wisely established. Like sleep coming over one and overtaking all resistance, *eros* disarticulates the organism and the intelligence within it. It may do so with the shaking, shattering force of Northern wind, as in Ibycus' verse:

> In spring the Kydonian
> apple trees flower, watered by flowing
> streams, where the maidens
> have their unravished garden, and vine buds
> rise and bloom under the shadowy branches
> of the vines. But for me love [*eros*]
> is at rest in no season:
> a Thracian North wind [*Boreas*]—
> ablaze with lightning—
> rushing from Kypris with scorching
> fits of madness, black, unrestrained,
> it brutally wrenches my heart [*phrenas*]
> at the root.[28]

Eros, then, is also a child-god, capricious and inexorable, like Dionysus displaying conciliatory tenderness as well as the power to incinerate and dissolve—undergoing pain and perpetrating it. Thus are set off the infinite vicissitudes in this world. Heat of love turned into lightning, raging storm, light darkening, cold wind blowing: from the delights of love to the destruction of Troy, *eros* is implacable.

In Plato's *Phaedrus* Lysias' speech underlines precisely the dangerous aspect of love, and the need to circumscribe and normalize the erotic relationship, maiming it in order to make it reliable, conventional, acceptable. In the *Republic* as well Plato gives voice to the deep concern

---

[26] *Theogony* 121–2; also 911.
[27] Lobel and Page (1955) fr. 130.
[28] Edmonds (1924) fr. 1 (= Wilkinson (2013) fr. 286).

around *eros*, and what *eros* may become when unbridled and uncultivated, allowed to roam about ravenous, devouring, obsessed by the drive to own. The figure of the tyrant expresses the unconstrained cupidity of appropriation and the misery, deprivation, and poverty this brings to the world and the despot himself. Yet, *eros* alone can address the dark side of *eros*. Socrates' second reply to Lysias in the *Phaedrus* (with the image of the winged chariot desirously drawn by the horses of *eros* across the earth and sky) as well as the overall development of the *Republic* show that, in confronting the ravages of *eros*, one will not have turned away from them, let alone denied or stifled them. One, rather, will have stayed with *eros*, divining its irreducibility to catastrophe, deepening the intimacy and acquaintance with it, and enduring its highly volatile unfolding. In this attitude towards the question of *eros*, it is as if we could see Plato dictating to Aristotle the program of his ethical reflection: the task of working with the inevitable and ineliminable—for *eros* is the energy and thrust without which there is no life. Hence the urgency of an analysis of the passions, of the desiring "part" of human psychism, in such a way that human thriving will never have been a matter of mere containment/repression of impulsivity. Has this been understood? The entire Aristotelian distinction between excellence (*aretē*) and continence has precisely to do with this orientation towards a unity based on harmonious integration, a unity that includes even resistance and intransigence, and is not obtained by forcing instincts into improbable molds, or by covering them over. And, in these provisos characterizing the Aristotelian meditation on the human *psychē* (on human aliveness), we discern the prodromes of what will have been called psychoanalysis.[29]

But we should linger a bit longer on the twofoldness of the human experience of *eros*: to seize the contrasting aspects, discernible and yet inseparable, indicating a unity pervaded by difference, not coinciding with itself. Love is breath, breeze, airy circulation. In the most diverse cultures it is described in terms of lightness, luminosity, free expansion and expansiveness, and hence spacious growing. We can hear this, for instance, in Sappho's voice, rising of its own accord and in the urgency of invocation, extraneous to the tortured work of modern poetry:

> Deathless Aphrodite of the spangled mind,
> child of Zeus, who twists lures, I beg you
> do not break with hard pains,
> O lady, my heart

---

[29] In the Aristotelian *corpus*, the analysis of the *psychē* and its motions is systematically developed in the *Poetics* and *Rhetoric*, not to mention the studies on sleep, dreams, and respiration in *Parva naturalia*.

> ...
> ...And fine birds...
> quick sparrows over the black earth
> whipping their wings down the sky
> through midair—...[30]

And again:

> ...your graceful grove
> of apple trees and altars smoking
> with frankincense.
> And in it cold water makes a clear sound through
> apple branches and with roses the whole place
> is shadowed and down from radiant-shaking leaves
> sleep comes dropping.
> And in it a horse meadow has come into bloom
> with spring flowers and breezes
> like honey are blowing...[31]

And again:

> you came and I was crazy for you
> and you cooled my mind that burned with longing.[32]

These fragments let transpire the yearning, the releasement into a vast disclosure, the desire that shakes one awake, the call at once enrapturing and imperious. Yet, at the same time, the presentiment of captivity and pain ("I beg you | do not break with hard pains, | O lady, my heart"), the quest for relief from a feverish condition: one shivers at once out of pleasure and out of fear. Eros "limb-loosening" (*lysimelēs*) "shook my | mind like a mountain wind falling on oak trees."[33]

Eros moves in the open and, thus, resonates with the imagery of summertime, its long days slowly gliding, sails filled with wind. But summer, the season of utmost disclosure and luminosity, already contains the indication of its contrary. The solstice, marking the threshold of summer, simultaneously announces the growth of darkness: at the time of light culminating, the shadow begins to lengthen again. From this point on, until the winter solstice, the day recedes.

Right after the summer solstice, to this day, in many Mediterranean countries (but in French Quebec as well) one celebrates the birth of St John the Baptist—a feast superimposed upon the fire ceremonies ubiquitous in the pre-Christian era, and preserving the same basic

---

[30] Carson (2002) fr. 1. (= Lobel and Page (1955)). [31] Carson (2002) fr. 2.
[32] Carson (2002) fr. 48. [33] Carson (2002) fr. 47.

features. From time immemorial, in various towns, cities, and designated places, one would light bonfires, arrange processions with torches, spend the night singing and dancing by the fire, to celebrate its triumph in the whole of nature, its fruitfulness and fecundity. At stake is not so much uranic fire (the fire of sky and sidereal distances), but altogether terrestrial and physical fire—and not even just the fire that brings the harvest to full ripeness, but the fire within the earth, in the incandescent nucleus where matter is transformed through fusion. This is the forge of Hephaestus, the divine blacksmith, in which metals, stones, and gems (the fruits of the earth) are formed. Simone Weil devotes moving words to this deity, underlining how the Greek archaic consciousness could seize the dignity and divinity of labor, even the hard and mysterious work of metallurgy, in the furnace: it is a god, however soiled and crippled, who takes care of it.[34] We shall meet him again.

In the Christian tradition this workshop becomes the infernal dwelling of the malignant. Yet, intertwined popular traditions as well as archaic Greek myth point in a different direction: there is a god always already in the despicable obscurity, deep within the bowels of the earth—the earth on which we walk as well as the earth that we ourselves are. Yet other traditions in the Far East link summer and its culminating, fruit-bearing fire to the dragon—an image both of the abyss (chthonic and aquatic, earth- and water-related) and of soaring heights, which recalls the specular intertwinement of the snakes on Hermes' caduceus, their ordering and balancing complementarity. The underground beast, whether serpent or dragon, may surface to destroy and devour with its fiery tongue; but it is also the guardian of hidden treasures; it itself is precious energy, indispensable vital force. Every attempt at reaching for those treasures and drawing upon those wellsprings must deal with it.[35]

Thus is physical, sexual love imagined, in its double function: it generates and destroys; frees and entangles; intensifies, heightens, dispenses beauty, induces growth, but also ensnares, confines, reduces, and threatens to annihilate. Physical love already harbors a sublime seed (a god dwells there): but it must be worked through, elaborated, known intimately; it requires cultivation, patient acquaintance. Every myth, every fable of dragons (of depths shrouded in darkness) alludes to such a work of polishing, bringing into an outline, divining what lies hidden, the dormant potentiality. From one end to the other, from dazzling luminescence to dismal shadow, it is love; what connects the two ends

---

[34] Weil ([1943] 1949); Weil ([1941–2] 1951).
[35] Granet ([1926] 1994).

is labor. Love in its most accomplished, comprehensive sense is the fruit of such a transformative operation. Thus, what Freud conceived as an instinctual duality (erotic, sexual, life-promoting impulses vs. aggressive, destructive, death-bringing ones)[36] is already all here, designated by a single word: *eros*. The popular tradition and the philosophical lineage agree on this: not two principles, but one—*eros*.[37]

Eros is always, in every sense of the word, folly (*mania*), says Plato. Trying to bend it to the requirements of reason, reasonableness, and convenience is useless—more: it is the sign of a deficiency in understanding and (what is more) of inauspicious presumption.[38] *Eros* does not come under human jurisdiction. It is passion and, as such, it captures, it preys upon us. It is not owned, but one is owned by it. Hence, it *always* involves a risk: for the distinction between savage fury (the domination of ravenous appetite) and divine inspiration (possession by a luminous god, a winged guide joining earth and heaven) tends to be unstable. Yet, however risky it may be, there is no access to vision (be it knowledge or visionary insight) without such a leap: the way of *ekstasis*. But it is possible to develop and refine one's experiences, gain some discernment and direction, so as not simply to proceed in a suspiciously abstract, unmitigated obscurity. The sophist, the tyrant, and the philosopher are all figures of the undergoing of *eros*, ways of coping with the threat *eros* entails—yet they are not the same and, shifting as these differences may be, they remain perceivable. Being human involves learning to attend to fire, neither fearing it nor being consumed by it, but drawing near and cultivating it.

Philosophy, as Plato develops it, may be seen as such a course of refinement: a science of *eros* (the "science [*sophia*] of Eros, whereby all living beings come to be and grow").[39] At stake is not possibly dispelling (let alone controlling) the mystery of love, but being insightfully led into it, drawing closer to its danger, while being granted protection in this exercise. Such a guiding science shows that at every step, above all at the elemental stage of passionate physical love, the utmost care is necessary. There will be no further movement if the love of bodies is not attended to in all its depth and resonance. The sublimation of *eros* turns out to be the

---

[36] *Beyond the Pleasure Principle* (1920), but adumbrated already in *The Interpretation of Dreams* (1899) and magnified in a brief, arresting text, *Why War?* (1932).

[37] Although Freud (*Analysis Terminable and Interminable*, 1937) claims a Greek heritage (namely, Empedocles) for his dualistic construct.

[38] The *Phaedrus* in its entirety articulates a polemic posture vis-à-vis the domination of convention: in the lack of love, the exercise of reason and composure ("mortal temperance, able to administer things mortal and impoverished") can only mortify the psyche, forcing it into a "privation of freedom" perversely and paradoxically "praised by many as virtue" (256e).

[39] *Symposium* 197a.

nurture and fuller realization of that which is already in and of itself sublime—but hidden here below, yet to be enacted.

This is evident in Diotima's teachings. In the *Symposium* she will undertake to bridge the bifurcation between cosmic energy (the god) and human experience (the *pathos*). And, indicating a way beyond the insularity of the human condition, showing the inscription of the human venture within comprehensive life, she will also in a way resolve the tension between the exhausting, imprisoning side of love, and the luminous, Promethean one.

Situating love embodied and impulsive within increasingly more ample domains of love, and ultimately within the other-than-human context, involves a thorough transfiguration of it. It allows the love between two to breathe in, to expand into the other than itself, and grow, while simultaneously keeping in sight the finitude of every relation and of those involved. As we shall see in turning to Plato's text itself, this affirmation of mortality, seized in its interpenetration with (and not in opposition to) immortality, is at the heart of Platonic thought. Far from giving rise to dangerous and surely pathogenic idealizations, putting unbearable pressure on the finite mortal, the Platonic teaching calls for an emancipation from idealization: it neither forgets nor devalues the human, but certainly does not subject the human to the formidable requirement of conformity to eternal models, infinitely pre-existent and unreachable. The mortal is surpassed, but neither humiliated by impossible demands nor left behind: it lives *in* the movement of transcendence, which always returns back to it and preserves its outline.

This love does not ask the mortal to embody the immortal, to live up to the immortal as a standard, but affirms the mortal as mortal and, simultaneously, as the bearer of a glimmer other than itself, open in a reverberation beyond itself. In other words: in following this way, one who loves does not turn to the beloved in order to satisfy one's own desire for the infinite, but rather in order to share such a desire with the other, to live such a desire together, in a communion that in(de)finitely favors and amplifies life. *Eros* becomes in this way the name of an unstoppable unitive thrust, in which love is born in what is proximate and minute, but in such an inception opens up to the all. It is in this way that the relation is fecund, that it disseminates itself, makes the world fecund, and brings other worlds to light. While, given the spellbinding force of time-honored interpretive habits, such outcomes might sound extravagant, or at least unexpected in a Platonic setting, the Platonic letter decisively corroborates them.

In the *Symposium* Socrates summarizes the way of love taught by Diotima, in which the terrestrial beginning is never left behind but always reinscribed in the movement of a gradually more inclusive experience of the beautiful:

> ... and the true way of proceeding, or being led by another, in the things of love, is this: beginning from the beautiful things here, in order to reach that beauty, gradually ascending, as if step by step, from one beautiful body to two, and from two to all beautiful bodies, and from all beautiful bodies to beautiful practices, and from them to beautiful learning, until from beautiful learning one comes to the apprehension of nothing other than the beautiful in itself, comprehending at last what the beautiful in itself is.... Do you think ... that it would be a worthless life for a human being to look at that, to contemplate it in the required way, and be together with it? Aren't you aware, rather ... that only there with it, when one sees the beautiful in the only way it can be seen, will he ever be able to give birth, not to appearances of excellence ... but true excellence, since he would approach the truth? By giving birth to true excellence and nourishing it, one would be able to become a friend of the gods, and if any human being could become immortal, he would.[40]

The culmination and ultimate outcome of the experience of love is not contemplation per se, but contemplation as fecund, as capable of generating a different life, a different way of being in the world (excellence, *aretē*, always characterizes a comportment, a demeanor, a way of being alive in the world). Ecstasy and rapture always turn back to this life here, renew it, reshape it making it beautiful, shining in a beauty that bears the traces of alterity, altogether irreducible to the mere observance of the laws and institutions of this or that geo-historical context. This is the love that does not consume but instead regenerates, itself inconsumable. It is in this experience that the mortal renews itself in its mortality *and* brushes with immortality.

This vision prepares the possibility—perhaps—of finding the resources for a task at the limit of the human, most improbable and yet necessary: to create the conditions whereby the beloved does not belong to us, but stays with us, for a while, for the time that is allotted; whereby the beloved stays with us freely, without constraint, freely loving us, loved in turn, in a shared *pathos* (*syn-patheia*). This is the love that does not devour but nourishes and amplifies life; the love that honors the beloved in his or her finitude, as a vessel of the infinite, as a human sign of the beyond-human (whether divine or natural), and hence accepts his or her partiality and shadow.[41]

---

[40] *Symposium* 211b–212a.
[41] Here also lies the radical meaning of *therapeia*: love, care, as availability to serve and honor the glorious immortals and the vulnerable mortals alike. In the *Phaedrus, therapeia*

For how would it ever be possible to own that which is free and cannot be dominated, nor enclosed—the soul, a breath in the wind—the soul that has traversed millennia, and from time immemorial has moved through innumerable encounters, losses, and good-byes?[42] Among other things, then, love becomes a matter of learning good-byes, of learning how to say good-bye.

14.4. The androgyne: from physical fusion to psychic completeness

The unitive force of *eros* is at the center of Aristophanes' fable, again in the *Symposium*. The playwright describes love as reconstituting originary integrity: it is the force that brings back together that which was separated.

Aristophanes' myth is well known: human beings were cut in half following Zeus' order—diminished, not altogether annihilated, so that they could continue to honor the gods with offerings and sacrifices. Divided, they roam the earth, each one of them seeking the dispersed other, in order to recreate the lost condition of wholeness. It was common practice in antiquity to cut a ring, coin, or other object in two, and give half of it to a friend or guest. Preserved and handed over from generation to generation, these parts would allow groups or individuals, even after centuries, to recognize each other as friends: the half was the memory of an originary love, infinitely open to becoming. The structure of the *symbolon* designates a fragile integrity always exposed to disintegration. It is a figure of unabated search, abiding desire, openness to the missing.

In this context is developed the figure of the androgyne that, to limit ourselves to the ventures of the West, from the Platonic inauguration

---

and *eros* overlap in the image of the lover approaching the beloved as a deity, with the same solicitude owed to the gods during rites and sacrifices (255a).

[42] Plato repeatedly traces the psyche's incessant transit from life to life, across death—as attested in the myth at the end of the *Republic*, the image of the soul as a winged chariot in the *Phaedrus*, and the vast discussion of immortality in the *Phaedo*, to limit ourselves to the most exemplary segments of the *corpus* in this regard. Here Plato sharpens the perception of the difficulty surrounding that which we call psyche, or even, most nonchalantly, soul—as if we knew what these word mean. Yet, far from a "personal" endowment (as the Scholastics posited, in a protracted debate of immense consequence), in the Platonic environment the soul is but the stratification of a boundless, even nameless, multitude—the movement of indestructible life ever returning, irreducible to any single figure, to any single mask. The soul is but a hypothesis, Lacan will have intimated ("Jacques Lacan: 1ère émission, Psychanalyse I.").

(through the alchemical traditions and the Renaissance) reaches the last century, where it is pervasively manifest—from Virginia Woolf's unforgettable *Orlando* to popular icons such as Ziggy Stardust and Annie Lennox. In the *Symposium* the androgyne is one of the three sexes of originary humanity: a part of humankind being sun-like and masculine, a second part proceeding from the earth and displaying feminine traits, a third kind, lunar in character, bearing both male and female features.[43]

The human being, thus, is a "symbol,"[44] and looks for completion, for the supplement that, alone, would release the inconceivable joy of integrity, of a whole connected with itself. Here then is portrayed the wrenching amorous experience in its languishing and longing for union, or even for the dissolution of two into one: the ancestral perception of incompleteness, inadequacy, and corresponding desire for participation and accompaniment, to the point of annihilation. Love is the physician called upon to heal this radical condition, this originary vocation to conjunction and insatiable hunger. Trying to alleviate the pain of dismemberment, *eros* literally undertakes to make one out of two and restore human nature. It is at this juncture that we encounter Hephaestus once again:

> Thus, whenever a lover of boys, or anyone else, happens to encounter the one who is their other half, they are overcome with amazement at their friendship, intimacy, and love, and do not want to be severed, so to speak, from each other even for a moment. These are the people who spend their entire lives with each other, though they don't know how to say what they want from each other. No one would think this is a mere union of sexual passion, as though that were the reason each enjoys and is so enthusiastic about being with the other. On the contrary, it is clear that there is something else—what, it cannot say—that the soul of each wants, though it does have a prophetic sense of what it wants and can speak of it in riddles. If Hephaestus were holding his tools and standing over the pair lying there together, he might say: "What do you want from each other?" If they had no answer, he might continue: "Is this what you desire, to be together as much as possible, so that you would not leave each other day and night? If you desire that, I am willing to weld and forge you into one and the same being, so that from being two you will have become one and can henceforth live as one being, both of you sharing a single life in common. When you die, you will share a death in common, there in Hades, as one being instead of two. Consider whether you would like this and would be satisfied should this happen." We know that when they heard this, no one would refuse, nor would they appear to want anything other than that. On the contrary, they would think they had discovered what they had really desired all along, namely, to be made one out of two by being joined and welded together with their beloved.[45]

[43] *Symposium* 189e–190b. [44] *Symposium* 191d.
[45] *Symposium* 192b–e.

The literal fusion of bodies certainly is not Plato's last word on this matter. Above we saw how Diotima establishes the persistence of the finite individual, precisely in the rapturous movement beyond—a movement entailing a unitive progression and indeterminately transcending the singular being, yet discernible only through the latter's profile, however impermanent and unstable it may be. Indeed, it could be said that the erasure of the distance and differences between lovers lends itself to the most disquieting distortions and morbid relational developments. Yet, well beyond the literal, physiological interpretation of the androgyne as the corporeal unity of the two sexes, androgyny becomes the cipher of a completeness (at once accomplished and hyperbolical, because infinitely open) that can sustain any division, end, or loss.

I would thus conclude with the bare evocation of androgyny in its symbolic (alchemical, psychic) valence. The integration of the countersexual element as a cipher of human completeness on the way to individuation is a crucial and pervasive theme in Jung.[46] But a reference to Virginia Woolf is perhaps a conclusion appropriate to these fragmentary and incomplete reflections, especially as her *Orlando* (1928) casts light on the connection between androgyny (i.e. the integration that perfects) and the possibility of good-byes, that is, of facing loss and separation without ceasing to love.

The novel ("the longest and most charming love letter" by V. Woolf to Vita Sackville-West)[47] tells the remarkable story of Orlando, a young aristocrat in Elizabethan England, who traverses the centuries up to the present, almost without aging. However, at some point in the eighteenth century (he is at that time in Constantinople as an ambassador), Orlando wakes up one day and finds out he has become a she. This will have numerous and unexpected repercussions. Beyond the question of identities (personal or otherwise), identifications, roles, masks, and outfits, Orlando is a figure of life: of life itself recomposing within itself all contradiction, moving through opposite regions of existence, passing into the body of a man, of a woman, through oscillating vicissitudes— while remaining at heart serenely unmoved, inviolate, whole. At a certain point, back in England and already in the nineteenth century, Orlando encounters Marmaduke Bonthrop Shelmerdine, Esquire, and instantly

---

[46] *Psychologie der Übertragung* (1946); *Mysterium coniunctionis* (1955–6).

[47] Nigel Nicolson, Vita Sackville-West's son, described *Orlando* thus, observing that in the novel Woolf "explores Vita, weaves her in and out of the centuries, tosses her from one sex to the other, plays with her, dresses her in furs, lace and emeralds, teases her, flirts with her, drops a veil of mist around her..." (Nicolson ([1973] 1998) 202–3).

falls in love with him. He reciprocates and they become engaged "a few minutes later":

> The morning after as they sat at breakfast, he told her his name. It was: Marmaduke Bonthrop Shelmerdine, Esquire.
> "I knew it!" she said, for there was something romantic and chivalrous, passionate, melancholy, yet determined about him which went with the wild, dark-plumed name—a name which had in her mind, the steel blue gleam of rooks' wings, the hoarse laughter of their caws, the snake-like twisting descent of their feathers in a silver pool, and a thousand other things besides, which will be described presently.
> "Mine is Orlando," she said. He had guessed it. For if you see a ship in full sail coming with the sun on it proudly sweeping across the Mediterranean from the South Seas, one says at once: "Orlando," he explained.[48]

Woolf spectacularly dwells on the play of mirrors between Orlando and Shel, exposing a complementarity between them that rests on the individual superabundance, if not completeness, of each. For, even aside from their encounter, each one of them always already harbors an other within and undergoes the unfathomable, inexplicable work of alterity:

> "Oh, Shel, don't leave me!" she cried. "I'm passionately in love with you," she said. No sooner had the words left her mouth than an awful suspicion rushed into both their minds simultaneously.
> "You're a woman, Shel!" she cried.
> "You're a man, Orlando!" he cried.[49]

And again:

> All this and a thousand other things she understood him to say and so when she replied, Yes, negresses are seductive, aren't they? he having told her that the supply of biscuits now gave out, he was surprised and delighted to find how well she had taken his meaning.
> "Are you positive you aren't a man?" he would ask anxiously, and she would echo, "Can it be possible you're not a woman?" and then they must put it to the proof without more ado.[50]

Until the day when, in the ongoing unfolding of life and undiminished love, they marry and, simultaneously, separate:

> ...and the Lady Orlando, with her ring on her finger, went out into the court in her thin dress and held the swinging stirrup, for the horse was bitted and bridled and the foam was still on his flank, for her husband to mount, which he did with

---

[48] Woolf ([1928] 1956) 250–1. [49] Woolf ([1928] 1956) 251–2.
[50] Woolf ([1928] 1956) 258.

one bound and the horse leapt forward and Orlando, standing there, cried out Marmaduke Bonthrop Shelmerdine! and he answered her Orlando! and the words went dashing and circling like wild hawks together among the belfries and higher and higher, further and further, faster and faster, they circled, till they crashed and fell in a shower of fragments to the ground; and she went in.[51]

WORKS CITED

Baracchi, C. (2004) "One Good: The Mathematics of Ethics," *Graduate Faculty Philosophy Journal* 25: 1–1.
Carson, A. (trans.) (2002) *If Not, Winter: Fragments of Sappho*. New York.
Edmonds, J. M., ed. (1924) *Lyra Graeca, Vol. 2*. London.
Gadamer, H. G. (1978) *Die Idee des Guten zwischen Plato und Aristoteles*. Heidelberg.
Granet, M. ([1926] 1994) *Danses et légendes de la Chine ancienne*. Paris.
"Jacques Lacan: 1ère émission, Psychanalyse I." *Un Certain Regard*. Channel 1. March 9, 1974. Television.
Kern, O. (ed.) (1922) *Orphicorum Fragmenta*. Berlin.
Lobel, E., and D. Page (eds) (1955) *Poetarum Lesbiorum Fragmenta*. Oxford.
Nicolson, N. ([1973] 1998) *Portrait of a Marriage: Vita Sackville-West and Harold Nicolson*. Chicago.
Weil, S. ([1943] 1949) *L'enracinement: prelude à une declaration des devoirs envers l'être humain*. Paris.
Weil, S. ([1941–42] 1951) *Intuitions pré-chrétiennes*. Paris.
Wilkinson, C. L. (2013) *The Lyric of Ibycus*. Berlin.
Woolf, V. ([1928] 1956) *Orlando*. New York.

---

[51] Woolf ([1928] 1956) 262.

INDEX

abyss 35, 197–9, 202–3, 226, 287, 290, 296
  abyssal 199, 203, 214, 225, 235
  abyssal object 197
Aeschylus 78–9, 97–8, 117, 171
aesthetics 5, 87–8, 146, 164, 172, 232, 243, 290
Aetna 196, 206
Agamben, Giorgio 2, 99, 103
ahuman 90
air 206, 230, 279
  elemental 201–2, 205, 221–6, 235, 291
  in Empedocles 16–17
  in Harman 204
  in Hölderlin 144, 147
  in Marcus Aurelius 202
  in Orphism 291
  in Sallis 222–4, 228
  in Stoic thought 251, 252, 263
alterity 277, 288, 299, 303
Anaxagoras 194, 287
Anaximander 2, 223, 224
Anaximenes 223, 224
analogy 67, 70, 75, 214, 262
ancestral reality 193–4
androgyne 300–4
animal 3, 10–12, 18, 32, 73, 78, 141, 160, 214, 233, 257, 287
  animal and plant 4, 21, 70, 160–1, 221, 225, 254, 256, 258, 292
  cosmic animal 260, 262–3, 265
  Derrida on 14, 90–2
  divine and animal 7–8, 59, 65, 75, 107, 125, 130
  as food 162, 165–8, 169–78, 181
  gendered 79
  habitat 101–2, 118
  human and animal 2, 7–8, 19–20, 49–50, 55, 57, 59, 63–8, 102–13, 125, 151, 159–61, 181, 214, 266
  ideal state 10
  instrumentalized animal 151–2
  language 71–2
  in Plato 19, 49–50, 55, 57, 59, 63–8, 70–3, 75
  political animal 102–13, 116, 118
  relationships among 99–100
  in Schiller 141–2
  sexuality 81, 229
  slave and animal 106

sounds 68–9, 125–6, 129, 131, 137
  see also speech; sign, non-linguistic
  see also monster
Anthropocene 2, 78, 214
anthropocentrism 65, 78, 90–1, 102, 118, 182, 283
anthropomorphism 161, 239
anthropophagy 161, 170–2, 181
anthrōpos 63–4, 66–9, 73, 136, 137
antihumanism 78–80, 88
Apollo 83, 88, 128, 150
Arendt, Hannah 31–46, 103, 104–6
Aristophanes 228, 291, 300
Aristotle 2–3, 8, 68, 190, 215, 231, 252, 260–1, 285, 287, 294
  animal 63
  biology 256
  body 243, 253–4
  cosmos 257
  De anima 125–7, 129–31, 167
  Eudemian Ethics 107
  female 10
  immanence 243
  Lacan on Aristotle 80
  materialism 190, 242, 267
  Metaphysics 223–4, 228, 287–90
  metempsychosis 167
  mother 283–4
  Nicomachean Ethics 63, 98
  Parts of Animals 250
  Physics 221–2, 271–7
  Politics 68, 98–118
  soul 167
  thauma 40
  time 271–7
  voice 125–7, 131
artifact 15, 33, 116, 142, 223
astoxenon 98
atopos 47
Auschwitz 31, 34–5, 38
  see also Lager, Nazi
autarchy 6, 8
autonomy 123–4, 127, 131, 135–7, 193
autophony 135–7
Averroes 289

Barad, Karen 15, 213, 214, 234–5
Barthes, Roland 50
barbarian 6, 8, 10, 136

Bergson, Henri 271–3, 277–82
bioethics 2, 238
biology 4, 12, 55, 108, 212, 216, 218, 231
   cosmobiology 240, 256–8, 262, 263
   see also *bios*; germ-cell
bios 2, 40, 99–103, 108–9, 111–13, 115
body 18, 69, 71–5, 117, 132–4, 167, 170, 232, 239, 242, 266, 268, 288
   body and soul 21, 58, 75, 110, 123, 132–4, 137, 163, 165–7, 180, 241, 260
   body politic 40
   devalued body 13, 15, 55
   gendered body 212, 217, 220
   material body 4, 14, 82, 132, 166–7, 169, 171–2, 206, 211, 217, 220, 232, 239, 261, 279
   maternal body 226, 235
   mind and body 15, 55, 166, 251, 254–5, 258
   organized body 71–5, 111
   representational body 8
   as self 11
   unified body 245, 249–63, 267
   see also corporeality; embodiment; incorporeality
breath
   see *pneuma*
Butler, Judith 22, 89–90, 124, 211–13, 215, 216–18, 230, 235

Callimachus 149–54
cannibalism 7, 169–70, 172, 178, 180–1, 262
causality 264–7, 287–8
character
   see *ēthos*
chorality 18, 141–56, 212
Cicero, M. Tullius 246–9, 255, 258, 265
cinaedus
   see *kinaidos*
citizen 8, 52–3, 98, 101, 115, 134–7
   see also *astoxenon*; politics
climate 14, 22, 78, 91, 205, 207, 213, 245
cohesion 250, 252–5, 258, 262–3, 267, 291
collectivity 103–4
communality 89
community 99, 143
complementarity 296, 303
connectivity 12, 240, 255, 260
consanguinity 170
conscience 42–3
context 194–5
contingency 4, 22, 39, 40, 79, 112, 115, 116, 199–203, 208, 253, 268

cookery 168–70, 172, 174
   see also animal as food; cannibalism; cuisine, Roman; vegetarianism
corporeality 123–5, 132–4, 137, 241–2, 244, 250, 251, 263
   see also body; embodiment; incorporeality
correlationism 191–2
cosmology 12, 195, 244, 248, 251, 256, 260, 262–6, 290
cosmos 1, 10, 11, 13, 18, 199, 245, 254, 283, 292
cuisine, Roman 174–80
cyborg 92, 166

daemon 11, 205
daimonion 47–60
Dante 289
Darwin, Charles 80, 212, 218, 229, 233
dehumanization 32, 164
Deleuze, Gilles 14–16, 23, 212, 241–3, 267, 279–80, 284
Demeter 151–5
democracy 97
Derrida, Jacques 14, 63, 75, 90–1, 124, 189, 235, 272–7, 278
didacticism 162–3
Dionysus 83, 293
Diotima 113, 145–7, 298, 302
disguise 128–9, 132
disorder 68
dissimulation 173, 212, 227–9
divination 247–50, 257, 265
divine 16–18, 67, 74, 83–4, 97, 144–7, 151–2, 159, 165, 167, 180, 220–2, 245, 268–9, 297, 300
   divine and animal 2, 7–8, 11, 106, 125, 131, 167, 172
   divine and daemonic 11
   divine and material 17
   divine and human 1, 2, 4, 106–7, 129, 293, 299
   divine cosmos 250, 252, 254–7
   divine image 83
   divine king
      see *tyrannos*
   divine sign
      see *daimonion*
divinity 84, 128, 151, 169, 172, 250, 254–5 290–1, 296
   see also daemon; *daimonion*; divination; nature, divine; nature, as providence
doxa 38–9
duality 133–4, 297

ecocriticism 3, 12, 195, 205, 206, 213
ecology 196, 203, 213, 228
ecosystem 82
eidos 215, 222
eikos 71
ekstasis 231, 297
embodiment 1, 4, 64, 71, 159, 165, 167, 168, 173, 250, 298
  see also body; corporeality; incorporeality
Empedocles 16–17, 82, 205, 206, 215, 221, 222–3, 297
entanglement 1, 18, 214, 216, 235, 259, 280
epistemology 5, 22, 59, 105, 168, 207, 234–5
Eros / *eros* 53, 82–5, 88, 219, 232, 287–304
Erysichthon 151–4
ethics 1, 201, 203–4, 213, 243, 258–9, 265–6, 281
  ethical subject 68
  interspecies ethics 12
  vegetarian ethics 162
  see Aristotle, *Eudemian Ethics*; Aristotle, *Nicomachean Ethics*
ēthos 2, 109
Euripides 17
evil 33–8, 42–6, 49, 70–1
evolution 4
externality 155
extramaterialism 242
  see also materiality; maternal; matter; new materialism

fact / facticity 33, 44, 89, 175, 190, 227
  see also truth
fate 264–7
femininity 6, 66, 135–6, 138, 301
  feminine principle 229
  femininity and the divine 223
  femininity and materiality 242, 283–4
  femininity and monstrosity 232
  feminine passivity 242, 280
  nature and the feminine 211–13
  see also gender; maternal; nature, and the feminine; performativity; woman
feminism 212–13
Fichte, Johann G. 148
fixity 164
fluid boundaries 129, 132
fluidity 170, 182
flux 161–4, 168, 181–2, 199, 202, 275–6, 291
food 161–2, 168–70, 172
Foucault, Michel 2, 14, 53–5, 78–9, 92, 199, 203
Freud, Sigmund 52, 80–5, 87–8, 91, 297

gadfly 49, 56–7
gender 124, 211, 216–18, 229, 235
  gendered animal 79
germ-cell 81–2, 88, 91
god/goddess/gods
  see divine; nature, divine; nature, as providence
graceless 70–1
Grosz, Elizabeth 13–14, 106, 211, 212–14, 216, 229, 235, 242–4

Haraway, Donna 191–2, 213, 244, 267
Hegel, Georg W. F. 79
Heidegger, Martin 31, 103, 153, 215, 217, 221, 222, 225, 227–8, 231, 274
Heraclitus 164, 199, 215, 226, 276
Herodotus 1
Hesiod 23, 126, 223, 288–9, 290, 293
heterogeneity 262, 263, 273, 277–8
Hölderlin, Friedrich 17, 141, 144–8
Homer 1, 123, 125–38, 215, 218–21, 223, 236
homogeneous 277, 279
homosexuality 9, 67, 229
  see also sexuality
Honig, Bonnie 5, 89, 90
hybrid 45–6, 50, 59, 159, 162, 163, 164, 166, 173, 179, 220, 231
hyperobject 195, 196, 197, 198, 205
hyper-reality 193

Ibycus 293
identity 125, 127–9, 135, 138, 199, 275
idyll 142–3, 147, 154–6
imitation 67–9, 73, 87
immanence 14, 15–16, 112, 240, 242, 243, 248–9, 251, 256, 261, 262, 264, 270, 271
immortality 203
incorporeality 14, 241–5, 251, 257, 260, 267–8
  see also body; corporeality; embodiment
interbreeding 163
interconnection 23, 92, 240, 248, 260
interobjectivity 198
interpellation 143, 144, 148, 152
intersubjectivity 50, 89, 91, 145, 198, 239
intimacy 100, 116–17
Io 165
Irigaray, Luce 6, 22, 211, 215, 225–8, 230, 232, 235, 271–2, 281–5

kinaidos 9
kinship 70–1, 98

Lacan, Jacques 52, 80, 85–7, 90–1
Lager, Nazi 35
　see also Auschwitz
Latour, Bruno 189, 191, 240, 244, 247, 255
likeness
　see *eikos*
Lingis, Alphonso 22, 212, 231–3
listening 47–50, 54, 56, 58
　see also voice
logos 41, 55, 57, 63, 66–9, 72–4, 98, 100, 102, 104–5, 107–9, 112, 115–16, 118, 124, 217, 227, 251, 256, 266, 288
Lucretius 164, 204, 241, 255

machine 12, 15–16, 32, 35, 37, 65, 79, 107, 166, 233
Marcus Aurelius 198–9, 202, 266
masculinity 138, 233
　see also femininity; performativity
masquerade 233, 302
materiality 1, 10, 14, 16, 82, 106, 108, 155, 196, 206, 212–13, 224, 227, 234, 239, 243, 268, 280
　see also extramaterialism; maternal; matter; nature, as physical world; new materialism
maternal 15, 23, 147, 220–1, 226–8, 232, 235, 283–4
matter 103, 240, 251, 258, 277–8, 283
　see also extramaterialism; maternal; materiality; nature, as physical world; new materialism
metaphysics 31, 33, 35, 40, 44, 191–2, 194, 201, 207, 215, 235, 272, 277
metempsychosis 160–1, 165, 166, 167
mimesis 9, 155, 233
　see also imitation; representation
Minotaur 150
misogyny 6, 13, 229, 284
modernity 18, 78–9, 81, 91, 92, 142, 234
moly 219–21, 236
monism 214
monster 7, 65, 130, 219, 232, 235, 292
　man as monster 37, 45–6
　monstrous in Plato 232
　see also animal
morphē 222
mythos 75

nature 12, 64, 162, 256, 258, 263, 279, 285, 291, 296
　denaturalized 67, 193, 215–17
　divine 16, 107, 131
　and the feminine 211–36
　in Hellenistic poetry 21

human and nature 17–18, 67, 69, 125, 131–2, 254, 256, 258
human nature 32, 74, 82, 87, 105–8
　as naturalized culture 67, 71, 110–11, 193, 215–19
　ordered 173, 179
　as physical world 17–18, 22–3, 111, 125, 134, 148–56, 175, 178–9, 189, 195–8, 203–7, 248, 287
　and *physis* 15–16, 22–3, 254
　as providence 23, 111, 150–6, 240, 243–4, 248, 251, 261–8
　renaturalized 214
　in Romanticism 141–4, 146, 148–56
　second 69
　as system 162, 173, 179
　see also performativity; *physis*
new materialism 2, 3, 189–90, 244
　see also extramaterialism; materialism
Nietzsche, Friedrich 3, 6, 17, 47–8, 82–4, 201, 218
non-human 1, 3, 4, 12, 14, 112, 145, 155, 161, 165, 166, 168, 173, 181, 229, 234, 239, 243, 265

object 190, 192, 194–5, 200, 205, 206, 207, 211–12, 234, 254
　see also abyss, abyssal object; hyperobject; subject
object-oriented ontology (OOO) 14, 189–93, 194, 195, 197, 203, 205, 206–7
　see also object; ontology
Odysseus 154, 219–21
Oedipus 15, 79, 84–8, 92, 147, 171
oligarchy 118
ontogeny 142, 146, 148, 230
ontology 3, 33–7, 44, 105, 107, 161–2, 189, 192–4, 197, 200, 201, 203, 211, 214, 215, 216, 225, 234, 241, 246, 259
　see also object-oriented ontology
order 64–6, 68, 73
Orphism 290–2
Ovid 159–82

Parmenides 23, 28–90, 222–3
Pausanias 1
perception 64, 99, 109
performativity 211–36
pharmakos / pharmakon 92, 219–21, 228
phenomenology 14, 196, 207, 211, 214, 215, 217, 222–4, 228–9, 231, 233–5, 272
philia 98–9
phylogony 142, 146, 148, 230
physikoi 3, 215, 222, 224

physiology 50, 302
physis 15, 101, 152, 215, 218–23
  in Homer 215, 218–20, 223, 228, 236
  and *technē* 15, 228, 234
  see also nature, as physical world; nature, and *physis*; *physikoi*
plant 2, 4, 10, 16, 18, 65, 70, 111, 174, 178, 181, 214, 219–21, 223, 225, 231, 254, 256, 258
Plato 31, 33, 34–6, 38–46, 47–60, 63–75, 123, 164, 199, 205, 215, 241, 256, 260, 262, 294, 302
  Apology 47–9, 51, 53–7, 59
  Gorgias 42, 47, 54
  Laws 19, 63–70, 72–5, 259
  Parmenides 16, 73
  Phaedrus 53, 55–6, 59, 71, 112, 293–4, 297, 299–300
  Protagoras 8, 125, 134–7
  Republic 34, 39, 47, 56, 59, 64–5, 69–71, 74–5, 116, 227–8, 250, 289, 293–4, 300
  Sophist 41, 73, 241
  Symposium 24, 47, 55, 290–2, 297–301
  Theaetetus 40–1, 48–9, 56, 59, 66, 73–4, 164, 232, 250
  Timaeus 72, 112, 205, 256, 259, 262, 292
  on the soul 167
  versus Socrates 35–6, 38–46, 50
pleasure 64, 83, 87, 91
plurality 33–6, 38–9, 43–6
pneuma 241, 245, 248–9, 250–5, 262–3
poiēsis 143, 148, 149, 150, 151, 154, 155, 219, 223
polis 2, 38–40, 101–2, 105–6, 113–18
politics 1, 31–46, 54, 56–7, 60, 97–118, 212–13, 235
  see also *astoxenon*; citizen
posthumanism 2–4, 33–8, 43–4, 65–6, 68, 75, 78–81, 88, 91–2, 160, 181, 189–90, 195–6, 201, 212
psyche 15
psychoanalysis 10, 14, 19, 77–92, 294
Pythagoras 159–82
Pythagoreans 81, 259

race 6, 9
rationality 107
  see also *logos*
reality 190, 192–3
reciprocity 143
Renaissance humanism 3, 5, 7
representation 67–70, 73
  see also *eikos*
rhizome 2, 16–17, 223

Sallis, John 22, 211, 214–15, 222–6, 232, 234
Sappho 293–5
Schiller, Friedrich 141–3
sēma / *sēmeion* 47, 51, 57–8, 246
  see divination
Seneca 171, 196–8, 203
sexual difference 6, 11, 15, 225–6, 235, 271–2, 281, 282–5, 297
sexuality 6, 8–9, 10, 133
Shelley, Percy Bysshe 148–9
simulacrum 204, 241
sign, non-linguistic 58
  see also animal, sounds; speech
slave 6, 8, 10, 106
sociality 143, 145, 149, 152
Socrates 17, 35–6, 38–46, 47–60, 69–71, 134–5, 294
  see also Plato, Plato versus Socrates
Sophocles 1, 5, 80, 85–8, 153–4
  Oedipus at Colonus 85–8
soul 18, 170, 202, 239, 254, 257, 266
  see also body and soul
space 97–9
speculative realism 14, 189–95, 200, 201, 203–4, 207
  see also object-oriented ontology
speech 68–74, 131
  see also animal, sounds; sign, non-linguistic
Spinoza, Baruch 15–16, 18, 235
subject 1, 6, 18, 20, 34, 44, 49, 58–9, 85–90, 91, 124, 133–4, 137, 141–6, 148, 152, 154, 156, 164, 194, 196–203, 205, 207, 212–13, 222, 227, 230, 235
  see also abyss, abyssal object; ethics, ethical subject; hyperobject; object; subjectivity
subjectivity 123, 127–9, 131–2, 135, 137–8, 143, 166, 168, 213, 216, 233
  see also abyss, abyssal object; object; subject
symbol 32, 87, 133–4, 230, 277, 300–1
sympathy 23, 99, 239–41, 243–68, 291
syzēn 98–9

taxonomy 161, 174, 176, 179, 182
technē 3, 13, 15, 251
teleology 102, 112, 217, 219, 222, 232, 240, 257, 284
telos 3, 89, 222
Thales 223
thanatos 83–5, 88
  see also *eros*

thauma 40, 58, 220, 228, 232, 236, 255
theater 22, 171, 204, 211, 227–9, 232–5
theōria / theōrein 39–41, 99, 227, 232
Theocritus 154–5
Theophrastus 2
Theseus 150
time 261, 263, 267, 271–85
topos 110–13, 115, 118, 218
totalitarianism 31–2, 35–7, 106
transhuman 55, 174
  see transindividual
transindividual 240, 264
  see immanence; transhuman
truth 32, 38–40, 52–4, 84, 112, 139, 194, 212, 215–16, 227–9, 232–3, 235, 244, 246, 250, 257, 259, 266, 299
  see also fact / facticity
tyrannos 92
tyranny 98, 294, 297

unity 40, 109–11, 240, 245, 249–54, 257, 259, 260, 262–3, 288, 291, 300
  see also monism

vegetable
  see plant
vegetarianism 160–2, 168, 171, 173–8, 180–1
voice 50–2, 54–6, 58–60, 66, 69–70, 123–32, 134–8

Weil, Simone 296
woman 6, 9–10, 18, 213, 214, 220, 283–5
  see also femininity
wonder
  see *thauma*
Woolf, Virginia 301–4
Wordsworth, William 143–4

Zeno 251–2, 255, 266
zōē 1, 63, 99–100, 103–4, 106, 110–11, 117

The manufacturer's authorised representative in the EU for product safety is Oxford University Press España S.A. of el Parque Empresarial San Fernando de Henares, Avenida de Castilla, 2 – 28830 Madrid (www.oup.es/en or product. safety@oup.com). OUP España S.A. also acts as importer into Spain of products made by the manufacturer.

www.ingramcontent.com/pod-product-compliance
Ingram Content Group UK Ltd.
Pitfield, Milton Keynes, MK11 3LW, UK
UKHW021137240326
469240UK00021B/168